THE
STOLEN
WEALTH
OF
SLAVERY

A CASE FOR REPARATIONS

DAVID MONTERO

Foreword by Michael Eric Dyson

LEGACY
LIT

New York   Boston

Legacy Lit
Hachette Book Group
1290 Avenue of the Americas
New York, NY 10104
LegacyLitBooks.com
Twitter.com/LegacyLitBooks
Instagram.com/LegacyLitBooks

First edition: February 2024

Legacy Lit is an imprint of Grand Central Publishing. The Legacy Lit name and logo are trademarks of Hachette Book Group, Inc.

The publisher is not responsible for websites (or their content) that are not owned by the publisher.

The Hachette Speakers Bureau provides a wide range of authors for speaking events. To find out more, go to hachettespeakersbureau.com or email HachetteSpeakers@hbgusa.com.

Legacy Lit books may be purchased in bulk for business, educational, or promotional use. For information, please contact your local bookseller or the Hachette Book Group Special Markets Department at special.markets@hbgusa.com.

Library of Congress Cataloging-in-Publication Data

Names: Montero, David, author.
Title: The stolen wealth of slavery : a case for reparations / David Montero.
Description: First edition. | New York : Legacy Lit, 2024.
Identifiers: LCCN 2023036573 | ISBN 9780306827174 (hardcover) | ISBN 9780306827198 (ebook)
Subjects: LCSH: Slavery—Economic aspects—United States—History—19th century. | Capitalism—United States—History—19th century. | African Americans—Reparations. | United States—History—Civil War, 1861–1865—Economic aspects.
Classification: LCC HT901 .M66 2024 | DDC 381/.440973—dc23/eng/20230804
LC record available at https://lccn.loc.gov/2023036573

ISBNs: 9780306827174 (hardcover), 9780306827198 (ebook)

Interior book design by Marie Mundaca

Printed in the United States of America

LSC-C

Printing 1, 2023

For my father, whose love of books nurtured my own.

CONTENTS

FOREWORD

WHAT IF I TOLD YOU?

By Michael Eric Dyson

"**W**hat if I told you?" the television announcer teased us with the first part of a question as athletic highlights rolled. The tagline has become iconic. It was used in trailers to introduce forthcoming episodes of ESPN's documentary series *30 for 30*, which showcased thirty films by thirty filmmakers to mark the twenty-four-hour sports network's thirtieth anniversary in 2009. The spectacular success of the series has made it a network staple. I was featured in a couple of the original films, including one about the rise and tragic death of college basketball superstar Len Bias from a cocaine-induced heart attack shortly after he was taken as the number two pick by the Boston Celtics in the 1986 NBA draft. He was forecast to rival the athletic prowess of Michael Jordan. Instead, he was stilled at twenty-two from an accidental overdose.

When the *30 for 30* audience heard the beginning of the question, they knew the second part would add a twist to a widely held perception of a sports hero or villain. What was flagged in Bias's case was the brutal transition from immortality to calamity and the question of potential that lingered in its wake. As images of Bias's balletic splendor flashed on-screen, the resonant baritone voice asked, "What if I told you that a sure thing can become a what-if?" In another film, devoted to Muhammad Ali's last fight, against WBC heavyweight champion and former sparring partner Larry Holmes, the question rang out: "What if I told you he wasn't the greatest?"

If the reversal of broad belief or accepted convention can happen in sports, it surely can happen as well with history and politics, especially when the subject is slavery, among the most vexing and complicated issues we as a nation confront. What if I told you that many of the beliefs you hold about slavery and race and whiteness and Blackness simply aren't true? What if I told you that the notion that nearly all the spoils of slavery went to the South and the North was relatively free of moral taint and economic exploitation is a grave untruth? What if I told you that the belief that most of the obscene wealth made by white businessmen during slavery was destroyed by the Civil War and that they didn't benefit from the long reach of the dollar well after the end of bloody hostilities is willfully wrong? What if I told you that the effort to distort Black history and ban books about our nation's imperfect past to offer a rosy picture of the present didn't begin with Ron DeSantis? What if I told you the book you hold in your hand offers these corrections to the record and a great deal more? Well, it is true, and David Montero surely makes it worth your while.

History, American history in particular, is not something we can take for granted, not something we can palm off to our children as the product of morally innocent ancestors who always said and did the right thing. History must be fought for, fought over, and fought through, and with—through the devastating obstacles placed in our paths by politicians and other figures out to hijack history for vain displays of power or ideological purity. And it must be fought with the best resources and tools we can garner through abundant study and honest reflection. We are at an especially perilous point in our progress as a nation. We must again decide if we will be bullied by charlatans of misinformation. We must ask if we will be vulnerable to educational poseurs who lack the skills to speak intelligently and justly on schools and history and books.

We are once again undergoing a sea change in the approach to our past and how we should view it and what we should do about what we learn. Social movements for change staked in race and gender and class and sexuality have riled up reactionary forces. These forces often bypass

rigorous inquiry and critical engagement as they short-circuit into intimidation and the urge to squelch open dialogue and bury genuinely free
speech. History suffers when merchants of menace dig into the local or
national till to fund efforts to stop the spread of deep knowledge. Too
often the sweep and sophistication of Black life are ignored, resented, or
rejected. In their place, the most saccharine and shortsighted views of
Black culture find hearty embrace.

Slavery has been particularly provocative because it is hardly a subject
about which one can be neutral. Neither is it a subject that easily lends
itself to ethical distance. It grabs you by the collar to make you recognize
that such insight comes at a cost—not, to be sure, through the surrender
of analytical skill, but in ditching blinders that shield you from the truth.
The Far Right's objections to viewing evidence and data in a fair light
has made them allergic to uncomfortable truths. They also have a hyster-
ical obsession with defeating "wokeism," which in many cases is merely
an enlightened grasp of the facts at hand. Conservatives expend far more
effort to rid the nation of the memory of slavery than their forebears spent
in getting rid of our country's original sin. They natter and prattle about
being made to feel guilty about what their mothers and fathers did, even as
they insist that what their mothers and fathers did wasn't all that bad. All
the while, complex and vibrant history is sacrificed on the altar of white
discomfort. What they cannot afford to know, they refuse to accept.

Vigorous, robust, heady history—the sort of history pored over
and struggled with and tested and interpreted and comprehensively
examined—is the only kind of history that can satisfy our need for true,
unsparing, and pitiless self-knowledge. Our understanding of slavery
should grow out of such a state of affairs. And deep moral awareness
should haunt any knowledge we deem worth possessing. Montero's book
makes clear that a healthy and productive view of slavery and its aftermath
must grapple with muscle, money, morality, and memory.

Muscle—Black muscle, Black bodies, Black embodiment, Black phys-
icality, Black strength, Black mobility, Black durability, Black energy—is
how slavery thrived. It is what white society exploited to do its bidding.
The foundations of American society rose on the relentless work of the
Black body to produce cotton, sugar, corn, wheat, flour, rice, tobacco,
iron, coal, turpentine. Black muscle built railroads, highways, houses,

churches, buildings, roads, and the like. Black muscle was at once pillo-
ried and despised and exploited and appreciated for what it could do for
the white world. Black muscle was repulsive to white society as an aes-
thetic and moral artifact of inferior engineering.

But the breathing, grunting, heaving, sighing, lifting, running, entertaining, and dancing of Black muscle—and its perpetual laboring—is
what built America and brought white vision, dream, and desire to life.
Black muscle was the technology of white imagination. As much as possible, white ambition was transferred to Black skin, skill, sinew, legs, but-
tocks, thighs, backs, heads, mouths, arms, fingers, and feet. The abuse of
Black muscle was routine. White sexual desire spliced into Black genetic
destiny to reproduce more muscle and body to realize white social and
cultural ambition.

The nonstop exploitation of Black bodies and the relentless working of
Black muscle created white money and massive white wealth. The unceasing exploitation of enslaved Black bodies generated untold millions, billions, even—adjusted to today's scale—trillions of dollars of white wealth.
Bankers, merchants, and heads of corporations reaped the benefit, especially those Northern figures who were thought to have kept their distance
from the horrors and compromises of slavery. Montero brilliantly unearths
how Northern figures benefited far more from slavery—and the forcefully
extracted labor of enslaved Black bodies—than Southern plantation owners. Northern businessmen who founded and ran Citibank and Bank of
America and built Wall Street and created corporations that generated
wealth that lasts to this day are the ones who took fullest financial advantage of slavery. Hardly any thinker before Montero offers as satisfying a
peek behind the veil of secrecy that shrouds white wealth and the pretense
to white innocence.

White innocence occupies a central role in the moral self-image of
many enslavers. These are men who could sleep easy at night believing
they had the backing of their religion, the blessing of their God, and the
benefit of their moral code. Nothing in their world suggested a disconnect
between their values and trading in Black flesh, exploiting Black muscle,
abusing Black limbs, and indulging their sexual appetites for Black bodies. That many of them belonged to manumission societies even as they
enslaved Black folk is the fatal flaw of their moral code, though, in truth,

it cost them nothing. Their outlook fostered a society where slavery could persist, where Northern businessmen could prosper, and where systems of subjugation could prevail. The moral composition of the Northern white mind was a study in jarring contrasts held in place by the refusal to see a problem where no human being existed—at least no human being that mattered to them. There was a Cartesian reversal at work when it came to the white perception of Black life: I do not think; therefore, I am not. When it came to Black bodies, white enslavers and Northern white beneficiaries of Black enslavement saw commerce first, commerce last, commerce always.

Then, too, the cultivated amnesia practiced by white enslavers was a boon for business. They were able to willfully forget the atrocities they committed in slavery; they forgot how hard Black enslaved folk had it; they wanted the government to forget their insurrection against the Union and their treasonous behavior; they wanted the newly unified nation, after the Late Unpleasantness had passed, to forget the violence and savagery against Black folk both in slavery and afterward. Today, their legatees continue the tradition of memory loss and willful forgetting. So much of the controversy over "wokeness" in the social and cultural sphere has to do with the will to forget practiced by those who seek to deflect history so that it may be washed clean and rewritten. That memory may be laundered, just as the billion dollars bounty of slavery was whitewashed by Northern businessmen who bore little of the public burden of the Southern plantation owner while reaping far more of the benefits. The addiction to amnesia clears the path to rewrite history, to minimize white shame for widespread devastation, and to erase the legacy and memory of Black folk in one fell swoop.

The beauty of Montero's book is that it rescues history, real history, American history, Black history, from the dustbin of neglect, denial, and ignorance and offers it a fresh hearing before the reading public. The wonder of this book is that it clarifies the costs of slavery with painstaking specificity and exhaustive particularity. He shifts effortlessly from broad-scope scrutiny of systems of racial terror to the intimate transactions of businesspeople who used Black muscle as capital, as collateral, as cushion and financial clincher. Montero destroys the myth that the South got the biggest piece of the financial pie and forever puts to bed the image of the relatively saintly white Northerner who was mostly abolitionist and certainly opposed to the exploitation of Black life. Montero shows that none of this is true. He argues that plenty of Northern white corporate titans were in on the plan to send Black folk back to Africa because, right along with banning books, they sought, when the getting was no longer as good as it had once been, to banish Black bodies and send us packing back to where we would supposedly prosper in our natural habitat. Never mind that many enslaved folk had been born in the United States. The few Black folk who were either convinced or coerced to return to Africa under those conditions mostly perished in the new promised land.

Montero nails it all: the muscle, the money, the morality, and the memory warfare. He brings dramatic conclusion to his astonishing tour of just how Black folk have been sold, used, abused, exploited, cast aside, forgotten, hated, and despised. He proves that we were used to make white folk wealthy beyond measure, especially many white Northerners, and that because of this, America owes Black people a significant debt. The appeal, and persuasion, and, really, the moral elegance of what Montero offers is that he names the names of individuals and corporations that made their wealth off of Black muscle and acknowledges the pioneering work of Black folk, especially Black women, in the fight for reparation. It is all so remarkable, so powerful, and so eloquently stated. While giving practical insight about how to recover the smallest of Black treasure, this book, then, is itself a treasure, a document of emancipation because of the story it tells, a handbook of hope because it tracks the real work that Black folk have done to get back even a fraction of what was stolen from us.

What if I told you that a white man offered a searing and detailed analysis of what other white people had done in history to Black people? Well, it is true, and in its own way, it is a majestic act of literary reparation for the sins we have endured.

Michael Eric Dyson is Distinguished University Professor of African American and Diaspora Studies at Vanderbilt University and author of twenty-five books, including seven *New York Times* bestsellers, among them *Tears We Cannot Stop: A Sermon to White America*.

INTRODUCTION

THE VAULT

By December 1908, City Bank of New York's home at 52 Wall Street had begun to cramp the company's outsized ambitions. The problem was the building's dour proportions: it was only five stories high, with squat masonry, a modest limestone facade, and small windows set in unadorned arches. For an entrance, it presented nothing more than an austere staircase running straight into the gutter.

City Bank had been occupying these same premises since its founding in 1812. Back then, it had only three full-time employees and one of the smallest capitalization levels of any bank in the United States. Now, nearly a century after servicing the cotton and sugar lords of America, it was the largest and most powerful financial institution in the world, with four hundred employees and capitalization 100 percent greater than any other bank in the United States.[1] Its president, James Stillman, whose father's cotton empire enriched the bank throughout the American Civil War, dreamed of much grander settings. And when the perfect deal came his way, he purchased a monumental building to be the company's new home: the Custom House, considered a crown jewel of classical American architecture. As luck would have it, the resplendent Custom House was directly across the street, at 55 Wall, so the distance of the move was to be short—only three hundred feet. But the bank still faced a logistical challenge unprecedented in the annals of the US financial system: How was it to physically transport the colossal deposits that had built up inside its vaults over the last century, the century when cotton, sugar, and slavery fueled the most explosive expansion of human wealth in world history?

There was $500 million in securities sitting in City Bank's vaults, worth more than $16 billion today, and they represented the density of America's vast corporatization and industrial development at the dawn of the twentieth century: railroads, steel, machinery, gas, electric utilities, and oil. More importantly, there was also $70 million in hard cash, what would now be worth $2.3 billion.[2] Most of that cash was in the form of actual gold, in fact 150,000 pounds of it—a veritable trove, evoking the bank's deep history, its roots penetrating to the briny origins of the nation, when America's early fortunes were made on the high seas, in war, trade, and kidnapping, and the fruits of those enterprises were carried back from distant lands, sealed in the hulls of great ships.

The vault of City Bank was a fulcrum resting astride two different times, two different eras—the old and the new, the past and the future—and Wall Street was the line. But how to cross it? Given so vast a fortune yet so short a distance, the officials of City Bank wagered that trucks or even wagons were pointless for the job. Instead, they detailed a plan audacious in its simplicity: they would hire one hundred men who would move all this treasure by hand, carrying it piece by piece, step by step, across Wall Street. The board decided; the date was set; the preparatory stages taken. For a brief time on the morning of December 19, 1908, all the wealth of the world's greatest bank would be paraded out in the open, flowing in the streets, laid bare for all to see.

How would all this loot now be stored, and what would become its fate? Before we follow its path, we should first be clear where it came from.

City Bank, though far from the fields of the South and its plantation ranges, was the nation's premier cotton and sugar bank. It was principally a bank profiting from the enslavement of Black people. That it survives to this day, more than two hundred years later, is only thanks to the extraordinary wealth that enslaved Black people produced—and that extraordinarily rich white men stole. The bank's original founders, nearly to a man, enslaved Black people; those who took the reins after them also profited

from enslaved people; and the heirs of those men, including James Stillman, grew up in the white privilege afforded by Black enslavement. More
to the point, the men who made City Bank made their fortunes not just
in the transatlantic cotton trade, *in* global slave industries, and *in* the
institutional torture of Black men, women, and children—but by forging,
through ship and coin, steam and rail, that very system of exploitation
itself.

Samuel Osgood, Isaac Wright, Benjamin Marshall: these "legendary"
progenitors of City Bank, still celebrated by the company today, were slave
entrepreneurs, shipmasters above all, before they were high "merchants" of
Wall Street. Their fortunes, derived from Black labor and circulated into
City Bank, were spat out again as loans to other slave-based enterprises
across the nation, institutionalizing the way of life that made white men
rich, through the destruction of Black people around the globe—though
one would never know this looking at Citibank's website, where nearly any
mention of this history is meticulously erased, locked away as if sealed in
a vault.

They are not the only ones with such a history, of course, nor the only
ones to shroud it in silence. City Bank was but one bank, among many
such banks, that dotted the street called Wall along the crest of Manhattan Island. Just one among a tight network of banking houses that functioned, in essence, as the headquarters of the largest industrial slavery
system the world has ever produced. Within feet of each other, Brown
Brothers & Co., Merchants' Bank, Bank of New York, Bank of America,
and many names still with us today, not to mention many others long
since forgotten, collectively ran this system from the gilded foyers and
polished boardrooms of the Empire City. They planted the deep roots of
the US financial system and drew up their great fortunes by pulling long
and hard on the veins of four million enslaved Black people thousands of
miles away. These companies have never publicly disclosed this fact. And
this is to mention only the New York banks, not the multitude of other
corporations—shipping, importing, insuring, manufacturing, machin-
ing, milling, harvesting, warehousing, distilling—that exploited enslaved
people, that built extraordinary wealth by doing so, that still exist today
because of that wealth, and that have never acknowledged how the labor
of enslaved Black people created their enduring prosperity.

Most of these companies share one more thing in common: they weren't located in the South. Nor were they owned by southerners. These slave-based enterprises were primarily in the North, at great physical distance from enslaved people themselves yet directly profiting from that enslavement. What's more, they were controlled by members of the East Coast elite, paragons of privilege and respectability who were both fierce defenders of slavery and ardent supporters of the Union, though, of course, some were Confederates too. These were some of the richest white men in US history—in fact, in world history—whose occupations had nothing to do with farming or plantations, but everything to do with exploiting a system that churned the unpaid, coerced labor of Black people into ever-greater wealth for other elite white men. Their machinations also included the exploitation of southern white plantation owners, farmers, and overseers.

In the year 2000, the distinguished historian Eric Foner lamented in an editorial about "the usually glossed-over participation of the North in America's slave system."[3] More than twenty years later, another distinguished historian, Sven Beckert of Harvard University, was still lamenting this fact, when he apprised committee members at a 2022 congressional hearing: "It is a mistake to think only about the southern states when thinking about slavery. Slavery's impact was national in scope."[4] The story we've been telling ourselves about America's enslavement of Black people has been obscured and troubled for a long time—and on many levels. It is the enterprise of this book to show that, among many existing problems, there are yet even more fundamental ones. The story we've been telling ourselves about slavery's wealth is set in the wrong place, with the wrong characters and the wrong time.

We have misapprehended slavery as primarily a southern story, its roots, consequences, and modern-day fallout confined to that physical space—a geography principally of the mind more than reality. The extraordinary wealth that millions of Black people produced for white men, though they produced it while trapped in slavery in the South and on southern land, did not remain in the South and did not principally benefit the South. That wealth flowed, like a mighty river, for decades, indeed centuries, into the North, a torrent worth hundreds of millions of dollars each year. And that current, that epic movement, is an essential part of this history. As such, the South is not where the story of slavery's stolen wealth principally takes place or *ends*; it is where the story of that theft *begins*. The pages of this book will argue that America's system of enslaving Black people to produce world historical wealth was and is an East Coast story *more than* a southern one.

Like any capitalistic enterprise, the system of enslaving Black people for profit had its levels, prioritizing the uppermost echelons of wealth production and its beneficiaries. Our prevailing history has been stuck looking at a certain midlevel echelon and its principal character: the southern plantation owner. We have clung to notions that the plantation, being the central site of *labor* in the enslavement system, was also the central and sole site of *profit-making*, despite copious evidence suggesting otherwise, copious evidence suggesting that even enslavers of the highest social eminence, contrary to popular belief, were often just making ends meet, beset with crippling debt and mounting costs.

In the world of slavery wealth, the "planter" isn't even the most consequential character to understand. And because our gaze is misplaced on him, we have failed to truly perceive, let alone attempted to quantify, the extraordinary magnitude of wealth that Black people forced into enslavement produced for the United States. To see that wealth requires perceiving the white men *at the top* of this capitalistic system, who truly created it, financed it, stole from it, and preserved it. These weren't the southern aristocrats who still dominate our collective imagination, a tiny percentage of whom owned plantations with an excess of one hundred enslaved people and resultantly produced generational wealth; and these were certainly not the slave traders, and less so the overseers, on whom our attention has understandably been focused, given their diabolical cruelty, but who were in fact the bottom of the chain.

The white entrepreneurs who extracted the greatest wealth from the system of enslaving Black children, women, and men did so at the greatest remove. They made their money not *on* the plantation but *through* it; not by being *near* to the cotton and cane fields but by being as *far away* from their management as possible; not by enslaving people themselves but by taking possession of what the enslaved produced, *after* the harvest, and controlling the transfer, the *destiny*, of Black people's labor. In America at that time, the mightiest affluence came from steering the effluence of slavery-produced wealth as it poured in bundles and bales from the deep furrows of the South, steaming over stolen Indigenous lands.

That wealth *itself* is what concerns us here. The corporate fortunes created by and then stolen from enslaved Black people by elite white men is this book's main character. As such, the basic organizing principle of this book, its analytic force, is to trace the rise of slavery wealth in the United States and follow it to where this vast fund of money ended up today. And though enslaved peoples began producing such wealth from their very arrival in America in 1619, this book focuses on the institutional profits of slavery as they arose in the 1790s, using corporate documents, statistical tabulations, and the business records of leading slavery capitalists.

The men who did this were market makers, earth movers, time benders—northern white men with their gaze tacked on the horizon of the east, over the great ocean. Shipbuilding, wind currents, and pounds-sterling-to-dollar conversion were their game. It was they who had the power to not only *finance* the largest, most coveted quantities of agricultural commodities the world has ever seen—hundreds of millions of pounds of cotton, sugar, and tobacco every year—but to *move* those massive quantities from one side of the earth to the other, from the interiors of the South, via the docks of New York, to the markets of Liverpool, Le Havre, and Antwerp, a logistical feat unprecedented in the history of the world. It was they who had the power to *exchange* these shipments, representing hundreds of millions of dollars' worth of enslaved people's time, from one physical form into another, into the legitimate currencies of elite white men, the cash notes, the railroad bonds, the Wall Street securities. It was they who took the largest slice of slavery's pie and lived in the greatest mansions the country had ever seen, leaving behind the country's greatest wealth for their progeny. They did so by owning the corporate structure that owned the southerners who exploited the enslaved: the credit houses that mortgaged a planter's farm and grew his acres; the brokering firms that commissioned cotton's record-shattering sales; the fleets of their age's most advanced ships that floated this precious cargo across the seas; the corporations that insured these vessels, the commodities on them, and the lives of the enslaved who made them possible; and the banks that swallowed up the prodigious flow of wealth, the ebb tide of enslaved people's energy, washing it back up on eastern shores. Some northern white men did all these at once, vertically integrating their enterprises around the theft of enslaved people's labor.

These are names rarely spoken of today—Moses Taylor and Percy Pyne; Anson G. Phelps; Alexander Brown and his sons, James, George, and William. Yet they still cast their long influence, like specters, through corporations that dominate our economy even now, corporations like New York Life Insurance, the mining company Freeport-McMoRan, Deutsche Bank, and Volvo. Or they are names celebrated distantly for their "success," because their wealth has been successfully distanced from their slavery, with the media vaunting their achievements in the public imagination without acknowledging their ties to Black people's subjugation: Mayer and Emanuel Lehman of Lehman Brothers Bank; George Peabody; August Belmont, agent of the famed Rothschild family; William E. Dodge, to name but a few.

We will have to ask ourselves why these names are almost entirely left out of the prevailing story we tell about America's long history of enslaving Black people for profit. Or why they're mentioned only in passing—always in passing—in the most celebrated accounts of slavery our nation has to date produced. It is an omission, it must be said, that has left our rendering of slavery woefully undertold. After all, how can we hope to truly understand the most heinous profit-making system the world has ever produced and its lasting impact on the Black people at its core if we don't look at the oligarchs, the profit masters, who extracted the greatest level of wealth from the top? It would be like trying to understand the ludicrous wealth generated by the tech industry by looking only at the software engineers and data center managers while never looking at Bill Gates and Jeff Bezos.

Knowing these names and their stories is critical because it highlights the most fundamental facet of the stolen wealth of slavery, a facet that's the central argument of this book: the wealth produced by four million enslaved Black people, which wasn't confined to the South, nor to the planters, but flowed continuously to the North, where it was harnessed by a small elite of northern white capitalists at a level unparalleled in the history of the world, also *never died, because it wasn't confined in time the way we've perceived it to be.*

As we've misapprehended the story of slavery's wealth geographically and anthropologically, we've done so temporally as well. We've misapprehended it as a story that ends in 1865, a fact made clear by opening most books on slavery and seeing how the chronology invariably stops at emancipation. Doing so creates an artificial breakage in historical time, cutting the umbilical cord linking our past to the present and the exploitation of Black people to corporate prosperity today. It also reinforces a dangerously outlandish misconception still widely held even now: that although the United States held the largest conglomeration of enslaved Black people anywhere in the world, amassed in the largest labor camps the world had ever seen, creating the most globally demanded commodities in world history and producing record-shattering amounts of wealth between 1790 and 1865 alone, this wealth somehow *disappeared* after the Civil War, apparently burning up overnight in the fires of conflict.

What particularly concerns these pages is precisely the opposite: how, *after* enslavement ended, leading white capitalists took the prodigious wealth wrought by generations of enslaved people, wealth illegitimately stolen from Black families, and transmuted it, like gold bar melted down to ore, into the "legitimate" industrial and financial corporations that catapulted the United States to the heights of global economic power after 1865. The core of this book is the story of the largest money-laundering operation in American history. And the purpose of telling it is to show that America's business of extracting wealth from enslaved Black people, far from being an antebellum phenomenon, is a present-day wound, a colossal theft that the United States in general, and corporations in particular, must address through reparations to Black Americans.

Central to this tale also is how Black activists in the early 2000s, starting with a lawyer named Deadria Farmer-Paellmann, sought out these truths, and how she revealed the origins of modern-day corporations as rooted in the bedrock of Black enslavement. She and other activists pushed corporations for the first time to acknowledge their complicity and provide restorative justice. Their unprecedented legal campaign helped give birth to the slavery reparations movement in the United States. The fruits of that work have never been more vital than they are today, and Farmer-Paellmann's story illuminates how corporations, by meaningfully committing to reparations, by reversing what has been their long record of silence, resistance, and obfuscation, can help effect a groundbreaking

shift in the country's long struggle to address the horrific crimes committed against Black people.

For now, a tightly sealed vault is where Citibank has placed not only
its treasure, but its history and roots in the generational wealth that it
stole from enslaved Black people. There that history has remained, figuratively beyond reach, beyond reproach, unquestioned, untouched,
wrapped in the ironclad prestige of an ironclad bank. Many of the major
corporations that power the American economy have done the same, as
the United States itself has done so collectively, sealing up the history of
Black wealth-making and its ties to modern corporations in a vault. In the
ensuing vacuum, history has been hijacked by myths, and were it not for
the pioneering litigation of Black activists like Farmer-Paellmann, the trail
might still be cold. The vault might still be fully sealed.

But it is not, and it is time that we pull back the door.

CHAPTER 1

HELL GATE

The wealth of slavery arrived each week to New York Harbor in the hulls of sailing ships. These were brigs, packets, and schooners, and they came from Charleston, New Orleans, and Chesapeake Bay. What they carried was not cash or coin, but the spectrum of precious commodities that enslaved Black people in the South were forced to produce: bales of cotton and tobacco, barrels of sugar, and bags of corn and Carolina rice. By 1810, only a few such ships had arrived in lower Manhattan, and they carried a total of $700,000 worth of cotton, a small but significant sum.[1] Yet by the 1820s, there were fleets of such ships, larger and more loaded down each year, and they hauled $4 million worth of cotton, the equivalent of almost $100 million today.[2]

This maritime trove grew and grew, such that ten years before the Civil War, two thousand vessels carried a bounty worth hundreds of millions of dollars up the coast to New York, as much as one-third of all the agricultural wealth that Black women, children, and men on southern plantations produced, the centerpiece of America's export trade. There in New York, these commodities were marketed, sold, and repackaged on thousands more oceangoing vessels, bound for England and other countries around the world.

This was staggering wealth, and though it had originated on plantations, it wasn't the South's anymore. Discharged on the slips of Manhattan's East River, not to mention in Philadelphia and Boston's Back Bay, this wealth became the domain of the North, feeding the ascendance and splendor of its Atlantic Ocean cities.

It wasn't by chance that Manhattan, though a thousand miles from the South, became the center of cotton, tobacco, and sugar shipping in the United States by 1820, and soon after that, the hub of financing and profiteering from Black enslavement in the nation. It happened because of a small set of white businessmen on Wall Street. It happened because of their ruthless design to make themselves richer, not by enslaving Black people themselves (though some did), but by commandeering the flow of products that Black people were forced to make.

These were men who kept their offices near the wharves. They lived in mansions of granite and marble on Fifth Avenue or Pearl Street or Broadway. They bore their era's most eminent names: they were Wrights and Aspinwalls, Minturns and Fishes, Taylors and Pynes, Gracies and Macys, Thompsons and Rogerses, Dodges, Phelpses, Browns, Howlands, and too many other white names to name. Many weren't born rich. Black people's stolen time and labor made them that way. By the 1820s, they constituted the pinnacle not only of New York society, but of white prosperity in the United States. They sat together on the same corporate boards and, through stock ownership, were further connected to an interlocking network of corporations, as well as society and charitable clubs. They were proudly committed to "culture," to white cultivation, *and* to enslaving Black human beings; doggedly racist; and later, rabidly anti-abolitionist. These men were mariners above all, their fortunes tied to the waters, to the shipping of cargo. The story of the rising wealth of slavery, bringing forward a new kind of riches that changed the country and the world, begins in an important sense with the sea.

A paragon among these men was Benjamin Marshall, and he distinguished himself early, a merchant capitalist presaging his age. Marshall was exceedingly rich, a famous banker and industrialist by the time he died in 1858. He was more than just an emblem of the terrible riches flowing north from the pits of slavery. He was one of the primary architects of this channel, setting in motion a process, soon amplified by others, that allowed white men to sell the products of Black enslavement on a greater scale than the world had ever seen. With wealth from slavery, Marshall was among the first to lay the financial foundation of New York. In the wake of his rise rose the prosperity of a city and an industry, shaping millions of lives to come. His story serves to solidify a sobering fact: the sprawling slave labor camps of the South could never have reaped such epic wealth, nor sown such epic misery, without New York, and New York could never have prospered without leeching onto this blood-soaked wealth. It was Benjamin Marshall and his circle—not exclusively, but primarily—who brought the vast money flows of slavery to the gates of Manhattan. And, with it, they built the country's lasting corporations, booming infrastructure, and strongest banks.

————

SINCE BEFORE THE time of the American Revolution, New York vessels had been sailing south, taking on the earliest cargoes produced by enslaved Black people (indigo, tobacco, deerskins, turpentine), then shuttling back to South Street's Maiden Lane. Nine days it took to sail from Manhattan to the port of Charleston at that time. Nine days by way of the East River, out the Narrows by Staten Island, finding the open waters of Sandy Hook, south past the Lower Bay, then along the forested coasts enfolding New Jersey and the Carolinas, hugging the capes of Lookout and Fear. It was a journey of some seven hundred miles, and a standard brig did it at a pace of less than one hundred a day. By 1775, some six hundred thousand enslaved people toiled in Virginia, Maryland, and the Carolinas; they produced one hundred million pounds of tobacco alone, at a value then of $4 million, or about $120 million today.[3] By 1790, with independence sweeping open territory and slavery expanding, more than eight hundred thousand Black people grew eighty million pounds of rice; white enslavers would soon have them cultivating sugar, and other crops as well.

Certainly, the South had ports from which to export these goods, chief among them Charleston, but it didn't have many. And, of course, there were southern merchants who owned ships, but collectively their tonnage

didn't amount to much. Shipbuilding was an old art, one that the southern states, by and large, didn't know and lacked the workmen to support.
Not so with New York, Boston, Philadelphia, and New England, whose
shipbuilding industry and numerous ports communicating with Europe
and the Caribbean were already more than one hundred years old.[4]
(New York's registered tonnage in 1799 was 120,253, compared to South
Carolina's 38,567; Massachusetts was 191,067, compared to only 286 in
Georgia.) As a result, New York's capacity to ship the South's growing slavery wealth wasn't only advantageously established after American independence, but it was growing, controlled by men who kept their vessels
at the docks off Beekman or Bowne or Crane, and their office fronts in
the warren of streets squeezed in and around that area. One of them was
Archibald Gracie, said to be "among the first merchants of this or any
other country—his ships visiting every port of the world."[5]

"A stout, fast-sailing vessel, burthen about four hundred tons, has
excellent accommodations for passengers, will sail from hence in all
next week for NORFOLK," advertised Gracie in 1784.[6] Originally from
Scotland, father to five, he had moved to Virginia for a time, sourcing
slavery-produced tobacco. With these proceeds, Gracie settled in New
York, where he purchased himself a ship to run more tobacco made by
enslaved Black people. Over the next twenty years, Gracie built a fleet,
and it sailed the ports of Baltimore, Richmond, and Norfolk, hauling to
Manhattan the bounty of what white southerners in that time produced
by Black people's hands, tobacco and flour principally. His ships sailed to
Cuba too, transporting sugar that enslaved people were beginning to cultivate on the island's plantations.

Slavery in its global manifestations was central to Gracie's shipping
empire; he enslaved no Black people in the South, yet slavery made Gracie
rich. He sold slavery-produced wares from his storefront on what was formerly dubbed Queen Street, in Manhattan, now known as Pearl. (His fleet
also sailed as far as India and China, and he sold Chinese tea and Indian
textiles.) From at least 1784, Gracie's vessels were also regularly sailing
between southern US ports and Liverpool, England, his three-hundred-
ton ship *Jeanie* and his four-hundred-ton ship *Industry* carrying tobacco
that enslaved people in Virginia had picked and packaged by hand.

In this way, New York businessmen were, from an early period, already linking together southern and British ports, with Manhattan placed in between, tracing the roughest outlines of a triangle—a triangle of trade that Marshall and his associates would later set in place. In the figure of Gracie, we see reflected a process of commercial evolution that would later accelerate during the antebellum period, a process that sows injustice to this day: trafficking the things enslaved people produced allowed white northern businessmen to own at first one ship and then many; with a fleet of ships, to transport even more enslavement goods, building a business empire; and with an empire suffused in the wealth of Black bondage, to buy into other commercial pursuits, diversifying into other forms of legitimate white wealth.

Gracie, just a few years from this period, would become a director of one of the most powerful institutions on Wall Street: Bank of America. To look at him is to witness then some of the earliest corporate foundations that the stolen wealth of slavery laid.

At 26 Wall Street, on the balcony of Federal Hall, George Washington took the oath of office as the country's first president in 1789. In short order, the republic had its first Congress, political party, and capital, and the right to profit from Black labor was enshrined in the Constitution for all, though compromises forbade white men from transporting Black people themselves over the seas. ("To buy and sell Africans is wicked, base, and detestable; to buy and sell colored Americans is in perfect accordance with the most exalted position in both State and Church," an abolitionist later noted about this hypocrisy.)[7] The architectures of US government, as with US commerce, in both the physical and conceptual sense, were being set in place, raised on the plinth of enslavement wealth with New York as host and home.

What power the Federalist Party exerted from that time and for the next two years under the hand of Alexander Hamilton was channeled for and by the prestige of merchants like Gracie. Hamilton and Gracie weren't only political associates, close friends, and business partners. (Together they founded the *New-York Evening Post*.) These were men at every turn deliberating on high-minded causes, the most portentous issues of their day—the new fiscal policy of Republicanism, the so-called rights of man, and notions of universal liberty and free trade. Yet while speaking words of high moral virtue in one breath, they exhibited the most base feelings of apathy toward Black people's afflictions in the next. Though committed to the civilizing force of democracy, they committed acts of searing cruelty in the face of Black people's humanity—humanity evident just before them, all around them, and, as we'll see, in their very homes.

How do we account for such contradiction? Toni Morrison, in her work *Playing in the Dark*, incisively explored just such a question, though through the lens of early American literature. Her insights are, with gratitude, put to use here, elucidating the grotesque paradoxes of this age. The duality of early America wasn't accidental, Morrison wrote, but imperative to budding notions of white liberty. Gracie's circle developed their very conceptions of freedom, honed their own sense of white freedom, precisely by projecting and parading it before those absolutely robbed of it. "The concept of freedom did not emerge in a vacuum. Nothing highlighted freedom—if it did not in fact create it—like slavery," Morrison wrote.[8] And so such men as Gracie, exemplars of the republic, lived by a duplicity designed to soften the knowledge that white men's ascent passed through the gates of Black people's hell. Gracie, the son of a lowly weaver, not only rose to the heights of this system of wealth and white supremacy. He built, as we'll see, one of its greatest monuments on a hill, where it confounds, and shimmers, and projects its doublespeak to this day.

In the 1790s, a man of riches like Gracie might trade what Black people made for English cloth, or Portuguese spirits, or furs. He might sell fifty casks of tobacco at his shop, tobacco that a man enslaved in chains near Tidewater, Virginia, had been coerced to make. Or he might broker its sale to New York agents representing French or British houses of trade. He might transport the tobacco to a foreign port, in one of his own vessels, along with ginseng and pearls.

What Gracie pocketed in return was gold or silver coins. Coins that might take the form of Spanish or US dollars, British pounds, Portuguese half joes, Dutch rijksdaalders, or French crowns—any number of the vast, at times, absurd proliferation of currencies then accepted in trade (this despite the founding of a national mint in 1792). Gracie, by 1798, had a large trove of such gold and silver coins. A single one of his ships transported to Spain cargo worth $137,620, or more than $3 million today; the ship itself was worth $342,000 in today's currency.[9] Not long afterward, Gracie was transporting supercargoes of silver itself, loaded up on large vessels bound to China and India to be invested overseas. Perhaps the rich mariner kept portions of his fortune in a strongbox at home or circulating through local banks. One thing we know Gracie did to protect and amplify his money was purchase real estate.

There was a bend in the East River known as Horn's Hook, roughly five miles from Federal Hall, a place still thickly blanketed with trees. In 1797, Gracie bought eleven acres of prime land there, in the vicinity of what is Eighty-Eighth Street today. The parcel cost him $5,625, one-third the cost of a ship, but its value, as an anchor for his class, grew and grew. There, on a rocky bluff, Gracie commissioned, by the famous builder Ezra Weeks, a wooden mansion of two stories, painted yellow, with a grand wraparound porch, one of the most magnificent estates of the era. It became known as Gracie Mansion, the very same Gracie Mansion that serves as the New York City mayor's residence to this day—the so-called People's House.

Popular history likes to recount that Gracie entertained lavishly there; that his home drew in Manhattan's tiny yet growing elite (in 1800, the city had only 33,131 inhabitants); that among his frequent guests over the years were Alexander Hamilton himself, John Jay, Founding Father and the nation's first chief justice, and Washington Irving, the writer. In fact, in the time before Irving wrote the masterpieces that would win him fame, Gracie's mansion was one of his favorite haunts.

The house's ornate facade faced the dramatic waters of a notorious strait, where rocks and fierce currents brought many a passing ship to its doom. Its name was Hell Gate. Here, Gracie's guests entered; here they waited to be feted, to be entertained.

We may avail ourselves of its vista as a point from which to take in the twisted moral waters, the zeitgeist of an age in which men like Gracie shaped America's lasting sense of character: in a newly independent nation, founded on freedom, its first capitalists rose to the heights of social and professional prestige, erecting grand houses through their deeper entrenchment in, and of, a system robbing Black people's freedom on an ever-increasing scale. This was a scale that Gracie's commercial activity was helping to grow, a scale that Gracie's mansion now reflected like a mirror.

The house came to symbolize the atrocities of slavery in more ways than one. Gracie had purchased by this point, with wealth steeped in

Black enslavement, at least five enslaved people for himself.[10] They served his guests and maintained his opulent style for no pay. At least one of them was a child. Yet Archibald Gracie was also a member of the New York Manumission Society, founded in 1785 to advocate freedom and education for Black people. He claimed to be an abolitionist. He contributed to the funding of schools for emancipated Black children in New York, the African Free Schools. But it meant Gracie made those contributions with money he derived from enslavement, as he kept a Black child in bondage.

It was a gross contradiction once again, a moral vortex, and all too typical of the age. Yet it was one that men like Gracie could ably live with, because all around them, prevailing social mores treated their duplicity as a kind of benevolence. The private right of white men to "extend" freedom to certain Black people while keeping it from others was considered a hallmark of civilization, not moral vacancy. ("We are convened to celebrate the triumphs of benevolence," self-congratulated an early pro-manumission tract.)[11] Paradoxically, one wasn't barred from joining the Manumission Society even if one enslaved people oneself; such a rule was not put into place until 1806. John Jay, in federal tax documents he filed in 1798, expounded in marginal notes almost proudly that, though he continually bought enslaved people, he intended to keep them only until such a time as their servitude "afforded a reasonable Retribution." After using them to recoup his investment, in other words, he then granted them freedom, a practice whose cruelty he appears genuinely to have viewed as magnanimity.[12]

Jay was president of the Manumission Society. And the organization's motivations overall were hardly benevolent: the programs Gracie and others funded were undertaken, as their early literature stated, with the intention to "keep a watchful eye over the conduct of such Negroes as have been or may be liberated; and…to prevent them from running into immorality or sinking into idleness." Such programs were designed, in other words, as a means of social and moral control, as the scholarship of John L. Rury traces.[13]

Alexander Hamilton, too, was an early member of the Manumission Society. For years, white scholars have hailed him as a revolutionary abolitionist, a so-called abolitionist Founding Father. But, as has recently come to light, Hamilton, too, enriched himself through Black enslavement, personally buying and selling Black human beings. Black enslavement "was essential to his identity, both personally and professionally," wrote Jessie Serfilippi in a 2020 research paper that, using Hamilton's personal ledger books, unearthed, for the first time, his enslavement of Black people.[14] In 1798, Hamilton even made $100 ($2,000 today) by lending out an enslaved Black boy to another party, and "collected money for the child's labor," Serfilippi said.[15]

As we'll see, many of the capitalists who later helmed the Manumission Society and other so-called abolitionist agendas also helmed the Wall Street powers that profited from, campaigned for, and vociferously defended the continuation of Black enslavement in the South. As with Gracie and Hamilton, so too with these other men. From this period, what white men signaled publicly about their opposition *in concept* to enslaving Black people differed entirely *in action* when it came to the business of keeping Black people enslaved and stealing Black wealth. Apropos, in 1799, New York passed the Gradual Emancipation Act, signaling that the time for legal enslavement in New York was eventually to end. In truth though, this law merely converted Black people so manumitted into indentured servants for the rest of their lives. (New York finally outlawed slavery in 1827.)

In 1801, Gracie took the step of freeing Abram Short, whom he had enslaved, as well as Sarah Short, Abram's wife. In 1802, Gracie then granted freedom to the couple's son, Charles Short.[16] It is unclear what became of the other two Black people Gracie enslaved. Despite his seeming benevolence, Gracie's involvement in and profiteering from the *business* of Black enslavement would become even more entrenched.

In 1799, the year he built his mansion, Archibald Gracie also incorporated, sold shares in, and served as president of the New York Insurance Company, founded at 66 Wall Street, one of the earliest corporate entities to provide insurance protection to vessels transporting slavery-produced goods. Its board included Joshua Sands, who ran ships from Charleston to England via New York, as well as John Blagge and John P. Mumford, shipping merchants for whom enslavement commodities like sugar, tobacco, and West Indian rum were critical to their business. White people's horizon for enslaving Black people was closing in New York, as in the rest of the North. But northern white men's capacity to traffic the things Black people were forced to make far away was widening, protected behind a new corporate shield of indemnity. In 1791, there had been no such insurance companies in the United States. By 1801, there were twenty-two, part of a burgeoning process of corporatization, born from slavery wealth, born to protect slavery wealth.

The laundering wheels were turning, illegitimate prosperity begetting more legitimacy, more whitewashed prosperity, more prestige for Gracie and his peers to soak up where the waters lashed the Hell Gate rocks. By a new century, the northern business of white profiteering from Black people's bondage was spinning its own centripetal force, gathering new numbers of men: the commissioner merchants, the brokers, the bankers, and the men to work the docks and warehousing, some from parts in and around the city, some from all the way across the sea. All of these individuals served the shipping trade, making a comfortable white living out of Black suffering in the South, hauling the loot to New York.

Washington Irving published few words about slavery, and those he did were confined to his short story "The Devil and Tom Walker," where he mentions that the devil is an enslaver. The only words he wrote explicitly on the subject, this trade all around him making friends like Gracie rich, remained unpublished, jotted in his diary during a boat trip down the Ohio river many years later. There he met, in Wabash, West Virginia, a "negro woman in log hut," whom he described as "a cheerful, contented being." Irving's party lingered with the woman for a time, eager voyeurs, and then one of them asked about her children. "The tears started into her eyes—she got up—crossed the hut—'I am not allowed to live with them—they are up at the plantation.'" There, Irving's diary cuts off. The "father of American literature," celebrated for his prolific probing of the American soul, never saw fit to write another word on this most fundamental American subject.[17] Irving, Gracie, Hamilton, and others like them were bequeathing, through the pillars of culture, commerce, and politics, a new world at once stunningly rich for white men of privilege yet willfully dumb, deaf, and blind to how white people filched from and abused Black people.

In the year 1802, Gracie, already one of the wealthiest men in New York, moved his "counting house" to 52 Pine Street. There he began importing a precious new commodity from lands freshly opening in the

South, the harvest of a new kind of plantation. Making his stake in this trade, Gracie was about to enter a category of white wealth utterly new in the history of the world, even by his standards. He publicized it for the first time in the *New-York Evening Post*, his newspaper: "Archibald Gracie... has just received, and for Sale—106 bales Sea-Island Cotton."[18]

New York City, like its mariners, had begun siphoning the first flows of wealth made by enslaved people as it seeped out of the post-Revolution South. And that wealth, through conduits like Gracie, was fertilizing the city's first corporate financial institutions. Yet there wasn't even any cotton to speak of. When cotton came, everything changed. And that was the moment that Benjamin Marshall would arrive.

———

SURVEYING THE RANGES of his new land three miles outside of Savannah, Georgia, Nichol Turnbull, "being at the time a stranger in the country, and little known," found himself anxious about his prospects, as he later wrote.[19] He spent that first season, the spring of 1789, making careful observations as to the surrounding climate, to know if there was something new on the land that might be done. Turnbull's holdings he called Deptford, and they had good frontage along the river—all told, 150 acres of marshland, plus 90 more acres on higher ground. During that time, Turnbull had sought out and found a quart of new seed from a man named John Smith of South Carolina, a seed called cotton that Smith in all probability had sourced from the Bahamas, where the plant had long been grown. That spring, Turnbull had one of the people he'd enslaved place a handful in the ground, on a single patch of earth among the lands he owned out at Whitemarsh Island. He waited, expecting little.

There was a time before cotton, a time when the islands off the coast of South Carolina shimmered in waves of blue indigo, before planters in the low country ceased trading that plant, replacing it with white gold. A time when cotton picked by enslaved people never left US shores. A time when white men had neither the surplus cotton to ship nor the ships to ship it. A time, to use sociologist W. E. B. Du Bois's terminology, before Black workers "began to grow a fiber that clothed the masses of a ragged world." A very long time in fact. It's well recorded that white settlers had the people they enslaved in Virginia cultivate cotton as far back as 1620. It's also well recorded that white men didn't export slave-picked cotton until after the Revolutionary War. When they did, America's cotton enterprise did not go well at first.

A famous story relates that when the English cotton merchant William Rathbone tried to import roughly twenty-eight hundred pounds of cotton to Liverpool in 1784, British customs officers seized the shipment on the grounds that it was fraudulent—they'd simply never heard of cotton being produced in the United States for export.[20] It wasn't until the following year, 1785, that a shipment of American cotton did reach Liverpool properly, arriving aboard a ship called the *Diana*, sailing from Charleston. Wrapped in burlap it came, pressed into a square—a bale—the better to fit tightly in the hold. This first shipment consisted of only one bale, or four hundred pounds. The next month another shipment arrived, this time from New York. It consisted of only two.

Two bales were the beginnings of the cotton business. Eight hundred pounds formed the origins of America's powerhouse wealth. Along a journey of four thousand miles, from the South to Liverpool, cotton continued to flow. Many hands passed this cotton, port to port, ship to ship, dock to dock. But among the first to touch it, to make it, to raise this wealth from the ground, were a woman named Lucy, a woman named Betty, and a teenager named Cato. Cato, Lucy, and Betty labored on a plantation owned by Nichol Turnbull; they were among Georgia's first enslaved.

Turnbull had come to Georgia in 1787, part of a larger flow of migrants pouring into that sparse and vastly unsettled land. He had arrived from Florida, the very rich scion of one of the wealthiest landowning families of that state. Others had been coming to Georgia since 1783, mostly from Virginia and North Carolina, poorer than Turnbull but by and large looking for cheap land that enslaved Black people would work. "The smallest planters buy some [slaves] as soon as they can, leave off doing any work for themselves, and grow lazy," observed one visitor at the time.[21] White slave traders forcefully marched nearly forty thousand enslaved Black people, on foot, south and west, to work the new lands men like Turnbull were opening up; they brought more than six thousand to Georgia alone. By 1790, the enslaved population had swelled to twenty-nine thousand, making up 35 percent of the state. As they did in Virginia, Maryland,

and South Carolina, white people tasked them to grow tobacco and rice. But the demand for those commodities wouldn't hold. Tobacco sales were flattening, and rice was beginning to fall as well, the result, among other things, of restrictive measures and punishing tariffs imposed by the Crown. Two years after ratifying the Constitution, the United States was, from the standpoint of trade at least, a poorer country than it had been before independence.

Much had to change, of course. But chief among those processes is that Turnbull's cotton quickly bloomed. "Finding it produced beyond my expectation," wrote Turnbull, "encouraged me to plant it as a part of my crop the year following." As early as June 1789, just months after he first planted it, Turnbull says, he began shipping quantities of his cotton across the sea to England, where Lancashire was just beginning to sprout its mills. The crop must have fetched a decent price, for Turnbull had his enslaved people plant forty acres of cotton next season, and the year after he had them prepare one hundred acres of ground.[22]

By their hand, and through their work, Deptford became unique among plantations, emblematic of America's history of wealth tied to Black enslavement. For Turnbull was among the first people in all the United States to experiment with cotton production on this scale. In fact, Turnbull, a man of boastful qualities, declared himself "the first founder and introducer of cotton planting since the Revolution."[23] This may not be true; possibly others came first. (John Earle and Colonel Andrew Deveaux, on the island of Skidaway, are considered contenders, and Patrick M'Kay, on the island of Sapelo, is another.) Conventionally, Turnbull is credited as among the first to experiment with cotton cultivation on a serious scale, which is to say, the first to experiment with coercing Black people to produce quantities of cotton sufficient for exportation.[24]

Just five years after their first attempt, enslavers like Turnbull sent 250,000 pounds of cotton to England. By 1793, the shipments had doubled to 500,000 pounds. And a year after that, the combined export of cotton enterprises like Turnbull's was an astounding 1.7 million pounds. Eli Whitney's cotton gin, an invention to quickly separate cotton fibers from their seeds, drove the explosion, and the increased rate with which it allowed enslaved people to clean cotton, combined with the increasing numbers of those enslaved, dramatically increased agricultural production

and efficiency across the South. Thus both cotton and slavery were effectively promoted on an industrial scale.

Within the span of just years, cotton sparked unimaginable wealth for
white people. The value of 1794's export crop was $500,000, or roughly
$12 million now. A precious commodity, produced with free labor, at the
exact moment in time when the world's demand for that commodity was
expanding, building to a seemingly limitless height.

British textile manufacturing absorbed every bale the US ships
brought, and demanded still more, indicating that there wasn't enough.
America's enslaved were expected to reap, and reap again. Steam mills
were spreading throughout England, eighty-two went up between 1785
and 1800 alone (the first went up in Manchester in 1789), and 350,000
people already worked there by 1788, records the historian Eric Williams
in the magisterial work *Capitalism and Slavery*.[25] Across India, the Americas, and the Mediterranean, humanity was changing, no longer spinning
its own cloth. The world thirsted for cheap shirts, processed pants, jackets,
and caps, and England was making them. Its mills thirsted for fiber to
render into cloth; the new slavery entrepreneurs—Turnbull in Savannah,
Kingsley Burden of Burdens Island, South Carolina, William Elliott at
Hilton Head, John Scriven of St. Luke's Parish, South Carolina—thirsted
for markets.[26] James Madison, in Annapolis in 1786, was enthused. "From
the garden practice in Talbot County, [Maryland], and the circumstances
of the same kind abounding in Virginia, there was no reason to doubt
that the United States would one day become a great cotton-producing
country."[27] The remedy lay one in the other, Great Britain to the United
States, across the oceans, with vessels as the bridge, and "the black workers
of America bent at the bottom of a growing pyramid of commerce and
industry," as Du Bois wrote.[28]

In this way, through the docks of Liverpool, British manufacturing
was saving the United States from a deficit of trade, and yet it was through
the docks of New York and Charleston that the British were saved, their
new economy gorged with material. "The New World, thanks to Eli Whitney, had come, not for the last time, to the rescue of the Old," observes
Williams.[29]

The coming of this moment itself—this peak alignment of supply and
demand, born out of England and the spinning heat of its looms—speaks

to the stolen wealth of slavery, the rueful story of transformative wealth exploited from Black people. That is the story that Williams's breathtaking research shows: how textile manufacturing was only possible because British capitalists, rich from West Indian slavery, from sugar, tobacco, and rum, had invested their money in steam and industry. Slavery wealth made England the textile and weaving center of the world, with Manchester as the center of it, and the world's cotton scraped across the docks of Liverpool. "It was the capital accumulated from the West Indian trade that financed James Watt and the steam engine,"[30] wrote Williams, and he showed, too, that the white business of enslaving Black people wasn't the business of creating wealth that disappeared. It was the business of creating white wealth that endured, white wealth from Black enslavement that seeped into the streets of Europe's great cities, building the palaces of Madrid and Lisbon and the Liverpool Town Hall, wealth that multiplied and shaped the world.

Stolen Black wealth had done that then; it was about to do so again now. Only this time it was "Mississippi, Manhattan, and Manchester," to use scholar Walter Johnson's terminology. "The history of Manchester never happened without the history of Mississippi," affirms Johnson. (And the history of both those places, it must be added, could never have happened without Manhattan, and vice versa.)[31]

Few human records exist to tell the epic from Deptford, to speak of the Black women, men, and children forced to work on Turnbull's land. Census records from the 1790s, many of them since digitized, are often a helpful tool, but those of Georgia have been lost or destroyed. What we know comes in part from newspaper advertisements that Turnbull himself placed and, otherwise, from a single document: Nichol Turnbull's will. On one hand, his will tells us much; on the other, precious little. Turnbull lists sixty-nine Black adults among his "property," as well as five infants. Here then are seventy-four lives that lived, including a driver named Bacchus, and three carpenters, two named Peter, one named Alick. Yet the document merely enumerates these people, stripping away their full names. The combined value of these lives Turnbull appraises at merely $18,400, a relative value of $419,000 today.[32]

From proximate accounts of that time, we know well the instruments of physical violence Turnbull was free to use, extracting blood and wealth from the Black people he enslaved. A visiting French dignitary, the Duke de la Rochefoucault Liancourt, traveled through Savannah in 1795, near Deptford. He captured the atmosphere of sadistic violence then prevailing in the region: "For the murder of a [Black person] with malicious intent, a white man pays a fine of three thousand six hundred and eighty dollars. If he have only beaten the [Black person], without intention of murder, till his death ensued, the fine is but one thousand five hundred dollars. He who maims a [Black person], puts out his eyes, cuts off his tongue, or castrates him, pays only a fine of four hundred and twenty dollars. It is easy to see, that a white man can, in such case, seldom be convicted; as [Black people] are incapable by law of giving evidence."[33]

In September 1799, the young man Cato, whom Turnbull enslaved, ran away for the second time. He was twenty years old. Turnbull, in an ad he placed offering Cato's captor a twenty-dollar reward, detailed Cato's first escape: "Cato is well known in and about Savannah, and will endeavor to get on board of some vessel, as once he secreted himself on board a ship bound to Grenada, and was returned to me thence."[34] Here was the opposite, yet the coeval, of Washington Irving. Together, the two book-ended the spectrum of white people's response to Black exploitation: One willfully blind to it, his privilege allowing him to have nothing to say. The other's gaze maniacally fixed on it, hunting down and rechaining a young Black life from the distance of nearly two thousand miles away.

By the end of forced marches in 1800, 893,602 Black people were enslaved in the United States, and the country's total population stood at 5.3 million.[35] That year, southern plantations sent twenty-seven million pounds of cotton to England—a crop worth $5 million, or a relative value of $106 million today. According to one estimate, cotton was fetching on average forty-five cents a pound, and would continue to do so until 1806.[36] These were record numbers, in terms of the Black human beings enslaved, the cotton they were forced to produce, and the value this new commodity commanded. And yet nothing compared to what they were about to become. Driven on this tide, the number of plantations like Turnbull's would continue growing; they would triple by 1830 from the time of the Revolution.

Within just its first fifteen years of cultivation, cotton generated more than $17.5 million in new wealth for white men, a figure equivalent to $372 million today. By 1800, it accounted for more than 15 percent of all the wealth the new republic made in export trade. It's reasonable to ask: What became of it? Where was it flowing, and who was making this money?

In this early period, and even later on, our search to find the presence of lavish wealth in the South will mostly be in vain. Instead, as numerous studies over the course of nearly a hundred years have shown, the new wealth of cotton and the new trove of slavery weren't pouring into the southern cities. They weren't building up the avenues of Charleston or augmenting Norfolk's roads—not to the extent one would expect. Some slaveholding families were growing rich, buying more enslaved people, planting new lands. But overall, the wealth of slavery wasn't seeping into southern industrialization. Nor was it seeping into shipbuilding, making the South its own world-class fleet. Wealth wasn't mounting in the vaults of the South's great rising banks; there were very few. As Nobel Prize–winning economist Douglass C. North showed back in the 1960s, urbanization and infrastructure in the southern cities were minimal, except for those few ports that specialized in sending slavery wealth away, principally Savannah, Charleston, and, to some extent, Mobile at this time. And the states these cities are in didn't grow much in population, ranking among the least populated in the nation. By and large, the southern states were characterized by growing swaths of agrarian land, worked by increasing numbers of destitute farmers and the enslaved, but overall containing, relative to the East and the North, very few people.[37]

A similar contrast arises when we look at corporations. In 2013, the scholars Richard Sylla and Robert E. Wright, at the economics department of New York University's Stern School of Business, compiled a database of all corporations formed in America's antebellum period. They found that, between 1790 and 1810, the period of cotton's initial rise, wealthy merchants throughout the North incorporated a total of nearly nine hundred businesses (banks, insurance companies, shipping, construction, etc.) with combined capital of nearly $45 million. During the same period, entrepreneurs in the South incorporated only 135 businesses, roughly one-seventh the number in the North, with only $19 million in capital, less than half that of the North. These statistics suggest that enslavers, plantation runners, and others connected to slavery, while generating wealth, weren't investing it at remarkable levels in the South.[38]

Between 1785 and 1800, the wealth of the nation *was* expanding. But the South wasn't where the story of slavery's wealth and its power was playing out. This was because enslavers like Turnbull, in order to sell their cotton at markets in the North and across the Atlantic, had to pay merchants a commission of 2.5 percent to broker such sales. Southern enslavers also had to pay for the services that sent their crop away, including docking fees, warehousing, baling, and, of course, shipping freight. Finally, they also had to pay to secure their cargoes, through the insurance policies that were becoming, thanks to shippers like Archibald Gracie, standard practice in that day. Cotton was quickly becoming a business, increasingly controlled by corporations—northern corporations. And in taking their cut, those corporations were forcing planters like Turnbull deeper down the growing pyramid, like a bale crushed into a ship's hold.

"For the slave owner and the landlord to keep a large or even reasonable share of these profits was increasingly difficult," Du Bois observed.[39] And this is to say nothing of banking and credit, of which there shortly would be much more to say. "Thus while the planters monopolized the cotton industry, drew to themselves the surplus of slaves, and apparently increased their wealth enormously, they were really but custodians of these returns, administrators of the wealth of Northern men who really ultimately received the profits of Southern plantations and Southern slavery," reported William E. Dodd in the 1919 book *The Cotton Kingdom.*[40]

———

AT THE END of 1801, Turnbull took out an ad to announce that Cato, now his personal servant, had fled from Deptford yet again. This meant that Cato had been recaptured sometime after September 1799 and that this was at least his *third* attempt to secure his freedom. Again, in ads placed in the newspapers, Turnbull offered Cato's prospective captor a twenty-dollar reward. Turnbull, surely bearing in mind how Cato had escaped the first time, added that any captain of any vessel harboring or carrying off Cato "will be prosecuted with the utmost vigor of the law." He signed it

November 20, 1801.[41] Turnbull ran the ad in the *Georgia Gazette* several times over the course of eight weeks. At least fifty-six days, then, Cato appears to have been free—from Deptford and Turnbull, at least. By the middle of January 1802, Turnbull's ads altogether ceased, and it's not clear whether Cato had been recaptured and reenslaved. Tellingly, though, Turnbull's will when he died did not list Cato among those he enslaved. Perhaps Cato found a ship in Savannah, a vessel with a captain willing to harbor him and sail him to a place of peace and hope.

By the light of a new century, hundreds, if not thousands, of enslaved people like Cato were running away, across the rivers, through the forests that still blanketed the land, or on ships that might take them north to places like New York and Boston, where Black people, like Abram and Sarah Short, were increasingly free. If they were lucky, they found their way along the same rivers, and perhaps even on the same boats, that carried their stolen wealth away—two destinies of the United States converging along the same lines.

Cotton production, meanwhile, exploded in the South, dripping off its docks, building at a dizzying degree. Here were thirty million pounds of product—the equivalent of fifteen thousand cars, fifty thousand horses, or five thousand shipping containers—to be moved one thousand miles to New York, and then three thousand miles across the Atlantic, at every season, at ever-greater volumes, and at ever-closer intervals. The trade became increasingly faster to market and faster in general, collapsing geography— a logistical challenge seldom seen in the history of the world. The question was: How would shipping keep pace with this system of wealth-making and production, a system tied to spreading misery and brute subjugation? And who would control the flow?

CHAPTER 2

THE TRIANGLE AND
THE TROVE

Benjamin Marshall left Huddersfield, West Yorkshire, for Manhattan, New York, in August 1803. He was just twenty, arriving empty-handed. Manhattan was still a windswept island, its urban core only one and a half square miles. Beyond Federal Hall were limitless green fields, dotted with mansions like Gracie's. Within sixty years, the span of Marshall's lifetime, the city would explode into a million teeming lives, a glittering realm of contradiction and class strife: palaces of glass and white marble; Broadway's glitz, the Bowery's reek; tens of thousands crushed into shanties by the water's rocks. For now, it had only five banks (there were twenty-eight in the entire country) and no grid. The streets were a labyrinth of ramshackle wood. ("In general the houses are mean, small and low...and a great many of them yet bear the marks of Dutch taste," observed one visitor.)[1]

It was also wracked by disease. In fact, cholera and yellow fever had overrun the island when Marshall set sail. Many people were leaving Manhattan, according to a doctor visiting from Edinburgh at the time. "It was reckoned that...half of the population [had] fled," he wrote. "The disease raged in narrow streets near the wharfs, where numbers of ill-fed and irregular people were crowded together."[2] Still, Marshall remained. He would manage to escape the widening contagion but was soon exposed to that different disease spreading mania all around him—the naked self-interest of fortune seeking through the ruthless degradation of Black people. Like Gracie, Marshall exemplified what Toni Morrison called "European settlers in the act of becoming Americans"—that is, people finding new and untold advantages of wealth and personality by "wielding absolute power over the lives of others."[3]

Fortunately for him, Marshall had two friends in New York, Francis Thompson, and Thompson's father-in-law, Isaac Wright, and they offered to lodge him in safety at their mansion "in the country," which is to say, in a still-bucolic part of Manhattan that later became Thirteenth Street. Marshall accepted. And so, freshly arrived, Marshall stumbled into the kind of association on which the platforms of history are made. It deepened not only his own financial prospects but also became a pin around which the crushing mill of cotton fortunes began to spin faster—first in New York, then the entire region, and eventually the world.

Marshall's friends, Thompson and Wright, were both older than he was, and Thompson was also an Englishman by birth. Wright owned ships, and Thompson had built a store close to the wharves, amid other well-to-do merchants, cabinetmakers, and purveyors of dry goods and cheese. He offered Marshall work in the store at 10 Beekman Street. Again, Marshall accepted, and again the arrangement suited him well. Thompson imported wool from relatives in Yorkshire, and this was a trade that aligned closely with Marshall's own.

Marshall wasn't a mariner, at least not at first. From the time he was old enough to work, he'd made his living in cotton, made a life, in fact, of heaving himself up the global cotton ladder. He'd started in manufacturing, spinning yarn and weaving cloth, as many in Huddersfield wove in their homes. At sixteen, he'd moved to Manchester, the textile center, deepening his ties to the trade. By eighteen, Marshall would have been familiar with the varieties of cotton arriving in England from eastern Turkey, Jamaica, Barbados, Guyana, and Brazil. No doubt Marshall would have encountered the new variety as well, the variety overtaking factories across Britain as the nineteenth century dawned: fine cotton, silky and abundant.

Black people enslaved in the southern US interior had reaped yet another record harvest, a harvest exported to England in 1802 at twenty-seven million pounds: loot worth $5 million then, loot worth roughly $132 million today, loot sufficient to make new fortunes and break old worlds. Not long after he encountered American cotton, Marshall became discontented to simply merchandise it from afar. He'd shuttled across the world on the wager that being closer to this prized crop's source would bring him fortune. In the United States, he hoped to work at selling cotton to England. On Beekman Street, in an office next door to Francis Thompson's, Benjamin Marshall began purchasing cotton produced by Black people enslaved in the South, with hopes of sending it abroad.

It wasn't an unusual choice, of course. Gracie and countless young northern white men had sought riches by selling wares that Black people had labored over for no pay. They tended to do so remotely, at a distance from the plantations furnishing their profits, the horror sites where Black people were beaten, worked to exhaustion, sexually assaulted, and emotionally abused. Marshall did so too at first, but then something changed in the way he pursued his business, something with greater ramifications for the building of America's slavery trove. He moved himself closer yet again to the core of production and violence, for he deduced that he could increase his profits immeasurably if, instead of buying cotton in New York, he traveled to the South and worked directly with enslavers to procure the crop. It was an opportunity to be seized in a realm of expanding exploitation, much like coming to the New World had been—to exalt himself higher in the cotton trade, making him even more rich.

And so, driven once again by that impulse, Marshall began traveling south each year, while still very young, buying up cotton directly from plantations, something other northern merchants at the time didn't regularly do. Ever the cutthroat youth, he personified one of the earliest links bridging the US plantation economy and the markets of Wall Street. "A pioneer," one historian called him, "among the hundreds who would later go south from New York on similar missions."[4] Marshall evidently found his southern experience important enough that he made it his practice to spend each winter in Georgia, a sojourn allowing him to dwell even more closely to cotton's source and study the process of its cultivation up close—which is to say, its cultivation through excruciating torments inflicted on Black people, an experience, evidently, that didn't weigh heavily on his conscience in any discernible way. Marshall continued this practice of wintering in Georgia because of a friendship he'd struck up there, a friendship with Nichol Turnbull.

There at Deptford, at the site of one of the earliest enterprises in slavery-produced cotton cultivation in the history of the United States, Marshall began to watch and learn. Through Deptford, the arc of his ambitions yet again began to grow. The capital he made from selling cotton he then invested in vessels themselves, carrying the earliest shipments of slavery cotton north, to New York. By 1811, shipping records show, Marshall himself was receiving on Wall Street consignments of cotton from Savannah and Charleston, and not long after, from more distant slave centers around the world.[5] In 1813, for example, he boasted in newspaper advertisements of having eighty thousand pounds of Bahia cotton for sale, cotton produced by enslaved people in Brazil.[6] It was a large consignment, certainly, with the potential to make Marshall even more wealthy, and he advertised that it was "lying in a Southern port." But that was the operative phrase: it was lying around, waiting for a buyer, like a dinghy trapped in the doldrums. Marshall was still merely an importer, a merchant at the mercy of buyers. He waited on demand, and such restless idleness conflicted with his designs.

Marshall wanted to source and sell cotton at a faster rate, maximizing its commercial flow. Sometime around 1816, he struck upon an idea. He'd seen firsthand that enslavers like Turnbull if aided by greater carrying capacity could substantially magnify their output, meeting rising global demand. Plantations like Deptford were growing not only in number across southern lands, but growing in size, in the number of coerced hands. The transportation logistics to accommodate the precious output, however, weren't keeping pace. Marshall saw the opportunity to reinvent these shipping arrangements, with a chance, once more, to configure himself more prominently in the harnessing of slavery's profits, propelling himself further up the cotton ladder.

And so an idea burst from the tableau of toiling unfree Black people he'd witnessed in Georgia under the lash. The feelings that welled up in Benjamin Marshall, amid all that suffering, weren't of violent indignation or Christian-tinged humanity; he did not call for liberation or abolition. Marshall's vision was of a ship. Not a ship of freedom to loosen the cord of misery that slavery created. A ship to tighten the cord, to amplify the production, to quicken the pace. A ship to break cotton out of a landlocked hold and bring it to the world through the docks of Manhattan.

Marshall's destiny would be bound to the abundant suffering around him. Again, he wasn't special in this callousness. But given his growing networks on Wall Street, his ties to the South, and the array of options and privileges laid before him, Marshall had made himself into something singular, and the material consequences of his rather mundane callousness became singular too. He was just thirty years old. His choice highlighted the ferocity of ideas, the terrible freedom everyday white men had— unrestrained by law, by commerce, by markets, by geography—to shape the world by entrapping Black people's lives. A new doctrine of wealth-seeking and success emerged from that power, tied to the new American identity, and it would echo through history, extolled and emulated through the ages.

Marshall's idea was to work directly with the South's enslavers, sourcing the products they forced Black people to make in labor camps growing both in size and in number, camps Marshall knew intimately. And he wanted to ship that cargo on a fleet of vessels that he would own across the world. Many merchants already did that, but their ships were small, and they sailed irregularly or on haphazard routes, and then only when their hulls were full. There was also much hand-wringing about potential bad weather. Undeterred, Marshall envisioned something far greater to anchor Black suffering to the world: several ships would sail across the Atlantic on a fixed schedule every month. They would be larger than the ships that existed, carrying more cotton than ever before; they would sail in revolving order, meaning a constant flow of goods; and they would sail on a fixed geodesic line, the same routes, the same dependability every time—an ocean-liner.

It was a confounding idea, truly, when all shipping was desultory back then and few mariners bothered crossing the seas on time. And Marshall devised this system to bring order and capacity to the delivery of enslavement's harvest, and through that routinization, to hone the entire slavery system like a machine. It would provide him and his cohort a bigger stake in enslavement's profit, dragging a larger conduit of it to the North, to New York. It would make him even more rich.

There were also national and industrial implications for what Marshall supposed. A fleet of regular vessels would streamline the significant but irregular flow of trade coming back from England: railroad iron, tools, textiles, machinery for cotton mills—all manner of goods needed to build a rising nation. Marshall's fleet would return those items to the United States aboard the very same ships. It would be a triangle of trade. A cotton triangle. From cotton ports to European ports, with New York in between. Marshall's idea laid the blueprint for one of the institutional foundations of what America's enslavement of Black people would become. What's more, it coincided almost precisely with pertinent financial configurations then emerging on Wall Street and in other cities throughout the North. Together, Marshall's idea and those processes allowed the North's banking and maritime dominance of the business of slavery to emerge.

———

DURING THE WAR of 1812, the hostility with Britain, the blockades, and the frequent seizures of ships caused cotton exports to diminish considerably for several years, and anxiety over the nation's trade and fiscal policy to grow. Merchants in New York were particularly incensed. While cotton was not moving, they also worried that the federal government's banking arm, the Bank of the United States, had dissolved. The renewal of the bank's charter was held hostage in Congress, where long-lasting squabbles raged over who should best control the banks: the federal government, or individual states.

Failure to renew the charter would mean the drying up of credit in a city already constrained by having just five other banks, a city whose banking prowess was inferior to that of Philadelphia, Boston, and Baltimore. New York was a city of shipping and trading merchants; they were eager to capture more of the South's cotton supply. At the time, "Wall Street was the centre, not of great banking institutions, as it is now, but of the great merchants of raw materials, [including] cotton," wrote *Moody's Magazine* in 1914.[7] Many merchants thus banded together; they organized for credit, and they appealed to the New York State Legislature to grant new charters for more private banks.

Their action took place in parallel to an important change in the structure and financing of the cotton market itself, a change also affected by the war. Planters like Turnbull had once sold directly to Liverpool, and British merchants on occasion had gone directly to the planters for their supply. But because ships were being seized on the high seas and seizures were expensive, shipping now involved significantly higher risks, which meant higher costs. It took more and more capital to sell southern cotton abroad, capital the old guard of enslavers and southern merchants couldn't readily raise on their own.

The cotton markets organized themselves with striking speed in response. By 1815, what had been the more direct system was done away with, and the New York shipping merchants controlled the trade by putting in place a long chain of intermediaries who could distribute the risk while also capturing the advantages nipping at the margins. They dominated in the end because New York Harbor was still the most advantageous port in the country from which to sail goods to the world.

A contemporaneous source describes the arrangement: "It has been the practice of the large shipping merchants to send annually to the south agents to purchase cotton and other staple commodities for exportation… The crops of the planters are usually contracted for by the merchants long before they come to maturity; the price being predicated upon a calculation of what their value would be."[8] It meant that from Wall Street, Archibald Gracie or Benjamin Marshall would send an agent to Savannah or New Orleans. The agent would then arrange to purchase cotton or tobacco through a "factor," a local representative who sourced the product directly from plantations in the interior. Marshall's agent would advance funds to an enslaver like Turnbull through the factor, based on the presumed sale; for this service, the agent took a fee of 2.5 percent. The agent in turn arranged to ship the cotton coastwise to his principal, Gracie or Marshall; and Marshall, upon unloading the cotton at New York, shared samples with agents of the London houses, who in turn were connected by a web of agents to the textile manufacturers of Manchester. Finally, Archibald Gracie or Benjamin Marshall had their employees load the cotton back upon a ship and sail it across the Atlantic.

It was a highly convoluted system made even more complicated by this: Hardly any of these transactions, at any point on the chain, involved actual cash changing hands. From this period on, the business of growing and selling staples produced through slavery, as well as buying land and enslaved people, all ran on promises, advances, and commissions, which is to say, faith. And all of these transactions were captured in a dizzying avalanche of bills and notes, each person assured their due when the sale was finally realized. A system, in other words, that those with access to capital or credit could easily exploit to the point of a planter's doom or a creditor's collapse. It was into this new system, a revolution in mercantile credit and mercantile banking, that the private banks of Wall Street were about to meld. They would begin feeding credit to various points on the slavery chain, both through the private affairs of their directors, and the banks' business lending to clients in the trade.

City Bank of New York had been among the first to receive a charter in the new scenario. Housed at the slender, stone-hewn building at 52 Wall Street, its inaugural project was financing the War of 1812 that had just broken out. (It lent $500,000 to the US Treasury.) But Citibank built its lasting reputation and finances through its seeping leverage in the commerce of slavery. Its fourteen founding directors were an amalgamation of Wall Street merchants who, through various personal and professional links, were intimately connected to America's business of Black enslavement, though that's a story that's never been told. The fact that many of them came to be in positions of power and privilege within the world of banking after first attaining positions of power and privilege in the commerce around enslavement is striking and instructive. What's more, the founding of their bank, itself profoundly shaped by the enslavement business, would also profoundly shape the future of cotton and Wall Street.

Among City Bank's first directors was Benjamin Bailey. Through his various companies—Bailey & Willis, Bailey & Bagert, among others—he transacted significant business in cotton, arranging ships and brokering sales for plantation enslavers. Bailey lived in a large house at 79 Chambers

Street. He patronized enslavement not just in the South; on a fleet of vessels, he brought sugar to New York from the slavery plantations of Cuba, and molasses to Wall Street from the West Indies. "Will proceed to any southern port for cargo," was one of his advertisement calls.[9] In 1809, manumission records show, Bailey enslaved a Black woman named Hannah, and later another Black woman named Dolly Floyd. In successive years, he also enslaved a man named Joseph Clark.[10]

It's important to note that Bailey's connections to enslavers, not to mention his wealth derived from slavery itself, would have been the very reason why he was invited to be a director at City Bank. From these early days of banking, as bank insiders like James Sloane Gibbons explained in 1858, directors were specifically chosen "for their wealth, commercial experience, and influence in attracting to the institution a good class of dealers."[11] Black enslavement and the bounty of agricultural trade it was furnishing was one of the fastest-growing revenue streams in both the country and the Northern Hemisphere. The Atlantic world, predicated on coercion, violence, and maritime trade, was an atmosphere where Bailey thrived; he would have been seen as an asset to the bank.

Similar findings encircle the biography of Peter Stagg, another City Bank director. Starting in 1800, his business was centered on the "West Indian trade," a euphemism for trafficking lucrative products made by enslaved Black people. Stagg sold tobacco made in Haiti (then known as Saint-Domingue), hides and coffee from Curaçao, and upland cotton from Charleston. He traveled regularly to source these products himself, forming close business ties to white enslavers throughout the hemisphere. In other words, men who routinely exploited Black people through abuse and exhaustion were the basis of Stagg's rising wealth, and that money running from them, through him, ran into City Bank.

John Swartwout was another original City Bank director. Citi used to describe him on its website as "among the more swashbuckling" directors, though as of 2023 it has removed that description. The bank has never disclosed that Swartwout, based at 85 Water Street, kept in bondage a Black woman named Jenny, as well as her children, Susan and Harriet, as historical documents show.[12] The bank has never disclosed that of its fourteen founders, nine in fact personally enslaved Black people, including five while they were directors. Collectively, these directors enslaved twenty-four Black people at various periods, who can be traced. City Bank, it's important to note, had until July 2023 never revealed any ties whatsoever linking its directors to enslavement, even though those ties ran deep, forming the backbone of the business and forging the network of associations that powered the bank's growing reputation.

The mercantile history of these founders is crucial when understood in the context of what a bank in these early days was meant to be, how it functioned. "The new bank, like nearly all banks of the day, was intended to be a kind of credit union for its merchant-owners," wrote Harold van B. Cleveland and Thomas Huertas, who worked at Citibank and published an official history with Harvard University Press in 1985.[13] These authors notably avoided the subject of the bank's ties to cotton, tobacco, sugar, and slavery (a subject to be picked up again).

For now, we can take what they say and fill in the blanks. A merchant like Bailey or Stagg, heavily invested in cotton sales and transportation, would "borrow from the bank to finance his purchase of goods," and then "repay the bank from the proceeds of the sale of the goods."[14] Merchant-owners like Bailey and Stagg weren't paid a salary such as a director of a bank today would receive. "Compensation came in the form of liquidity and access to credit and services."[15] In other words, the bank existed as a private pool of money for Bailey and Stagg, money that they in turn were paying to enslavers in the South and the Caribbean.

It stands to reason that City Bank, through these directors, enabled enslavers throughout the plantation zones of Jamaica and Havana and Charleston and Savannah to expand their operations considerably, which meant subjecting more and more Black people to torment and abuse. What's more, merchants like Bailey and Stagg repaid City Bank with the proceeds of the sale of goods like cotton, sugar, and tobacco. In other words, they relied on the proceeds of slavery, thereby directly growing the bank's slavery trove, a pool of tainted money that in turn washed out into Wall Street and then to enslavement businesses throughout the hemisphere.

It wasn't just City Bank's directors who were so involved, but its customers too. Documents from City Bank's earliest ledger books are rare and difficult to come by. Some early documents, however, surfaced in a public trial in 1859, including a small cache of pages from the 1814 ledger books of the bank's cashier, G. B. Vroom. They show that City Bank, from its earliest days, and because of its earliest clients, was putting money directly into various slavery industries in the South. The ledger shows $5,443 (roughly $83,000 today) going out to "R & J Oliver," the brothers Robert and John Oliver, who ran Baltimore's largest tobacco concern, at the center of which were extensive plantations and dozens of enslaved Black people. The bank lent a total of $6,216 ($94,600) to the merchant R. F. Muller, a veteran of the "West Indies" trade in slavery commodities. By 1809, Muller had built a business importing hundreds of bales of cotton to New York. After 1815, he was chartering vessels to St. Martinique and other slavery ports to import coffee, rum, and molasses.

City Bank was also lending large sums of money—$99,897, or $1.5 million today—to Prime, Ward & Sands, a premier Wall Street cotton brokerage financing southern enslavers, and connecting their supply to overseas markets. How many other slavery-connected firms flowed through the financial veins of City Bank? The documents are but a passing glimpse, a brief peek inside the vault, but they suggest that those flows were consequential and lasting, running deep in the business of Black bondage.

In the decade after its founding, City Bank continued to fuel the rise of directors steeped in such business. Among them was James Magee, already one of the city's top twenty cotton merchants. Between 1808 and 1810 alone, he consigned 231,600 pounds of cotton, an immense sum, from Savannah and shipped it on board his vessels, via New York, to Liverpool.[16] Magee's cotton connections likely led to him being elected a director in 1817. Fidele Boisgerard, originally from Charleston, was already importing rice and cotton from New Orleans when he was tapped by the bank to be a director in 1813. Two years later, no doubt flush with "credit and services" from City Bank, he began running a regular packet ship, the *Ann*, to Charleston, and was soon sailing it to Bordeaux.[17] (Boisgerard died in 1817.) Benjamin Desobry started out as a cotton trader in Baltimore. He later moved his office to 86 Maiden Lane in New York. In 1818, the same year he became a City Bank director, he started advertising ships to France with large consignments of 150 to 200 bales of cotton, which he received on his brig, the *Levant*, from Savannah and New Orleans.[18]

City Bank, from its earliest origins, functioned as a capital thread in cotton's rise, which is to say, slavery's rise and institutionalization within the US economy. So, too, did Bank of America, Bank of New York, Phoenix Bank, Merchants' Bank, and many of the other institutions beginning to ascend after 1812 along Wall Street. Like City Bank, they were formed by and drew in as directors men who enabled and profited from Black enslavement by shipping and trading the agricultural wealth unfree people produced. Every time they took on a cargo or commissioned a sale, these men, from their desks on Wall Street, effectively took a cut of a Black person's stolen time, turning this time into funds to be invested elsewhere. Such directors at Bank of America included not only Archibald Gracie but the leading cotton shipper George Newbold and an eminent cargo hauler improbably named Preserved Fish. ("He is said to have been picked off a wreck while floating down a river, and named Preserved Fish in consequence.")[19] All had extensive ties to plantation enslavers across Georgia, Virginia, and the Carolinas, ties they brought into the bank, ties they hoped to strengthen with Bank of America's credit.

New York's banking industry overall was founded by such men. From 1814 to 1832, John Ogden was a director of Merchants' Bank, located at 40 Wall Street. During that entire time, he ran his own cotton firm out of Liverpool. "He did a great business, owned ships…and sent cargoes of cotton, flour and other goods," reports one contemporaneous source. Henry Post, who ran a large cotton shipping enterprise with William Minturn, was cashier and later president of Franklin Bank.[20] "For these men, using banks to lend and borrow money (and to diversify their assets) was a natural by-product of their role as 'merchant princes' who regularly needed capital to keep cargo ships plying between New York and Liverpool, Hamburg, Charleston, Mobile, Havana, Batavia, Canton, and other ports," write Steven H. Jaffe and Jessica Lautin, historians with the Museum of the City of New York and authors of *Capital of Capital: Money, Banking, and Power in New York City, 1784–2012*.[21]

Almost from the start, the private nature of these banking operations caused considerable concern among many quarters, reflected in written accounts at the time, particularly about how these banks—registered under public charter and ostensibly acting in the public trust—were conducting themselves in the cotton enterprise. One of those accounts, a trade review published in 1820, exposed how banks often worked *corporately*, through decisions made at the board level, to advance credit that heavily financed cotton and enslavement but did so through exorbitant interest rates. The trade review, while not mentioning specific New York banks, suggested that many indulged in this practice:

> Another method by which the means to carry on the cotton trade were procured was through the assistance of the banks....The directors agreed to make the required loan upon the applicants paying the six months interest in advance, and engaging to remit the ninety days paper of the bank to the south, and put it in circulation. In this way the banks actually loaned money upon an usurious contract, and in fact received interest at the rate of more than one percent, a month.[22]

John M'Cready, the author of the review, concluded that the banks, by privately negotiating these speculative deals, were derelict in their duty of discharging the public trust. "The incorporated companies of this country are to a great extent mere associations of men for private speculation, protected by the operation of law," M'Cready argued. He added, "Lord Coke says, that corporate bodies have no souls."

It can safely be estimated that between one-third to one-half of all the bank directors of Wall Street by 1815 were directly profiting from the enslavement of Black people, and that the sale of the commodities Black people produced from southern plantations was a central pillar of their operations.

———

THE MONEY DERIVED from advancing funds to enslavers, and from transporting the commodities of slavery, showered the Eastern Seaboard by 1815, making the fortunes of many eminent names. Boston had the

Cabots, the Westons, and the DeBloises, their noble maritime fortunes intricately laced to the cotton sources of the South, not to mention the Baring Brothers bank's rising agent Joshua Bates. Philadelphia had Stephen Girard, whose bank, Girard Bank, one of the richest in the United States, he built from the proceeds of slavery, not only stolen from the Caribbean, but from a plantation in Louisiana where he enslaved thirty Black people. ("The princely Girard owed his fortune to the slave accumulation of St. Domingo; and there are few 'old families' North whose fortunes are not dated from slave connections," relates a contemporaneous account.)[23] There was also Thomas Cope, founder of a long and prosperous shipping line, as well as William Brown, heir to a consequential transport and credit business based around slavery and founded by his father, Alexander Brown.

The elder Brown was himself on a steady rise, based in Baltimore and soon to position his empire at the center of the growing enslavement system on Wall Street. In Baltimore, Brown was connected to another man by the name of Elisha Riggs, who was partner in turn to George Peabody, and by that web of alliances, they were all connected to a third man, W. W. Corcoran. Peabody, Riggs, and Corcoran became some of the most affluent cotton brokers and transporters of their day, bringing in riches that financed even more consequential pursuits in banking, philanthropy, and the arts. By the efforts of these men, and the networks they controlled, enslavement was tied even more heavily to the ports of Philadelphia and Boston for a time than to New York, though that was soon to change.

The cotton transportation business already thrived, clearly. The triangle was running. But it did so, prior to 1817, despite inefficiencies and standards of practice that appear wayward and glaring today. For one, a shipmaster sailed to whatever port he might pick up cargo; he sailed again only when his hull was full, and then only when the weather permitted. In 1854, the writer John Livingston observed: "The ancient mariners of that period of our commercial history considered it a presumptuous defiance of Providence to promise the departure of a ship for a regular day, without reference to winds of weather."[24]

The system was designed to avoid calamity, or the risk of sailing empty—of losing money. But it also meant that money, particularly amid the rising cotton flow, was ultimately left on the table. "A half dozen [ships] might clear for Liverpool in a single week and after that there might be no sailings for five or six weeks," wrote historian Robert Greenhalgh Albion, in his definitive work on the New York port.[25] The same was true in reverse. Once at Liverpool, vessels waited to fill their hulls; the sailing back to US ports was sporadic and restless, meaning business was lost. For Benjamin Marshall and his partners, this was no way to run an industry transporting the most precious commodity in the world, based on an enslaved labor force fast becoming the largest in the world.

In 1818, Marshall, together with Francis Thompson, his nephew Jeremiah Thompson, and Isaac Wright, launched their new line of ocean liners. They explained in a letter to one of Liverpool's leading cotton houses: "These Ships shall leave New York, full or not full on the 5th, and Liverpool on the 1st, of every Month throughout the year."[26] Regular service, dependable timing, shipping that ran like a machine, something never done before. It constituted nothing less than a revolution in transportation and the business of slavery.

The first of their ships to set sail for Liverpool was called the *James Monroe*, and its hull was filled mostly with apples, and only seventy-one bales of cotton. But, as advertised, despite the paucity of its cargo, it sailed, nonetheless. Its flag was a red blazon with a black ball at its center. As a result, the first of the regularized transatlantic ocean liners became known as the Black Ball Line. Three other ships followed the *James Monroe*, each about one hundred feet long and four hundred tons in carrying capacity. All lost money in the beginning, being too capacious, and too empty. But Black Ball's owners had the capital to wait it out.

Success did come, roughly by 1820, and it changed shipping, enslavement, and New York forever. "From the sailing of this packet," wrote Grant Thorburn in 1845, "we may date the day from whence the commerce of New-York began to increase seven-fold."[27] The Black Ball ships were soon loaded up, as the idea of regular cotton shipments caught on, spawning an industry of competitors and imitators—the Red Star Line in 1821, the Blue Swallowtail in 1822, among others—that opened numerous additional lines across the Atlantic, and down the coasts to southern plantations as well. All sides of the cotton triangle began to flow regularly and exponentially.

A "commercial marine" emerged, as the *Southern Literary Messenger* of Richmond later called it, "which whitens every sea, and carries the products of American industry into all ports open to her flag."[28] In an important sense, ships had given birth to America's slavery wealth. Now, slavery wealth helped fund an explosion of more ships. They consisted not only of ocean liners but a range of vessels meant to transport the South's slavery commodities to New York and the rest of the North, and from there to England and back again. (Between 1820 and 1860 the number of vessels built grew by 27,956—much of it to transport cotton, tabulated Thomas Prentice Kettell, a nineteenth-century political economist and writer known for his pro-slavery views.)[29]

So began an ever more concentrated flow of cotton passing through New York, and for this reason, by 1820 New York surpassed Philadelphia and Boston as a center of trade.[30] South Street and its docks sat at the center of the world's most important economic triangle, the greatest wealth engine the world had ever seen.

By 1821, the total value of all US exports was $54 million. Cotton accounted for $20 million, and of that, roughly 20 percent, or $4 million, was exported through New York. In 1805, when Marshall first entered the cotton trade, only forty-five ships sailed from New York to Liverpool. They carried three million pounds of cotton. By 1827, 132 ships reached Liverpool from New York, carrying more than thirty-nine million pounds—a more than tenfold increase.[31] It has been calculated that in 1825, New York received "nearly one-third of the whole [cotton] crop of the United States."[32]

No wonder the shipping magnates of Wall Street emerged as the richest merchants in the city; the profits they drew from carrying cotton, tobacco, and other slavery products to the world were immense. "The ocean freights for many years, earned by Northern ships in transporting cotton, have averaged over twenty millions of dollars per annum," estimated the British writer George McHenry in 1863, using statistics then available.[33] It meant a figure somewhere around $450 million per year in today's currency.

The emerging institutional link between cotton, slavery, and Wall Street in this period was nowhere more poignantly reflected than in the relationship between City Bank and the personage of Isaac Wright. Wright, whom a socialite once described in a white satin vest and cravat, with "gray hair tied behind with black ribbon," had long been a prosperous cotton shipper.[34] In 1825, as his fortunes rose even higher through Black Ball, he was elected a City Bank director. Thus, the bank profited considerably from its close relationship with the revolution he, Marshall, and Thompson had unleashed. Meanwhile, Wright and his business, Isaac Wright & Co., prospered from the bank's services and pool of credit. In fact, so important was Wright and his slavery-dependent business that he was elected president of City Bank in 1827, serving in that position for five years.

The central role City Bank played in underwriting Wright's shipping line is one the bank itself has proudly, though deceptively, emphasized for decades. "The first regular transatlantic shipping service was established with the aid of the City Bank under Isaac Wright, its fifth President, a milestone in the history of American Commerce," the bank touted in a full-page advertisement in 1937, commemorating its 125th anniversary.[35] The bank was careful then, as it has been ever since, to avoid highlighting that, in doing so, it helped launch a revolution in the commerce of slavery, a milestone that directly facilitated the exploitation of Black people to expand exponentially.

It is now well appreciated that the drug cartels of Mexico became the richest, most powerful in the world not by producing cocaine themselves. The coca was grown by someone else and refined into cocaine thousands of miles away. The Mexican cartels became rich through shipping and supply, through moving product by revolutionizing the transportation system at the heart of their illicit global trade, making it standard and reliable. This is what Isaac Wright and Benjamin Marshall, with the facilities of City Bank, did for slavery.

Year after year, Black Ball and its competitors, by streamlining their shipping, matched the prodigious trajectory of cotton output. In 1818, enslaved people produced 125 million pounds of cotton, and the ships carried 92 million pounds abroad; in 1820, the ships moved 127 million pounds; by 1827, 204 million pounds. Year after year, the ships kept pace. To do so, Black Ball's owners and others constructed bigger and bigger ships, and more of them. ("Each of these valuable ships will carry upwards of 2200 bales of cotton," Jeremiah Thompson announced of a new fleet in 1826.)[36]

This regularized, massive flow of cotton constituted not only a revolution in the physical transportation of enslavement commodities. A corollary effect was that standardized schedules also "revolutionized the flow of consignments, correspondence and intelligence," as one historian noted. [37] The ships carried news and mail, precious information in an analog world, which helped merchants and lenders draw a quicker picture of markets and sales, though often not an accurate one.

The prospect of greater reliability was soon to inspire a new epoch in the enslavement industry, emboldening merchants to speculate more brazenly on cotton (often to disastrous effect), simultaneously spurring enslavers to take out riskier and more frequent loans. Because of the ships, a greater channel of transatlantic capital would begin to flow, "the physical 'cotton triangle'...inevitably mirrored by an equally large system of international and interregional payments."[38] Regularized ships made New York and Wall Street keel to the order of generating more wealth, purchasing more enslaved people, then acquisitioning more land and more cotton to buy more enslaved people and generate more wealth. And on and on it went, a cycle as tormenting and powerful as the pounding of the sea.

Southern merchants were incensed and shaken by this spectacle, making calls for a fleet of their own. "Those who first established the packets, have placed New York on a commercial eminence, and put a sceptre in her hand, which she delights to hold," fumed the *Southern Literary Messenger.*[39] The paper said also: "If the South would contend with the North for her portion of this trade, the race must be run with the New York packets....[The South] must rival, nay eclipse, that carried on by the New York *liners.*" [40]It was a call to action that, though repeated continuously, didn't materialize in a direct southern fleet for several decades.

Other than Marshall, the men most responsible for institutionalizing the cotton triangle at the heart of America's slave industries—Francis Thompson, Isaac Wright, and Jeremiah Thompson—were all Quakers. In *Capitalism and Slavery*, Eric Williams observed that "slave dealing was one of the most lucrative investments of English as of American Quakers, and the name of a slaver [ship], *The Willing Quaker*, reported from Boston at Sierra Leone in 1793, symbolizes the approval with which the slave trade was regarded in Quaker circles."[41] This approval remained true up until Marshall's time.

Between 1818 and 1828, Jeremiah Thompson sold and shipped so much cotton abroad that he was considered the foremost cotton exporter in the United States—referred to by some as the country's first "cotton king"—as well as the nation's largest shipowner. And yet Thompson, though single-handedly responsible for transmuting so much of Black people's pain and labor into Wall Street's wealth, was also a member of the Manumission Society of New York. In fact, he'd first become a member as early as 1810, when his ties to plantations and their evil harvest was first solidifying.[42] For nearly two decades, this prodigious cotton trader had professed the cause of emancipation (to this day, some sources refer to him as an abolitionist), providing funds and support for Black people's freedom, contributing to tracts, and attending meetings, even as he helped expand the business of keeping Black people enslaved. To the following passage in a manumission tract, Jeremiah Thompson had signed his name:

> This nefarious traffic, which severs the dearest ties of domestic life, fills the bosom of affection with hopeless anguish, tears the unprotected victim from his country and his home, and plunders him into wretchedness bordering on despair, ought to awaken in us, an attention that cannot sleep, a diligence that cannot tire, an ardour that will not abate, a perseverance that will not slacken, and courage that cannot fear.[43]

What self-deceptions did such men use against the evidence of their own senses, to slumber their attention, to numb their conscience, in order to conduct this vile business? Ultimately, we don't know. The private papers and writings of Marshall, Thompson, and Wright have not survived. And so we cannot understand, through their own documents at least, how they justified profiting from a "nefarious traffic" they knew so well to be so cruel. Maybe their delusion doesn't need to be guessed at; patently, it can be seen as the basis of their commerce, a heartlessness that became the legacy they left behind in the rise of Wall Street and New York.

The wealth of enslavement was changing. Men who'd made their early fortunes on the waters, extracting wealth from enslavement at the level of transport, were propelling themselves up the ladder to capture an even greater share of the profits.

It isn't that "planters" didn't see this trend, didn't note it in their ledger books, how northern men dominated the extraction of southern enslavement wealth. They burned with the indignity of this lament: "The South thus stands in the attitude of feeding from her own bosom a vast population of merchants, ship-owners, capitalists and others…who drink up the life-blood of her trade," an Alabama congressman said.[44] Yet they had done little to stop it. By the time they made their voices known, it was already too late. The vast trove of wealth made by subjugated unfree people was inexorably flowing north. And cotton, though now the mainstay, eclipsing faith and attention in all else, was just one part of that flow.

CHAPTER 3

A NORTHERN SLAVERY ARISTOCRACY

Throughout the 1820s, northern men, rich from the business of slavery, intermarried, braiding slavery wealth with bloodlines, making themselves stronger, making themselves into dynasties, and fostering generational wealth—wealth that would outlast slavery itself. Benjamin Marshall married a daughter of Jeremiah Thompson. Jeremiah Thompson married a daughter of Isaac Wright.[1] The Kings married into the Gracies, the Grinnells into the Minturns. The daughter of Anson G. Phelps married William E. Dodge. They also employed each other's sons. All the while, they corporatized together, sitting on each other's boards.

In New York, they pooled their resources and built in 1826 the Merchants' Exchange Building on Wall Street, just east of William, a physical center for their congress. And there many of these men—vice presidents, treasurers, directors, fathers-in-law to each other's daughters and sons—sat and governed the commerce of the nation. They helped drive an extraordinary proliferation of new businesses, a new era of incorporation. "The demand for acts of incorporation is continually increasing," New York's former chancellor, James Kent, observed in 1827, "and the propensity is the more striking, as it appears to be incurable…and we seem to have no moral means to resist it."[2]

Between 1810 and 1830 alone, northern businessmen formed twenty-four hundred corporations, with a total capital of $275,538,074, or $8 billion today. The result was a dense concentration of corporate wealth, such that by 1828, New York banks and insurance companies were assessed for tax purposes at $23,984,660, meaning they owned 21 percent of the city's total wealth.[3] By the late 1820s, men enriched from slavery formed a mercantile elite, a network of power and privilege under the domed lighting of the merchants' room connected to the South and powered by the workings of two million enslaved Black people. To say that these merchant princes constituted a northern slavery aristocracy is not merely a euphemism. It's borne out in fact, for many of these Wall Street luminaries were enslavers themselves.

Every morning, Samuel Tooker rose in his chambers in a wooden two-story house, at 5 Bridge Street, and then dressed for the day's affairs. He was attended almost certainly in those hours by a Black man whom he enslaved, a man who appears in the 1820 census records but who's never named. Tooker was one of the most prominent grocers in all of New York, with a large shop on South Street. In that shop he sold wholesale quantities of items like brandy and flour, beef, and hams.[4] He ran besides this a real estate business, leasing out stores and grocery stands. His business dealings appear to have been sufficiently robust as to make Tooker well regarded and rich, and it was because of his elevated position that he remained a long-running director of City Bank. Tooker had helped found the bank, in fact, in 1812, a time when he ran a business outfitting ships for war; he remained a director until 1823. City Bank's credit no doubt helped Tooker's business, providing him the means for affluence, including the means to purchase the man whom he kept enslaved. Every evening, Tooker almost certainly ordered this man to help him undress, to prepare his food, to wait on his cares and longings, part of the suite of privileges he enjoyed as a white corporate director in New York.

By 1820, there were only slightly more than five hundred Black people still enslaved in New York City. The fact distills an important and study-worthy moment in time. In 1790, white people had enslaved more than 20,000 Black people in New York City. By 1810, that number had dropped to 1,446, and then down again to roughly 500 by 1820. The overall trend, in other words, suggests that white people in New York, acting on a consort of gradual emancipation laws, were freeing the Black people they enslaved. (A portion of the reduction, we can also assume, was because Black people died.) Enslavers in 1820 like Samuel Tooker, then, were those *least* willing in the city to grant freedom to the Black people they enslaved. These men were the last holdouts, the hardest-core enslavers in the history of New York. It shows that slavery was more alive in the North, more proximate to the workings of the northern economy, indeed Wall Street banks, than many northerners in this period perhaps wanted to accept or perhaps were even aware of.

In addition to Samuel Tooker, at least two other City Bank directors, both living in New York, were enslavers: cotton magnate James Magee and Edmund Smith, both directors from 1817 to 1825. Each of these white men kept in their homes a Black person robbed of freedom, presumably as a personal servant. (The US Census Bureau furnishes no biographical data about the Black people these men enslaved, not even their names.) According to the 1820 census, the prominent merchant Cornelius R. Suydam held five Black people in bondage as of that year. Suydam would become a City Bank director in 1825. Among other well-known Wall Street figures, Joseph D. Beers, a cotton and securities broker, also enslaved a Black person in 1820. In Philadelphia, the banker Stephen Girard, arguably one of the richest men in the country at the time, enslaved a Black person. So, too, did Gurdon Mumford, one of the founding directors of the New York Stock Exchange.

By cross-referencing the 1820 census with that of 1810, we learn that some men who had enslaved Black people in 1810 no longer did by 1820, suggesting that perhaps they had granted freedom to those they'd enslaved. Manumission records from the Office of the Register of New York County show that Abraham Bloodgood, one of City Bank's founders, had enslaved a Black woman named Isabel but manumitted her on August 12, 1812, just a month after he became a director of the bank.[5] (Manumission records, unlike census records, often detail the names of enslaved Black people.) In total, Bloodgood had enslaved two Black people in 1810, but none by 1820.

The opposite is also true for another City Bank director: Edmund

Smith enslaved no Black people in 1810. It was while he was at City Bank, however, that he evidently purchased, as his personal property, a Black person that he held in captivity within his home.

This is by no means an exhaustive sampling or search, but it suggests preliminarily that somewhere around 10 percent of the northern mercantile elite may have been enslavers, referring to dozens and possibly hundreds of the highest levels of the commercial class directing the national economy. Whatever the actual figure may be, that leading bankers, like Stephen Girard, and Wall Street figures, like Joseph D. Beers, Gurdon Mumford, and others, were enslavers themselves puts the sharpest emphasis possible on a critical point: the North's economy, despite what many of us believe today, and many people in the Atlantic states then wanted to believe, was as grossly intertwined with Black people's suffering and exploitation as the South's.

———

BY WHAT RIGHT did these rich merchants in the North, to say nothing of the rich enslavers in the South, continue to take what was not theirs, to profit from the stolen labor of Black people?

By the right of omission.

There was no policy or doctrine, no act of Congress, or order from the White House that checked the building of slavery's trove. Legislative acts throughout the 1790s, and again in 1807—namely the Act Prohibiting the Importation of Slaves—forbade white men from *transporting* Black people from Africa as enslaved property.[6] (By presidential decree, the US sloop of war *Cyane*, armed with twenty-four heavy guns, patrolled the western coast of Africa, to intercept any ship involved in this transportation.)[7] But because the US Congress didn't have the power to regulate internal trade—that was the domain of the states—white men were free to transport unfree Black people *within* US territory.

There were, to be sure, many who rose in the chambers of Congress to condemn the *practice* of bondage, of white men enslaving Black lives. President John Quincy Adams, for one, was famously against the institution, "that outrage upon the goodness of God."[8] Yet no one rose to condemn the *commerce, the riches* based on this crime against humanity. "What have been the views of American commerce in respect to freedom?" asked Rev. Theodore Parker, an abolitionist, many years later. "It has been against it, I am sorry to say so. In America, the great commercial centres, ever since the Revolution, have been hostile to freedom."[9] No legislative, judicial, or executive measure condemned the money flows themselves, the rising tide of this epic wealth, which was flowing north. No senator rose to say that cotton shipping and sales should be stopped, that corn sales should be stopped, tobacco exports stopped, the multimillion-dollar transportation of these products stopped, that this commerce firmly fixed as a primary means of American prosperity should be shut down. Certainly, the reality of Black enslavement would have no purpose without this commerce; the institution of slavery, hundreds of years old, would have no reason to exist were it not for the business of producing agricultural bounty wrung from Black people's hands. Yet Adams nowhere in his memoirs laments the cotton brokers of Wall Street or the shipping merchants who aided them; he nowhere lambastes how enslavement embellished the riches of corporations.

To be sure, changes would come. The horizons of slavery geographically compressed and dimmed. In 1827, the New York State Legislature, after decades of "gradual emancipation," formally outlawed the enslaving of Black people by white men, a move echoed in legislatures across the North. But even then, these laws didn't prohibit white merchants on Wall Street from profiting still, across state lines, from a Black person's continued captivity in the South. Far away, the sloop of war *Cyane* kept patrolling the commercial boundaries of enslavement. Yet no legislation seriously proposed interdicting the interregional, international commerce powered by enslaved people's labor that had become a principal, indispensable branch of American wealth at home. By the 1820s, the right to pursue slavery wealth in the United States, from any corner of the republic, was inviolate. The question was, at what cost?

The precious core of this wealth was cotton, though cotton wasn't the only crop being harvested and traded. What made cotton special was its abundance, constancy, durability, and portability, coupled with world demand. So great was the demand, so reliable the production, that Great Britain could steer its national policy by it. In the United States, the federal government erected a battery of tariffs to promote cotton's growth, and to promote, also with subsidies, the transportation system of ships that allowed the export of cotton to thrive. Treaties were hammered out, reprised, and renewed time and again with England and France, among others, to ensure that American merchants could sail their own vessels loaded with cotton, tobacco, and rice to these foreign ports, conducting vigorous trade. Cotton and cloth from other ports of the world were heavily taxed at the US border, discouraging their growth; on the other hand, taxes and barriers so levied on American cotton were vigorously appealed. (In 1810, the federal government fought to repeal an act in France that prohibited the importation of American cotton and tobacco.) Thus did American maritime commerce come to be based principally, though not entirely, on cotton. "The carrying of the cotton crop," remarked an account in the 1850s, "has been the basis of the Northern freighting business, and the national tonnage has swollen…step by step with the cotton product."[10]

Between 1795 and 1830, white men harnessed enslaved Black people's stolen time to create a total output of cotton that was, in the aggregate, according to the best statistics we have available, valued at $524,260,000 in 1830 dollars. To put this into further context, the value of cotton amassed in this period far surpassed the total authorized capital of all corporations created in the United States between 1790 and 1830, which collectively totaled $473,136,048.[11] And that is only the value of the cotton itself; it doesn't include Black people's lost wages and other associated costs (a subject to be discussed later). Tabulated in today's currency, the cotton trove alone would amount to, by the most conservative estimates, $15.2 billion, though this means only dollars converted to dollars, accounting for inflation. It doesn't consider how this money would have grown when invested into other pursuits, as it surely was. Finally, this is the total in just the first thirty-five years of cotton's life, and we are talking only about cotton, and only about half of its life as a commodity produced by Black people during nearly a century of bondage.

The truth is, in talking about enslavement, we talk about cotton too much. There's relative accord among economic historians (where views often do not agree) that cotton, being the leading US export at this time, generated significant wealth and acted as an important stimulus to economic growth and national income in the United States. But cotton represented, again according to concordant scholarship, less than 10 percent of the gross national product throughout the 1830s, and the remainder of the antebellum period, in fact. (For comparison, manufacturing expanded between 1815 and 1859 to account for roughly 20 percent of GDP.)[12] The economists Alan L. Olmstead and Paul W. Rhode point out that corn was a far more valuable agricultural commodity than cotton, only it wasn't shipped abroad in nearly the same numbers.[13]

That said, we don't need to speak of cotton as being the *main* driver of the US economy or the *main* driver of growth in this period (it wasn't), to appreciate that it was, undoubtedly, a critical factor in the furnishing of unprecedented riches for white people across the nation, particularly white people who weren't even in the South, and that it was a *colossal driver* in economic development overall. One of the main reasons for this was that cotton, as the nation's leading export, was exchanged abroad for hundreds of millions of dollars in iron, foreign capital, and other goods imported back to the United States. And that transfer pushed the economy to grow.

This is not to undercut the extraordinary wealth that cotton generated for white men, but to begin to position cotton more precisely within the larger, overall financial juggernaut that the business of enslaving Black people would become. Enslaved people cultivated a multitude of riches far beyond this one plant (as important as it was), a reality to which we'll soon return. Enslaved Black people produced rice, wheat, flour, corn, and sugar. In 1819, they cultivated $7,636,970 in tobacco for export ($160 million today); in 1820, $7,968,000 ($182 million today); in 1821, $5,648,962 ($134 million today); in 1822, $6,222,838 ($142 million today). US tobacco exports were clearly dropping, yet these were still tremendous numbers.[14]

Enslaved people produced tar, turpentine, and molasses as well. They made rum, whiskey, and gin in distilleries. "The profits from this trade fertilized the entire productive system of the country," wrote Eric Williams in *Capitalism and Slavery*.[15] He was referring here to slavery and the British industrial system, but the same truth was mirrored across time, over the Atlantic.

Enslaved people were forced into the country's mines, to harness ore and coal. They fired bricks in kilns. Increasingly, they were forced to work on laying iron tracks and performing a myriad of other labors related to the growth of the country's railroads. They felled trees, cleared land, hewed lumber. Enslaved people's hours, their stolen days and nights, were the basis of an entire wealth-generating system, "the foundation stone" as Du Bois wrote, "not only of the Southern social structure, but of Northern manufacture and commerce, of the English factory system, of European commerce, of buying and selling on a world-wide scale."[16]

We have seen that this encompassed not only shipping and shipping merchants but that slavery profits had begun to meld with banking and manufacturing; these funds would soon encompass new industries like mining, iron, and gas. To consider briefly the total array of slavery wealth (as we will later in more detail) is to contemplate funds amounting to hundreds of billions of dollars, and more likely many trillions. The questions to be asked in pursuit of possible answers are: Who took the greatest share of this money? What did they do with it? And where did it go?

From cotton profits alone, it's evident that enslavement wealth by the 1820s contributed to both private wealth and public income in dimensions that were vast and consequential, some obvious, others incalculable. No doubt it's impossible to account for all the places where the great pools of slavery funds splashed into legitimate ones. There's no accounting in a vortex. What monies Benjamin Bailey reaped from enslavement and then placed in his City Bank account, he invested out again into the stock market. The profits George Newbold derived from shipping slavery-produced commodities he remitted back to Bank of America. Money from a host of such merchants then flowed into the Bank of the United States, and that bank in turn lent these funds to a thousand different enterprises, at a thousand different addresses and homesteads across the country, brightening white people's lives, opening new doors for their children's futures.

Witness, as far back as 1819, the US secretary of the treasury, William Crawford, writing to bank presidents in the South about the web of these transactions: "Many of the loans made by the [Bank of the United States] have been to cotton planters, and it is believed that many of the debts due from this class of citizens will be paid by shipments of cotton to New York," he wrote, "the proceeds of which will be placed to the credit of the Treasurer of the United States in the Branch Bank at that place."[17] The official business of the Bank of the United States, in other words, was run on cotton, remitted with the proceeds of Black bondage. The hidden pathways taken by Black people's stolen time—readily perceived, yet unknowable in all its reaches, all its places—is the history of American money.

By the 1820s, slavery wealth had soaked into the nation's vastness, and the Treasury profited, along with state and city governments, from the revenue that came down. A branch of American prosperity, seldom discussed, much less visualized, is surely the history of the riches of enslavement sweeping into northeastern cities through the tax base. "New cities were built on the results of black labor," Du Bois wrote.[18] From the hand of someone unfree and Black, fettered on a plantation, to the bale hoisted on a ship, heaved by Black people, coastwise to the North through the docks, this wealth flowed like an arrow, and a duty was then collected on each bale or barrel of rice, each bushel of corn, each pound of sugar by a clerk at a customs house. There were also charges for storage, for weighing (12.5 cents) and freight (1.5 to 2 cents per pound), cordage and carting. Commissions, shipping, and insurance took a further 5 percent from the net; baggage and transportation to local ports (say, Mobile) before onward passage to New York, another 1.5 cents per pound. It's easy to see why New York alone, according to estimates, took, in the form of fees and other income, one-fourth to one-third of all the revenues that cotton alone generated in the United States.

In New York, Philadelphia, and Boston, the custom houses also collected duties the other way: from goods returning via the triangle, goods imported back from the cotton, tobacco, and rice trade. The shipping lines of the North—the Black Ball, the Swallowtail, the Dramatic Line—brought tons of metals and textiles from England, plus barrels of wine and bolts of cloth from France. Equally importantly, they brought goods essential to the function of slavery, such as clothes and leather and farming instruments used by the enslaved.

All these products were procured from the slave commodities exchange, and a duty on each of these items was paid. The power of enslaved people in the South drove the dynamic like a boomerang, but it was the cities of the East and North that collected the spoils, coming and going, like a catchment. And so Thomas Hart Benton, a US senator from Missouri, rose in the House chamber in 1828 to grouse about the imbalance. Or, as he said, "that quarter, whose cotton, tobacco, and rice, constituting seven-eighths of the agricultural, and three-fifths of the total exports of the country"—he was talking about the South—"gives employment to numerous ships and mariners of the East, enriches many of their merchants, and builds up their cities, and brings back the chief part of the imports which pay the twenty odd millions of revenue into the Treasury, which are expended elsewhere"—by which he meant the North. [19] Twenty million dollars paid to the Treasury from imports exchanged on enslavement goods would be equivalent to $583 million today. It meant the cotton triangle rendered today's equivalent of billions of dollars in customs income to the government over a decade.

With more than 1.5 million Black people pressed into labor by the 1820s, the luxuries of the North compounded. More streets for white people were created, docks were expanded, and the first gas lightings took place in Manhattan and Boston with monies sieved from slavery. [20] Wealth abounding is what Frederick Douglass, arriving as a free Black man to a shipping town in Massachusetts, noted readily all around him, in marked contrast to the southern poverty, from where he'd come:

> In the afternoon of the day when I reached New Bedford, I visited the wharves, to take a view of the shipping. Here I found myself surrounded with the strongest proofs of wealth. Lying at the wharves, and riding in the stream, I saw many ships of the finest model, in the best order, and of the largest size. Upon the right and left, I was walled in by granite warehouses of the widest dimensions, stowed to their utmost capacity with the necessaries and comforts of life....From the wharves I strolled around and over the town, gazing with wonder and admiration at the splendid churches, beautiful dwellings, and finely-cultivated gardens; evincing an amount of wealth, comfort, taste, and refinement, such as I had never seen in any part of slaveholding Maryland. [21]

The proliferation of ships was the surest sign of this wealth, a metaphor for its rising tide throughout New England. Shipbuilders were busy building fleets in the sea town of Medford, Massachusetts. They had built at least seventy-five between 1806 and 1820 alone, including the *Emily* for William Bayard, cotton merchant and early Bank of America director, and the *Pedlar* for Joseph and Samuel Cabot, of the

Boston maritime dynasty.[22] Such fleets were built with the proceeds of the so-called Southern trade, with subsidies from the US Treasury, to further stimulate that trade.

The riches of enslavement seeped into private fortunes as well. From at least 1815, tax lists in New York were made public, and the finances of northern men rich from the commercial products of slavery were popularly discussed in books and broadsheets. We know, for example, that Archibald Gracie's estate was assessed at $60,000 in 1815 ($1 million today), Benjamin Bailey's at $37,000 ($642,000 today), and Benjamin Marshall's at $50,000 in 1825 ($1.35 million today).[23]

The taxes these men paid would have been small, however; there were then no federal or state taxes, only a local tax of roughly 1 percent of total assessed wealth. Each of these assessments, it's also important to add, were self-assessments, made by the merchants themselves, and therefore notorious for being underreported by half or more. As historian Edward Pessen noted in 1971: "Tax officials bemoaned the practice of great merchants, men known to be owners of vast real-estate holdings and substantial shareholders in banks and insurance companies, coolly to swear that they possessed no personal wealth whatever."[24]

What these figures tell us is that the fortunes of the northern slavery merchants were even greater than officially deemed (double to six times, according to various estimates), that they were rooted in durable forms of wealth (fortunes that would last for generations), and that they were concentrated in a very small number of hands (a mercantile elite). By 1828, there were roughly 450 families worth between $25,000 and $100,000 in New York, representing roughly 1 percent of the city's population. Together, they controlled $25 million worth of the city's wealth ($700 million today). A similar picture adheres in Boston, where 260 families, worth between $50,000 and $200,000, controlled more than $20 million in wealth ($560 million today) while constituting 2 percent of the population.

Here, then, are the origins of unequal wealth distribution in the United States, and the riches that northern men plundered from slavery—headquartered as they were in free states, no less—must be seen as a powerful contributing factor. Certainly, not all the 1 percent families were directly tied through commerce to Black enslavement, but many were. They were a class unto themselves, a northern slavery aristocracy, and the pinnacle of an increasingly crushing class system. For comparison, white carpenters in this period earned wages of between $0.58 and $1.25 a day; bricklayers, $1.50 a day in New York and South Carolina; masons, $1.21 a day; agricultural laborers between $0.47 to $0.58.[25] Even if such laborers managed to find employment for three hundred days a year, which most did not, their annual earnings, at most $450 a year ($10,000 today), were a paltry fraction of the nation's affluent cotton and tobacco men. And yet, such wages were still a vast fortune, of course, in view of the plight of millions of Black people, toiling under cruelty for no pay.

WHAT DID NORTHERN people think of their own role in this diabolical system of wealth? Many, we can presume, were apathetic. Many, no doubt, were unaware, particularly given that the press, largely tied to powerful slavery entrepreneurs like Archibald Gracie, had said hardly a word by the 1820s about northern commercial involvement in slavery's riches. There were, moreover, virtually no organized and prominent abolitionist groups at this time drawing attention to the issue. Concerned northern citizens tended to be like William Hillhouse, a delegate of the Continental Congress from Connecticut, who published this harrowing account in an early anti-slavery pamphlet entitled *The Crisis*:

> A peck of corn a week is allowed a slave—this, with now and then a pickled herring, constitutes, I am told, on many plantations, the only allowance, and on others the most material part of the allowance, for the slaves the whole of the year, except during the season of sweet potatoes, when these, the cost of raising which is very trifling, are substituted. The cost of cloathing a [Black] child is so trifling as to be hardly worth mentioning. On many plantations they are naked, as the climate is warm, except where the mothers provide some covering; without any expense to the owners. In others some coarse cotton, the growth of their plantations, is allowed.
>
> On the rice plantations, the slaves are fed with refuse rice, which is not fit for market.[26]

The vast literature today attesting to these deprivations (autobiographies, written accounts, interviews with formerly enslaved people) underscores that white enslavers maximized profits through gross neglect, minimizing, to a criminal and often lethal degree, the necessities they provided to the Black people they enslaved. Rufus Houston, enslaved in Alabama, recalled, when interviewed years later by the Works Progress Administration, how his enslaver "would sometimes after a very hard day's work take a piece of meat or an old meat skin and rub it over our mouths to fool the people as though he fed his slaves better than the others. When they were fed they would be huddled like cattle and their food put in troughs."[27] Jennie Haggens, enslaved by a man named Hartie Thompson in Centerville, Texas, described in another WPA interview that: "The houses were made of logs, moss, and dirt, with dirt floors. The slaves of Mr. Thompson were often driven to a trough like hogs and [there] they would eat such as they were given to eat."[28]

In this period, northerners outraged by slavery, like William Hillhouse, almost always focused on southern culpability, projecting outward, creating distance. Their tendency to do so belies a critical fact. Among all this rising wealth, among the many privileges northern people enjoyed because of slavery, was perhaps the most important of all: It was their privilege *not to* question their own privilege's origins in slavery. Over time, this would change. But more common in this period was that northern white people, especially those traveling to the South, tended to perceive the hellish travails of Black people in slavery as wholly disconnected from their own luxuries and comforts, a distortion with far-reaching effects.

In 1816, James K. Paulding, a writer from New York (Paulding would later become US secretary of the Navy), made a voyage through Virginia and came upon the following wrenching scene, an example, he later wrote, "of the tricks men will play before high Heaven, when not only custom, but the laws, sanction oppression." A cart was being pulled in the afternoon heat on a road. Inside the cart were five or six Black children. Paulding published his account in a popular book called *Letters from the South*:

> The cart had no covering, and [the children] seemed to have been actually broiled to sleep. Behind the cart marched three black women, with

head, neck, and breasts, uncovered, and without shoes or stockings; next came three men, bare-headed, half naked and *chained together with an ox chain*. Last of all, came a white man...on horseback, carrying pistols in his belt, and who, as we passed him, had the impudence to look us in the face without blushing. I should like to have seen him hunted by blood-hounds.[29]

The white man, Paulding later learned, was transporting the Black children and adults to sell them at a slavery market in Maryland. What truly galled Paulding was not that such things took place—even in New York in 1816, there were enslaved people; there just weren't slavery *markets*. It galled him that the business of transporting Black people, for white people to buy and sell, took place openly, in midday, without shame, "without blushing." He wished, in fact, that white southerners only did such things at night, that the business of slavery was hidden away.

What stands out here is the sense of timing, that a northern white man was forced to confront such atrocities for the first time and that, through a widely read book, he publicized it, compelling others to consume these horrors. It reflects that the northern public was still separated from slavery, but that writers like Paulding were bridging that separation. This separation was not merely physical and geographical. It was a mental line of separation in northern white people's minds: Slavery, they told themselves, was a repugnant phenomenon peculiar to the South, its injustices and financial benefits somehow isolated there. The North was more and more free, its prosperity based on free industry and labor; consequently, it was less and less tied to, let alone responsible for, this economic system and its horrors.

Certainly, there were distinctions to be made, given the obvious fact that the North had far fewer enslaved Black people than the South. (The 1820 census records zero enslaved people in Vermont, Ohio, New Hampshire, Massachusetts, and Maine.) What's more, in the eleven northern states of the union, free Black people, numbering around 112,000, enjoyed a canopy of legal protections and social advantages otherwise scarce in the South: "anonymity and economic opportunity," in the words of scholar Julie Winch, in addition to Black churches, schools, and communities.[30] And yet, even as of 1820, there were more than ten thousand

African Americans still trapped in bondage in New York State, and more than seventy-five hundred in New Jersey. It means that many thousands of white northern men, and in some cases, white northern women, directly enslaved Black people themselves, benefiting from their servitude.

What's more, in northern cities like Philadelphia, many free Black people prospered. But they did so encircled by white hostility—hostility that intensified as their community grew, including hundreds fleeing from the South, and as both the city and commonwealth became a thriving haven for freedom. (Pennsylvania had more than thirty thousand free Black people by 1820, ten thousand in Philadelphia alone.) More than two hundred thousand free Black Americans in this early national period, whether living in the North or the South, faced lifelong racial discrimination, denial of citizenship, and political disenfranchisement, facts cogently documented in vast bodies of literature.

James Forten, born a free Black man in 1766, embodied the nuances of this predicament. Forten served his country in the Revolutionary War, fighting for American independence. He then became owner of a thriving sail-making business on the wharves of Penn's Landing in Philadelphia. Among Forten's many clients were the leading captains and ship makers of Philadelphia, and his workforce was both Black and white. He had sizable real estate, money sufficient to lend out, and other comforts when he published *Letters from a Man of Colour* in 1813. "There are men among us of reputation and property, as good citizens as any men can be, and who, for their property, pay as heavy taxes as any citizens are compelled to pay," Forten noted.[31] According to research by the scholar Christopher J. Bryant, most free states taxed Black people at essentially the same rate as white people. Southern states, on the other hand, imposed much higher and blatantly discriminatory taxes on Black people.[32]

Forten was prosperous, an esteemed, even celebrated citizen. (It's well documented that he jumped into the Delaware River, on seven occasions no less, to save people from drowning.) He was indicative, more importantly, of a rising Black middle class. Yet as affluent as he was, he felt compelled to publish his *Letters* because his rights were constantly under attack from state-sponsored racism, and never more so than in 1813. Pennsylvania lawmakers that year, scheming to prevent more free Black people from migrating to the commonwealth, had put forward a bill requiring all persons of African descent to register with local authorities, seeking to imprison and possibly even sell into enslavement any Black person found to have broken the law. For instance, failing to produce the documents required to register would have constituted a jailable offense. So continued the long history, active since the Revolutionary War, of white authorities seeking to codify free Black people as a "grievous affliction," or "a danger to societal and economic interests," and in that way to create grounds for incarcerating and otherwise removing them, writes Bryant.[33]

The proposed Pennsylvania law ultimately didn't pass. But it was one arrow in a sling. And happening as they were in free states, these measures showed that the wall supposedly separating the inhumanity of southern slavery from the freedom and benevolence of the North was more porous than white people in the North would have liked to believe. Certainly, as we know, there was no wall, legal, political, or otherwise, separating northern cities from the harvest of slavery's wealth. No such separation stemmed the flow of money pouring from southern plantations to Wall Street, and from Wall Street back to plantations in the form of services and credit. It was one system, one triangle, each piece critical to the other, though, of course, the flow of money north was harder to perceive, its violence not as readily apparent as a white man forcing a coffle of chained Black people at gunpoint down a country road.

It was ironic that the North should see itself distinct from the rapacity and injustice of enslavement. As far back as the birth of the republic, the Founding Fathers readily perceived the North's complicity, though they also took exacting measures to downplay it. Historian Yohuru Williams tells us that Thomas Jefferson's early drafts of the Constitution included a passage that was to condemn the institution of slavery and its enablers, including King George, with bristling phrases like "execrable commerce" and "piratical warfare."[34] Yet Jefferson, in order to protect northern interests as much as southern, struck this passage, thus infusing our founding document with the foundational sin of omission.

"The removal was mostly fueled by political and economic expediencies," Williams explains. "While the 13 colonies were already deeply divided on the issue of slavery, both the South and the North had financial stakes in perpetuating it. Southern plantations, a key engine of the colonial economy, needed free labor to produce tobacco, cotton and other cash crops for export back to Europe. Northern shipping merchants, who also played a role in that economy, remained dependent on the triangle trade between Europe, Africa and the Americas that included the traffic of enslaved Africans."

Williams reports too that Jefferson, writing decades later in his autobiography, detailed northern interests, as much as southern, as the motivation for striking so important a passage. "Our Northern brethren also I believe," Jefferson said, "felt a little tender under those censures; for tho' their people have very few slaves themselves, yet they had been pretty considerable carriers of them to others."[35]

The merchants of the North certainly remained "considerable carriers," of the products of enslavement more than enslaved people themselves, yet certainly these were two sides of the same coin. Looming implicitly at the center of the contract governing the United States, then, was an acknowledgment that slavery's hold over the nation was holistic, as indispensable in its furnishings of wealth to the North as to the South; that sharing the spoils of this barbarous system, through a triangle, was a key point of accord at the basis of our union; and that, given how carefully the framers considered the financial interests of both the North and the South, they perceived, correctly as it turns out, that this triangle and its sharing of slavery wealth wouldn't change.

Black people, of course, long knew that what wealth the country enjoyed, top to bottom, was the fruit of their labor, that the bounty taken from their suffering was the foundation of white prosperity North to South, even if white northerners refused to see it. In the first decades of the nineteenth century, they began to say as much, to publish as much, and the timbre of the call deepened over time. James Forten was again a prominent voice. Forten, who was famous for saying "that here we were born, here we would live, and here die,"[36] wrote in 1817, together with the Black leaders Absalom Jones and Richard Allen, also of Philadelphia, a resolution asserting Black people's claim to the prosperities that Americans enjoyed widely because of Black labor. They also called for Black citizenship, one of the earliest appeals of its kind. It was published in the *National Advocate*, a newspaper in New York.

"Whereas our ancestors (not of choice) were the first cultivators of the wilds of America, we, their descendants feel ourselves entitled to participate in the blessings of her luxuriant soil, which their blood and sweat manured," they wrote, further stating: "We view with deep abhorrence the unmerited stigma attempted to be cast upon the reputation of the free People of Colour...'that they are a dangerous and useless part of the community,' when, in the state of disfranchisement in which they live, in the hour of danger they ceased to remember their wrongs, and rallied around the standard of their country."[37] This last reference was to the Revolutionary War, in which not only Forten but also Allen had served. (Allen had hauled salt on a wagon from the mines of Rehoboth Bay in Delaware, with which he supplied the Continental army.)

Perhaps most consequentially, it was the southern states, as we have seen, that fervently inveighed against the North's eager participation in the spoils of slavery. They burned, in fact, with indignation over it. They decried the North's "ostentatious display of humanity," its hypocrisy in benefiting from enslavement while disavowing any role. "Let them do us common justice, therefore, and we are willing to share the odium, if any there be, equally even with themselves," chided Edwin Clifford Holland, the editor of the *Charleston Times* in 1822.[38]

As proof of the North's "tenderness" for slavery, to use Jefferson's term, Holland elaborated in his reporting how northern vessels, in open violation of established law, were not only transporting the commodities of slavery but also still eagerly transporting enslaved people themselves to the South. "They should be the last to upbraid us when we can point to cases of clandestine commerce with Africa, on their part, *long after the abolition of the Trade*. The [ships] *Science*, the *Endymion* and the *Plattsburgh*, *all of them fitted out at New-York*, were taken possession of by the proper authorities of the United States in the year 1820, for a violation of their laws in this respect."[39] What Holland said was true. Even forty years later, authorities were still seizing New York vessels involved in the transportation of enslaved people. Mysteriously, the vessel's owners, presumably rich men, almost always avoided prosecution.

Yet the northern white public had long refused to acknowledge its role in the trade. This disavowal itself was one of great privileges that white northerners derived from enslavement: to live in cities enriched by the labor of Black people while escaping any critique over the source of that prosperity. Relatedly, it was the privilege of northern magnates to capitalize on slavery without being exposed as collaborators, without being questioned widely—as yet, anyway—as merchants of misery amplifying slavery's horrors. This disconnect, a kind of cognitive dissonance, was a critical factor in why slavery and its riches continued to expand, and an important reason why—though much later, when abolitionists took aim at this dissonance, and consciously targeted the money flowing north—the prospects for abolition also began to change.

It is worth adding that this dissonance is also a factor, as we will see, in why America's history of slavery remains distorted today. The false notion that the North was hardly involved in enslavement continues to prevent a full reckoning of slavery's costs to Black people and its overall benefits to white people.

———

It was a fixation of *Charleston Times* editor Edwin Clifford Holland that Denmark Vesey, a thirty-four-year-old free Black man, accused of plotting an insurrection in 1822, had allegedly intended to seize Charleston's vast riches before razing it to the ground. Holland, in a long monograph published on the conspiracy, and based on official magistrate interrogations obtained through torture, had Vesey and thirty-four enslaved accomplices first capturing the city's robust shipping industry, then taking hostage its prized mariners (to pilot the plotters off to freedom), before finally setting upon and robbing all the city's banks. What made Holland livid—and we can imagine, also his readers—was not just Vesey's supposed bloodlust, Vesey's yearning, so Holland and his fellow Charlestonians alleged, to kill countless white enslavers; it was also this robbery, this scheming to take Charleston's wealth, which Holland went on to connect, employing many twists and conspiratorial angles, to a vicious northern attack on southern economic sovereignty.

It mattered not to Holland that there had been no insurrection, that Vesey and the thirty-four enslaved Black men were rounded up on scanty evidence, tortured, summarily found guilty, and hanged. On the contrary, Holland, the Charleston mayor, and the regional press put this down to uncanny police preparedness. Holland took the opportunity to blame any number of elements: free Black people as agents of the North; enslaved

Black people as ungrateful to the South; northern missionaries ("apostolic vagabonds") for spreading among enslaved people, through scripture, a demand for freedom; and northern politicians for denouncing slavery during the rancorous debates, the so-called Missouri Question, that had seized Congress two years earlier. (Holland and many southerners posited that those debates, by calling attention to the evils of slavery, had inspired enslaved people across the country to revolt.)

Finally, Holland came to the pith of his rant: "The true causes of all the clamor upon the part of the Northern and Eastern States upon the subject of slavery, can be referred to no other definite feeling than a desire to wrest from the Southern and Western States the ascendency that their wealth and talents have given them in the councils of the nation; and, by diminishing their representation, to secure to themselves the whole management of the affairs of Government." [40]

The Vesey affair did ignite something, though not an actual plot; it showed smoke blazing high over the embers already burning between North and South, a conflagration involving not merely the wealth of slavery and its control, but, more importantly, its costs. Enslaving Black people produced extraordinary wealth for white men, but at what cost? What cost to white people's security, to their law and order, to their wealth, to their comforts, to their white majority, to the very stability and cohesion of the union, with only second thoughts given (when given at all) to the costs, in blood, in time, in wealth, in families, in torment, to Black people as well? "The tenure by which we hold our slaves, is daily becoming less secure, and more the subject of acrimonious animadversion," prognosticated Whitemarsh B. Seabrook, later the governor of South Carolina. "The skeptic need not longer doubt of the proximity of danger." [41]

These were long-burning questions, long-burning embers. They cradled the nest of paradoxes at the heart of America's historic slavery wealth. Almost from the inception of plantation slavery after the Revolutionary War, and certainly from the time the profitability of cotton exports began to bloom, white thinkers of various persuasions, both southern and northern, fixated on the troubling yet integral feature of the system of slavery they had built: that the benefits of its wealth came at an ever-higher price and that, paradoxically, the reward for slavery's success, this climbing ever upward of its sumptuous profits, was to plant the seed for its own eventual destruction. The Founding Fathers had said as much, again not in the Constitution, but in writing elsewhere. Their thinking belied the paradoxes, the twists of logic mirroring the twisted fate of wresting liberty at the price of Black enslavement, prosperity at the expense of excruciating torment for Black people.

Slavery, according to Jefferson, couldn't last, yet it also could not be abolished easily. It was like holding a "wolf by the ear, and we can neither hold him, nor safely let him go," Jefferson wrote in 1820.[42] The more indispensable it became—to the wealth of the colonies, to the republic, and now to the early nation—the more impossible it became to sustain as well. The United States had needed more and more enslaved people to make more and more wealth, for more and more white people. But more and more Black people under the chain increased the chances of violence, white people feared.

In Jefferson's estimation, enslavement would eventually lead to the outbreak of racial war. Emancipation was urgent, he and other framers had reasoned since the late 1780s. Yet they added, confusingly, if emancipation were to happen, it would have to be gradual, not immediate, despite its urgency. At the same time, however, emancipation was also impossible, according to James Madison, rendered so "by the prejudices of the Whites, prejudices which…must be considered as permanent and insuperable."[43] Yet again, every attempt must be made at the impossibility of emancipation, the framers urged, because time was running out, the fires were burning. What, then, was to be done? And done how? And done for whom? To do what to whom?

Clearly, we should not expect coherent thinking from men who, while propounding on the ills of slavery, enslaved and profited from Black people themselves. A confused tapestry is what was inherited and passed down. In 1806, John Parrish, an outspoken Quaker missionary from Philadelphia, continued this hand-wringing in a written tract: "It has been frequently asked, 'How can the United States get rid of slavery?' This is an important question. The immediate liberation of all the slaves, may be attended with some difficulty; but surely something towards it may now be done."[44]

William Hillhouse, the early abolitionist from Connecticut, wrote his own treatise of conflicted thoughts in 1816, with his turmoil producing a clear framework for the thinking of the age. Hillhouse was exercised by the Missouri debates. Missouri's acceptance to the union, its tipping the representational balance of power toward slavery, its encouraging of slavery's expansion westward—all were flashpoints for him, as for many in the North, proof, once again, that surely something "may now be done." Hillhouse was disgusted by slavery's greed; the Latin epigraph of his work was *Auri sacra fames*, "the accursed greed for gold." Yet even a tract as ferocious as his provided no practical remedies for Black people's liberation. He merely held out vague hope, at some vague time, by some vague decree, for the gradual emancipation of enslaved Black people. In the meantime, his work did what tracts by many white authors, even those opposed to slavery, tended to do at the time: it descended into the reservoir of Jeffersonian prejudice and fears, seeing the price of slavery's riches through the lens of white people themselves and what it might cost them.

Hillhouse, almost as much as Holland, worried about one thing above all: white people's safety. Already enslaved people's violent resistance to oppression had shaken white people's sense of security. Such resistance included not only revolts in Charleston as far back as 1739 followed by Gabriel's Rebellion, in Richmond, in 1800, but also Toussaint Louverture's successful revolution in Haiti. More rebellions were sure to come, Hillhouse warned: "...Africa and her sons will retaliate their sufferings on the heads of their oppressors; who by themselves or their predecessors, for more than two centuries, have made them drink, to the very dregs, the bitter cup of affliction." [45]

In the meantime, the rising threat wasn't perceived as being just from *enslaved* Black people; equally threatening was the rising number of *free* Black people, many of them jobless and without prospects, Hillhouse fretted. For Hillhouse, as for others, the crux of worrying about white safety was worrying about white people's safety *in numbers*. He tracked rigidly, as others had done, the census statistics showing that the Black population was growing; it was growing because slavery was growing, and because more and more Black people were free. He grew vexed at the thought. Inherent in any remedy to address the ills of slavery, in Hillhouse's mind, as in the period at large, was a prevailing need to protect the white majority of America: "The effect of slavery in the United States is to lessen the ratio of the white, and to increase the ratio of the slave or black population." [46]

And even though Hillhouse was in support of emancipation, it was emancipation with a clause, freedom with a price: enslaved Black people should be freed but also sent away from the white republic of the United States.

It was an idea already gaining ground across the nation. The North and the South may have arrayed themselves opposingly over who should control the wealth of slavery and benefit from its power to apportion representation in government. But on the matter of free Black people, and "what must be done with them," the two sides found a disturbing, far-reaching, and ever-increasing alignment.

It was not long after Missouri was accepted into the union that Ohio, in 1823, passed a resolution proposing gradual but complete emancipation of all enslaved people. Similar resolutions were supported by Delaware, New Jersey, Indiana, and Rhode Island, which signaled that such legislation would soon sweep through the North. The resolutions that Congress then tabled in preparation for Black people's eventual emancipation were foretelling. In 1825, Senator Rufus King of New York, one of the Founding Fathers, proposed raising a national fund, paid for through land sales, to relocate free Black people to a territory, then unspecified, within the United States for their "settlement."[47] In other words, he proposed to banish Black people away. George Tucker, US representative from Virginia, sharpened the point, proposing to nullify the claim of Indigenous people west of the Rocky Mountains and settle any and all emancipated Black people on Indigenous land.[48]

In either case, in the minds of white power brokers and thinkers, North and South, Hillhouse to Holland, the final stop on the long road to freedom for Black people, after having immeasurably enriched the nation, was to be one of exile, propelled by white supremacy and caustic fear. For now, proponents of this banishment scheme had yet to devise how practically to pull it off. But by working together to figure it out, they united powerful elements in the North and the South, at a time when slavery was otherwise beginning to rip the country apart.

In just a few years, Black abolitionists would organize, and the power of their message against this "remedy" would draw white abolitionists to their cause. Black resistance would even turn some of the northern capitalists toward abolition, though, truthfully, this was very few. The vast tide of northern merchants would prove to be adamantly pro-slavery. They already were. We know this despite what tithes they gave to manumission societies, what words they may have uttered in the cause of emancipation, what charities they created for free Black schools. We know this from the record of their actions and choices, a record that is long. For decades, they received and consorted with southern men who completely usurped the freedom of Black people. As an abolitionist later wrote, "Multitudes who imagine themselves opposed to slavery lose their hearts through their pockets."[49] And Wall Street directors enslaved Black people themselves, as we have seen. These merchants, whether in New York, Boston, or Philadelphia, *were* heartless; they were not fighting for the dismantlement of the enslavement system, including their own profits, the source of their own riches. On the contrary, they continued to side with the South to protect the business and profits made from this exploitation of Black people, a business that was their own. In a later period, a period soon to come, they formed and financed societies to prevent the outbreak of war as means of further protecting southern slavery interests. In other words, their interests.

In the meantime, in this restive period when white leaders anguished themselves calculating slavery's costs, these same commercial power brokers and businessmen began putting their money toward something else, an investment as indicative of who they were, what they believed, and what they wanted the United States to be as the slavery system they worked so hard to sustain. At a time when slavery profits were at an all-time high and Black people's calls for liberty and citizenship were ascending, Wall Street and its most prominent bank directors pooled their vast resources to prevent Black people from ever making America their home.

CHAPTER 4

"PARTING ASUNDER PARENTS AND CHILDREN"

On the morning of February 6, 1820, a three-hundred-ton vessel set sail from New York Harbor, of great consequence to the history of slavery and the struggle for Black freedom. It was the merchant ship *Elizabeth*, and it had embarked for Sierra Leone in western Africa. Preparations for its voyage had been years in the making, and the ship, officially chartered by President James Monroe, was met on departure with great fanfare, a crowd of six thousand crushing at the Hudson River docks to see it off. Samuel A. Crozer, a white physician from Philadelphia, was busy about the deck that morning, helping to secure on-board supplies, tools, and stores for the long journey. He would serve as the voyage's attending doctor and principal agent, alongside Samuel Bacon, a white priest and Harvard-trained attorney. In New York, Crozer's associates on Wall Street had furnished him with the sum of $1,448 in expenses, to be used, as he later reported by letter, "for making preparations for the comfortable establishment and subsistence of the first colonists who shall need the aid of the Society." [1]

The "colonists" of which Crozer wrote were eighty-eight Black people making the first journey of its kind in US history; "the Society" was the American Colonization Society, an elite organization of politicians, southern enslavers, and Wall Street directors who, finding common cause in the project of Black removal from the United States, had overseen much of the preparations for this day. This included arranging the "settlement" to which the *Elizabeth* now sailed, a patch of land supposedly sanctioned, through prior contact, by the inhabitants of Sherbro Island, off the coast of Sierra Leone. The society's managers chose Sierra Leone based on precedent: British authorities had been deporting free Black people, including people from Jamaica, to Sierra Leone since the late 1780s.[2]

There were thirty-three African American men, eighteen women, and thirty-seven children assembled on board the *Elizabeth*, roughly thirty families.[3] Some had been born free, though many had been enslaved, among them Daniel Coker, a twenty-year-old Black man who had escaped from slavery in Baltimore and settled in New York, where he became an ordained minister. Like Daniel Coker, these Black émigrés had boarded the *Elizabeth* based on a promise: the American Colonization Society had declared that on Sherbro Island, they would live without interference, utterly free from white oversight, on abundant lands provided by "rich and benevolent patrons."[4] In return, however, they had to agree to leave the republic forever, no longer enslaved but never to be free residents of the United States.

The *Elizabeth* struggled to make passage from the harbor that day, so thickly was the Hudson blanketed in sheets of ice. When at last it broke out to sea, the journey proved increasingly arduous, and several times during the ensuing weeks, all on board gathered to pray. "The binnacle was washed off, and compasses broken," Reverend Bacon later described. "Sometimes the ship was before the wind;—sometimes she was rolling in the trough of the sea; sometimes they lost all command of her."[5]

It was at the middle of the passage, among the tumult and raging waves, that Crozer and Bacon, the white agents, told Daniel Coker and the other Black passengers, after much coaxing, the hidden truth: the society's settlement, and all the many future ones it hoped to establish in the coming years, in the name of removing free Black people from the United States, would forever be ruled by society agents—a Black overseas colony, in other words, managed by white overseers. Bacon feared the passengers would mutiny, but Daniel Coker, taking them aside, convinced them to persevere, to see what might come, he recorded in a later diary.

A sense of calm eventually settled over the remainder of the journey, though it wouldn't last. Within weeks of reaching Sherbro Island, many of the first Black émigrés, along with Bacon and Crozer, would be dead from hardship and disease.

The sailing of the *Elizabeth*, paid for by rich white enslavers, pitching about the waters in an ill-conceived effort to carry Black people, full of hope, far away from the United States, was at once a metaphor and the beginning of grotesque fantasy, the origin of myth and tragic farce. A metaphor for the delusional scheme that white leaders, both on Wall Street and in Washington, believed could resolve the personal guilt, the financial stakes, and the intellectual hypocrisy of enslaving Black people in a nation founded on the principle of liberty. It was part of the fantasy of constructing an all-white republic, a promised land expunged of all Black people. It was driven by the myth that with the right amount of money and business skills, this hateful scheme could actually be achieved. And it was a tragedy because many Black people believed in the society's farce and sought solace in the hope of freedom offered by colonization. They did so even as rich merchants and corporate emissaries—directors at City Bank, Bank of America, and leading cotton firms on Wall Street—underwrote voyages that exiled thousands of Black people forever from the promise of American liberty. Ultimately, many ships like the *Elizabeth* sent many hundreds of Black people to their deaths.

The capital of slavery, managed from Wall Street, underwrote this enterprise. It ran for a hundred years and was unlike any undertaking in the American experiment. To understand the evolution of the wealth of slavery, indeed the evolution of the country itself, is to understand the unfolding of this grim plan, "an enterprise so vast in its conceptions, so momentous in its results," as one colonizationist said.[6] Its practical implementation was far more limited than the society hoped, yet its potency for fomenting political ideas, for cohering powerful white alliances, grew and grew, its ultimate endeavor being to create a lasting sense of insecurity among Black people, convincing them that there was no place for them in the United States other than slavery—an endeavor, of course, that failed. Here were the early ideas of white supremacy turned to an odious new design; here was the bedrock notion that whiteness, being threatened by growing numbers of free Black people, required "solutions," funding and coercion for its protection, lest white people be replaced, a notion still alive today, now in the guise of the "great replacement theory," which a white supremacist specifically cited, in May 2022, before killing ten Black people with an assault rifle at a supermarket in Buffalo.

From very early in the life of the republic, American colonization would intensify as white leaders came to perceive the end of slavery as inevitable, as their fears grew about rising numbers of free Black people, and as they clamored to protect their slavery wealth and its ultimate dividend: the purity and prestige of whiteness. But so, too, would Black resistance to the society grow. And by organizing against American colonization and the Wall Street capitalists backing it, Black leaders created some of the earliest Black networks, community organizations, and public protests calling for abolition, Black liberty, and African American citizenship in the history of the United States. Tracing the flow of money into colonization, from out of the business of enslavement, illuminates two parallel histories: how corporations, bank directors, and government officials, all privately enriched with the money stolen from Black labor, publicly banded together to spend this transformative wealth on a far-reaching project to ensure white supremacy in the United States; and also how, in the face of rising Black and abolitionist movements, they failed.

———

ONE OF THE earliest known American references to the idea of colonization was made in 1811 by Thomas Jefferson. "Having long since made up my mind on the subject of colonization," he wrote, "I have no hesitation in saying that I consider that as the most desirable measure which can be adopted for *draining off this part of our population* [italics added]; most advantageous both for themselves and for us."[7]

By "draining off," Jefferson was referring to removing Black people away from the United States, to colonies in Africa yet to be settled, by white American financiers and patrons. In other words, deporting Black people en masse. As the scholar Jeffrey Fortin points out, the Anglo world was steeped in such history, long codified in racialized writing and enacted in policies of protecting whiteness through the "transportation and removal of unwanted peoples in the British Atlantic empire."[8]

On the subject, Jefferson was exceedingly well read. Passed through him and other Founding Fathers, the idea of using Black enslaved people's labor to build riches, a flourishing white society, but then evicting *free* Black people from America's shores lived robustly at the center of political discourse throughout the life of the early republic. In 1854, in his famous speech at Peoria, Abraham Lincoln was still entertaining the idea of colonization. He said: "My first impulse would be to free all the slaves, and send them to Liberia,—to their own native land." Lincoln could apparently not conceive of an America offering Black people their rightful home. "What next?" he said later in the speech. "Free them, and make them politically and socially, our equals?" he asked. "My own feelings will not admit of this; and if mine would, we well know that those of the great mass of white people will not."[9] The stance of Lincoln, who raised money for colonization efforts even well after emancipation, affirms how the idea of "draining off" Black people from the United States endured, entwined with private business interests as an executive consideration well beyond the Civil War and well into the twentieth century in fact. (Colonization efforts ended in 1904.)

The project of colonization persisted not only as a political proposal, not only as discourse. Colonization was put into action as an ongoing scheme because it was well funded, and because it was a scheme driven, among other things, by the resources of Wall Street: an elite white project, supposedly for the benefit of Black people, yet ultimately an agenda designed to constrain and invalidate the growing notion of Black freedom. (Salvation from God's wrath was also a consideration for white supporters.)

Enslavers, cotton growers, and various merchant constituents had been organizing colonization meetings since as far back as the early 1800s, from the time there was cotton, and wealth from its exportation began to grow. These meetings were held in churches and Masonic lodges throughout the country, in Concord, Boston, Charleston, and Natchez—that is, both North and South—attended by both men and women via loosely affiliated regional chapters. In gatherings, white people spoke of saving the "savage continent" of Africa by converting Black people to Christianity and sending them back "home," and thus "pouring on that barbarous region of our globe, the 'light of immortality and life.'"[10]

In 1817, regional chapters coalesced into the national governing body called the American Colonization Society, a sign itself of how popular the white fantasy of Black deportation had become and how central it was to the issue of slavery. Robert Finley, a New Jersey pastor, and Elias B. Caldwell, his brother-in-law and an attorney in Washington, DC, are among those credited with founding the national society. They established their headquarters in the capital, the better to lobby the White House and Congress. It was Reverend Finley, often the group's mouthpiece, who notoriously crystallized its racial animus: "Their number increases greatly, and their wretchedness too," he said of free Black people. "We should be cleared of them."[11]

Immediately, the society's efforts drew the support of President James Madison, who later served as the group's third president, as well as President James Monroe. Countless governors joined the society, as well as newspaper editors in the South and in New York. The society also boasted Supreme Court justices and congressional leaders, including Henry Clay, the Kentucky Whig Party leader who, an enslaver himself, ardently championed the cause in the Senate. (Clay became the society's president after Madison.)

To enumerate the list of white people supporting the aims of this body, its agenda of forcing the banishment of Black people from the United States, is to enumerate the very list of the country's most politically powerful men. But influence wasn't enough; they needed money as well. Reverend Finley, accordingly, called for "rich and benevolent contributors." The society's platform of white supremacy would stand on many pillars: Jefferson drove the ideology; Clay, Congress; Madison and Monroe, the White House; James Watson Webb, editor of the *New York Courier and Enquirer*, its editorial mission; Reverend Finley and many church fathers, its evangelical spirit. But it was Wall Street bankers and merchants who would provide much of the capital, the business management, and the financial skills to make it a reality.

The terms and conditions, so to speak, of colonization were confusing and murky, suggestive even of benefits. The society claimed to be working *against* slavery, recognizing its inevitable end. But it was vehemently opposed to emancipation in the United States. It claimed to be working on behalf of Black people yet assailed Black people's reputation at every turn. The society's plans were supposedly pious; at the same time, they were degrading and coercive to Black people's rights. White people no doubt believed they were doing good by colonization, yet the goal they sought was odious. The society's aim was to constrain Black people's agency; even so, many Black people—Daniel Coker and countless others—found fruitful new lives through it. Colonization's many contradictions collapse into confusion because it was, in a sense, a grotesque hall of mirrors of the prevailing, conflicted white sentiments of the time. Ultimately, the society provided its white adherents a kind of moral veneer, one that further obscured the sin of slavery they were supporting.

To be clear, some regional colonization societies provided funds to enable the manumission of enslaved Black people. But they offered Black people freedom only in exile, not freedom at home. Similarly, some white people stipulated in their wills that, upon death, the Black people they enslaved were to be emancipated, but only "on condition of their removal to Liberia." (The practice continued well into the 1850s.)[12] This was a choice that hundreds, and eventually thousands, of African Americans chose to make. Though what Black people like Daniel Coker, acting on their personal agency, sought through colonization—to "escape the oppressive conditions in their native land" and as a "means of finding a safe home," in the words of Rhondda R. Thomas, professor of literature at Clemson University—and what the white managers of the society intended it to achieve were two different things, the difference between choosing to be an émigré and being forced to migrate.[13] This is to say, expanding Black liberty in the United States wasn't the society's chief intention; deporting as many Black people as possible—indeed, all Black people—was.

The society made this plain rhetorically, practically, and consistently. In its 1820 annual report, society managers outlined how all Black people, "both BOND and FREE," could be transported abroad at the rate of 40,000 a year, and that this could be achieved with the aid of the federal government, namely through the levying of a tax on distilled spirits. Such a tax would "furnish half a million of dollars, annually" they resolved, and, most importantly, the "proceeds would, in less than a century, purchase and colonize in Africa, *every person of colour within the United States* [italics added]."[14] The scale of the society's ambitions, rendered clearly in writing then, was the total eradication of Black people from the United States by 1920.

This wasn't all. In Liberia, the society envisioned a world unsettling in its parallels to slavery: on growing tracts of land, they hoped to found plantations where formerly enslaved Black people, converted to Christianity and ministering to the "pagans," would farm rice, cotton, and other products, though in principle, these now "free colonists" would be allowed to profit from their agricultural trade as they saw fit. For good reason, Black abolitionist James Forten called colonization "the circuitous route through which [free Black people] must return to perpetual bondage."[15] It was one of the most calculating missions for achieving complete white supremacy that elite white men, both northern and southern, ever undertook in the history of the republic. "One of the great movements of the time," said Henry Clay, dedicated to the entire separation of the two races. [16]

Again, it was not just as an idea, but a reality to be achieved. In fact, the colonization scheme, as conceived by the society, constituted an unprecedented logistical undertaking, one requiring a great many sailing ships and extensive capital, working to expel Black people from American shores in constant, revolving motion. This also meant that many mariners would undertake many voyages across the Atlantic. The society's projected goals, in other words, eerily paralleled the original transatlantic slave trade, only now in reverse. What's more, colonization harnessed the very shipping enterprises that had arisen to manage the immense volume of enslavement commodities flowing across the globe, run by merchants around the wharves of Wall Street.

There can be little doubt that these maritime considerations were an important reason why so many Wall Street shipping merchants were later drawn to, and elected directors by, the American Colonization Society and its branches, and an important reason why the society's activities intensified with their involvement. Jonathan Goodhue, for example, the eminent cotton shipper and director of Bank of America, became the treasurer of the New York branch of the society as early as 1819. George Gallagher, partner in one of the city's largest shipping firms, became a manager of the society in 1820, active until 1827; he was meanwhile a director of City Bank nearly that whole time, from 1817 to 1825. These were among the "rich and benevolent" patrons answering Reverend Finley's call. They put their skills, status, and connections to formidable use, just as the organization intensified its primary mission: the mission of turning beliefs and closely held fears into threats.

The rising Black population, the society warned in recurrent publications, was a menace to the white majority, "a horde of miserable people, the objects of universal suspicion, subsisting by plunder" it said. If granted emancipation, free Black people would incite enslaved Black people to revolt, the society claimed, a "threatening prospect of future danger" to the white population. What's more, the society said, Black people would never be accepted by white people as their equals; they would never find gainful employment and schooling, so they should feel threatened enough to want to leave America forever.[17]

There was to be no solace for Black people in this paradoxical arrangement: their only "choices," the society told them, were to remain in the United States and be enslaved or to achieve freedom through banishment. The northern riches reaped from slavery, coupled with Wall Street's expertise, would prove invaluable in spreading these fears, in pushing colonization's diabolical hopes.

———

IN 1819, THE American Colonization Society, having hired leading attorneys in Washington to lobby President James Monroe and Congress, won a decisive victory. Congress granted its approval, through an official act, to establish Liberia, not only as a US colony for the settlement of formerly enslaved people, but for any African person "seized in the prosecution of the slave trade by the commanders of the United States armed vessels."[18] The nuance of this power is striking. It meant that US Navy vessels (it was for this reason that the war sloop *Cyane* was patrolling the African coast) could seize any African person, found being held against their will on any illegal slave ship bound for the United States, and, regardless of their country of birth, effectively deport them to the society's colony in Liberia. ("There is no power expressly vested in the Executive to provide, after such delivery, either for their support or protection," the congressional act added; any deportees would have to fend for themselves.)[19]

Congress appropriated $100,000 to give effect to these provisions, or $2 million today.[20] That it did so stresses the dangerous functioning of this group, a body both quasi-governmental and also private, with strong connections to the executive and legislative branches yet run by commercial interests. In fact, it is hard to determine where the line between official US government policy and private colonization policy ended and where the aspirations of the American Colonization Society differed from those of overall white society. The functioning of government, the evolution of the republic's ideals, the wealth of slavery, and the project of Black removal had virtually become one. For good reason, Samantha Seeley, associate professor of history at the University of Richmond, has called this "one of the more understudied movements in the history of American slavery and freedom."[21]

It was not long after Congress's approval that the disastrous voyage of the *Elizabeth* followed, transporting the first eighty-eight "emigrants" and leaving them at Sherbro Island, 130 miles south of Sierra Leone. Once there, after local tribes refused to grant the land they had earlier promised, Daniel Coker and the rest of the émigrés, finding themselves corralled in a marsh, had to fend for their lives. (The death of white society agents Bacon and Crozer had made Daniel Coker de facto leader of the group.) Many perished within weeks, including nineteen almost immediately of fever. Others were killed by local inhabitants, or died due to the colony's unsanitary provisions, its only water derived from the marsh.[22] Daniel Coker, however, survived, and continued to record events in his diary. He remained committed to the cause of Black colonization until his death in 1846.

"True, many of the colonists who first emigrated died," the society reported in a subsequent newsletter, boasting nonetheless of success. It published Coker's journal as a propaganda tool, both as proof of the mission's accomplishment but also as a reflection of Black people's willingness to migrate. Of those not dead on Sherbro Island, the society reported: "They have since however been removed to a more eligible situation."[23]

This "more eligible situation" was a settlement seized by force. Following the disastrous events at Sherbro, society managers again lobbied Monroe, and the president (critics called him a "zealous colonizationist") sent a US naval officer, Lieutenant Robert Field Stockton, to Liberia with instructions, essentially, to procure land for the society by any means necessary.[24] This, Lieutenant Stockton did. During his intrusion into Cape

Mesurado, Stockton pressed the Dey people and their monarch, King Peter, to negotiate with him for the sale of land. A history of Stockton published in 1856 relates that when King Peter refused, Stockton pursued him to his home, there drawing a "pistol and levelling it at the head of King Peter, and directing him to sit silent until he heard what was to be said."[25] If the king refused to sign the contract thrust upon him, Stockton told him, he would be dead by morning. King Peter signed over the land.

With the raising of an American flag, the Dey land was officially designated as Liberia, its capital christened Monrovia in honor of President James Monroe. The society had wrested its banishment colony through assault, threats, and the price, reportedly, of $300, all with official US sanction and resources.

THE "SUCCESS" OF the first US colony in Liberia attracted a broadening swath of the country's most prominent men. There were many preachers and pastors, congressmen, and other politicians who joined the society's call, along with several of the country's largest enslavers—men like Stephen Duncan, who enslaved more than one thousand Black people on his Mississippi plantations. Even more telling was the makeup of the society's officers, the men elected to manage its affairs. According to one estimate, almost three-fourths were enslavers themselves, a facet of the society that's been well explored. Almost totally unstudied, however, is the fact that many of the men drawn into the society's orbit after the establishment of this first colony—and particularly its leadership—were Wall Street corporate leaders, shipping magnates, and bank directors, men running the corporate structure that facilitated Black enslavement from the North.

In fact, the person who would become most synonymous with, and consequential to, the American Colonization Society after this period wasn't a preacher, a southern politician, or an enslaver. He was Anson G. Phelps, corporate titan of Wall Street and rising industrialist, as well as one of the city's foremost supporters of fundamentalist Christian causes. Few men in the United States were as enriched by Black suffering and bondage as Phelps; few were as intensely committed to the cause of Black exile as he. "There are very few in the United States who have devoted so much of pecuniary contributions, time, and labor on behalf [of coloniza-tion], as Mr. Phelps," a society address later pronounced.[26]

Phelps had begun regularly attending colonization meetings as early as 1817. He recorded that year in his diary his zeal for the society, writ-ing that he hoped it would be "one of the means to give the heathen to Thy son." Phelps was then thirty-seven years old, commercially ascendant, and ardently self-obsessed.[27] His lengthy diary, marked by a pen scrawl-ing densely over compact pages, exhibits a religiosity bordering on mania, with Phelps constantly begging God to render him more holy, beseeching the Creator meanwhile to bestow more beneficence for such holiness.

Phelps's most fervent prayers were all for himself. His narcissis-tic self-reflexivity, applied to the colonization scheme, makes clear that Phelps, with great vigor, undertook the cruel work of deporting Black peo-ple because, in almost peevish anticipation, he expected from God dra-matic rewards for fulfilling the designs of white supremacy. Certainly, he pressed these motives to an extreme degree, and yet Phelps captured the ethos of cruel piety all too typical of his age. It was a generally confounding Christian sentiment, a lethal mix of willful blindness, self-righteousness, and selfishness, justifying so much of America's studied ambivalence toward the business of slavery, particularly in the colonization plan.[28]

Phelps began donating liberally to the society at a rate that would steadily grow, according to estimates, to almost $3,000 a year, or between $85,000 and $100,000 today.[29] Phelps was by then an exceedingly rich merchant, his wealth derived from purchasing large cargoes of cotton from southern plantations, shipping them to Liverpool, and exchanging the cotton for precious metals, primarily tin, which were then imported back to New York—the very heart of the cotton triangle. His two-story mansion on First Avenue, surrounded by thirty acres of manicured greens, sat in the middle of what would become Kips Bay, between Thirtieth and Thirty-First Streets. He was meanwhile a director of the American Fire Insurance Company and the North American Trust and Banking Company. Rich from cotton, his metal business would later morph into mining, and eventually into that quintessential industrial concern known as Phelps Dodge, a multibillion-dollar corporation acquired in 2007 by FreeportMcMoRan, the giant mining conglomerate. His path illuminates the evolutionary pinnacle of what a white man enriched by slavery wealth could become, and the white supremacist goals, underwritten with that wealth, that many white industrialists of his time hoped to achieve.

Phelps's involvement in colonization intensified, tellingly, in parallel to his becoming more entrenched in business dealings with southern enslavers and plantations. While he worked for the supposed amelioration of enslaved people, Phelps, along with his partner Elisha Peck, controlled a financial stake in a line of Charleston packets, which handled a great deal of the cotton he shipped to Liverpool. These enterprises made Phelps a millionaire by the 1830s, one of only six in the country.[30] In parallel, the official business of Phelps Dodge also became enmeshed with the official business of American colonization. One of Phelps Dodge's commercial vessels, the *Victory*, was often used for American Colonization Society business, including to transport important society agents, such as secretary R. R. Gurley, back and forth between New York and Washington, DC.[31] "During the late [eighteen] thirties and forties," reports a biography of Phelps's son-in-law, William E. Dodge, "Phelps Dodge & Co. handled part or all of the business affairs of the American Colonization Society and its New York branch; they had charge of funds, made purchases, and so forth."[32]

Never too busy for the society, Phelps took several leadership roles within the organization. In 1835, for example, he simultaneously headed a committee dedicated to growing the society's presence in places like Pennsylvania while overseeing another committee managing the removal of dozens of enslaved people from Savannah, Georgia, to Liberia.

A pastor later said of Phelps: "He did not expend his money in vain and futile schemes for the abolition of negro slavery, but gave freely from his abundant wealth to the promotion of practicable objects of benevolence, particularly the Colonization Society."[33] It is worth pausing over that detail: Phelps could have given liberally to abolitionist causes, to the many rising groups calling for the total and immediate emancipation of Black people; he did not. Though calling himself a "friend of the colored people," he became, in fact—by choosing to lavishly support the banishment of Black people—an object of increasing scorn for African American leaders, including Martin Robison Delany, the editor of the *North Star* newspaper, who later called Phelps "that malignant libeller of our race, A.G. Phelps."[34]

Likewise, Phelps's business partner and son-in-law, William E. Dodge, didn't endorse the abolition of slavery. He supported sending Black people away, and his business endeavors were undertaken within that vision. Dodge would later harness his wealth, derived from slave industries, to launch a political career based on the platform of white supremacy. "This country is not the place for the colored man," he years later told a meeting of the Colonization Society. "It will be a forced effort to attempt to place him on a par with the white man. I am more and more convinced that God made Africa to be the home of the Negro."[35]

Several of Dodge's and Phelps's Wall Street peers were already active in the management of the American Colonization Society when they joined; their numbers steadily grew. These were men who signed on to the society's vision that Black removal was critical to American progress, to ensuring the purity of America's whiteness. "In fact, if we mean to accelerate the progress of civilization, it can only be done by colonization," one of their tracts read.[36] Grove Wright, a City Bank director, served as treasurer from 1823 to 1829, taking over from Jonathan Goodhue.[37] George Newbold, a director of Bank of America, became a manager of the New York society in 1824. Cornelius R. Suydam, whose family had deep roots in cotton shipping, became a society member in 1839. Suydam was still a director at City Bank at the time.

In total, dozens of Wall Street's leading bankers, presidents, directors, and merchants, men who sieved immense riches from slavery, both financed and managed the repugnant colonization cause, raising thousands in funds and pledging a great deal of their personal time and money, over decades, to achieve the expulsion of Black people from the republic.

Black activists were particularly incensed by the role of these business leaders. "The Northern and Middle States are called upon for donations to enable the monarch of the south to bury his slaves in the sands of Africa," Hayden Waters, a leader in the African American community of Otsego, New York, told a church gathering in 1830. "Thus far, northern capital is instrumental in parting asunder parents and children—no more to meet."[38]

The society, while purporting to work on behalf of Black people, simply ignored Black outcry and criticism, pushing on. In 1833, the society's New York chapter formed a new committee to raise $20,000 ($636,000 today), for the purposes of founding yet another exile colony near Cape Mount in Liberia. The settlement was to bear the name New York. Among the men elected to head the committee were several with mercantile ties to slavery, including George Griswold, Samuel Ward, and Pelatiah Perit.[39]

At a meeting held to announce the drive, Ward and others made explicit their support for southern enslavers. "As citizens of the United States, we [have] no right to interfere with the claims of property of our southern brethren. The constitution recognizes their right to slave property...and they are entitled to its enjoyment."[40] They added that "delivering our country from the evils of a free colored population" through Black exile was the only feasible way forward, not emancipation.[41] These Wall Street magnates made explicit, in other words, that they intended to use their elite positions and influence, coupled with their deep pockets, to protect the business of slavery and ensure the white supremacy of the United States through Black removal.[42] That evening, Wall Street leaders pledged $4,000 ($127,000 today) on the spot for the new deportation colony; Samuel Ward and George Griswold were among the leading donors, pledging $200 each, or more than $6,000 today.[43]

MISGUIDEDLY BENIGN INTERPRETATIONS over the years have said, ironically, that a kind of liberal-mindedness, a deep caring, even a zeal to end slavery drove Phelps's participation in colonization, along with other Wall Street men. Libraries and official government histories, not to mention corporate public relations accounts, have likened Phelps and these men to philanthropists, even abolitionists, because, like Archibald Gracie and Jeremiah Thompson, they funded what they positioned as benevolent causes for Black people. Until at least 2008, the Department of History at New York University sponsored the Anson G. Phelps Lectures, lectures dedicated to elucidating the contribution of early Puritans to US history—lectures designed to honor Phelps and his civic contributions. This includes the fact that Phelps, between 1848 and 1858, sat on the governing council of the University of the City of New York, the predecessor to NYU.[44] The fund for the eponymous lectures was endowed by Phelps's grandson James Stoker.[45] No record can be found of the Anson G. Phelps

Lectures exploring Phelps's ties to enslavement through cotton shipping, or exploring how Phelps's wealth, made from enslaved Black people, may have helped benefit NYU. Nor has any lecture been given that problematizes Phelps's untiring support of a century-long operation calling for the expulsion of Black people from the United States to ensure the supremacy—in numbers, wealth, and political power—of white people.

More critical readings challenged the American Colonization Society's motivations publicly, and did so, in fact, from the very start. One source of keen refute was John Quincy Adams. Adams had occasion to speak with many colonizationists at the White House while serving as Monroe's vice president. After one such meeting, he penned in his diary the following lines:

> There are men of all sorts and descriptions concerned in this Colonization Society: some exceedingly humane, weak-minded men, who have really no other than the professed objects in view, and who honestly believe them both useful and attainable; some, speculators in official profits and honors, which a colonial establishment would of course produce; some, speculators in political popularity, who think to please the abolitionists by their zeal for emancipation, and the slave-holders by the flattering hope of ridding them of the free colored people at the public expense; lastly, some cunning slave-holders, who see that the plan may be carried far enough to produce the effect of raising the market price of their slaves.[46]

Adams, who grappled for years with the growing popularity of the society, came to detest the organization. "That fraudulent charitable institution, the Colonization Society," he wrote, elsewhere adding, "the whole colonization project was an abortion."[47]

Various elite, white-led abolitionist groups likewise discounted the motivations of the society. The American Convention for Promoting the Abolition of Slavery, led by prominent lawyers Peter A. Jay and Hiram Ketchum, expressed its opinion that "they have not been able to discern, in the constitution and proceedings of the American Colonization Society, or in the avowed sentiments of its members, anything friendly to the abolition of slavery in the United States." [48]The society's plan, they added, was wholly unrealizable, as it would require tens of millions of dollars to transport even a fraction of the population of free Black people from the United States, a sum that the society didn't possess and likely had no hope of procuring. "The plan of colonizing the free people of colour proposed by the society, is impracticable, and if it is practicable, it will be attended with fatal consequences to those who shall embark in its purposes."[49]

Their observation was correct on both counts. Despite robust funding, plus the management skills of Wall Street's most accomplished directors, not to mention political backing of the highest order, the society never succeeded in removing to Liberia more than a few hundred Black people each year.

The reasons why Black people chose to leave ran a wide gamut, some from hope, some from despair, some from being tricked, explains Professor Rhondda R. Thomas: "Some people are looking for a fresh start. Some people are looking to get out of America because it was so racist. And even as free people, they can't realize their aspirations as full citizens, and all the rights and privileges that are associated with that. Some of them are going because they want to be attached to the motherland, where their roots are," she says. "I think some of them are lured away by the Colonization Society, with the promises of a paradise."[50]

For those who did board the society's ships, the deportations resulted in catastrophically high death rates—almost half of all the Black people deported, according to some estimations. Black people, some as young as ten years old, died far from home of agonizing diseases, in some instances torn from their families. By any measure, the American Colonization Society was a failure, though this didn't stop it from carrying on its activities vigorously for another eighty-five years.

What can this mean? It suggests that the society's greatest success wasn't its practical achievement, and that practical achievement wasn't likely its foremost purpose. William E. Dodge supported colonization for decades, despite acknowledging that its goal of total Black removal was impossible. In fact, according to a biographer, Dodge summarized that view in the following racist remarks: "He used to say, with a laugh: 'Why, all the shipping of the world would not suffice to ferry half of them to Africa!'"[51]

Colonization was racist white fantasy. The society operated on the level of funding myth and the incandescent specter of violence, much as white supremacist groups do today. Its success was to keep alive, as propaganda for white people, an ever-persistent threat *about* Black people, that they would one day eclipse the white majority; and to keep alive an ever-persistent threat *among* Black people, that all Black people would one day be expunged. In other words, its effort was to make the Black experience in the United States unlivable. To this effect, it continued throughout the 1830s and '40s to generate donations and other revenue of up to $50,000 a year ($1.6 million today); it continued spending thousands of dollars on printed material and speeches; Anson Phelps, William Dodge, and its other members continued to meet nationally, disseminating, and funding its repugnant cause.[52] Lincoln, still musing about colonization so many years later, is proof of *this* success.

Colonization failed in the end, though, because of one critical factor above all: opposition by Black organizers and Black people themselves proved so vehemently effective against it. This opposition lit the fire for lasting networks of Black resistance, the fire for the beginnings of the abolition movement itself. And it was for this reason that Black people by and large, despite the vast coercion machine that the society, with its Wall Street funding had become, were almost entirely unmoved by colonization's offerings, and unwilling to migrate.

Just after the society's formation, Black organizers in Philadelphia, including Richard Allen, Absalom Jones, James Forten, and John Gloucester convened a meeting in 1817 at the Mother Bethel Church to discuss the Colonization Society's views. Forten had actually been contacted by Rev. Robert Finley, the society's spokesman, who hoped Forten might help to popularize the society's cause. Forten, realizing that it would be prudent to put the issue before his community, reached out to others to organize a meeting. The turnout was astounding: three thousand Black men attended, nearly every free Black man in the city of Philadelphia. (As of 1810, there were slightly fewer than nine thousand Black people living there.)

Forten and the organizers had called the meeting because, at least at that point, some *endorsed* the concept of colonization—though of a certain kind—having been influenced by Captain Paul Cuffe, a wealthy

Black shipbuilder in New Bedford who visited Sierra Leone and advocated for free Black colonies in West Africa. (It should be stated that Cuffe's ideas were markedly different than the society's.) Forten and church leaders expected the Philadelphia gathering to endorse this idea too. But that wasn't the case. After the assembly took in the nuances of colonization, as envisioned by white society anyway—that the society's goal was to deport *all* free Black people, or at least as many as possible, whether they wanted to leave the United States or not—they voted unanimously to condemn it.

"There was not one soul that was in favor of going to Africa," Forten wrote to Cuffe.[53] On the contrary, the assembly pressed James Forten to issue a resolution rejecting colonization, or any measure "having a tendency to banish us from her bosom."[54] Black abolitionist Theodore S. Wright later observed that "the people of color in Philadelphia...in an assembly of three thousand, before high heaven, in the Presence of Almighty God, and in the midst of a persecuting nation, resolved that they would never leave the land."[55]

The Philadelphia resolution proved an epochal event. Wright tells how his father traveled from Schenectady, New York, to Philadelphia to learn more about the resolution, his journey indicative of a "spirit which prevailed among the people of color...They lifted up their voice and said, this is my country, here I was born, here I have toiled and suffered, and here will I die."[56] Colonization leaders continued chartering dozens of ships, while hundreds of silk-vested, top-hatted Wall Street directors continued pouring cash and coin into the society's coffers. At the same time, however, the range of salient Black voices denouncing this exile grew, and organized Black action to end slavery, combat racial segregation, and promote equality strengthened over the course of a decade.

In March 1827, Samuel E. Cornish, pastor of New York's First Colored Presbyterian Church, and John Brown Russwurm, then recently graduated from Bowdoin College (Russwurm was one of only three Black graduates in the country at the time), together founded *Freedom's Journal*, the nation's first Black-run and Black-owned newspaper. Its emergence reflected the dynamic constellation of Black intellectuals to which Cornish and Russwurm belonged; it was made possible by social networks that had been building within the free Black community since the American Revolution. "There was a social infrastructure that could support a

national newspaper," highlights the writer Jacqueline Bacon. "Generations of leaders had laid the groundwork for the periodical by building
community institutions, demonstrating the power of rhetoric in forming
a national consciousness, and asserting the right to determine their own
destinies."[57]

Freedom's Journal announced Black weddings, advertised Black businesses, and reported on a variety of domestic and foreign news, with distribution in Canada and Haiti as well. Its founding coincided with New
York's finally granting emancipation to the state's remaining enslaved people, a joyous event the paper covered widely.

Colonization wasn't why Cornish and Russwurm founded *Freedom's
Journal*, but it became an important focus of their coverage, given the
threat the American Colonization Society posed to Black people and the
resources the society expended—including running two newspapers of its
own, the *African Observer* and the *African Repository and Colonial Journal*. *Freedom's Journal* drew sustained attention to the society's threats and
effectively discredited, before a wide audience, colonization's otherwise
vastly popular and war-chested ideas.

The efforts culminated in 1829 with the publication of the vision-
ary work *Appeal to the Coloured Citizens of the World*, written by David
Walker, a Black clothing-store owner in Boston and the son of an enslaved
man. Walker had lived through the execution of Vesey and the ensuing
terror of Black people; after fleeing Charleston, where he was born, he'd
traveled throughout the country, witnessing the plight of African Americans. He'd been both a contributing writer and the Boston agent for *Freedom's Journal*.

At his store, located on teeming Brattle Street, he discussed in meetings with Black people the conviction that the United States was Black
people's birthright, shaping this idea into an opus. At its heart, *Appeal* was
a searing critique of the American Colonization Society, which Walker
dismissed as "a plan got up by a gang of slave-holders to select the free
people of colour from among the slaves, that our more miserable brethren
may be the better secured in ignorance and wretchedness, to work their
farms and dig their mines, and thus go on enriching the christians with
their blood and groans."[58]

Colonization's religious hypocrisy ("Is it surprising to think that the

Americans, having the bible in their hands, do not believe it?") allowed Walker a wider lens for conveying the necessity of Black liberty and Black citizenship in the United States, and he did so by homing in on the idea of slavery and its vast wealth, on what African Americans had rightfully earned and what they were owed. "The greatest riches in all America have arisen from our blood and tears...tell us now no more about colonization, for America is as much our country, as it is yours."[59]

Walker proposed freedom through violence if necessary. "Remember Americans, that we must and shall be free...," he wrote. "Will you wait until we shall, under God, obtain our liberty by the crushing arm of power? Will it not be dreadful for you? I speak Americans for your good."

Appeal was one of the first Black pamphlets of its kind. It appeared with singular force, in singular language, with a resonance to meet the uniquely threatening reality that the Colonization Society, increasingly led by Wall Street, was becoming. "It was merely a smooth stone which this David took up, yet it terrified a host of Goliaths," wrote Black abolitionist Henry H. Garnet.[60]

Walker's pamphlet circulated widely, due in large part to its reprinting in major northern newspapers, but also thanks to Walker himself. From the South, enslavers and politicians had made great effort to silence *Appeal*'s author, labeling him pro-militant, violent, and an insurrectionist. A group in Georgia offered a $1,000 reward for killing Walker, $10,000 for bringing him in alive.[61] But Walker's efforts at selling and distributing his work (he gave copies to Black sailors heading out of port from Boston, and sewed others into the clothes of Black people who visited his store) dovetailed with the growing nodes of organized Black resistance, and this ensured *Appeal*'s reaching a wide audience.[62]

One of its lasting impacts was to inspire a new generation of abolitionists—Black and white—including Maria Stewart, a Black woman who helped publish *Appeal*, and William Lloyd Garrison, who had originally been a member of the Colonization Society, supporting its goals, but who later broke completely with the idea of colonization in favor of abolition. Garrison would come to call *Appeal* "one of the most remarkable productions of the age."[63]

Walker died suddenly in 1830 of tuberculosis, just as suddenly as the spark of his vision was loosed and before witnessing its full legacy in all its bloom. His *Appeal* marked a critical moment in time. "It demarcates the historical threshold between two eras," writes Gene Andrew Jarrett, dean of the faculty at Princeton University. "It also stands at the inception of an antebellum period, invigorating black abolitionists with invectives of racial nationalism, inspiring them to oppose the rising American Colonization Society, and broadening the rhetorical possibilities of the pamphlet form as slavery became increasingly untenable for the nation."[64]

———

"WHY SHOULD THEY send us into a far country to die?" the Reverend Richard Allen wrote in a letter published in *Freedom's Journal* in 1827. Allen, one of the Black organizers of the Philadelphia gathering so many years before, amended an important observation: "See the thousands of foreigners emigrating to America every year: and if there be ground sufficient for them to cultivate, and bread for them to eat; why would they wish to send the *first tillers* of the land away? Africans have made fortunes for thousands, who are yet unwilling to part with their services; but the free must be sent away, and those who remain must be *slaves*."[65]

"Africans have made fortunes for thousands." "Thousands of foreigners emigrating to America every year." It wasn't lost on Reverend Allen, descended from "the first tillers of the land" that the merchant princes of Wall Street, even as they underwrote the most extensive banishment of Black people in US history, were welcoming record-shattering numbers of white Europeans to America's shores. In fact, many of the shipping magnates who supported colonization—George Griswold, Robert Minturn, and Jonathan Goodhue among them—owned the heaving packet ships and ocean liners capable of carrying three hundred passengers over the Atlantic, which made the vast, epochal scale of European immigration possible at all.

In 1817, following the launch of the Black Ball Line and its competitors, twenty-two thousand immigrants arrived in the United States, predominantly from England, Ireland, and Scotland; fifteen thousand arrived in New York and Philadelphia alone. Many had traveled aboard the same ships that had taken cotton out to England and France, ships that used to carry precious goods and materials on return, and now a rising white workforce. In 1819, another nineteen thousand white immigrants arrived. [66] The Naturalization Act of 1790, allotting citizenship to any "free white person" who lived in the United States for just two years, meant these white men, women, and children were almost seamlessly granted rights and legal protections that Black Americans, despite fighting for the nation's very independence and existence, were not.

The shipping tycoons helming this mass migration were, in a very concrete sense, fulfilling a Jeffersonian ideal: in 1784, Jefferson had written that, to offset the loss of enslaved labor that would eventually result from emancipation, the United States should send vessels to "other parts of the world for an equal number of white inhabitants; to induce whom to migrate hither." In this sense, Wall Street's participation in colonization was motivated by a much larger, much more global vision of white dominance and its political and economic aims, as Jeffrey Fortin, now an associate professor of history at Emmanuel College Boston, explains. The sweeping flow of capital, goods, and people was intended to create "an Atlantic world where being white meant largely unrestricted movement across national borders, immigration, and access to citizenship and protection from forced migration," writes Fortin.[67]

White immigrants would become an ever more important piece of the triangle at the heart of this Atlantic world that colonization hoped to secure: a sprawling zone of riches made possible by the extirpation of Indigenous people from Western lands, the dispersion of enslaved Black people into those territories, and the exile of free Black people. The American Colonization Society said it hoped colonization would "provide and keep open a drain for the excess of [Black people] beyond the occasions of profitable employment"—and by "employment," it meant enslavement.[68] Once settled, white immigrants, many of them poor, were to toil endlessly in a burgeoning consortium of manufacturing and industrial corporations, funded from the proceeds of slavery, and controlled by the slavery entrepreneurs of Wall Street.

———

ON FEBRUARY 27, 1833, Maria Stewart rose before a large convocation at Boston's African Masonic Hall. Stewart, who had helped David Walker

publish his *Appeal*, was becoming one of the most famous Black activists in the United States and one of the first Black women to lecture and
publish widely on the issue of Black equality. Protesting colonization was
central to her mission, and she made clear, in powerful speeches, the connection between white wealth and Black exile: "They have obliged our
brethren to labor; kept them in utter ignorance; nourished them in vice,
and raised them in degradation; and now that we have enriched their soil,
and filled their coffers, they say that we are not capable of becoming like
white men, and that we never can rise to respectability in this country.
They would drive us to a strange land."[69]

She also made a point of calling out the spurious nature of the American Colonization Society's funding efforts: "If the colonizationists are
the real friends to Africa, let them expend the money which they collect,
in erecting a college to educate her injured sons in this land of gospel
light and liberty: for it would be most thankfully received on our part, and
convince us of the truth of their professions, and save time, expense, and
anxiety."[70]

Stewart highlighted a striking point. Despite claiming to be a benevolent association, the American Colonization Society spent virtually no
money in the United States for the direct benefit of Black people; no
money on schools, hospitals, or housing for African Americans, whether
free or enslaved. The Pennsylvania Augustine Society for the Education
of People of Colour, one of many Black organizations dedicated to building Black schools, had existed since 1818. Yet the society had never offered
it, or any organization like it, aid of any sort.

In contrast, to manage its mass expulsions abroad, the society had
become a veritable colonial corporation, a deeply funded multinational
enterprise. It had several administrative offices in multiple jurisdictions
throughout the United States.[71] It had also financed the construction of
several public buildings in Liberia, as well as a series of Christian missionary schools and churches, including a Sunday school for children, plus
salaries for thirty-five scholars. It even paid for the upkeep of a defensive
military organization in Liberia, composed of a uniformed corps, two
infantry companies, and two artillery companies, plus a detachment of
twenty guards, "for the purposes of manning the Battery."[72]

When Anson G. Phelps had first joined the society, its donations and

other revenue amounted to $14,000, or $334,000 today.[73] Parallel to his
involvement and leadership, the society's revenue climbed to $62,000 by
1840, or $2 million today.[74] (Soon afterward, in 1841, Phelps was asked
to join the society's board of directors.) This was a great expenditure of
money, white wealth from Black enslavement contributed by directors of
Bank of America, City Bank, the Bank of New York, and others for the
purposes of exiling Black people thousands of miles away and subjecting
them to Christian indoctrination.

It is revealing to point out, furthermore, that the leading abolitionist organization in the country at the time, the American Anti-Slavery
Society, had a budget commensurate in size—$38,304 in 1837; $35,466 in
1855—to the Colonization Society's.[75] This was money actually expended
on freedom for Black people, money to which Phelps and Dodge and
Goodhue and countless other Wall Street directors, notably, weren't contributing. During her address, Maria Stewart highlighted this fact too,
quipping wryly of the society: "But ah! methinks their hearts are so frozen
towards us, they had rather their money should be sunk in the ocean than
to administer it to our relief."[76]

Again, Stewart's striking point occasions a moment of reflection.
It has been estimated that between 1817 and 1836, the American Colonization Society spent a total of $332,586 funding the removal of Black
people to Liberia. This equates roughly to $10.6 million today. During
the same period, the US government itself spent $264,710, or $8 million
today, underwriting the society's efforts.[77] That together these two forces,
interlacing private interests and public office, public money and private
donation, spent the combined total of nearly $19 million financing Black
expulsion, and did so in just the first two decades of the scheme's existence, constitutes an atrocious chapter in America's long history of making
the United States unlivable for Black people.

By 1838, the American Colonization Society had deported five thousand Black people to Liberia, including an estimated one thousand who
had formerly been enslaved. This number would more than double by
the Civil War.[78] It's worth considering that this figure is remarkable from
several points of view: On the one hand, that the society failed to exile
more Black people crystallizes the effectiveness of Black organized resistance to this enormously powerful, well-funded group. It also speaks to

the delusional quality of the Colonization Society, a disconnect between its fantasy and its actual achievements. And yet, five thousand is still a significant number of Black people who chose, under various circumstances, to leave—some no doubt acting upon their own hopes and designs, others coerced, pressured, or duped.

"I think that they thought they would have more autonomy," says Rhondda R. Thomas, "and that this was just the vehicle to get them into a new situation. And they did not fully comprehend, or the colonizers did not fully communicate, the motivations. Their motivations were never altruistic. Ultimately, they're trying to get free Black people out of America, so the nation can be a slave society."[79]

It wasn't just that Wall Street bank directors and shipping merchants helped the society; the society benefited their businesses, their vision of prosperity, the goals for the United States, all of which were tied to achieving white supremacy by stealing extraordinary fortunes through Black enslavement. For good reason, William Lloyd Garrison called the American Colonization Society "slaveholding and pro-slavery combined in organized warfare upon colored liberty."[80] To threaten slavery was to jeopardize the immense financial proceeds of the cotton triangle and the wider export of trade it supported. Simultaneous to physically ejecting Black people from the body politic and fabric of the nation, the impact of the society and of the Wall Street leaders who poured their wealth into it was to cast doubt and division over the prospects of abolition and emancipation—to disseminate, ultimately, the ideology that the United States was not, and could never be, Black people's rightful home.

As such, the national debate began to speak of the threat of violence, the prospect of the South seceding, and even the prediction that the United States would dissolve. This "disunion" would happen, warned the writer James K. Paulding, "*whenever* the misguided, or willfully malignant zeal of the advocates of emancipation, shall institute *as it one day doubtless will*, a crusade against the constitutional rights of the slave owners."[81]

CHAPTER 5

A MERCHANT PRINCE

By 1830, New York had left its origins of ramshackle wood behind and had become a city of marble and luster. Philadelphia, Boston, and Baltimore had too. There was marble for statues, monuments, and hallways, to fete the living; marble for gravestones, mausoleums, and sarcophagi, to honor the dead. Marble flowed to New York from Edwin Greble's yard in Philadelphia, and some from New England quarries farther away. Ships arriving to port from Livorno, ships that had shot the white wealth of cotton across the sea, brought back the veined white marble of Carrara. On Broome Street, Fisher and Bird specialized in marble mantels for the home, including fireplace mantels, but also slabs cut to the fashion of the day.

All of this marble was drawn into the Empire City, pulled up its stairs, and set in place for the merchant princes, the mariners who had dragged the spoils of the southern ports north to Manhattan. "There is no nobility in this country. There is a class of princes, and they are the highest in the city," wrote journalist Joseph Alfred Scoville in 1864. "There are the princes Goodhue, Aspinwall, Aymar, Perit, King, Grinnell, Minturn, Howland, Boorman, Griswold."[1] These were all cotton men, bound to the South, to slavery.

In 1830, Nathaniel Prime built a new marble chamber for his cotton house on Wall Street, with offices on the upper floor, and the banking room of Prime, Ward & King gleaming below. Marble and mansions were going up on Broadway, one of the city's first thoroughfares; it ran for two miles, in a straight line, an unbroken expanse—unfettered, like the ascent of slavery's trove.

Mansions rose too among Fifth Avenue, supposed monuments to distinction and class, but retiring in the shadows of their construction where the trees remained, many in the city smoldered. The oldest, richest families in New York—the Van Rensselaers, the Fleets, the Livingstons, clinging to title, to land, and riches made possible by Black labor—sneered at this age of upstarts, even though the main wealth of *this* time was the same as *their* time, "coined from the sinews of the slave."

The mansions disgusted, too, the art critics, of whom there were many now to judge the fineness of New York, though what disgusted such critics wasn't the stolen lives of Black people that had made the houses possible; they judged that the houses were ugly deviations from classical norms. "The dwelling-houses of our merchant-princes, are, with a few honourable exceptions, simply exhibitions of a very uncultivated taste," wrote one. "The offspring of untutored minds, they bear upon their fronts the impress of ignorance and presumption."[2] Elite white society, free to criticize itself, looked no deeper than the facades of its houses, blind, like Irving, like Hamilton, to a full accounting of the ledger of the heart.

But many understood what these houses *truly* meant. Their being erected at so high a price to enslaved people didn't go unnoticed by the free Black people of New York, of whom there were more than ever, nor by the city's abolitionists, whose numbers were also rising. They saw "'men of great stakes,' merchant-princes…giving aid and comfort to the slave-catcher, without losing their place in polite society."[3] New York was becoming a city of many worlds: A city of marble but also of mirrors, reflecting shards of horror back upon itself. A city of resistance. Such that this one place produced the story of two factions: one born out of hatred for the merchant princes and their slavery wealth; the other, heir to it, heir to the northern men, rich from the bounty of southern enslavement, who weren't just shipmasters and merchants anymore. They were becoming the nation's most powerful bankers and corporatists.

———

THERE WAS A mansion at 80 Leonard Street, halfway up the block from Broadway near Church Street, "a large double house, with a court, and an entrance for horses and carriage from the street."[4] Few records exist to detail it fully, but we know it boasted fifty rooms when later it was converted to a hotel. It was the home of James Brown, son of Alexander, a patriarch among the country's first millionaires, whom some sources likened to a Medici of old.[5] Alexander Brown had emigrated from Ireland in 1800 and worked as a linen salesman in Baltimore. But by 1804, after cornering that trade, he turned his energies, and that of his sons, to the vast commerce of slavery.

James, the fourth-born son, "a man of the simplest tastes...[despite] immense wealth" was around forty when living at Leonard Street. His brother John was in Philadelphia; his brothers George and William were in Liverpool. His mercantile family positioned at all corners of the Atlantic, James Brown was moving to the heart of it, to become the future of it, "an active participator in every important financial event in the history of this country," according to a nineteenth-century accounting by the *New York Times*.[6]

The path of James cuts through upheaval and flux, showing how the Wall Street businesses at the center of enslavement were evolving, and that rising to the top of the wealth pyramid, as others fell away, were a corporatized and concentrated few, financing the subjugation of growing numbers of Black people bent at the bottom. Each day, James Brown said goodbye to his wife and six children after breakfast, walked down the palace stairs to a "one-horse coupe" parked on the street, and headed south on Broadway to work.

His movement melded to a larger stream, other affluent men who "crossed the city to reach a dark counting-house in the centre of traffic," as Alexis de Tocqueville described, in what we might call the "cotton commute."[7] There were now "omnibuses" in Manhattan, large carriages carrying thirty men or so down Broadway, to the wharves, to the buzzing center of the North's cotton hive. "Hundreds of the first merchants, who reside two miles from Wall Street...step from their marble stoops, after breakfast, into one of the omnibuses and find themselves in Wall-Street before they have finished picking their teeth!" marveled a contemporaneous account, ringing with the prosperity of the time.[8]

Not all men worked in cotton commerce—some traded in tobacco and rice—but cotton touched most everything, a truth soon to become clear in a very short time. To read such accounts is to witness, then, the normalizing of routines that white prosperity had wrought: men heading down to Wall Street in the morning, in their powdered wigs, returning in the evening to their comfortable homes, to their dinners, regular like the waters, yet based on the worst pith of inhumanity, the business of possessing living souls.

The volumes of Scoville, among the most impressionistic accounts of the time, provide a glimpse of how entwined cotton then was with the everyday business of moneymaking on Wall Street. How the merchant Ward Cowing sailed to Mobile, Alabama, each season, or out to New Orleans, buying cotton, bringing it back for Dudley & Stuyvesant. How the firm of Spofford, Tileston & Co. shipped shoes to enslavers both in Cuba and the southern states—shoes for enslaved people cutting sugarcane—receiving sugar from the island in return, cotton, and rice from Charleston. Each day, Noah Talcott, proprietor of Talcott & Lyman, set out tables covered in blue paper at his office, and laid out "hundreds of samples of large lots of white cotton" for buyers.[9]

These cotton exchanges, as well as the sales of tobacco and rice, worked on credit-making backed by notes. "The goods and credit of the merchant are represented by promissory notes, which are bought, and sold, and pass from hand to hand, almost like bank bills," observed William Worthington Fowler, beginning his career around this time.[10] The business of enslavement had become the business of advances, running on promises. "It is credit which has furnished the merchants of New York with by far the greater portion of their available means, by which they have been able to monopolize so large a portion of the Southern trade," wrote James D. B. De Bow, the publisher of the *Commercial Review of the South and West*.[11]

James Brown had first joined this rush in 1825, sent by his father, and he had taken a storefront on Pine Street. (Historical sources say he worked in "dry goods," a deceitful euphemism.) The family started out as shippers, sailing slavery cotton and tobacco on a fleet; their ships included the *Tobacco Plant* and the *Natchez*, a nod to the plantations they served. By the 1820s, their Liverpool firm, William Brown & Co., was the second-largest receiver of cotton in England, which is to say, in the world.

Year after year, Alexander, the father, pushed the business, and he pushed his sons. "While all the family were conspicuously sagacious financiers, Alexander Brown's was the guiding and controlling mind that decided all questions of doubt or difficulty," reports a nineteenth-century history of the firm.[12] Alexander had employed their capital, not to mention decades of learned business experience, capturing various points along the cotton supply chain: a network of agents throughout the major ports Charleston, Mobile, and New Orleans; linkages to the leading cotton factors, men who annually sourced thirty million pounds or more; and relations with some of the South's most notorious enslavers, among them Thomas Bibb, former governor of Alabama, "a planter on a baronial scale," owner of two thousand acres, with dozens of enslaved people.[13]

The Browns drew business and acclaim by avoiding, even at the sake of profit, risks that other merchants did not. The father, especially, was circumspect to an extraordinary degree. The Browns also built a commission business, proffering advances to factors, earning 2.5 percent on an extraordinary volume of consignments. Between 1826 and 1827 alone, the firm moved 59,829 bales of cotton, valued at $2,670,000, or $72 million today. This cotton the Browns transported on their own ships to Liverpool, where William brokered it to the mills. After a time, they offered yet another service, this one exchange of currency, making pounds sterling available to American merchants selling cotton in Liverpool. They earned several more percentage points that way.

As he aged, Alexander tasked his sons to take the reins. By the 1830s, what the family created was perhaps the only enterprise of its kind in the world: a network of interlinking corporations, family-run and vertically integrated around enslavement, though the family did not enslave Black people themselves, at least not yet. Today, there is a street named after William in Liverpool (he died Sir William, having received a baronetcy from the Crown) and a skyscraper suite in Manhattan bearing the family's name: Brown Brothers Harriman.

Men like Jeremiah Thompson, George Newbold, and Jonathan Goodhue owned fleets and sailed cotton around the globe on strong commercial networks. But few men commanded so many sides of the Atlantic slavery triangle as the Browns *and* profited so fulsomely from the trade. Importantly, they did so by pioneering tactics—continuous growth, strategic expansion, calculated risk—considered standard corporate practice today. Mastering a system that destroyed Black people's lives and mastering the psychological distance of never acknowledging that destruction is one important way that white men first learned to flourish in the business of the United States, the business of Wall Street.

It was risk that induced Alexander Brown to worry about shipping. Through his network of agents in New Orleans and his factors in Charleston, he had been closely watching the cotton markets and taking careful note. In fact, Alexander Brown had thrived by learning from how others failed. In a letter to his son William, he admonished that too many merchants, seeking a higher reward, chose to own the cotton they carried on their vessels and, as a result, were too exposed. "The moment the property leaves the port they are divested of all hold to secure [payment] of their drafts which it may take months to determine," wrote Alexander. "Young adventurers" especially, the patriarch averred, played fast and loose with northern credit and were apt to "fall so generally into the mania of speculation." [14]

It had happened to great houses considered indomitable once before, to no less a figure than Archibald Gracie. Gracie's son, William—a young adventurer—had bought large quantities of cotton on credit, borrowing $100,000 from the Bank of New York.[15] William had used his father's mansion, there at the mouth of Hell Gate, as collateral. When he lost spectacularly, Archibald Gracie, seeming stalwart of privilege and wealth, sold his famed estate to pay off the debts. By 1823, the Gracie house was shattered.

That cotton toppled so august a figure foreshadowed how treacherous the waters of the business had become. The Browns were therefore apt to keep to a rule, only ever owning a very small percentage of the cotton they moved. It meant forgoing a spectacular return if the price of cotton shot high but also calamity if it collapsed. Their profits came down at a low and steady rate—a constant drizzle, not a dramatic rain. Alexander determined finally that the wealth to be made in the business of enslaving Black people wasn't in transporting the goods they produced at all; those persisting in that commerce courted disaster. Brown knew the landscape that he gazed upon. His forecasting proved prescient. In 1825, a great disaster came, and he was ready.

More cotton flowed across the seas than ever, more than ever was planted by enslaved people in the fields. But more than ever was not enough. A frenzy for wealth consumed both sides of the Atlantic, and large sums of cash flowed south, from even the most patrician of Wall Street firms. These included the old-guard bank LeRoy, Bayard & Co., which advanced $50,000 that season, or $1.35 million in today's terms, to Vincent Nolte, a powerhouse cotton buyer in New Orleans.[16] Jeremiah Thompson, for another, pushed his operations to the extreme. His ships grew bigger and longer each year, and he had more and more of them, no less than fifteen sailing across the world. But he took on heavy advances to fill them, meaning heavy borrowing and heavy risk.

It was clear that the volume of cotton the United States produced through enslaved labor *would* increase. It was believed that the price would too. And yet, in early 1824, influential merchants on Wall Street and their counterparts in England began mistakenly panicking over what they perceived as a shortage in Liverpool's stores. In New Orleans, Nolte, accustomed to moving forty thousand bales a year, began holding back his supply.[17] This redoubled the imagined crunch and sent British demand, consequently, to all-time highs, a combination of panic and demand that in turn sent speculation and borrowing into overdrive, further driving up the price, and the speculation. Wall Street was about to have one of its earliest booms and busts.

From the South, newspaper editors eyed the goings-on with agitated alarm. They decried especially the "new-fashioned money-manufacturing establishments" involved.[18] They were talking about Wall Street insurance companies, which though forbidden by legal charter from offering banking services per se, skirted New York's lax laws and advanced funds to enslavers. In 1824, for example, three New Orleans plantation owners became the largest borrowers of Mercantile Insurance, where Benjamin Marshall was a director. The firm had been founded in 1818 at 43 William Street, near the corner of Wall, by Jacob Barker, a prominent New York cotton transporter. Mercantile Insurance was a firm with no business offering credit to men who kept Black children in chains.[19] The loans were backed with cotton, with the lives of Black people as collateral.

Driven by unscrupulous credit like this, the price of cotton reached 29.5 cents a pound by 1825. But that was the peak; that was it. In April, American cotton began rolling into Liverpool, outpacing the previous year's supply, making it clear that the panic had been unfounded. "There was no deficiency in the supply of cotton," a newspaper observed, "but on the contrary, a great superabundance."[20] The market rapidly collapsed, the price of cotton falling first to 15 cents and then 8.8 cents. Men who had borrowed and men who had lent, expecting cotton to produce mythical returns, found that when finally sold, it fetched less than one-third what they had hoped. There was no money to pay, much less to collect.

Panic spread. Most watched with alarm, though others snickered that rife speculators—young adventurers—were about to get their due. "Many an insolent upstart will it tumble from his carriage," crowed the British writer William Cobbett. "New York will amply share in the sweepings of the hurricane; and the base and insolent traffickers of Pearl-street, in that city, will get a pull back to their career of profitable plunder."[21]

The sine qua non of such plunder, of the whole system, was the unremitting toil of more than two million enslaved Black people. Five Wall Street firms alone owed $2.5 million after the cotton collapse, or more than $65 million today, estimated a Boston newspaper at the time. The total size of the cotton debts, estimated around $5 to $6 million, or $135 million today, were but a fraction of the overall cotton market. The fall-out continued for months, then years, reflecting how deeply cotton and slavery, particularly on Wall Street, were connected to everything. "Many who have not had anything to do with Cotton, are brought to the verge of ruin by the purchase of bills drawn by Cotton shippers," Robert Lenox, a director of the New York branch of the Bank of the United States, wrote to Nicholas Biddle, the bank's head.[22] "Hundreds of houses failed," added Scoville.[23]

The upheaval revealed several important dimensions of Wall Street at that moment in time. The largest banks—City Bank, Bank of America, Bank of New York, among others—all weathered the storm. Fraternities of merchants protected by a private, liquid pool, they had done their job, and done it well. It showed that many, though not all, of Wall Street's most consequential slavery entrepreneurs had found protection under a growing corporate umbrella. Isaac Wright, for one, cofounder of the Black

Ball Line, had been a director of City Bank since 1825. Cotton suppliers like Wright, moreover, were housed not only in banks but in a dizzying proliferation of insurance companies and corporate boards. (A New York commercial directory from 1827 lists forty-two insurance companies housed around Wall Street, including Aetna, Equitable, and Farmer's Fire Insurance.) Their power to make wealth from facilitating enslavement was redoubled by doing it together, by selling shares in their concerns. They were diversifying, and as a result, they faced less and less personal risk.

Benjamin Marshall, notably, was not devastated. He had taken his capital from shipping slave commodities and bought shares in the Phoenix Bank and Farmer's Fire Insurance, in addition to Mercantile Insurance. In fact, Marshall had bought enough to get himself elected to all their boards. More importantly, in 1826 Marshall funneled his enslavement wealth, a decade's worth reaped from partnership in the Black Ball Line, into a critical new industry: he founded a cotton mill along the Hudson River, capitalized at $300,000, or the equivalent of $8 million today.[24] It was "the first attempt made in the country at producing yarns of the finer grades."[25]

Like the Brown family, Marshall was moving away from the center of cotton commerce, though not from cotton altogether. His move foreshadowed how vast sums of money derived from cotton and slavery would flow into the country's rapidly expanding manufacturing sector, setting in place a pillar of the US economy. The South's capacity to coerce goods from enslaved Black people was perhaps more important than ever to Marshall's business, to his personal riches, though now from the manufacturing side. He had been living comfortably on Thirteenth Street. But by the time of the crash, he had left Manhattan altogether and settled in Troy, upstate New York, to run this new concern.

It was individual cotton magnates who were hardest hit. And none more than Vincent Nolte. He had claimed to be the single largest cotton shipper in the South. Now his business was ruined. Nolte traveled all the way to England after the collapse to meet with his creditors, including Baring Brothers, for terms; he was rebuked at every turn, he detailed in his memoir.[26] Likewise ruined was Jeremiah Thompson, considered the largest cotton shipper in the North (some sources claimed the world). "He is said to have shipped half the export of [cotton] from New York for the last three years," wrote the *Newport Mercury* in 1827.[27] Unlike the Browns, Thompson owned the cotton he shipped, and with it, all the risk. When boom turned to bust, he found himself saddled with massive debts, persona non grata at banks around the world. "An immense amount of Mr. Thompson's bills have been noted for non acceptance at Liverpool. His engagements are said to exceed $1,200,000," reported another newspaper later that same year.[28] It meant a debt of $32 million today, a catastrophic loss, causing an international stir.

The aging Quaker had been punched down by his own greed, seeking more from the riches of enslavement than even the greediest around him. Thompson died a few years later, but not before having to sell his stake in Black Ball, the shipping line that had made possible his, and the nation's, astonishing wealth. Jonathan Goodhue, the Bank of America director, was the purchaser.[29] "As thunder-storms are often useful to purify the atmosphere," wrote the *Niles' Weekly Register* of Baltimore, "so blowings-up like these may be necessary."[30] The end of an era had come.

Another was beginning. For the crisis underscored one thing more. It was not just the merchants and cotton buyers financially afflicted; on the other side of the coin, so were enslavers, and that meant that the lives of Black people were further catastrophized too. One such enslaver was a man named Christopher Adams. He kept seventy Black people in bondage on his Belle plantation in Iberville, Louisiana. Adams had been one of the three heaviest borrowers from Mercantile Insurance, where Benjamin Marshall was a director, putting up his property and enslaved people as collateral. After the crash, because Adams owed the Wall Street firm $32,522 or roughly $880,000 today, Jacob Barker and Mercantile Insurance sued him for default. At one point, marshals showed up at his plantation, seeking to foreclose on his lands and cattle and take possession of the men, women, and children that he'd enslaved. Adams fought the case, and it dragged on for years, all the way to the US Supreme Court. The lives of Belle's Black people hung in the balance all that time.

Documents from a court case give us the briefest glimpse of who they were, including a man named John Winfrey and another named Jack Wright. There were also many children: Aleck, ten years old; Ned, thirteen years; Manuel, eight years; Celeste, twelve years; and the toddlers Rosine, Giles, and Margarette, ages four, three, and one, respectively. A

federal court upheld Mercantile's right to seize these human beings as collateral and recoup its loss, which meant the corporation could break apart
Black families as it pleased.[31]

So began a period when southern enslavers fell deeper in debt to
Wall Street corporations, with the result that those New York firms began
to record in their ledger books, collected through foreclosure, not only
white men's properties and houses, but Black people. We don't know what
became of the men, women, and children in the Mercantile case. Documents cease speaking their names; their trail disappears down a pit of
debt and injunction, suit, and countersuit. There are only questions that
reverberate, questions that remain. Part of the incalculable ledger of what,
in the American pursuit of wealth from slavery, Black people lost.

In Congress, the South Carolina senator Robert Hayne surveyed the
tumult on Wall Street with alarm. He noted that, as a consequence of
cotton speculation, northern banks were poised to "get the whole estates of
those who have failed in New Orleans."[32] Hayne had also learned, he said,
that among such banks was one in particular: the Bank of the United States
itself—in other words, the US Treasury, as the Bank of the United States
was 20 percent owned by the federal government. The bank, it turned out,
had lent money to enslavers and plantations, and because of foreclosures
had become owner itself of those estates, and of enslaved people.

Research by Sharon Ann Murphy, a professor of history at Providence
College, shows that the Bank of the United States had come to enslave
dozens, if not hundreds, of Black people, through foreclosure, since as far
back as 1809.[33] The Bank of the United States had placed itself, alongside Wall Street corporations, "at the heart of the buying and selling of
human property," she wrote, "one of the most reviled aspects of the system
of enslavement."

What disturbed Senator Hayne wasn't the moral aspect of this predicament, of the US government acquiring Black lives because of bad credit;
rather, he was incensed by the legal confusion that had allowed it to
happen—confusion because the country had no uniform bankruptcy law,
and because usury laws in places like New York were allowing speculators
and banks to run amok in the business of enslavement. Hayne lamented,
in what turned out to be an accurate forecast, that these kinds of foreclosures would continue indefinitely, meaning more banks and corporations
would swallow up southern plantations to their roots, people and all. He

noted also: "The banks are made the instruments of giving a fictitious credit to insolvent men, and thereby enabling them to ruin those who, deceived by false appearances, lend money, or sell goods, to such men."[34] Hayne seems not to have considered that unscrupulous business practices were becoming a key ingredient for success on Wall Street. The ultimate fallout would be to Black lives.

From Baltimore, Alexander Brown was watching—and learning. In 1825, he had written letters to his contacts in Mobile, Alabama, noting the many firms that had gone bust. Alexander, together with his son James, saw new opportunities for business emerging in a landscape where men were driven to indiscretion and ruin by greed. The Brown firm, having so meticulously focused "on steady employment for their ships," as historian John Killick notes, by the late 1820s took a decisive tack. They began selling off their ships, reconfiguring their capital, and "leaving shipping operations to specialists."[35] They were evolving into something new. No longer subject to the vicissitudes of ocean commerce and the ups and downs of trade, the Browns would become lenders themselves: a bank. They would start the first private bank in the nation that specialized in commercial finance for the growing business of slavery, since banks like City Bank and Bank of America, though deeply enmeshed in southern slavery, were still primarily focused on mercantile trade.

Their transformation would prove illuminating: that men rich from shipping slavery goods would now lend money to spread slavery's hold across the land reflects the path that America's tainted trove of money, and the US banking system in general, was taking and how the business of slavery was evolving. And via that transformation, by moving out of shipping, the Browns allowed a new cast of more institutional, ruthless players like Baring Brothers, the Barclays, and the Rothschilds to emerge at the heart of cotton transport and commerce.

CHAPTER 6

CALAMITY

Arthur Tappan was forty-four years old and a silk merchant when he committed himself to the abolitionist cause in 1830. He did so because of a criminal case. Tappan had read of a twenty-five-year-old named William Lloyd Garrison in Baltimore: how Garrison had revealed in a newspaper that a New England merchant, Francis Todd, had used his ships, and the cover of his merchant respectability, to transport enslaved Black people from Baltimore to New Orleans; how Todd had sued Garrison for libel after Garrison published the piece; and how Garrison was convicted and thrown in a Baltimore jail, where he'd been languishing for eight weeks. (Garrison was unrepentant behind bars, writing from his cell: "A few white victims must be sacrificed to open the eyes of this nation, and to show the tyranny of our laws.")[1]

Interestingly, Todd, the shipping merchant, didn't sue because he disputed the facts of what Garrison had written—for the facts were that Todd's transportation of enslaved people had been entirely legal, upheld by state laws. Todd sued because he didn't want to be publicly outed. He didn't want the screen of northern respectability protecting him to be punctured and his reputation besmirched. Ultimately, the case drew such widespread attention because Garrison had exposed to public opinion the ties binding northern merchants and northern commerce to the heart of slavery, showing, as he said, "that a New-England abettor was as liable to reprehension as a Maryland slaveholder."[2]

Reading the story, Arthur Tappan was so unsettled by the injustice that he paid one hundred dollars to have Garrison released. When the two men later met, Tappan was struck by a young man of unusual vitality and purpose. There were by then many dozens of anti-slavery societies and many hundreds of white anti-slavery spokesmen, but almost none like Garrison, the supposed "madman and incendiary." Garrison called for what most other white men did not: immediate and total emancipation, and the recognition of Black people as Americans.

The fire he tended had been lit by David Walker, and even when critical of Walker's appeal to violence, Garrison couldn't escape mirroring him, Walker's stridency becoming his own: "Every Fourth of July celebration must embitter and inflame the minds of the slaves...furnish[ing] so many reasons to the slaves why they should obtain their own rights by violence."[3] Garrison had himself been a former colonizationist. But now, with a special hatred for the Colonization Society's scheme of expulsion, he, like Walker, denounced them publicly and widely, including once before a crowded hall in which no less than Anson Phelps had sat.

Upon his release from jail, Garrison told Tappan that he planned a newspaper, the *Liberator*, focused on the dual objects of his scorn: "the conspiracy of the slavocracy against human rights, and the cruel delusive character of the American Colonization Society," Lewis Tappan later recorded.[4] The endeavor, "when commenced," noted African American abolitionist William Cooper Nell, "had arrayed against it the 30,000 churches, and clergy of the country—its wealth, its commerce, its press."[5] Arthur Tappan signed on his support, as did several Black abolitionists, including James Forten, who, enclosed with a touching letter, sent Garrison money for twenty-seven subscriptions and asked for extra copies to pass among his friends.[6]

The *Liberator* first appeared in January 1831. Already the abolitionists were a detested group, in a widening orbit of hatred, South to North, that Walker and Garrison had stoked. It grew even more after the events of August 1831, when Nat Turner, a preacher of unusual charisma, enslaved in Virginia, led his followers in killing more than sixty white people across Southampton County, the largest such uprising in the history of the United States. No sooner were Turner and his cohort arrested and executed than leaders across the South instantly blamed Garrison for the violence. "Those enslavers who sought comfort in myths of natural Black docility hunted for those whom they considered the real agitators: abolitionists like Garrison," explains Ibram X. Kendi in *Stamped from the Beginning.*[7]

Turner's uprising proved a watershed movement, not only by giving pro-slavery leaders cover to impose new laws restricting Black people's right to seek education, freely assemble, or practice Christianity without white supervision, but because it provided them ammunition to ratchet up enmity toward abolitionists and intensify support for colonization and the "removal of the free people of colour...as an antidote to all our ills."[8] Threats abounded for abolitionists wherever they tread after that, even as far away as New York.

Some two years later, Arthur Tappan and his brother Lewis assembled at Astor Place in Manhattan on the evening of October 2, 1833. There they were joined by the Reverend Joshua Leavitt, the journalist William Goodell, and the merchant John Rankin. Garrison was not with them that night. Together these men, who formed the nucleus of the city's earliest white abolitionists, hoped to make a significant historical contribution: they were meeting for the purposes of organizing the American Anti-Slavery Society, the first national organization in the country that in calling for the immediate emancipation of enslaved Black people would also act as an institutional counterweight to colonization. Its members were Black and white; they included Samuel Cornish, former editor of *Freedom's Journal,* and Rev. Theodore S. Wright, the first Black man to graduate from Princeton Theological Seminary.

The Anti-Slavery Society had chosen as its venue that autumn night Clinton Hall, a large library near present-day East Eighth Street. They had made their arrangements well in advance. Yet upon arriving at the hall at seven o'clock, they found that it was locked, and that a large placard had been hung, advertising that a different meeting was to take place in the same hall at the very same time. It was addressed "TO ALL PERSONS FROM THE SOUTH" who had an interest in the meeting being proposed by the abolitionists. It was, moreover, signed "MANY

SOUTHERNERS." The signature was strange: there wouldn't have been that many southerners in New York to warrant such an appeal. The placard's subject matter was also ominous: it called on all men of the city to attend who might "feel disposed to manifest the *true* feeling of the State [of New York] on this subject."[9] Tappan and his group, sensing danger, decided to leave Clinton Hall.

For days in the lead-up to October 2, the abolitionists had feared something like this. They had been the subject of unrelenting public outrage and scorn. Many of the leading New York papers had run columns maligning Tappan and his colleagues, including Garrison, accusing them of stoking violence and championing, through emancipation, the breakup of the union. "Garrison boldly urges the utter overthrow of the churches, the Sabbath, and the Bible," wrote the *New York Herald.* "Nothing has been sacred with him but the ideal intellect of the negro race."[10] Many of the papers, in fact, had for days urged readers to break up Tappan's announced abolitionist meeting. "The object," Lewis Tappan later wrote, "was evidently to outnumber the friends of freedom at their own meeting, and crush in the shell the anti-slavery enterprise."[11]

For prudent reasons, therefore, Arthur Tappan hastened to move the gathering to the Chatham Street Chapel, a place of worship nearby where one of his colleagues was a trustee and held a key. Accordingly, they informed as many people as they could—though, in the end, not many—of the change in venue, and then, all told, a group of about fifty, both Black and white, hurried to Chatham Street. There they assembled in the small lecture room of the chapel, where, after the iron gate was shut and locked and candles lit, their meeting began.

Back on Astor Place, the streets around Clinton Hall grew tense, crowded and heavy with danger. Among the leading voices that had been inciting rioters to target Tappan's meeting that night was none other than the American Colonization Society, particularly the chair of the New York branch's executive committee, William L. Stone. Stone happened to be also the editor of the *New-York Commercial Advertiser,* a powerful paper. Just that morning, he'd printed the following editorial reprising the abolitionist's proposed meeting: "Is it possible that our citizens can look quietly on, while the flames of discord are rising,—while even our pulpits are sought to be used for the base PURPOSE of encouraging scenes of *bloodshed* in our land? If we do, can we look our Southern brethren in the face and say, we are opposed to interfering with their rights? No, we cannot."[12]

The editor of the *New York Courier and Enquirer*, James Watson Webb, also a colonizationist, went a step further, calling directly on citizens to put down the abolitionist meeting with violence.[13] He added specifically that they should show up to Clinton Hall at seven o'clock.

The incitement had worked. By seven o'clock that evening, a virulent mob—pro-slavery, anti-abolitionist, and sympathetic to the Colonization Society—began swarming around Clinton Hall. After finding the doors to the building locked, they soon filed raucously into Tammany Hall, a larger venue nearby, and those who couldn't fit inside spilled out into the surrounding street. The crowd's size was estimated at five thousand. They were led by members of the Colonization Society itself, including John Neal, a lawyer who served as secretary, and later treasurer, of the society's branch in Portland, Maine.

Inside the lecture room of the Chatham Street Chapel, as candles burned, Arthur Tappan led his group in prayer. Then together they resolved to form a society for the immediate abolition of slavery. Inside Tammany Hall, John Neal led the largely drunken crowd in resolutions denouncing abolition, and in mongering fears of white massacre by Black people. "We take this opportunity to express to our Southern brethren our fixed and unalterable determination to resist every attempt that may be made to interfere with the relation in which master and slave now stand, as guaranteed to them by the Constitution of the United States," Neal said.[14] He went on to accuse the abolitionists of calculating to "produce a dissolution of the Union," and said they "should be called, not Anti-Slavery, but Anti-Colonization Societies."

The crowded hall had been whipped into such a fever, with visions no less of civil and race war ("If the blacks of Southern States were at once to be set free, the whites would become slaves," another speaker had railed) that many called for violence. "Let us go there and rout them!" many at last cried when informed that the abolitionists were in fact meeting close by.[15]

Thousands of rioters, drunk, angry, and zealous, then streamed from

Tammany Hall, stomping in the night toward the small chapel on Chatham Street. They soon surrounded the building where Tappan and his fifty companions were finishing up.

The colonization mob could see candles still flickering inside. They tried to batter down the iron gate, growing more and more irate that in fact it would not budge. "Ten thousand dollars for Arthur Tappan!" they shouted. "Where are they? Find them! Find them!"

Inside, Tappan and the abolitionists had now determined to flee, but first they instructed the chapel's janitor to open the iron gate, lest the mob break it down. This the janitor did, and Tappan and the others had just enough time to run from the lecture room, finding a passage through the chapel and out the back. One member of the mob, Lewis Tappan later learned from the janitor, pursued the fleeing abolitionists close behind, so close that, holding a lamp in one hand, a drawn dagger in the other, he almost struck one of them from behind.

The abolitionists were lucky to escape. Even so, Arthur Tappan decided to run back inside the chapel, and there he witnessed the following scene.

Pandemonium had overtaken the room as rioters proceeded to smash the chapel's chandeliers, benches, and lamps. They hollered and hooted in frenzy. The mob's size was difficult to calculate, but as many as could fit into the chapel had seized, by the shoulders, a Black man who hadn't managed to escape in time. (No historical sources document his name.) Still hooting and hollering, they pulled him into the chapel's pulpit. The white rioters forced the only Black person in the room to perform a mock meeting as if he were Arthur Tappan himself. They demanded that he make a speech, laughing all the while at his expense, a "riot-cum-minstrel act," as Douglas A. Jones, professor of English at Rutgers University, called this harrowing scene.[16]

He at first refused, but the screaming crowd wouldn't let up, so at last he complied. As the crowd quieted, he then said: "You doubtless know that I am a poor, ignorant man, not accustomed to make speeches. But I have heard of the Declaration of Independence, and have read the Bible. The Declaration says all men are created equal, and the Bible says God has made us all of one blood. I think, therefore, we are entitled to good treatment, that it is wrong to hold men in slavery, and that—"[17] He didn't need to finish. His words so arrested and disarmed the drunken rioters that, almost miraculously, the mob, seemingly spent of its frenzied rage, ceased its hooting.

Within a short time, the mob dispersed through the chapel's iron gate and out into a street blanketed by night. New York's first colonization riot was over, its venom drained by the valor of a single Black man, his name now lost to history. The American Anti-Slavery Society was born.

New York City would erupt several more times like this, mobs breaking up abolitionist meetings, including again at the Chatham Street Chapel in 1834. White mobs savagely beat Black men in the streets. They broke down the doors of Arthur Tappan's house (he again narrowly escaped), dragged his furniture into the street, and set it on fire. The mayor of New York at the time, Cornelius W. Lawrence, a high-ranking Colonization Society official, did little to quell the violence, and meanwhile condemned the abolitionists, the victims, for causing it.

The American Colonization Society continued inciting mobs, perhaps even paying the rioters out of its coffers. In New York, a war was "now waging between the Abolitionists and the Colonizationists," William Jay, the anti-slavery luminary, later wrote.[18] William Lloyd Garrison himself, fittingly, was more incendiary: "That Society has been the grand instigator of all the violent acts of the southern slaveholders, and of the populace in our principal cities, against those who dare to proclaim the truth of God with all fidelity, and who urge the duty of immediately breaking every yoke and letting every captive go free."[19]

It was in this world riven not only by talk of a dissolving union but by actual dissolutive conflict that the call for abolishing slavery, for the emancipation of Black people, rang louder—a sound echoing through the streets of New York, the nation's leading newspapers, and the office suites in the banking palaces of the city. And it was in this world also, and in this city, in a time becoming more fully sensate to the sufferings of Black people, to the evils of enslavement, to its drawing prospect of disintegrating the union, that James Brown and his family, slave financiers, chose to expand their empire of cruelty from Wall Street.

———

IN 1833, BROWN moved the family firm to 59 Wall Street, near the corner of Hanover, on the upper floors of the Joseph Building. It placed him just across the street from City Bank, and directly adjacent to the Custom House, where City Bank would later make its home. Bank of America was close by at number 44, as was Merchants' Bank. The choice of geography wasn't accidental. James Brown aimed to be among the men of "excellent paper" filling the banking houses of that lane. He, his father, and his brothers were marking their decisive step away from *transporting* the goods of slavery to *financing* slavery itself.

They continued shipping consignments of cotton to Liverpool, but under stricter terms, and as a smaller and smaller dimension of their business. By 1836, they would jettison all such ties, cease all shipments, and close out related accounts. Their transition from mercantile business to commercial banking was becoming complete.[20] How the Browns evolved as a commercial enterprise was a microcosm of how Wall Street, northern corporations, and the US economy itself transformed at this moment in the early nation, a commercial evolution driven with the start-up capital seeded from slavery.

In 1834, not long after the move to Wall Street, one more event cemented the firm's transition and James Brown's ascendancy within it. Alexander Brown, the patriarch, died at the age of seventy. His demise, voluminously covered in the press, privately lamented throughout the Atlantic, signaled the passing of an age, and the coming of a new one: there had been a formative capital stage of slavery, when merchants and vessel owners had institutionalized the enslavement of Black people into a thriving global business. But that was now falling away. Certainly, this was because the uncaring minds responsible for legitimating this callous commerce—Archibald Gracie, Jeremiah Thompson, Isaac Wright, Francis Thompson, Stephen Girard, Benjamin Bailey, and now Alexander Brown—were literally dying. But it was also because the nation's torpid indifference, a kind of moral screen that had cloaked the North's enabling of slavery for more than forty years, was being ripped off—by Maria Stewart, Hayden Waters, Samuel Ringgold Ward, William Lloyd Garrison, and a rising new generation of abolitionists. The sons of the original abettors of enslavement on Wall Street would carry forward their forefathers' brutal legacy, deepening the capital entrails linking corporations to Black people's bondage while pushing their slavery-tied banks and corporations to evolve. But they did so, increasingly, on contested ground.

James Brown, a fixture of New York society and pinnacle of Atlantic esteem, inherited one of the world's most powerful slavery firms and one of America's greatest slavery fortunes. The will of Alexander Brown offers a striking glimpse of those riches: his portion of the Brown firm was then estimated to be worth $4.6 million, or $142 million today. His will furthermore revealed that Alexander Brown's personal estate was valued at $913,020, or $28.5 million today. Alexander Brown was "possibly the richest general merchant in America," writes historian John Killick. According to one historical source, only three other men in the United States—John Jacob Astor, Stephen Whitney, and Stephen Van Rensselaer—were richer than Brown when he died.[21] No doubt he was one of the white men most enriched by the business of slavery in the history of the United States. And yet his fortune was but a fraction of the wealth his sons would continue to make for thirty years or more, turning wealth from slavery into industrial investment and laying the foundation for the multibillion-dollar corporations that the Brown firm today has become.

From his new office suite a thousand miles from the South, James Brown made deals and lent money that allowed the horrors of slavery to magnify and grow. The firm's capital then stood at $5 million, or $152 million today. Brown employed it in a steady stream of cash to northern cotton merchants and southern factors alike. Throughout the 1830s and '40s, for example, he provided revolving lines of credit to many of the South's biggest enslavers, including John Routh of Concordia Parish, Louisiana (he enslaved 163 Black people); John D. Amis of Lowndes County, Mississippi (224 enslaved); Peter M. Lapice of St. James Parish, Louisiana (134 enslaved); and William Stamp (175 enslaved).

The credit lines involved were considerable. In the case of Lapice, Brown had lent him $400,000, or $12 million today.[22] According to research by Killick, Brown extended $100,000 each year ($3 million today) to the factors Martin Pleasants & Co.[23] As early as 1827, the Browns had been advancing $100,000 or more a year to Thomas Bibb, whose Belle Mina plantation, with twenty-five hundred acres, was one of the largest in Alabama. The Brown firm also extended $200,000 a year (nearly $6 million today) to Yeatman, Woods & Co., considered the largest cotton firm in New Orleans. The Browns renewed these credit lines, totaling several million dollars, year after year throughout the 1830s and '40s, an astonishing outpouring of wealth derived from slavery and poured back into slavery.

There were few businesses connected to Black people's bondage, interwoven with sugar, tobacco, and cotton production, that the Browns' avalanche of money didn't touch: they funded land companies opening up western territories in Mississippi for plantation, financed New York brokers and shippers, and became strong holders of southern bank bonds, principally in New Orleans and Natchez. "We made several large loans to banks and individuals to sustain them," George Brown wrote to his brothers from Baltimore in February 1835. "This has been a year of great prosperity for us."[24]

The Browns, while superlative lenders, weren't the only ones providing credit to enslavers. Hundreds of other Wall Street firms and northern banks did the same, including the Bank of the United States itself, run by the Philadelphian Nicholas Biddle. Together this gush of capital fed an even more spectacular tide of greed, and one with ultimately catastrophic effects yet again. Whereas once enslavers had hoped to make profits over the course of seasons, now, one observer pointed out, "the producers and the speculators…not satisfied with regular business and moderate profits, must try to get rich in a single year."[25] They borrowed and borrowed; the banks lent and lent.

What did enslavers do with this borrowed money? The simple answer is that, in the late 1830s, they bought more and more Black people's lives on credit, resulting in one of the largest, most disruptive, and most tragic expansions of slavery in the history of the nation. It was estimated by the *Natchez Courier*, a Mississippi newspaper, that white traders in this period, feeding the cotton greed, sold more than 250,000 enslaved people from the upper slavery states of the South between 1835 and 1837, moving them to new plantation lands across Mississippi, Alabama, Louisiana, and Arkansas.[26] Observers pointed out that each of these Black people's lives would have cost an average of $600, meaning that this enormous and vile transaction would have cost $150 million, possibly more, a sum that equates to $4.6 billion today.[27]

Nearly all of it was financed through credit, with enslavers in the lower states mortgaging their plantations and enslaved people as collateral to obliging banks—and northern banks at that. "This trade was carried on by the aid of Northern capital," reported the *United States Gazette*, a Philadelphia newspaper. "Northern banks and brokers were involved, the United States Bank was involved."[28] All were willing to speculate, including Brown Brothers, because they could play with Black people's lives. They could squeeze Black people's labor for more profits. They could make up for spectacular loss, should it come, by selling the human beings whom they exploited.

In the meantime, there was a consort of other profits for the Brown firm to make. James Brown and his brothers also fortified a consequential business that their father had begun, the firm's so-called bill business, focused on Liverpool. "Americans who wished to import goods from Great Britain and the East, if their reputation abroad was not sufficiently well established to make direct purchases, applied to Alexander Brown for credits on the Liverpool house," an official history of the Brown firm explains.[29] Essentially, it meant that the Browns acted as a currency exchange, negotiating for a commission of 2.5 percent the exchange of cotton and tobacco for pounds sterling. The global economy of cotton, the economy of the South, the economy of enslavement, and of the northern Atlantic cities couldn't operate without such exchanges, which allowed hundreds of millions of dollars in goods, worth billions today, to be imported into the United States along the cotton triangle. It wouldn't be an exaggeration to say that American prosperity in this moment hinged on sterling exchange, and that James Brown—his network, his capital, and his management skills all honed through the business of Black enslavement—represented an outsized portion of that prosperity.

The firm's bill business with Liverpool, begun in 1830, reached $2 million, or nearly $58 million today. Just five years later, in 1835, its bill business generated $7.8 million in revenue, or $226 million today. Certainly, there was money to be made in physically shipping cotton to England. The Browns' new enterprise reflected, however, that there was even more money to be made in the *triangular flow of money* that financed enslavement.

As prominent as they had been in cotton shipping, the Browns, according to estimations by Killick, controlled at most 15 percent of the entire cotton trade, given the market's size, complexity, and scope of competition. As financiers of the triangular trade, however, they dominated. Between 1830 and 1850, they would come to control up to 50 percent of the entire market in letters of credit, becoming the single largest purveyor of foreign and domestic exchange in the United States. They were the pinnacle of the business of enslavement for decades. They achieved this by being eminently trusted by the South's leading factors and enslavers, by lending on strict terms yet prodigiously, and by harnessing strategically their vast endowments made possible by the unrequited toil of enslaved people. They did it, most of all, by being heartless and consistently relentless in the face of Black suffering. Indeed, the Browns became, when the next great financial calamity did eventually sweep over the nation, enslavers themselves.

That calamity, the Panic of 1837, was even more acute and far-reaching than the financial shock wave of 1826. Many elements contributed to it: a depression in cereal prices; President Andrew Jackson's refusal to renew the charter of the Bank of the United States, sending credit markets into a spiral; and a congressional act that altered the ratio between gold and silver. But bearing intensely on all these other pressures was once again cotton and speculation. Enslavers had bought more and more enslaved people with bank aid. At the same time, they had demanded greater and greater advances on the cotton they would produce. As a result, they had run up both the price of cotton and, with it, their irredeemable tab of credit. Surplus supplies of Indian and Egyptian cotton, among other things, had then caused the price of cotton to collapse by half or more, down to six cents a pound. Enslavers were saddled with debts they could not hope to pay back. The chain of upheaval—recall that enslavers had borrowed at least $150 million to purchase more Black lives to exploit—stretched from Mississippi to Manhattan once again.

The Browns themselves weren't ruined, but they were firmly tested. So great was their control of the credit market, so critical a fulcrum to the Atlantic slavery system, that naturally the Browns were tremendously exposed, as they held £800,000 worth of useless notes for US firms. Their collapse wasn't out of the question, and this prospect alone sent further shock waves throughout global commercial circles, particularly in England. Two-thirds of the Brown Brothers firm's engagements were dedicated to the sterling exchange, representing $10 million, or $280 million today. This was money facilitating an enormous portion of Great Britain's economy and that of the Atlantic triangle. Quintessentially, the Brown firm was too big to fail. After the Bank of England eventually interceded, arranging a bailout of $10 million to cover the Browns' exposure, Brown Brothers paid the money back within six months, so robust was their comeback.

All across the South, the panic ruptured the system of agents and factors that had, since the War of 1812, allowed leading New York and British firms, including the Browns, to siphon such riches from slavery. (Yeatman, Woods & Co. was among the factors that failed.) The widening fallout meant that southerners of various stripes were destroyed by debt, others by the seizing up of credit. According to one estimate, nine-tenths of all merchants in Mobile, Alabama, shuttered their operations. In vast portions of the South, there was no credit to be found at all. Lamented the *Vicksburg Whig*: "The best men in the country find it impossible to raise any amount of money, except at the most ruinous sacrifices."[30]

What this flashpoint shows is how the unrelenting churn of money at the heart of slavery—money flowing north from plantations to brokers and banks; money flowing south from Wall Street, habituating enslavers to chronic debt—powered the US economy as a whole. According to the *Bankers Magazine*, more than 250 firms in New York alone failed in 1837, their liabilities exceeding $100 million ($2.8 billion today). It is a staggering sum, a sum revealing how deeply the business of Wall Street was enmeshed in the business of Black enslavement.[31]

"I was in Wall Street an hour," observed Henry Clarke Wright, a white abolitionist, in June 1837. "Slavery seemed to be stalking through that street, exulting over broken fortunes....There were then slaves in the South to the amount of over nine hundred millions of dollars. This was all stolen property, obtained by violence, and robbery, and murder. Yet our northern merchants trusted the thieves and robbers, depending mainly on their stolen property for pay. Now this little city, New York, Boston, and all the North, are being punished for being partakers in the sin."[32]

The greatest tumult, once again, was to Black lives. Many enslaved people were reduced to the brink of starvation, because bankrupt enslavers lacked the means to feed them. Newspapers reported enslaved people fishing in rivers for their subsistence. "There are at this moment thousands of slaves in Mississippi, that know not where the next morsel is to come from," reported the *Philanthropist* of Cincinnati, Ohio.[33] Across the landscape of ruin that southern labor camps had become, the first thing white enslavers did was sell the Black people they had enslaved, an atrocious exercise of white privilege.

The stories resulting from this time still have the power to sadden and shock. In 1837, the grocery-store owner Rezin Orme, in Washington, DC, was faced with bankruptcy, because men who owed him money, ruined themselves from the panic, were unable to pay. Orme opted to sell a Black woman he enslaved, Dorcas Allen, along with her four children, and he intended to use the proceeds of the sales to move to Ohio, to start a new life with his wife. James H. Birch, the notorious slave trader who took possession of Allen, transported her across the Potomac to Alexandria, Virginia, locking her away in the district's largest slavery pen, pending her sale. There followed an excruciating torment, a personal apocalypse. That night, August 22, 1837, Allen killed the two youngest of her children—Maria Jane, aged four, and William Henry, aged two—by strangling them. She had decided that she'd rather that they die than be sold into enslavement and possibly taken from her. She had tried to kill her two older children as well, and then also slit her own throat, according to reports, but neither she nor the older children died, and they were then discovered by the night watch.

The poor mother was then dragged before a jury and tried for the murder of her children. After pleading temporary insanity, Allen was actually acquitted of the crime, but that only meant that, as a result, the court released her back to Birch, and he again arranged to sell her and her children.[34] Her nightmare would have begun all over, had it not been that her husband, Nathan, a free Black man, had all the while been working tirelessly to purchase his wife's freedom from Birch. He raised much of the money himself while also receiving fifty dollars from John Quincy Adams, the former president. (Adams, after first reading of the Allen case, could not let it go, and even while writing in his diary that pursuing Allen's freedom would ruin his career in Congress—he was already isolated as an abolitionist—he recorded his many steps to help win her release.)[35]

How many Black mothers, after 1837, faced the nightmare choices of

Dorcas Allen? How many thousands of times over again, in cities across the country, did the mortgaging of enslaved people's lives to satisfy white people's debt result in tragedy? Our recorded history doesn't tell us, but surely it is vast, indeed countless. Countless Black children torn from their parents, wives from their husbands, husbands from wives, friends from friends, communities ripped apart forever, never to meet and talk and hold each other again, a grief more profound and immeasurable than any financial loss.

From the North, abolitionists took up this issue with fervent outrage. Through their writing and agitation, they produced a kind of watershed moment around the events of 1837, their eyes especially trained on the tainted capital flowing through slavery, its ill and devastating effects on Black people's lives. The abolitionists publicly reviled not just how enslaved people were being sold after the Panic of 1837, but *to whom*. That is, they began to consider a critical but previously overlooked fact amid this societal-wide credit collapse, an inescapable reality given how much the debt now saddling the South was owed to rich white men in the North: "The natural result of this extraordinary bankruptcy at the South," Tappan's Anti-Slavery Society reported that year, "would be to throw the ownership of large numbers of slaves upon Northern capitalists."[36] Prior to 1837, capital had flowed by the millions from northern corporations and lenders to feed the insatiably destructive appetites of the southern slavery system. Now, following 1837, the process went into reverse: amid a titanic transfer of assets from southern enslavers to satisfy their northern debts, many of Wall Street's leading figures came into legal possession, through seizure and default, of enslaved people's lives.

Among those northern capitalists was James Brown himself. The panic ruined many fortunes, and yet, as they so often did, the Browns came out on top. Their debtors, unable to pay in cash, remitted almost $1 million worth of cotton to the Browns in 1837 ($28 million today). As a result, the brothers opened an entirely new office in New Orleans to handle this flow, Killick points out.[37] The Browns also took care to draw closer, socially, and financially, to protect their reputation and their assets. Accordingly, James Brown arranged a prosperous, well-placed marriage for his daughter, a union to become the talk of affluent circles of his age. His brother, Sir William, arrived in New York by ship from Liverpool to celebrate the event. Sir William also brought the groom—his own son. James Brown married his daughter to his brother's son (Alexander Jr.)—in other words, her first cousin. Thus the Browns consolidated their house, concentrating their wealth, consummating their corporate structure, through intermarriage at a time when they became richer because Black families were increasingly being torn apart. [38]

Because the Browns had lent extensively throughout the 1830s, and liberally, they held on their books a wide range of plantations mortgaged as collateral and, with them, large enslaved labor forces. After the Panic of 1837, James Brown had from Wall Street litigated extensively through the southern courts to seize these assets and enforce contracts, court records show, resulting in a tremendous run of foreclosures, downsizings, and mergers of enslavement plantations, all of which became his legal property. "My intention," Brown coldly wrote to a Louisiana court about the foreclosure of Peter M. Lapice's plantation, a man he had known and worked with for years, "was to make my claim good in the best way I could, for my own exclusive benefit, and without any regard for the future rights, benefits or interest of said Lapice."[39]

Brown and his brothers came to own a cotton plantation in Concordia Parish, as well as a sugar plantation in St. James Parish; plantation lands in Brushy Bayou; and the Bayou Lafourche Plantation, among many others.[40] Together, their holdings came to exceed twenty-five thousand acres. It means these Wall Street bankers were among the largest plantation owners in the history of the United States. The number of Black people the Browns enslaved, amounting to at least three hundred, and likely dozens more (precise records are difficult to come by) placed them among the top 1 percent of enslavers in the country. It cannot be said that they were oblique bystanders in a business that happened to be connected to enslavement; they actively and willingly built their enterprises around the exploitation of Black lives.

It's difficult from the vantage point of today to conjure the image needed to digest that James Brown, arguably then the most prominent banker in the United States, if not the world, head of the country's premier investment bank, and a sage advisor to politicians and state governments throughout the union, had, by the 1840s, become busy himself with a deep hand in the southern enslavement economy: hiring and paying overseers to manage his enslaved labor forces, consulting with plantation staff about the expansion of sugarhouses and the manufacture of sugar, managing a large roll of monthly payments from cotton and sugar plantations, hiring southern-based agents to collect outstanding debts, and foreclosing on numerous plantation properties. The Browns had other choices, other business lines. They trafficked opium from China. They traded in gold (an August 1836 newspaper detailed the ship *Europe* sailing from Liverpool to New York with £30,000 of gold for Brown Brothers & Co.).[41] They were beginning to manage large-scale investment banking projects, including the first-ever Baltimore railroad. Is it naïve to suppose that James Brown, prompted by the turmoil of 1837 and the suffering of Black people—suffering increasingly detailed and broadcast in New York's major newspapers, not to mention throughout the nation—could have chosen to jettison this cruel business, much as the firm had done with shipping? That he could have listened to his conscience and chosen to move away from slavery altogether, concentrating on other lucrative pursuits?

Years earlier, Alexander Brown had written to his son the following piece of advice: "Better to lose the business than have an uneasy mind."[42] Yet James Brown had no uneasy mind about the business of slavery. He carried it on for at least another fifteen years. In fact, his office on Wall Street became more and more central to the firm's business. "New York is the principal place to negotiate bills and it has been found most advisable to have the Southern accounts transferred there," wrote James's brother George Brown from Baltimore in 1837. "This state of things unfortunately throws most of the labor on James but it cannot be helped."[43] The profits of forced Black labor remained so enticing to James Brown and the Brown firm, even as it evolved into other "legitimate" pursuits, that Brown refused to forgo them, and that is an indelible, though often ellipsed part of the firm's history too. Brown had become so busy through the prosperity afforded by Black people's enslavement that he wrote, gallingly, to his brother to complain about being so pressed: "We have enough to do now and more than I want. I have been a slave this winter."[44] It was one of the only times James Brown ever bothered to reference the fettered people he exploited, and only to reference himself.

John R. Killick reports that James Brown, upon tallying his wealth in 1842, detailed that his investments in the South totaled more than

$1.5 million; $348,000, or nearly a quarter, was in the form of plantations.[45] Brown's wealth, converted to today's currency, would amount to $55 million on the low end. It means that, quantifiably, and conservatively, $12.9 million of his private wealth was directly derived from the enslavement of Black people forced to work on plantations that he owned. What remains ultimately unquantifiable, however, is how his loans, in expanding the overall pool of slavery wealth in the United States, institutionalized and normalized as a business the enslavement of human beings based on racial caste and how his capital mainstreamed into the everyday flows of US finance the practice of brutalizing Black people.

Precious little is known about the Black people who made James Brown rich. But one account survives, almost miraculously: James Lucas was born in 1833 in Wilkinson County, along the Mississippi River near Artonish, Mississippi. In 1937, the Works Progress Administration found him and interviewed him at his home on North Commerce Street in Natchez. Lucas was 104 years old. He was the oldest formerly enslaved Black person living then in Natchez. His interview reveals that Lucas was one of the people the Browns came to enslave.

"I was born in a cotton field in cotton picking time," Lucas told his interviewer, adding that other enslaved women quickly "fixed" his mother up after she gave birth, "so she didn't hardly lose no time at all." His mother's name was Silvey, and her mother, he said, had been brought to the United States enslaved on a ship.

Lucas shared that the family was enslaved together on a plantation called Lochleven. In 1845, James Brown seized, through foreclosure, 22,652 acres of land that comprised the Artonish, Lochleven, and Lockdale plantations, located contiguously on a bend of the Mississippi known as Homochitto Cut-Off. These lands had been turned over to Brown Brothers when Lucas, who worked as a house servant, was twelve. "They had to mortgage us to Brown and Brothers, around St. Joseph," Lucas told his interviewer. He remembered the foreclosure, and remembered it well, he said, because his former enslaver, William Stamp, drank and couldn't hold on to the property.

James Lucas was one of at least 175 Black people whom the Browns enslaved at Lochleven, sales deeds show. Lucas remembered the overseers and other agents at the plantation as being wickedly cruel, "meaner than bulldogs," he said, and he never forgot how they put enslaved people in stocks and whipped them.[46]

It would have been James Brown's overseers who did this whipping. During the period that Brown employed them, he himself became a prominent patron of high-minded philanthropic causes. Notably, Brown was not a colonizationist (at least, no surviving American Colonization Society records reference his name). Rather, his most passionate pursuits were the American Bible Society and the temperance movement, a movement advocating personal abstinence from alcohol and the probation of all spirits. (In 1835, Brown Brothers pledged $1,000 to the New York State Temperance Society.)[47] Temperance preached from the hallowed grounds of Christian ethics, and James Brown seems to have been particularly drawn to its mission of human responsibility, even at a time when his conscience allowed him to profit from the Black people he enslaved.

The buying and selling of cotton had made the Browns experts "in the handling of letters of credit and bills of exchange, a business they came to dominate after 1845," writes historian Kathryn Boodry in *Slavery's Capitalism*.[48] Managing overseers and the output of traumatized Black people, their "success" in financing enslavement augmented their global reputation of trust among white peers, including other banks and merchants throughout both the United States and England, lending them the imprimatur of "financial excellence." The Browns, characteristic of glaring hypocrisies in their age, championed teetotaling with bottomless greed and cruelty.

Such hypocrisy didn't escape the withering lances of the American Anti-Slavery Society, and though never mentioning James Brown by name, abolitionists began to cut apart the sanctimoniousness of temperance patrons who, though professing Christianity and denouncing the national sin of drink at one end, said nothing about the national sin of slavery on the other. "In ancient times it was set down as one of the deepest crimes of a depraved people that they 'sold the righteous for silver, and the poor for a pair of shoes,'" chided an abolitionist pamphlet. "Yet our American Christians do much the same thing in effect; they sell women and children 'for cash'…and perhaps gave the money to the temperance society."[49] James Brown squarely fit this description, even though he always escaped public censure. Other prominent Wall Street men, however, soon did not.

———

ON DECEMBER 22, 1838, a merchant named William Trapp held a public auction on the main street of Greensboro, Alabama, where he sold for cash that day a Black woman about thirty years old, as well as her infant, "eleven months old." He also auctioned for cash a Black girl "about 10 years old," and another Black girl "about 8 years old." Trapp advertised this "Public Auction of Negroes" in the *Alabama Beacon*.[50]

Trapp had arranged the sale not for himself but on behalf of a man named Charles Whelan, an enslaver and merchant in Greensboro. Whelan had defaulted on several loans, and, as he was unable to pay, he had put up for sale this unfortunate mother and child, plus the two little girls. The cash that Trapp raised from the sale he was then to pass on to Whelan's creditors. So was conducted a horrific, yet fully legal, financial transaction that, using enslaved people's lives as collateral, formed a solid pillar of debt payments in the United States at the time. Here were more Black children, their names unrecorded, torn from family, sacrificed to the unfathomably heartless system of achieving American financial balance. The southern newspapers, particularly after the calamity of 1837, brimmed with cruel advertisements like this, an evil so commonplace as almost to escape notice.

Except in Trapp's case, the transaction didn't go unnoticed. Rather, Trapp's advertisement caught the eye of abolitionists in Boston and New York, and for a particular reason: Trapp had published the identities of Whelan's creditors, and it turned out that they were both merchants in New York: Lewis B. Brown and J. W. Leavitt. It was on behalf of these Wall Street men that the enslaved mother and children were ultimately sold, reported the *Emancipator*, an abolitionist newspaper printed from Nassau Street by Tappan's American Anti-Slavery Society.

Lewis B. Brown was the lesser known of the two creditors, running a clothing shop on Pearl Street. But J. W. Leavitt—John Wheeler Leavitt—was a particularly prominent figure in national commercial circles, owner of "one of the longest established firms in Pearl Street."[51]

The *Emancipator* called great attention to this fact. It had clearly shocked the abolitionists to learn of Leavitt's involvement. It appears to have been the first time they'd discovered that northern businessmen of such high stature, pillars of New York's financial community, were collecting outstanding debt through the sale of Black American children and women in the South.

Collapsing the geographical line as it did, North to South, the episode crystallized a moment in time: the North, largely in self-denial, at times sanctimonious, awoke to the snaking wealth of slavery coiling around its own neck. "It shows what we at the North have to do with slavery, and why we need to preach anti-slavery at the North," wrote the *Emancipator*'s editor, Theodore Dwight Weld. A new era in the fight for abolition was born.[52]

Weld and the paper later reprinted their findings as *Northern Dealers in Slaves*, a now largely forgotten but piercing and invaluable booklet, one that became the basis for abolitionists to swing the "sword of truth," as they put it, at the otherwise untouchable heart of slavery, "striking through many individuals, for whom respectable connections and high reputa-tion...would plead that they might be spared the pain and the exposure"— which is to say, the northern merchants deeply complicit in slavery's profits. "We are impelled by a sense of duty, to lay open the entanglements in which our northern men are bound hand and foot, and tongue, as the vassals of slavery," they wrote. And so began a fascinating exposition that shines further light on the hidden inner workings of slavery, wealth, and Wall Street at the center of US history.[53]

What exercised the *Emancipator* to begin with was the legality of these transactions, involving as they did men on Wall Street. "No man can properly send a demand to be collected in a slaveholding state, without giving positive orders to his agent or attorney, that slaves shall not be taken for payment, either by conveyance, trust, or execution," it wrote. "But in this case, the deed of trust is legally supposed to have been accepted by the creditors, for whose benefit it was made; and so the sale was necessarily made under their orders, given either by themselves or their *authorized* agent...It was therefore, both in a legal and moral intent, a sale of slaves, on the 22nd of December, 1838," the newspaper concluded—a sale con-ducted by John W. Leavitt himself.[54]

The *Emancipator* didn't mention at the time (for reasons unknown), a critical detail: John Wheeler Leavitt, in addition to running his own merchant firm, was also a director of Bank of America. He was, moreover, an active member of the American Colonization Society, not to mention active on the executive committee of the American Temperance Society. These facts put an even stronger point on the *Emancipator's* exposé, which continued: "Who gave [John W.] Leavitt...the right to take from this mother the child she bore with the pain of her own body, and sell it to a stranger 'for cash'?"

The *Emancipator's* discovery reveals that not only Brown Brothers, but many Wall Street banks, were directly, and deeply, enmeshed in the business of selling Black people, and we can infer this because we know that their banking operations were indistinguishably tied to those of their directors. It is hard to imagine that whatever money Leavitt had lent to Whelan had not involved, in one manner or another, the credit facilities of Bank of America. And it is not beyond reason to suppose that Leavitt, a high-level bank director, would have lent money, through the facilities afforded him by Bank of America, to numerous other enslavers throughout the South, particularly at a time when hundreds of New York firms and banks were doing so. After the tumult of 1837, many other enslavers would have sold Black people to pay Leavitt off, though these transactions wouldn't have come easily to light.

The *Emancipator* added that "probably the great body of New York merchants would do just as readily and as openly." And they were right. Its article, citing a range of advertisements from southern newspapers, enumerated a tragically long list of enslaved people in the South who were sold as credit against loans owed to "merchants and bankers in the city of New York."

"One negro man named Abraham," excerpted the *Emancipator*, "one Starling, one negro woman Maria and child, levied on as the property of David Fluker, to satisfy an execution in favor of H & D. Parish."[55] H & D. Parish were the brothers Henry and Daniel Parish, two of the wealthiest cotton traders in the United States. In the 1830s, their annual operations reached over $300,000, roughly $9 million today.[56] Their firm, advancing credit throughout the South, was based at 126 Water Street in Manhattan.

Daniel Parish—no doubt thanks to his high connections in southern

plantation circles—was, moreover, one of the longest-serving directors of
City Bank, from 1834 to 1863. It means that Parish was running City Bank,
availing himself of the bank's liquidity and services, and the bank availing itself of his appalling business, when Abraham, Starling, Maria, and a
Black child were rendered his legal property, their lives sold for his profit.
The money Parish made from the sale of these human beings almost certainly found its way into business transacted by and through City Bank,
enriching the bank and Parish alike.

The details of another slavery auction read: "One negro man named
Peter, and one Tom, levied on as the property of E.F. Lyon, to satisfy an
execution in favor of J.D. Beers." J. D. Beers—Joseph D. Beers—was one
of the oldest and most venerated names among the New York merchants
at that time. He ran a stock brokerage firm from 20 Wall Street, was president of the North American Trust and Banking Company (where Anson
Phelps was a director), and had significant real estate holdings throughout the city. Beers would become a particularly unscrupulous figure in
the dispossession of Indigenous people from their lands, further opening
southern territory to enslavers, as a director of the New York and Mississippi Land Company.

In its article, the *Emancipator* poignantly imagined a banker like
Beers, with money in hand after selling Black human beings, buying
gifts for his wife and children, going home to present them, and shrug-
ging off questions about the origin of the cash. The rueful scene crystallized how the interior life of wealthy white families and prominent
nineteenth-century entrepreneurs, as with the cities in which they worked
and lived, was made possible by a pool of collateralized debt based from
Black people's lives. "By a simple application of the Golden Rule, determine at once," wrote the *Emancipator*, "whether it is right for Northern
Christian merchants to make their gains and collect their profits by such
proceedings as this."[57]

The *Emancipator* detailed only a few of the names that then came
to light, in this one period. But we can assume, given the tens of millions
of dollars lent by northern banks to enslavers, that there were many more
such transactions, many more Wall Street directors enriching themselves
through the direct sale of Black adults and children. We can infer that
this stream of cash would have enriched these banks as well—banks still

known to us today—becoming part of the investable funds of these businesses, and that this flow of money would have been a tremendous contribution to Wall Street's profits throughout the antebellum period, helping it to thrive up until this day.

We can imagine, too, as did William Wells Brown, a prominent African American abolitionist, how portions of this money, reaped from the abomination of slavery, would have been employed on Wall Street for another purpose: to launder white men's reputations. "And I should not wonder," Brown, who lectured widely, contemplated in a famous speech, citing specifically the Whelan and Leavitt case, "when the bones, and muscles, and sinews, and hearts of human beings are put upon the auction-stand and sold for his benefit, if he [meaning Leavitt] could give a little to the church. I should not wonder if he could give a little to some institution that might throw a cloak over him, whitewash him, and make him appear reputable in the community."[58] William Wells Brown was right: White men made rich from slavery would deploy vast portions of their wealth over decades—indeed, generations—to smother, blot out, and otherwise obfuscate the crime at the heart of their prosperity. And, as we'll see, those funds continue to launder reputations to this day.

What ultimately shocked the *Emancipator* was not just that merchant-directors on Wall Street were enriching themselves by selling Black mothers and doing so legally; what shocked them was that the practice was conducted so openly, so callously, and that New York merchants felt no shame about it. In fact, the *Emancipator* noted that Leavitt and the other merchant, Lewis B. Brown, having freely admitted to approving these transactions, saw nothing untoward about engaging in them.

William Lloyd Garrison had been thrown in a Baltimore jail, paradoxically, for publishing the truth—a truth his accuser didn't deny. Denmark Vesey was hanged by the barest thread of rumors. A $1,000 reward was put on David Walker's head. Yet rich white businessmen like Daniel Parish, Joseph D. Beers, and James Brown faced no legal sanction, let alone prosecution, in an American society that prized prosperity and professional achievement far above the fate of the enslaved.

Abolitionists began to home in on this hypocrisy. They began to see that the fight for abolition, if directed only at southern interests, would only go so far, that the northern men and women buttressing this system also had to be attacked if the whole institution was to be brought down. That meant stripping away their impunity, at least in the court of public opinion. And so there followed from the *Emancipator*'s initial foray into this subject a rich, inspired, and increasingly caustic body of abolition- ist literature focused on northern riches. Where before there had been only silence, they connected dots, exposed travesties, and showed every- day human culpability in the North, even though the abolitionists rarely named specific names. Here is the Anti-Slavery Convention of American Women calling out northern women for profiting from Black bondage: "Multitudes of Northern women are daily making use of the products of slave labor. They are clothing themselves and their families in the cot- ton, and eating the rice and the sugar which they well know has cost the slave his unrequited toil, his blood and his tears."[59] Together, the women at the convention appealed for a northern boycott, holding a mirror to how deeply enmeshed slavery already was in the workings of commerce and the business of everyday life.

———

A MARBLE PALISADE, an empire of ships, a city of cotton and tobacco banks is what the New York headquarters of US slavery had become. Its prince was ascending once again. In the middle of the 1840s, James Brown bought the entire lot of 59 Wall Street and, after tearing down the existing building, spent a reported $1 million of the firm's slavery fortune building a new bank. It was considered one of the finest in New York, if not the world. A palace wrought from marble and ensconced with black walnut, fine-worked iron, soaring frescoes, and inlaid gold.[60] Did this mer- chant prince ever face a public rebuke? Did he travel from his palace on Leonard Street to his palace on Wall Street wholly unperturbed, both in mind and by the public? Was he ever shouted down as he stepped from his one-horse coupe to the street? It is difficult to know, as there's no trace in historical newspapers of abolitionists or any group publicly calling out Brown by name. But the episode uncovered by the *Emancipator* provides an important layer of nuance.

New publications, like the Quarterly *Anti-Slavery Magazine*, suggested that slavery financiers such as James Brown were no longer conducting their business with a critical pillar of support: the blanket approval of northern society.[61] Instead, they made their decisions in an atmosphere of greater public awareness, of increased tension and opposition. And that tension and related backlash began to run both ways: as fire directed by the abolitionists toward the slavery capitalists, and by the capitalists back at the abolitionists.

We know that James Brown would eventually join the fray explicitly, on the side of slavery. And we know that William Lloyd Garrison became an ever more determined and detested man on the side of the abolitionists. The merchants of slavery commerce, accordingly, organized to fight back, turning the North, and New York in particular, into a principal bastion of hardened slavery support. One Boston merchant, speaking with an abolitionist sympathizer, went on to explain pointedly the spirit of this growing war: "There are millions upon millions of dollars due from Southerners to the merchants and mechanics of this city alone, the payment of which would be jeopardized by any rupture between the North and the South. We cannot afford, sir, to let you and your associates succeed…And I have called you out to let you know, and to let your fellow laborers know, that we do not mean to allow you to succeed. We mean, sir," the merchant said with emphasis, "we mean, sir, to put you Abolitionists down—by fair means if we can, by foul means if we must."[62]

CHAPTER 7

BURN EVERYTHING IT FINDS

Sometime in the winter of 1841, Daniel Hillman Jr., an iron baron in Tennessee, sent a team of enslaved workers deep into the virgin woods along the Cumberland River. They were colliers—charcoal cutters and pit workers—and they huddled under the canopy with axes. Their breath was heavy in the morning light. The hacking began. There, the forest crackled with the sundering of tree limbs, the sieving of bark, the shredding up of stems. Up and down fell their blades. An hour passed. Next, they felled the pecans, then the hackberry, then the ancient copses of oak. All toppled sideways, and in the dirt landed their great crowns. These were trees older than maps, older than living memory. But in this one season, Hillman ordered them all ripped out to the roots. Some would later be floated downriver, to become frames for fine houses, hulls for great ships. But they were only a few. Most were burned. Dragged by the colliers to hollows in the earth and burned.

These pits, Hillman ignited to a ferocious degree—as his father had taught him, and his grandfather before that—stoked with cord Black people had cleaved for hours and days from the nearby woods, the precious fuel of a smelting fire. From the fire rose the foundations of Empire Furnace, one of the longest-running industrial ironworks in the South, churning out tons of iron sheet and boilerplate, all through the day and night, and giving birth simultaneously to one of the greatest corporate dynasties and family fortunes in the history of the United States. And all of it made possible by the ceaseless subjugated labor of 255 Black people. Whole sections of primeval forest Hillman felled and charred to fuel his furnaces, to force iron from rock and spread the spark of modern industry.

Five hundred miles to the south, along the eastern bank of the Mississippi River, Stephen Duncan, a banker and cotton magnate, also sent teams of enslaved people deep into the woods to hack and defoliate large tracts of land. He decreed that the oak be split, quartered, and sawed into lumber. The scraps, he burned. The lumber, he made his enslaved people mill and build into living quarters for themselves—plank dwellings mostly—plus other buildings for his slavery enterprise.

As far back as 1834, Duncan had acquired 2,815 acres of Choctaw land, in an area the Choctaw had called Issaquena, their word for Deer Creek. He acquired them cheaply, for almost as many dollars. In the long hours of the day, he tasked his enslaved people to cut the forests; in the gloom of the night, they burned the trunks to ash. Deer Creek became flat land. With more clearing, Duncan planted more cotton and, with the proceeds, bought more enslaved people, then more acres, including large plantations lost in the ravages of 1837. By that cycle, he evolved into everything a white man dedicated to enslaving Black human beings, on deforested Indigenous land, hoped to be: rich beyond the measure of any previous time; father to a privileged family; director of a farming, real estate, and banking empire; pinnacle of Mississippi society; president of the Mississippi State Colonization Society, with an iconic mansion in Natchez, called Auburn, and investments stretching to Wall Street.

Duncan's labor camps were many, clustered all along the river, and he gave them names like Carlisle, after his hometown in Pennsylvania, and Duncannon, to memorialize his grandeur. All told, by 1840 Duncan's overseers worked 366 enslaved Black people on fourteen thousand acres of defoliated land. He would soon be the single largest "planter" in the world, a euphemism masking the industrial size of his operation, wealth, and cruelty. The Black people he enslaved produced not only cotton, but sugar, molasses, and corn, the broadest range possible within the spectrum of America's enslavement wealth. Locals called the vast stretches of Duncan's slave lands "the Reach."

In an arc stretching one thousand miles, from Missouri to Delaware, slavery's reach by the 1840s was longer and deeper than ever before. The Panic of 1837, breeding collapse, consolidation, and renewal, meant the system was more organized, more productive of staples and services, more brutal and more destructive to Black people's lives, predicated on the wholesale destruction of the natural environment, while also generating more wealth for white people than at any time in US history. The more than 2.5 million Black people enslaved in the United States, their very bodies worth to white men several billion dollars, constituted now the largest coerced labor force ever amassed in the world. They worked on millions of acres of land seized from Indigenous peoples, a zone of productivity unprecedented in scope and output in the Americas, if not the globe.

Yet their productive capacity, furnishing hundreds of millions of dollars in epic wealth each year (billions today) was controlled by fewer and fewer hands, concentrated in a smaller number of elite white families, perhaps at most four thousand, like the Hillmans and the Duncans, agro-industrial businessmen at the top of the chain. As W. E. B. Du Bois observed: "In the second quarter of the century Southern slavery was irresistibly changing from a family system to an industrial system."[1] The slavery system wasn't only organized along industrial and corporate lines, producing record levels of wealth. Increasingly, enslaved people were set to work in America's burgeoning industrial enterprises themselves, their labor giving birth to new forms of innovation, growth, development, and riches: forging metal and milling lumber; laying railroads and digging canals; mining gold, coal, and lead; refining sugar and flour; and working on steamers and docks—which is to say, building the industrial base that made the United States the wealthiest, most powerful country in the world.

The work enslaved people did in this time contributed exceptionally to America's growing riches, not merely because they were held captive in exceptional numbers by white people, but because white people, forcing them to do this work in ceaseless shifts, often around the clock, and for no pay, reaped tremendous outcomes of goods and improvements, in a fraction of the time, and for a fraction of the cost, more than anywhere else in the world. Such were the lasting fortunes made by a new generation of slavery entrepreneurs that some of these men became the single most influential corporate investors in the United States. To consider the scope of the wealth produced by Black people in this time then is to behold how it fueled the expanse of a robust economy at the height of its bloom.

————

THE FIRST STOLEN wealth was land. The earliest history of white wealth-making in the United States is a history of horizontal slaughter, of nature set to doom. Indigenous lands taken by white men were rich in boxwood, in cypress, in hickory, in ash. These were ancient forests, teeming with animals, with minerals, loaded with carbon dioxide, abounding with natural wealth. They were destroyed. "When I first began my work," wrote John P. Parker, a Black inventor, formerly enslaved, "all northern Kentucky was still covered with virgin forest...[but] the forest gradually disappeared."[2] Said Louis Hughes, enslaved on a Mississippi cotton plantation for fifteen years: "The trees...were cut down...piled into great heaps, called 'log heaps,' and burned." "The burning was done at night," Hughes added, "and the sight was often weird and grand."[3] Up and down the Mississippi River by the 1840s, among the canebrakes of the low country and, higher up, among the belts of pine, the nights of the American South burned with the ambition of white wealth-making, with the heat of Wall Street.

A verdant realm is what Stephen Duncan had taken back in 1830, ten miles along the eastern side of the Mississippi. Animals had been abundant here, as were old-growth trees. Duncan bought his first tract of land cheap, from the US government—150 acres for $188.50—as white men could at that time. A few days later, he bought an additional 470 acres for $586.50. In 1831, the federal government auctioned more than 2.7 million acres in this way, taking a purse of $3.5 million ($108 million today). Buying land was easy: there were five US Land Offices across Mississippi alone, from Augusta to Chocchuma, proffering an explosion of "new" tracts. These lands were abundant because worlds had been destroyed: the Choctaw, Chickasaw, and Cherokee peoples, who had thrived in, protected, and contested these forests, were all gone.

Forced removal, the so-called concessions that had been separating

Native peoples from their pristine forests for three decades, forged the arc of land that cradled the savagery of slavery: the Treaty of Fort Adams, in 1801, ceding 2.5 million acres of Indigenous land; the Treaty of Mount Dexter, in 1805, ceding five million acres more. As early as 1818, land companies, with backing from Congress and credit from the US Land Office, had sold more than one million acres alone for $7.2 million (the equivalent today of $151 million). Points out Emilie Connolly, assistant professor of history at Brandeis University: "Removal-era land speculation fed on a landed abundance and liquidity created by state destruction of the Chickasaws' economically prosperous society."[4] In 1820, the Treaty of Doak's Stand ceded an additional five and a half million acres of Indigenous land. Then came 1830, and President Andrew Jackson happily signed the Indian Removal Act. The westward advance of white wealth, population, and power was legalized. White settlers sent one hundred thousand Indigenous people on the Trail of Tears; fifteen thousand of them lost their lives, and fifty-five million more acres of their land and flora fell to wholesale destruction. The cotton lands expanded. Reported the British writer George McHenry in 1863: "The discovery that the bottom lands of the valley of the Mississippi could grow cotton much cheaper than any yet tried, caused a great speculative excitement in the south-west, and created a corresponding land mania in the north-west, inducing persons to lay out farms and project cities in tracts still covered by primeval woods."[5]

White enslavers had been cutting thick swaths and burning their way through America's ancient forest since the colonies. Much of American recorded history—repeated over and over in settler diaries, US government surveys, pamphlets, and the accounts of Black people formerly enslaved—echoes with the collapsing of the land. As early as 1750, Johann Martin Bolzius, a German-born minister, witnessed in Georgia how slavery and unbounded wealth had spread through fire: "If one wants to establish a plantation on previously uncultivated land, one orders [enslaved people] to clear the land of trees...The [enslaved] must hack the branches off the trees, and also pile them in heaps. Now when one observes that all branches and bushes are quite dry, one puts fire to them and lets them burn up. Since the land is full of dry leaves, the fire spreads far and wide and burns grass and everything it finds."[6]

Enslavers bent on riches put the burning principle into practice across

Alabama, clear-cutting the Coosa Valley, the Black Belt, and Horseshoe Bend, and along the Tombigbee River too. They did it because the land most propitious for cotton and sugar was flat, open ground fully exposed to the sun, for intense heat was required to grow these staples. The Piedmont of North Carolina was deforested; Mississippi's Yazoo Swamp; in Tennessee, swaths of Cherokee lands—Etowah, Coosawattee, and Hickory Log—were cut up and set to flame. "Not unfrequently will one planter deaden and destroy a thousand acres in one season," observed *Hunt's Merchants' Magazine and Commercial Review*, an observation from which the magazine concluded: *"The pine forests are being rapidly swept away."*[7] Through this path of destruction, white enslavers pulled "the centre of slave cotton production...southwesterly," traced sociologist Charles Post, from "coastal South Carolina and Georgia in 1815, to western Georgia and southern Mississippi and Alabama in 1830."[8]

In 1831, Peter Pitchlynn had been among the first Choctaw people to leave the ranges around present-day Columbus, Mississippi, forced to walk the Trail of Tears. (Pitchlynn, like many Choctaw, had enslaved Black people himself.) In 1846, he returned to Mississippi. He couldn't recognize his ravaged home, cut up for cotton. "This was once a healthy country, but now it is a very sickly one," he wrote to his brother. "I scarcely know any of the places which were once familiar to me."[9]

Here the frontier of slavery met the advancing frontier of modernization and industry in the United States. The result was a melding of industrial Black enslavement with the collapse of climates and ecosystems, for the purposes of corporate profit and industrial expansion. The scale of this destruction paralleled the scale of white men's ambition; it was a devastation as unprecedented as the white wealth it would create and the Black lives it would shatter, the genealogical lines and family trees it would sever and sunder at a million points. It is important to recall that the vast reaches of the slavery lands—miles of endless fields, barren and churned like a grave—didn't naturally exist; they had to be made. That is to say, everywhere they took land, white men forced Black people to cut the way. The number of labor hours expended to make such devastation has to be considered. The shoulder hours, the hours Black people spent in swinging axes—even enslaved women. In his 1853 memoir, Solomon Northup eulogized Black lumberwomen held in subjugated labor, how "the largest oak or sycamore [stood] but a brief season before their heavy and well-directed blows. At piling logs, they were equal to any man."[10]

In all of recorded human history, humans had never cut down so many trees as white men fixated on slavery in the United States did. Available statistics paint a picture that is clear: slavery's expansion unfolded side by side with ecocide on an industrial scale. Indeed, slavery on an industrial scale was only possible because of ecocide, and ecocide the result of industrial-grade slavery. Between 1650 and 1790, white men tasked Black people to cut roughly twenty-five million acres of trees in the colonies.[11] Between 1798 and 1850—the rise of the cotton belt and the cotton boom—the pace accelerated enormously, and enslavers razed fifty-five million more acres.[12] They planted, in the wake of these cindered forests, forges like Hillman's and reaches like Duncan's, plus sugar refineries, whiskey distilleries, sawmills, and, increasingly, railroads. The destruction was unrelenting. Again, it was possible only because the Black people tasked with doing it were hardly given rest.

By the 1850s, southern economists could boast: "The cotton fields of the United States, extending from the Atlantic to the Rio Grande, embrace in their wide extent 500,000 square miles."[13] Between 1850 and 1859 alone, the peak of cotton cultivation, white entrepreneurs would go on to raze thirty-nine million more acres of trees, nearly one-third of the total since 1650 in one-twentieth of the time.[14] And not only trees. The research of historian Mart A. Stewart catalogues how slavery "brought an end to canebrakes" as a feature throughout the South.[15] "The whole country was then an entire canebrake," the writer Fortescue Cuming described Kentucky as being in the 1780s.[16] In the prairie lands of Alabama in 1817, "the most frequented roads through the richest lands were covered across by a leaning and overhanging and interlocked tops of the tall canes, growing on each side, rendering the passage of travellors slow and difficult," reported Edmund Ruffin, a Virginia enslaver.[17] These were ripped out to the roots.

All that time, in a blaze lasting for a century, "much good timber was burned and destroyed, because there was no market for it and the trees stood in the way of cultivation," the US Department of Agriculture later concluded.[18] The charred landscape of the South became a funeral pyre, a monument to greed, a lost people's grave.

Somewhere in the geological record, in the breast of the land, rests a hidden tally of this woe, barely recalled to us now, an unknown quantity of sorrow. Perhaps a full reckoning of the trees can never be known, but it should be considered. It is also part of the record of what was stolen, of what was taken, of what was lost.

By 1840, the ships of the American Colonization Society were sailing, banishing free Black people in droves, while the ocean liners, returning from England, disembarked wave after wave of white immigrants on US shores. Andrew Jackson's project of "Indian removal," culminating in the wholesale expropriation of the forests, worked hand in glove with the banks of Wall Street and James Brown, their capital plying armies of enslaved people to burn white people's path deeper west, deeper south. The triangle was spinning, and alighted now by industry and slave production along industrial lines, the slavery trove piled higher.

SEVERAL OF THE primary industrialists of the United States were white business owners who moved south with their families from New England in the early years of the nineteenth century, seeking fortunes in the new lands and, more importantly, in the widening ability to enslave Black people and exploit their labor. Through that unrequited labor, many of these men formed stout branches of family trees that survive even now, trees soaked in slavery wealth, in the hardship of shackled Black people. In many of these cases, the branches of the family tree gave birth simultaneously to eponymous corporate formations and industrial firms, which, infused with and only made possible because of slavery wealth, propelled industry forward considerably in the years both leading up to and following the Civil War. Black people's lives, their storylines, their family ties, are a crucial yet erased force in the biographies of these vaunted families, many of whom are still exceedingly rich today.

Among the richest and most prominent then, and still now, were the Hillmans, a billionaire family today based in Pittsburgh. In the antebellum age, the Hillmans pioneered the mass production of iron in the South, forming one of the principal networks of industrial development in early America. The lines of the family are old, strong, and proud,

according to the family itself, a lineage much consecrated and still celebrated by its heirs. Today, in fact, they are considered among the largest
and most discreet venture capital investors in the world, with institutional
stakes in Amazon, Google, and General Electric, not to mention eighteen
philanthropies that funnel out millions each year. But to become so, in an
evolution of carefully forgotten stages, the Hillmans first extracted their
great fortune, later taking it north, from Black people forced to reap iron
from the hematite rock of western Kentucky, Tennessee, and Alabama, in
a century of forging that decimated the Cumberland River woodlands and
countless Black lives.

The original patriarch of this family was known as "Old Daniel Hillman." Proudly, the Hillmans have written that his forebears worked iron
for seven centuries, back to the Netherlands and the family's roots. The old
man was originally from New Jersey but moved south in the 1820s, hoping to escape debts and reverse financial misfortune. He and his wife had
three sons and a daughter; Daniel Hillman Jr. was then in his teens. There
is no record that Hillman Sr. was an enslaver himself. But slavery proved
critical to his success, becoming more and more central to the family's
story, to its role in casting America's industrial might, and to its great and
lasting wealth.

In 1830, a man named Abner McGehee enticed Daniel Hillman to
come to Roupes Valley, Alabama, near present-day Birmingham. McGehee owned a large plantation on over ten thousand acres of land, where
he enslaved at least seventy-one Black people, including eleven children,
census records show. Already he was transforming the cotton wealth they
produced into yet other pursuits, becoming the single largest investor in a
new project just then beginning: the Alabama railroad.

By investing in such frontiers, McGehee personified the early channels
of slavery funds then pouring into US industry. He hoped to accelerate that
process even further, turning Alabama into a center of iron production,
and so he hired Daniel Hillman Sr., whose reputation had traveled far. It
was Hillman's ingenuity and skill that built a dual-chambered bloomery
on Roupes Creek, two brick furnaces where metal blooms—molten slabs
of fizzling brightness—were pounded into iron, shaping the destiny of the
South. But it was McGehee's riches from forced Black labor that made it
a success.

Enslaved Black people had long worked in the small forges and furnaces that dotted this region. In surviving historical documents is recorded their work toiling to fell the timbered creeks, deepening pits for firing coal, and charging the blast furnaces with ore from the nearby hills. Their role in the expansion of iron making throughout the United States had been consequential and constant since the eighteenth century—notably, in the early furnaces of the Chesapeake. (According to some accounts, the first enslaved African peoples mined ore in New Jersey as far back as 1676.)[19]

No documents survive to speak of those enslaved African Americans who may have worked under Hillman at his bloomery, there at the birth of iron in Birmingham. But their presence, based on prevalent facts, must be assumed. They were put under the chain in this new industry, their labor exploited, so that an older industry could spread its reign: that of slavery itself. For at his bloomery, with its water-driven hammer, Hillman mined tough metal and turned out horseshoes and plows, farming instruments critical to the production of cotton.[20] These ironworks, in time, gave rise to a small industrial town, supplying the nearby plantations, the surrounding trees increasingly destroyed to feed the forge. Daniel Hillman Jr. himself apprenticed there with his father (he had spent much of his youth cutting cord for charcoal), but his father died soon afterward, in 1831, when Hillman Jr. was twenty-four.

It is long established in lore that generations of Hillmans prospered, launching the United States and themselves to the heights of industrial riches, because the elderly Hillman left to his son a singular and prodigious knowledge of ferrous metals. So attest most authoritative accounts of iron making in the South, as well as the genealogical record published in 1905 by members of the Hillman family themselves, *Ancestral Chronological Record of the Hillman Family*.[21] Enshrined into the origin story of one of America's great fortunes, in other words, is the notion that the recurrent success of the Hillman industrialists, and their brood, came down to their effort and talent alone. Such stories sidestep the more important truth: The network of deep-pocketed enslavers whom the elderly Hillman connected to his offspring, their contacts and their wealth, turned his son Daniel Hillman Jr., then setting out for Tennessee, into the patriarch of the billionaire family of present day. And most

important of all were the Black people Hillman Jr. himself would soon
come to enslave.

————

THE PASSING OF one Hillman generation to the next, from slavery deeper
into industry, coincided with larger, epochal shifts in American prosperity. The industrial capacities of the country were just then about to leap
forward. No doubt industrialization was already underway in the United
States. But profits from slavery, tens of millions invested by the Benjamin
Marshalls, the Anson Phelpses, James Brown, and, later, Hillman and his
network, were helping to drive even greater specialization and mechanization in manufacturing, particularly of textiles. This led to a proliferation of
new machineries and factories, with the added result that iron was becoming, to paraphrase historical geographer Anne Kelly Knowles, a more central strand in the "national narrative of industrialization."[22]

Soon, the mining and construction capacities of the country would
reach peak increases, each more than doubling in value between 1839 and
1849, spawning new roads, canals, and, increasingly, railroads. Just as it
had unleashed a revolution in farming and cotton production unparalleled in history, an explosion in shipping and transportation, a revolution
in exports and foreign trade, a revolution in mercantile networks, banking,
and credit, not to mention a sweeping and catastrophic transformation of
the land, the billions of dollars reaped from slavery would help power the
industrial revolution of the United States.

Historian Robert S. Starobin, in his pioneering study of industrial slavery in 1969, dispelled the myth that enslaved people "labored exclusively
on large southern plantations," that cotton was the only wealth they produced, and that "the sectional conflicts between 1790 and 1861 were simply struggles for supremacy between Southern Agrarians and Northern
Industrialists."[23] Unfree Black people—as many as two hundred thousand,
Starobin's work revealed—were indissolubly tied through an iron chain to
America's growing industrial enterprises, to the riches these enterprises
wrought, and to the highly productive corporations they spawned. This
reality is no more poignantly captured than in the story of what Daniel
Hillman Jr. was about to become. Crossing into Tennessee's Cumberland

River valley, Hillman Jr. both pushed and was pulled by this rising wealth like a rivulet to a stream.

That enslaved people's labor so stimulated the fires of US moderniza-tion was a fact widely affirmed in that time itself, certainly by southern enslavers, but also by the northern businessmen who abetted them. "The position which the Southern United States hold to the commercial and industrial world, is one of the most remarkable phenomena of modern times," reflected James D. B. De Bow, a southern economist of notably rank, strident, and racist views. His bigotry distilled the prevailing senti-ment of white people of that time: "When we reflect upon the origin of black servitude in America," he wrote, "...when...it began to weave that thread of cotton which has gradually enveloped the commercial world, and bound the fortunes of American slaves so firmly to human progress, that civilization itself may also be said to depend upon the continual servi-tude of the blacks in America."[24]

The rising order of industrialization promised that unfettered riches, even more than the colossal amounts already pilfered, waited to be stolen from the toil of Black people, to be ripped from the land. Iron was one key to those riches, a key to the achievement of modern civilization itself, a civilization yet based on the barbarism of continual slavery. The limits of the wealth to be had were limited only by how far and how hard white entrepreneurs were willing to exploit Black people and push slavery's reach. The questions again arose, however: Riches at what cost? Affluence at what price? Wealth for whom?

———

By the late 1830s, Daniel Hillman Jr. secured a contract in Dickson County, Tennessee, partnering with the iron maker Anthony W. Van Leer, who was originally from Pennsylvania. Hillman began managing Van Leer's Cumberland Furnace and Fairchance Furnace, which is to say, managing their enslaved labor forces. Foreshadowing Hillman's own path, the melding of slavery and iron had made Van Leer rich. In 1830, he'd enslaved only four Black people; by 1840, he enslaved 148. The growth of his enterprise reflected how the key to industrial productivity through-out the region, and increasingly the nation, was the increased pilfering of

Black people's minds, bodies, and time. Ironmen like Van Leer, though once heavily reliant on white ironworkers, increasingly gave up hiring them by the 1840s, deeming their labor too intractable and too expensive in the wake of strikes and wage increases.

For good reason, the furnaces of the South became known as "iron plantations." Up and down the Cumberland River alone, white ironmen came to enslave eighteen hundred Black people by the 1850s.[25] Tennessee metal soon became prized across the country, so much so that Congress officially deemed it as comparable in reliability, following a series of tests, to the best irons then being produced by the dominant, much larger forges of Pennsylvania.

What was the key to Van Leer's and Hillman's "success"? The answer wasn't innovation: iron making was an ancient, even crude process; it hadn't changed remarkably since 1715 (though the introduction in 1829 of hot-air blast was a notable advancement). What changed was that white managers like Hillman worked enslaved people to exhaustion, around the clock, six days a week, for months on end—often to death—to escalate output and production. These unbroken hours, Black workers spent in hellish fire pits, burning cord into coal, packing coal into ovens to smelt ore, and draining off the noxious flows of slag. Black laborers sourced ore constantly from bare rock in the hills. If lucky, shallow ore could be pulled from open pit mines; if not, it had to be tunneled from deep underground, with the ever-present danger of suffocation and collapse. Standing in pools of stagnant water, dust clogging their lungs, Black people (they tended to be men) pounded metal for days on end to meet the soaring demands of America's new iron age.

Works like Van Leer's specialized in pig iron, so called because when poured in molten rivulets and left to solidify in place, the metal took the appearance of a sow feeding her young. It was aptly named, for these hard irons became the basic sustenance of our nascent industrialization, and, when later reforged and refined, took on the thousand different forms— "from the gigantic steamer which crosses the Atlantic, to the smallest of ornamental shirt buttons"—then making modern life possible across the republic.[26] Van Leer and Hillman, in fact, shipped their pig iron as far as Pittsburgh, establishing the earliest connections between the Hillmans and the city today synonymous with their name.[27]

Few northern white people had ever set foot in the sprawling zones of industry that constituted the slavery system in the South. Few had ever seen a Black person enslaved, toiling under lash and chain for no pay. ("We reached Norfolk next day in the afternoon. I never had seen a slave, and as soon as the ship was secured I landed and took a stroll through the town," a voyeur recalled flippantly in one of the New York papers.)[28] There remained two separate zones in the United States, the world of enslaved labor and the world of free cities, and the gulf of perception was bridged only by ships or long voyages by wagon. In reality, however, they were one system, interpenetrated through goods and capital and greed, feeding each other, much as the iron flowing north from Tennessee. "The *roots* of this institution are at the south," said the Boston Female Anti-Slavery Society, "but its baleful *shadow* is over *us*."[29]

It was a feature of America's business of Black enslavement to become more and more pervasive yet, paradoxically, more and more invisible, silently infecting its maladies over more and more essential things. Cotton cultivated by nameless enslaved people had changed the way white people celebrated themselves in cloth and dress throughout US cities. Industry and iron produced through slavery were now changing the *cities* themselves. It is a legacy we are still beholden to today that Americans, living in relative prosperity, expect never to see the people who make the things that make life enjoyable for them, and the *not-seeing*—the not-seeing the frenetic activity of sweatshops, and the invisible hands bent over meager pay—is integral to that enjoyment. Its roots were planted back then. The ironworks of the South gorged the cities of the North with iron pounded by enslaved hands—iron for water and gas pipes, for better living; iron to fill the air with higher buildings and the docks with bigger ships.

The long reach and overdrive of slavery came to characterize the bulk of America's most important industries. The twenty-five hundred Black people enslaved in the country's coal and iron mines worked around the clock, seven days a week, in two twelve-hour relays; in other words, Black people kept these operations running twenty-four hours a day. In Virginia, the work in coal mines was halted only on Sundays, Starobin quotes a mine operator as saying, "when the water [was] drawn as often as necessary to keep the works below from being flooded." [30]

Teams of enslaved people worked so fast at building roads, digging ditches, and forging canals and turnpikes that corporate navigation works, including some owned by the federal government and the US Navy, exclusively used their labor. Rather than hiring enslaved workers on contract, as they had in the past, these works came to purchase large enslaved labor forces themselves. The same applied to all sorts of mills—rice mills, flour mills, and sawmills chief among them. A staggering thirty thousand enslaved people—a number greater than the population of most US cities at that time—worked in grinding rice and wheat into flour. As a result, southern flour became a critical national staple. These enslaved grinders worked continuously, day and night, up to sixteen hours a day, six to seven days a week. And that's how Americans received their daily bread. "The rule…was unremitting toil, with illness or accident the only respite," Starobin wrote.[31]

It was by managing industrial enslaved labor like this that Daniel Hillman Jr. became prosperous for the first time. Strategically, he conducted that slavery wealth into even more, for he fused his bloodline with that of an elite family of enslaver-politicians. In 1840, he married Ann Marable, who'd grown up surrounded by privilege and slavery, on a plantation where her family held captive thirty-six Black people, a plantation called Escape in Montgomery County, Tennessee.

The unpaid work of Black people ran long and deep in the Marable line. Ann's father, John H. Marable, had inherited enslaved people and plantation lands both from his forebears and his wife's. Slavery wealth helped launch his career in Congress when he represented Tennessee's Eighth District between 1825 and 1829. According to a website focused on tracing genealogical records from Tennessee, Ann's father had once "won" a Black child in a game of poker in Washington, DC [32] (presumably while serving in Congress, no less), a heinously common practice in the antebellum period. That child, Pole Marable, was sent from Washington and confined to housework at Escape, the rupture to his family unknown. Did he have siblings? Were his parents alive? There are no traceable records that can say. What is known is that Pole Marable, forced to take his enslaver's name, was still held at Escape when Daniel Hillman Jr. arrived.

The couple married on the plantation, according to genealogical records and family accounts. They lived at the plantation for many years, served and surfeited by the Black people forced to work there, Pole Marable among them. In 1841, Ann Hillman gave birth, at Escape, to their son, John H. Hillman. He would later head one of the nation's premier industrial concerns, the Pittsburgh-based Hillman Coal and Coke Company. It was with fortunes from that firm that the family became steel tycoons.

The Hillmans' other son, Thomas T. Hillman, later an important industrialist himself in Alabama, was also born and raised at the plantation. According to an early twentieth-century account, in fact, it was the job of two enslaved Black men to carry Thomas Hillman all around the grounds each day after he was seriously injured in a horse-riding accident. They often carried him on their backs, and did so for several years throughout his youth.[33] The same account, written by journalist Ethel Armes, celebrates this detail to the point of trivializing it, quoting a Hillman family friend as callously joking, "All during [Thomas] Hillman's youth he hunted, in this way, carried on the back of one or other of these negro men, and, by the way, he held the record in fishing." Cruel indifference to the Black people they subjugated was part of the family's own lore.

That legacy continued for decades. The Hillmans and their children would all eventually leave Escape in the 1850s. But Pole Marable never did. He remained at Escape until 1892, long after emancipation, when he was very old, unable to hear or see and with nowhere else to go. While out walking unattended, a Tennessee newspaper records, he was struck and killed by one of the passing trains, harbingers of progress that men like McGehee and Marable, rich from crushing up lives like Pole's, had increasingly financed on plantation lands—a tragic reflection, one among multitudes, of the devastation the Hillmans left in the wake of their steep ascent.[34]

In 1841, Daniel Hillman Jr. rose higher toward the pinnacle of wealth and standing. Thanks to partners, capital, and land acquisitions made possible by his in-laws, namely Ann Marable's uncle, he acquired Empire Furnace and Fulton Furnace. Together, they became the centerpiece of one of the most productive industrial complexes in the South, indeed the nation. There's no doubt that these enterprises made Hillman Jr. rich beyond the measure of his forebears.

In 1844, he built another furnace, Center Furnace, the third in his empire. By 1845, he began buying vast tracts of new woodlands—seventy-five hundred acres in Kentucky alone.[35] He cut up and burned these forests, smelting ore, then bought more land, consolidating more industry. He bought up nearly all the early ironworks of the Tennessee Valley, including several rolling mills and presses, and floated all the machinery in 1845 up the Cumberland River, establishing a sprawling new works in Lyon County, Kentucky. The *Times-Picayune* later called him "at one time the wealthiest man in western Kentucky."[36]

All the while, Daniel Hillman Jr., rich from slavery, transformed the Hillman family, for the first time, into enslavers themselves. He acquired throughout the 1840s at least 253 Black people to toil in his furnaces, census records show. Many of them died, and so Hillman continued to purchase even more, the total number of people he enslaved being closer to 270. This was one of the largest enslaved labor forces anywhere in the country, six times larger than his father-in-law's and nearly double that of his former boss, Van Leer.

By most calculations, Hillman would likely have spent roughly $150,000 then, or $5 million today, to enslave these people for life. (Court records show that when he purchased four enslaved people in 1846, Hillman paid a total of $2,243.34, meaning roughly $560 for each Black person.)[37] To speak of Hillman's industrial development is also to consider the cruel industriousness that he applied to snatching these 270 lives—270 people robbed of the right to speak and to act for themselves. The hours Hillman spent in writing letters and otherwise communicating with slavery auctioneers and traders, determining the location and availability of these unfree people, negotiating terms; the hours he spent traveling to view those whose freedom he would pay to steal; the hours spent chaining and transporting them along the Cumberland River; the countless blocks of time and energy expended corralling them in his brick furnace complex, day after day.

No doubt Hillman recouped his vile wager. By 1852, his slave-driven works led the regional market, and he received commissions all over the country. His iron was loaded on ships bound for fabricators and factories across the North. Hillman iron wrought by enslaved African American men eventually became the bridges of Pittsburgh, the cast-iron foundations of mansions in New York, and the skeletons of ocean liners sailing the seas from Boston.

Within Hillman's personal evolution are traces of the country's evolution, of the potency of slavery wealth to shape the national course, from agriculture toward industry, from small-scale forging to mass production. Old Daniel Hillman's bloomery had produced three hundred pounds of iron a day.[38] The Empire and Fulton Furnaces alone produced more than eighteen thousand, or a total of 6.6 million pounds a year, at a value of $72,600 ($2.6 million today).[39] Hillman Jr.'s sons, cradled in the privileges of slavery, would carry that evolution even further. Their corporations, seeded with slavery wealth, enabled the mechanized mass production of iron and steel, a new echelon in America's industrial and financial development.

The Hillmans have their *Ancestral Chronological Record*. Black families enslaved by them have but stories scattered in pieces, fragments on the internet, testimonials buried by time. Today, there are communities of Black Marables, and communities of Black Van Leers and Van Liers, many of whom trace their name's origin to the enslaver Anthony Van Leer, Daniel Hillman Jr.'s business partner.

Military records from 1864 reveal something further: Daniel Hillman Jr. enslaved a forty-four-year-old Black man named Gustavus Hillman, originally of Virginia. He later enlisted with the US Colored Heavy Artillery Regiment during the Civil War, and as of 1890, his widow, Rachel Hillman, was still alive and receiving Gustavus's war pension.[40] In all likelihood, Gustavus was forced to carry his enslaver's name.

That few records speak for these men and women is a statement speaking volumes itself, an epic on how the wealth of slavery, as it forged and preserved the aura of the great white families, allowed the names of African Americans to be lost, usurped, and swept away.

A Kentucky newspaper from 1911 contains but a passing reference to Jake and John Reeder, two enslaved brothers who worked at Fulton Furnace; they were said to be "the strongest couple anywhere to be found," hoisting barrels of flour in each arm and carrying them from riverboats to the furnace.[41] Neither census records nor court documents could be found to provide any further trace of this pair.

Proceedings from the Supreme Court of Illinois in 1899 reveal that Daniel Hillman also enslaved Edward Baker, and that after emancipation, Baker married, had children, and acquired property.[42] In 1853, William Shouse was also enslaved by Hillman, military records show, and he remained so for another ten years, until he liberated himself during the Civil War to fight for the Union.[43] Hillman later submitted a claim to the US government seeking compensation for such "desertions," for sixty of the Black men he'd enslaved would leave to take up arms against the Confederacy.

Among those who "deserted," military records show, were two enslaved men named Joseph and Montgomery Marable, their names an echo of the past, Hillman's past, and an indication they had once been enslaved by Hillman's father-in-law.[44] They were likely "inherited" by Hillman after his father-in-law died, a link in the chain of dynastic slavery wealth.

Burning his furnaces to extremes and fleecing his Black workers of pay, Hillman could produce iron more quickly and cheaply than his competitors, and that was the key to his success. Tennessee and Kentucky iron—which is to say, Hillman iron—came to compete with the extensive metalworks of Pennsylvania, not in terms of output, but by undercutting these industrial forerunners in price. (Pennsylvania alone accounted for more than 50 percent of US production.)[45] The cost to Black people's lives was incalculable. Many are reported to have died of cholera, scarlet fever, and exhaustion.

Kentucky death records capture the passing of at least sixteen of the Black people Hillman enslaved between 1852 and 1859.[46] The records from 1859 list the names of five men—Billy, Calop, Bill, Edward, and Dudley—all of whom died of scarlet fever.[47] In other records, however, Hillman didn't bother to provide a cause of death; a note in the margin of the record says that "Mr. Hillman had nothing to report," so the entries are simply left blank and unfilled. In the fields all alongside Center Furnace, up until the 1960s, could be seen many of these people's graves, shallow and unmarked, their bodies interred just feet from where they gave their last to the Hillman fortune.

By the 1850s, as many as ten thousand enslaved Black people worked in iron-making firms like Hillman's. Many became the highest-level artisanal metalworkers in the country, their labor indispensable to new frontiers of mechanization and modernization that iron wrought in the United States. Emanuel Elmore Jr., the son of a man once enslaved, recalled seeing his father's prowess at the forge. His father worked at the Cherokee

Iron Works in Spartanburg, South Carolina. "If you could have seen pa's hammer, you would have seen something worth looking at," Elmore told the Works Progress Administration in 1937. "It was so big that it jarred the whole earth when it struck a lick."[48]

Iron production surged in the United States, from 165,000 tons in 1830, the year Old Daniel Hillman founded his bloomery, to 800,000 tons in 1848, the year his son Hillman Jr. became a tycoon. By the 1850s, the iron industry reached a height of $50 million a year, or $1.68 billion today. The southern states produced roughly 25 percent of all that iron, meaning Black laborers contributed extensively to America's iron value in the decade before the Civil War.[49] They helped put the United States, once heavily dependent on England and Russia for metals, on the path to iron self-sufficiency, a key to the country's industrial development.

This increased capacity of iron production, coupled with new forms of its production (the use of higher-burning mineral coal and anthracite instead of charcoal began after the 1840s), made iron cheaper to produce and thus more widely available. Increased production in iron in turn stimulated the coal and gas industry. It is estimated that financiers, including, as we'll see, many connected to slavery on Wall Street, invested upward of $100 million developing the nation's coalfields.[50] Roughly one-third of iron was furthermore consumed by the railroads. In the 1840s, there had been no US-made rail. By 1855, the United States produced 135,000 tons, while continuing to import roughly the same amount.[51]

"The seas are traversed by iron ships," Abram Stevens Hewitt, a leading American industrialist at the time, proclaimed, "the land travelled over by iron carriages upon iron roads. We have iron engines employed for nearly every mechanical purpose. Water is brought along our streets by iron pipes, and all our thoroughfares illumined by means of gas conveyed to us through a similar channel. Many of our houses have iron floors and iron roofs, whilst the windows are closed with iron shutters."[52] Not mentioned by Hewitt, or other industrialists celebrating the age, was the iron scourged into fetters, into iron chains, the collars that shackled African Americans forced on coffle lines across the South. Or how it made the axes that, arriving in shipments by the thousands from manufacturers in places like Connecticut, Black people were forced to use to decimate wider and wider swaths of trees.

SUCH HAS BEEN the fortune that the Hillmans extracted from enslavement, preserved and unbroken for nearly two hundred years, that the Hillman progeny have lived ever since as billionaires, civic leaders, and Republican Party doyennes. Several foundations and Pittsburgh landmarks are today endowed in their name, including the library of the University of Pittsburgh and the Hillman Cancer Center. The living heirs reside in discreet mansions, including an unmarked estate in the hills outside of Pittsburgh, while others head philanthropies and quietly travel the world. *Forbes* has estimated the Hillmans' wealth (as of 2017) at $2.6 billion. The family's reputation is firmly cemented to the nation's history. Yet today it is strategically forgotten, carefully airbrushed from popular accounts, that John H. and Thomas T. Hillman, two of America's great industrial barons, synonymous with modern innovation and success, prospered chiefly because they were carried on the shoulders of Black people subjected to an ancient, barbaric cruelty.

Many industrial families made their wealth this way: the McCormicks in Raphine, Virginia, whose McCormick Harvesting Machine Company, built with capital from enslaved labor, has today evolved into a multibillion-dollar concern; the Pratts of Alabama, their cotton gins, produced on an industrial scale by enslaved people, giving birth to parallel operations in iron, mining, and smelting; and the DeBardelebens, whose extensive network of industrial concerns, developed with seed capital from forced labor, survive under different names today. The research of scholars W. David Lewis, J. Mills Thornton, and Robert J. Norrell, among others, traces how vast flows of capital were conducted out of the "plantation order" into modern industry across Georgia, the Tennessee Valley, and Alabama. "Among Alabama's 55 leading investors in industrial and transportation ventures between 1840 and 1860," observed Lewis, "were several slaveholding planters and cotton factors."[53]

James Brown had financed enslavers so that those enslavers, himself among them, would grow rich. Here, then, was the next stage in that process, the next step in America's financial evolution. These enriched "planters" were building factories, plants, iron forges, mines, and sheet-metal presses. Like iron itself, made through the alchemy of conducting one form to another, the next more durable than the last, they were taking the riches, the money, pilfered from Black people's hands, and transmuting it from slavery to industry, and soon from industry to corporatization and investment.

Daniel Hillman Jr.'s wealth endured because he invested it into higher uses, into things that lasted, things that, as with iron, remained. He formed a conglomerate of new iron and coal concerns and, in the meantime, together with his brothers, purchased seventy-two thousand acres of land. The totality of these holdings, though rooted in the South, eventually became the foundation of one of the most lucrative industrial empires in the North. Hillman also took measures, through his strategic investments, will, and trusts, to protect and pass portions of this wealth to his sons. In 1865, he would give Thomas, on Thomas's twenty-first birthday, a $50,000 interest in the business, worth $1.4 million today.[54] The Hillmans' corporate partnerships endured through the Civil War and the dawn of the twentieth century, forming the bedrock of the wealth the family enjoys today.

Families like the Hillmans, long before the conflagration of Civil War came, it is clear, were taking pains to preserve and magnify their wealth, to posit it in vehicles and instruments unbounded by geographical or temporal limits, vehicles arising themselves from new industries, in the selling of stocks and bonds, investment, corporatization, and "the technology of wills and trusts," as one scholar has put it.[55] The reach of slavery wealth was intended to be broad and movable. Its reach was meant to be eternal.

CHAPTER 8

THE REACH

Trees toppled across the South, and white enslavers forced Black people in greater numbers to the picking and smelting lines. The energies of three million enslaved people were organized into an industry, industrial enterprises were increasingly fertilized by slavery, and the output of the system was shipped across the world. Consequently, the wealth of white Americans everywhere rose. "It is believed that, looking to the great aggregate of all our interests, the whole country was never more prosperous than at the present period, and never more rapidly advancing in wealth and population," President James Polk informed Congress in the State of the Union address in 1848.[1] Neither world affairs nor domestic concerns, Polk added, "had arrested our onward march to greatness, wealth, and power." The truth of Polk's message was embodied in no better symbol than the president himself, a man progressively enriched by the profits of coercing Black people to work for no pay.

Polk had owned a cotton plantation in Tennessee. He sold it to buy a new one in Mississippi, on stolen Indigenous land in the rush after Jackson's Indian Removal Act was passed. The sale enriched him even more. While occupying the White House, he plowed his new proceeds back into slavery, arranging to purchase and enslave nineteen more Black people in Mississippi. At least thirteen were children. The president of the United

States, sitting in the Oval Office, took elaborate pains to conceal these facts, arranging surrogates to make the deals, as Lina Mann, a historian with the White House Historical Association, has written.[2]

The lure of its riches being greater than ever, America's business of slavery continued to draw from great distances white men to its shores, as it had since Benjamin Marshall's time. Among those who arrived in 1850 was a passenger aboard a ship from the small German hamlet of Rimpar in the then kingdom of Bavaria: Mayer Lehman. After disembarking, this young immigrant traveled to Montgomery, Alabama, where his brothers and other men known to him had formed a small community, a network of traders and grocers specialized in the sale of cotton that enslaved people made. Montgomery was then a center of its production, and its town center, Court Square, was consequently a center for the buying and selling of Black people, hundreds of whom were paraded down the wood-clad streets each month.

Mayer Lehman, then twenty years old, took his place among this thriving outpost of slavery capitalism and, together with his brothers, opened a shop there on Court Square. His involvement in the cotton trade, small at first but growing rapidly with time, transformed his family's fortunes, creating a still-intact dynasty. His fortunes from slavery also helped transform the South, and later, the banking industry of Wall Street. The siblings called their business Lehman Bros. & Co.

Slavery was transforming the destiny not only of presidents and immigrants, but the finances of the nation overall. In 1812, the revenues of the US Treasury had been so meager as to compel the federal government, then preparing for war with England, to borrow $16 million from banks in Philadelphia and New York.[3] By the 1840s, thanks to slavery, the nation's financial outlook had dramatically changed. The stupendous cotton export, the volume of imports brought back to the United States on exchange, and the duties collected on these foreign goods, amounting to $32 million in 1834 alone, swelled the national coffers. So rich was the growing republic that it paid off its foreign debt to the tune of more than $100 million.[4] Explained Guy S. Callender, the economic historian, in 1902: "No other country had ever paid off a national debt."[5]

Northern states continued to disavow that they either enabled or benefited from this tide of wealth, but southern enslavers and their proponents knew this not to be true. They continued calling out northern hypocrisy in public protestations, but they also began to do something more: they began documenting, rather meticulously, the financial flows saturating the North from the evil institution of which they claimed to have no part. As a result, it became a salient feature of American slavery in this period that a vast array of the country's public and private institutions kept consistent, prolific, and detailed records not only of Black people's enslaved labor and its output, but of the commercial value these commodities produced. This included volumes of datasets and statistics compiled by the US Department of the Treasury, as well as the US Department of Commerce, the Bureau of Agriculture (today the USDA), and the US Census Bureau. Documenting the wealth of the slavery industry became an industry all its own.

It also included a robust stream of works, articles, and compilations exactingly rendered by leading newspaper and magazine editors attuned to these statistical riches, the most prominent of whom in the North was an editor named Thomas Prentice Kettell. His southern counterpart was a writer named James D. B. De Bow, editor of the eponymous *De Bow's Review*. In 1856, Kettell produced one of the enduring tomes of his age, a two-hundred-page statistical treatise emblematic of the South's quest to marshal, almost as a weapon, data legitimizing its grievances against the North. Though a New Yorker, Kettell was fervently supportive of slavery and the South. His aptly titled *Southern Wealth and Northern Profits*, together with studies by De Bow and a host of publications—the *American Cotton Planter*, *Hunt's Merchants' Magazine and Commercial Review*, the *Niles' Weekly Register*—spotlighted, almost as tragic drama, how the vast labor fields of southern slavery (Kettell calculated the total at more than fifty million acres) were producing wealth untold and unseen in the history of the world. Though, as we'll see, the question Kettell and others insistently asked, as his title suggests, was where this wealth was going and who ultimately was reaping it.

Much of this documentation survives. It is at once a record of preservation, but also of destruction, a wealth of information floating over an abyss of history, the riches Black people made meticulously catalogued and detailed, even as their names and stories were systemically erased. Such statistical observations had been recorded since the late 1790s, and certainly from the 1820s, but nothing on the scale of this, a documentation endeavor whose bureaucratic, organizational efforts mirrored the intensifying industrialization of a labor system whose brutalization would soon trap as many as four million Black people's lives.

There are problems to be sure with statistical tabulations taken from such an era—an era not known for the reliability of its figures. There are questions of accuracy, questions of provenance, questions of statistical corruption, questions of bias above all, and so on. But these are, on the other hand, some of the only statistics of their kind that exist, compiled from the official records of our government at the time and, as such, serve as a rudimentary accounting. To the extent that these stats are trustworthy, they allow us to put figures to the value of slavery's production, thus gaining some semblance of the size of this horrible institution's wealth. Such a tabulation isn't meant to quantify that horror itself but to give a sense of the riches that white people made through calculated brutality. To be sure, a dollar put to slavery's output cannot contain all that enslavement took from Black people, all that countless communities and individuals lost.

After the Panic of 1837, the price of cotton never reached above twelve cents a pound again, yet the overall production, in tons, unceasingly increased. With cotton lands greater than at any time in history, and more enslaved people to cultivate the bolls, US cotton production exploded to 654 million pounds in 1840, more than five times the harvests of 1820. In 1841, the cotton that Black people cultivated, and that was exported abroad, was valued at $61 million, or $1.87 billion today. By the year 1850, that figure would nearly double, reaching $120 million then, or $4.1 billion today. Available statistics show that in the nine years between 1841 and 1850, Black laborers toiling to extremity in the South produced a total bounty of cotton that was worth $752 million then or, conservatively, $23 billion today. Over the next ten years, between 1851 and 1860, enslaved people would go on to create a cotton bounty amounting to $1.675 billion then, meaning more than $51 billion today.

These were staggering sums, and their scale is even better appreciated when viewed in relation to public finance figures, private wealth production, and capital investments in the United States at the time. As it happens, a congressional investigation into American wealth, undertaken and released in 1853, gives us a sense of such figures, allowing us

the chance to make such a comparison. Congress undertook this assessment because it was concerned about issues of possible corruption at
the time, including the fact that foreign nationals, namely financiers in
Great Britain, owned a very large stake of the country's wealth. Relying
on Treasury accounts, its findings revealed that stock ownership in the
United States—comprising the stocks and bonds of 113 cities and towns,
347 counties, 985 banks, 75 insurance companies, 360 railroads, 16 canals,
and 15 other corporations—amounted to $1.4 billion then.[6] It means that
the wealth enslaved people created through cotton in just ten years—
$1.675 billion—constituted more wealth than white people held in all
the major stocks of the United States. What's more, the very bodies of the
more than three million Black people that white people enslaved, worth a
combined value of some $1.8 billion, easily trumped the value of Ameri-
ca's corporate wealth.

Homing in on bank capitalization and road construction proves even
more illuminating. The total amount of money invested in 985 bank stocks
by 1853 was reported at $266,724,955;[7] the capital invested in road con-
struction in 1852 (with 12,628 miles under progress) was $252,560,000.[8]
In just two years alone, 1855 and 1856, Black people cultivated cotton for
white enslavers worth $256,500,000 then, nearly as much as this bank
stock, and more than all the roads being laid in the nation in 1852. Year by
year, slavery created wealth for which there were few parallels in our history. For good reason, the US Department of the Treasury itself reported
in 1852: "[Cotton] is the main source of the prosperity of the mechanic,
the artisan, and other laboring classes, as well as that of the merchant and
manufacturer, in every section of the Union. Everywhere it has laid, broad,
and deep, and permanent, the foundations of the wealth and strength of
the United States, and of their independence of foreign nations."[9]

Let us consider these cotton figures in their aggregate. All told,
between 1790 and 1865, the period for which we have reliable statistics,
Black people's stolen labor cultivated harvests of cotton that were valued
at a total of $3.9 billion then. (This figure includes both cotton exported
abroad and cotton consumed domestically.) At a very conservative conversion rate, this equates to $171 billion today that was produced in the life
of the cotton industry before the Civil War. The figure is astonishing in its
own right. Even so, it doesn't account for how this astronomical amount of

money would have multiplied and compounded through investment and interest over time. The true figure is more likely several trillion dollars, and perhaps even higher than $50 trillion, according to conversion estimates using the tools of the website MeasuringWorth.com.

To be clear, we are speaking only of cotton. And, of course, cotton was but a portion—though a large one, to be sure—of the overall agricultural wealth that Black people's stolen time created. There was also sugar. In 1803, when the United States purchased Louisiana from France, there was hardly any sugar production to speak of. Within just thirty years, Black people's energy, exploited by white men across the reaches of the South, produced outputs of sugar that totaled one-sixth of all the supply in the world. The United States became a sugar power to compete with Cuba and Brazil. In the process, it forever changed the production and consumption of foods, global tastes, and corporate fortunes.

In 1850 alone, Black people working in sugarcane fields produced a record harvest of 237 million pounds of sugar, which combined with molassses and other products, had a value that year of $13,738,190.[10] That would be equivalent to at least $531 million in today's currency. The total value of sugar produced by Black people in the slavery years of the republic totaled something on the order of $1 billion, or more than $28 billion today.

There was also rice. In 1821, enslaved people across the Carolinas and in Mississippi produced rice with an export value of $1,494,307 ($35 million today). By 1840, the number had risen to $1,942,076 ($60 million today). In the decade between 1840 and 1850, that output exploded, with enslaved people producing $23,589,774 worth of rice exports ($729 million today). All told, the value of rice produced by enslaved Black labor in the United States and exported abroad amounted to $78,918,986 ($2.28 billion today). [11]

Finally, there was tobacco. Available statistics reveal that the value of tobacco produced by enslaved people between 1817 and 1856 amounted to $315,231,962 ($9.13 billion today).[12]

It is possible that these figures do not capture the entire scope of such agricultural productions, given that more cotton, sugar, rice, and tobacco was likely produced than recorded. Yet already these figures present exceptional furnishings of material wealth. And they are but a portion, for this is to say nothing of wheat, corn, hemp, indigo, whiskey, gin, and countless other commercial products produced in the zones of enslavement. Taken together, the total value of merchandisable wares produced by enslaved people in the period between 1790 and 1865—and we are excluding the values of their lost wages, and the value that white men placed on their bodies themselves—likely exceeded $6 billion at that time, or $215 billion today, a figure that is more accurately in the trillions if we factor in growth through investment and preservation.

———

WHAT THOMAS PRENTICE Kettell, James De Bow, and many others sought to ascertain was not only how much wealth such as this the South was producing but who was actually reaping the benefits. Using statistics available to them at the time, Kettell, De Bow, and others were led to conclude that this wealth was not pooling in the South, building the foundations of southern industry, southern shipping, or even southern banks. In each of these areas, the southern states, compared to the North, lagged noticeably behind. This seemed not to make sense: paradoxically, the South, though serving as the abode of all the nation's enslaved laborers and the progenitor of so much national wealth, was far less affluent, developed, and industrialized than the North. Such a scenario led the abolitionist Theodore Parker to conclude: "There is no State in the Union but it is poorer for Slavery."[13]

In fact, both northerners and southerners, whether pro-slavery or pro-abolition, widely observed a theme in this period, and it contradicts our current tightly held perceptions: slavery was creating wealth, but the men truly profiting from it were not, broadly speaking, the so-called southern planters, the owners of plantations and managers of the enslaved. What Kettell and others found looking at such men was that they were chronically in debt, many on the verge of being broke. Slavery, at least for those directly inflicting its barbarities and daily oppressions, was often a penniless pursuit.

This had been a feature of the enslavement system for a long time. In 1826, no less a figure than Thomas Jefferson, aging Founding Father and enslaver of four hundred Black people, had written from Monticello to his bankers on Wall Street to say, regrettably, that his loan payments would be late. Jefferson's creditors were the patrician firm of LeRoy, Bayard & Co., founded in 1787. The author of the Declaration of Independence had first taken out personal loans with them in 1790, while ambassador to France. The US government, then a fledgling enterprise often in arrears, had been unable to pay his salary. Like thousands of enslaving profit-seekers around him, this most eminent of statesmen also couldn't avoid the slick pull of Wall Street's easy money, the spiraling vortex of its damning credit. The original amount of Jefferson's loan had been only $45, but the small loan was "too carelessly neglected from that time," as Jefferson explained in a letter, and his principal eventually ballooned to more than $6,000 ($126,000 today).[14]

This happened in large part because Monticello, where enslaved people were forced to produce flour, wheat, and tobacco, was a labor camp grossly unfit to meet its own rising costs and crushing debts. It remained incapable, well into the 1820s, of furnishing the material means for Jefferson to pay down his Wall Street debts, namely in the required quarterly remittances. (The plantation's account books list total debts by 1821 of more than $31,000, or $774,000 today.) In his letters, almost frantically dispatched from Monticello, Jefferson fretted over meager sales of tobacco, haggled with buyers, and pressed his Richmond agents to devise timely sales of flour, urging the proceeds to be sent on to Wall Street.

Plantation life, the act of enslaving others, did not for Thomas Jefferson ultimately furnish a good living. All through those years, he supplicated his bankers in chaste, often dotingly polite letters, bemoaning his inability to pay. Chronically, he asked for more time. Often he sulked about selling portions of his property to meet his obligations; almost always LeRoy, Bayard & Co. agreed to his concessions, forestalling such sales. "Most Cheerfully do we accord & sooner than expose the author of the Declaration of Our Independence, to unnecessary sacrifice of property," they wrote in 1822.[15]

Eventually, the Founding Father ran out of such time. Jefferson, though one of the country's largest enslavers, with a vast landed estate and agricultural operations, died, according to historical consensus, a somewhat impoverished man, the culmination of a life of chronic indebtedness. Even when he managed, though only after thirty years, to pay down by $4,000 his debt to LeRoy, Bayard & Co., Jefferson was struck again by financial calamity. The insolvency and death of a friend in 1820, whose plantation went bust, exposed Jefferson, as guarantor of that estate, to $20,000 more in liabilities, or $477,000 today, at an annual interest of $1,200. Jefferson called this "the coup de grace" to his own rapidly diminishing prospects.[16]

It may be that this Founding Father was possessed of a uniquely terrible business sense, either lacking in personal discipline to make regular payments or given to imprudent financial forecasting, or both. Or it may be that the financing of slavery estates, and the credit required to make them run, amounted to treacherous business.

Whatever the case, that Thomas Jefferson was on the hook to a Wall Street banking firm, evidently unable to make sufficient profits from slavery, reinforces the point that Kettell and others labored to make: enslavement was highly profitable, though often not for the enslaver himself. De Bow, for his part, calculated that a typical southern plantation owner, with one hundred enslaved people, might generate $7,000 in a season from cotton sales but lose $5,250 in expenses, or 75 percent, including commissions to factors, the cost of shipping the cotton to market, taxes, the cost of feeding enslaved laborers, and fees for overseers. The money left to such a "planter" was further diminished because, De Bow argued, most also had to pay off debts, particularly for advances received. If their cotton failed to sell at the prices for which they'd been given these advances, they could be ruined. "The natural, indeed the inevitable effect of this state of things upon the plantation States," De Bow argued, "has been to subject their industry to an indirect tax, which has consumed so large a portion of their annual profits as to deprive them, in a great measure, of the means of accumulating the *capital* equally essential to the success of commercial pursuits."[17]

Kettell's and De Bow's point wasn't that all plantation owners were penurious. The lavish dwellings and affluent lifestyles of many southern slaveholder families is firmly documented, reflected even today in the still-standing mansions they built in places like Natchez, Charleston, and Savannah. Kettell's and De Bow's point, in underscoring the fees and costs of plantations, was to highlight that the profits of enslavement were going somewhere else, to someone else.

In the process, their inquiries help raise an important question about the nature of the enslavement business, and that is the extent to which plantations were profitable at all. This is a question that scholars have long explored and strenuously debated since antebellum times. One modern consensus, led by historian Ulrich B. Phillips in the 1950s, concluded that by the close of the 1850s it was "fairly certain that no slaveholders but those few whose plantations lay in the most advantageous parts of the cotton and sugar districts and whose managerial ability was exceptionally great were earning anything beyond what would cover their maintenance and carrying charges."[18]

Other studies have suggested that a plantation's profitability was correlated to its size, with plantations of 293 acres or more exhibiting a positive rate on return, while those with 181 acres or less did not.[19] These studies, broadly speaking, tend to show that some plantations were highly profitable while many others were not, and that is not surprising, of course. But overall, what they do is point to a critical, underlying issue of concern to us even now: popular conceptions of slavery think of the plantation itself as the essential and primary locus of profit-making within the slavery system—in fact, as the only locus of profit-making, exclusively synonymous with the beginning and end of the flow of enslavement's wealth. But what if this is wrong? What if, as Kettell, De Bow, and many abolitionists as well also emphasized, plantations were not, as a rule, a particularly profitable point on the enslavement chain? Or at least, not as straightforwardly profitable as modern conceptions have made them seem?

It is worth exploring the question. It illuminates, in novel ways, dimensions within the flow and character of slavery wealth—dimensions that are important to understand if we hope to appreciate two interrelated questions about this history: Who really made money from slavery, and where did it go? One way to approach this understanding is to look at those plantations that *were* astoundingly profitable, that did generate large amounts of cash for their owners over a significant period of years. And what better way to do that than to examine the plantation enterprises of the man considered the largest enslaver in the history of the United States: Stephen Duncan, with his sprawling Mississippi holdings, the Reach. By the eve of the Civil War, Duncan and his family had come to enslave twenty-two hundred Black people on more than fourteen thousand acres of land. The

scale of this imprisonment is startling, the output of its forced labor astonishing: According to one of his biographers, Duncan's plantation complex produced in a single year 1.47 million pounds of sugar, 2.88 million
pounds of cotton, 60,000 bushels of corn, and more than 61,000 gallons of
molasses. The sugar and cotton alone that Black people produced at the
Reach was worth $438,000 in 1860, or $14 million in today's terms.[20]

Duncan's was surely not a plantation operation that struggled to survive. It was an industrial-sized labor camp, its sprawling acreage and labor
forces assembled over a period of thirty years. It was practically an agri-
business conglomerate, and Duncan, its corporate president. What this
means, among other things, is that the Reach was by no means an average
plantation and therefore is certainly not useful as a basis for understanding
the "typical" enslaver in the South. On the other hand, its superlative size
and success tell us much about slavery's wealth, including the tiers inherent within this system, the scales of market share, and the kinds of people
who were growing rich from plantations. The Reach's success, moreover,
allows us to trace what large-scale enslavers did with their money—where
it went, so to speak.

If we consider the fact that Duncan's twenty-two hundred enslaved
people produced in the year 1860 2.88 million pounds of cotton, and if
we consider that the total output of cotton produced in the United States
in that year was 2.154 billion pounds, we're left to conclude, roughly
speaking, that Duncan's operations were responsible for 0.13 percent of
the nation's total cotton harvest. On one hand, this is astounding, and the
fact that one plantation operation produced so much elucidates, within
the enslavement business, the scale of possibility; on the other hand, that
even Duncan, someone with such vast amounts of land and labor, could
account for only 0.13 percent of supply, gives us a keen sense of the limits
of this business, namely the limits of market share.

Looked at another way, we also deduce that Duncan's bales of cotton in 1860 were valued at $317,196 while the total value of cotton crops
produced in 1860 was $246 million. So once again, he accounted for .013
percent of the overall value of cotton crops that year. The point is: Stephen Duncan's plantation complex was generating abundant amounts
of revenue from cotton, and while certainly not small, these cotton revenues were small relative to the market's overall size. If that was the case for

Duncan, the nation's superlative enslaver of Black people, we can imagine the constrained output and market share of much smaller plantations down the chain.

Note that in making his calculations about plantation expenses, De Bow used as an example a plantation with one hundred Black people enslaved, in other words, quite a sizable amount. We can infer that plantations with even fewer "hands" would generate even less revenue, struggling all the more.

Duncan's example shows us that it was those plantations endowed with extraordinary amounts of land, labor, and resources that generated extraordinary profits, the essence of Ulrich B. Phillips's observation. And that is important for this reason: there were few plantation owners in the United States who operated anywhere near Duncan's scale, and thus who could have possibly harnessed his level of wealth—very few indeed, according to William Kauffman Scarborough, author of *Masters of the Big House*, a study of the largest enslavers in the history of the United States.[21] Using census records and other documents, Scarborough set out to create a kind of ethnography, a snapshot both of the lives of affluent plantation families and the patterns according to which they invested their wealth.

Scarborough found that 339 white families in the United States enslaved 250 or more Black people. It means that in the United States, particularly by the 1850s, there was a very tight concentration of large plantations at the top of a pyramid, producing a robust agricultural output, and thousands of smaller plantations, spread throughout the southern states, producing a modest amount of cotton or sugar and, perhaps, as many observers have suggested, struggling to make ends meet.

William E. Dodd, in *The Cotton Kingdom*, spoke of a "rapid concentration of economic power in three or four thousand families who lived on the best lands and received three-fourths of the returns from the yearly exports." It was his estimation that a "thousand families received over $50,000,000 a year, while all the remaining 666,000 families received only about $60,000,000."[22]

Individually, these smaller families may not have generated great profits, but taken as a whole, their thousands of farms, making up the arc of the plantation system, produced a fantastic outpouring of agricultural wealth—$60 million, if Dodd is right, or $2.15 billion today—wealth that was literally compiled by the tons on the docks of the South each season, physically concentrated and compressed into the hulls of thousands of ships that then sailed away.

It was this movement that so concerned Kettell and De Bow. Their thesis was that southern wealth from slavery, broadly speaking, was flowing out of the South; it was flowing north, on those ships, and through paper notes, in circuits of credit and exchange; it was being taken in the form of northern commissions and storage fees; it was concentrating, most specifically in New York. Kettell, using US Treasury figures, calculated that the South exported to the North more than $462 million in goods each year ($16 billon today), and that northern businessmen reaped $231 million of the profits ($7 billion), or half. "The proceeds," he concluded, "are the basis of large moneyed operations at the North." He added: "All the paper, foreign and domestic, growing out of the crops, to the value of at least $1,000,000,000 per annum, draws directly or indirectly upon New York."[23] Kettell was crystallizing that to truly appreciate the story of slavery's wealth, it was not enough to look only at where this wealth *began* its journey: the plantation, a point on the chain where profits actually tended to dim. The true story of its value was to be found in looking at the journey's *terminus*, on Wall Street and other parts of New York.

It was a very similar argument that abolitionists, as we've seen, had begun making as far back as 1837, the time of the great financial crash, and from the 1850s onward, it was amplified by a wider range of voices, becoming a more mainstream view. "It is safe to say that two-fifths of this business, $200,000,000 at the least, is managed and controlled by New York merchants, or their agents, and that it affords a profit to the large and small dealers of that city of twenty per cent on the whole amount, say $40,000,000," affirmed such a writer in 1861.[24]

What physically made possible this movement of wealth, constituting a kind of yearly capital flight? It was that northern merchants, particularly on Wall Street, not only continued to own the ships—ships essential to carrying the bane harvests of enslavement—but also that these merchants owned more of these ships than ever. "In the decade before the Civil War," reports one source, citing figures from an 1852 congressional hearing, "more than 2,000 U.S. merchant ships, totaling 1,100,000 registered tons, and 55,000 seamen were employed in the coastal navigation that brought cotton from southern ports to New York. Another 800,000 tons of American shipping and 40,000 seamen were employed in the transoceanic cotton trade."[25]

The annual physical relocation of enslavement commodities, from deep in the interior of the South, through the Empire City, to markets dispersed throughout the world—the logistics involved, the manpower, the capital—remained one of the most immense and intensive enterprises in all the annals of US commerce. The South itself, meanwhile, still had no sizable fleet to speak of. What funds and profits southern enslavers were making from the systemic coercion of Black laborers they were manifestly not reinvesting into a transportation system of their own, nor, for that matter, into insurance companies to indemnify their cargoes. Most of those companies, to which southern plantation owners were paying fees of between 1 and 2 percent of their cargoes, were clustered in New York City, not Charleston, or Savannah or Natchez. "Is it the fault of Northern insurance companies that the South has no New York City with its $50,000,000 invested in the insurance business?" a trade magazine mused in 1860.[26]

The same could be said of financial institutions. The assertion that capital was draining out of the South was reinforced by observers who studied the nature of southern banks, namely the discrepancy between the level of their deposits and the revenues generated by enslavement commodities. Pointed out William E. Dodd, in The Cotton Kingdom: "Though the cotton, rice, and sugar of the South sold for $119,400,000 in 1850, the total bank deposits of the region amounted to only some $20,000,000. Ten years later, when the value of the crops had increased to more than $200,000,000, less than $30,000,000 were deposited in the banks of the cotton and sugar belt."[27]

Overall, the South, despite being a region productive of voluminous wealth, contained far fewer banks in the late antebellum period as compared to the North. Between 1850 and 1859, Kettell detailed, the number of northern banks increased from 516 to 934, and their combined capital reached $261 million. The South, on the other hand, created less than one-half the number of banks in the same period, and their combined capital, $104 million, was far less than half that of the North's. The wealth of slavery, so it seemed, wasn't amassing in the bank vaults below the Mason-Dixon Line.

"It is not a matter of surprise, under all these circumstances," the author of *Southern Wealth and Northern Profits* concluded, "that notwithstanding the large production of wealth at the South, capital accumulates there so slowly. All the profitable branches of freighting, brokering, selling, banking, insurance &c., that grow out of the Southern products, are enjoyed in New York." Kettell then added: "And crowds of Southerners come north in the summer to enjoy and spend their share of the profits."[28]

His summation points to a further element that, while certainly not representative of southern enslavers as a whole, was significant and meaningful enough to constitute an institutional feature of enslavement wealth in this period. Why was there so little money in southern banks as compared to the banks of the North? Because many of the South's richest men, in a decades-long dynamic reaching its nadir in the 1850s, had been transferring their capital to New York, sending their vast share of the profits of enslavement to bankers on Wall Street. Enslavement was a system in which wealth flowed in multiple directions, multiple ways: as much as a mighty torrent poured from New York, from the offices of men like James Brown, washing over the southern shores, the plantations of the bayou, and Chesapeake Bay, millions of dollars also left the South each year, toward New York, flowing the other way.

Stephen Duncan, even as he oversaw the Reach, was a banker himself, sitting on the board of several financial institutions in the South, including the Bank of the State of Mississippi and the Agricultural Bank of Natchez. Naturally, he circulated a significant portion of his capital through these banks, financing local land purchases and the purchases of ever more Black people. Duncan, meanwhile, lent large sums of money to other enslavers, taking Black people as collateral in return. But Duncan also consistently funneled large sums of capital to banks in New York each year, thereby buying up real estate, corporate stocks, and government bonds.

The richest men around him, a circle of lavishly affluent enslavers, men possessed of monumental plantations like Duncan's and known as the Mississippi Nabobs, did the same. Collectively they remained throughout their lives intimately connected to New York City's financial institutions, forming a living circuit of slavery capital flowing north. Like Thomas Jefferson before them, their primary banker was on Wall Street,

though the fortunes of these men never foundered like the aging Founding Father's. The Mississippi Nabobs all shared the same banker, in fact.
He was Charles Leverich, vice president of the Bank of New York, and he
kept their accounts in the most pristine standing over a long career.

Leverich was a telling story himself, one of four brothers, proprietors
of a family firm of great fame. Two of the brothers lived in New York, and
the other two in New Orleans. Together, they engaged in factoring, cotton purchasing, credit advances, and the management of large-scale plantations for enslavers throughout the South. They also owned plantations
and were enslavers themselves, their wealth, collectively, amounting to the
equivalent of more than $10 million today.[29] The Leveriches were at once
utterly unique and yet aptly reflective of the financial ties through which
southern enslavers endowed New York with their profits in this age.

Through Leverich and the Bank of New York, Levin Marshall, one of
the Mississippi Nabobs, funneled cash into northern railroad securities,
bonds, and real estate. His net worth exceeded $220,000 by 1860, or $7.4
million now.[30] Marshall's wealth came from enslaving 817 Black people on
sugar and cotton estates in Mississippi and Louisiana. With the proceeds
of their stolen labor, he built a mansion both in Natchez and another one
on Long Island called Hawkswood. Marshall kept a ready supply of cash
on account with Leverich, including nearly $52,000 between October
1851 and July 1852, the equivalent of almost $2 million today.[31]

Stephen Duncan kept similarly extensive funds with the banker and
engaged his services to manage his plantations, tasking Leverich, for
example, to purchase shoes and clothing for one thousand of the people he enslaved. In all the letters Duncan wrote, according to numerous
scholars who have studied them, he almost never mentioned the people
he enslaved, the human beings who made his prosperity possible. When
he did, it was almost exclusively to report they had died; he did so not out
of human concern but out of financial worry. The silence, as with so much
in this vile business, speaks more than the words. Duncan was more apt
to write to Leverich of the fine French cheeses, wines, and champagnes
he wanted, and that Leverich should send these on to Auburn, the Duncan mansion in Natchez, along with chandeliers and sumptuous furnishings from high-end stores in New York. In 1851 alone, Duncan deposited
$91,000, or $3.3 million today, into his account with Leverich.[32] The blithe

felicities afforded by Black people's forced servitude, there at the highest levels of the chain, wouldn't have been possible without the bespoke services of such New York firms. Wall Street bankers were the soft glove to the crushing hand wringing merchandise and riches from Black men, women, and children's stolen freedom.

The other Mississippi Nabobs were, as with Duncan himself, certainly no stand-ins for the average planter, and it would be difficult to say how much their northern investments generally and their reliance on Wall Street banking in particular were characteristic of enslavers in this period. And yet, though representing wealth and capital transfer at the highest echelons, the Mississippi Nabobs certainly weren't alone, as the work of William Kauffman Scarborough and others, including Morton Rothstein and Alana K. Bevan, shows. Additionally, historian Paul Wallace Gates traced how wealthy plantation owners plowed millions of dollars into buying northern land, paving the way, among other things, for railroad development in places like Chicago.[33]

In his own study, Scarborough found northern banking and financial connections among 73 of the 339 leading enslaving families he identified, and he detailed the equivalent of millions of dollars flowing from their plantations and other slavery enterprises into northern corporate stocks and bonds, hotels, real estate, and factories. With their wealth, these men, much as Thomas Prentice Kettell apprised, were enriching cities, banks, and industries far beyond the South. "Scarborough's study," Bevan underscores, "offers proof that some of the most influential and wealthy slaveholders lived in a cross-regional world."[34]

The connections show that the wealth of slavery, being a wealth of destinations, didn't often inhere at the level of the planter at all; that those "planters" truly endowed with wealth, luxuriating at the upper reaches of this system, were hardly worthy of the name; they were financiers and conglomerate heads more than farmers, "master[s] of capitalism who incorporated slavery as an integral part of [their] economic base," as Stephen Duncan's biographer, Martha Jane Brazy, calls them.[35]

The northward course of southern slavery's riches, conducted as they were in the form of cotton on a thousand ships, or one bank transfer at a time, denotes the notion that enslavement, being itself a system of epochal flow, cannot be perceived as a static story, a story rooted in place, a story fixated only on its *beginning*—the South and the plantation—but a story whose prevailing destiny, naturally, is what came at the *end*, where this vast and historical wealth ended up, geographically, and what it came to be, over the course of time.

The terminus of that journey was the harbor of New York and the brick-faced lanes of Wall Street. What grew there in the years before the onslaught of the Civil War, sourced from the bounties of slavery, protective of slavery, and pushing the country itself toward war, were the foundations and fortunes of a new force in the life of the American experience, the emergent reign of modernizing, industrializing, heavily capitalized corporations.

CHAPTER 9

THE MERCHANTS' DOME

The Merchants' Exchange Building sat on a stretch of Wall Street between William and Hanover, a solid block of blue granite, with a dome that soared more than 120 feet in the air, and a portico of eighteen massive Ionic columns. Inside, its rotunda was vast enough to hold three thousand people, which is to say, three thousand of the city's most elite white men. The original building had burned down in the great fire that swept New York in 1835, auguring the calamity on Wall Street that came soon afterward. Like the fortunes of the cotton kings, the Merchants' Exchange had been rebuilt by 1843, "the most splendid public edifice in the city."[1] By 1850, it had resumed its place as the nation's central temple of commerce, a gathering hall for its leading financiers and entrepreneurs—particularly its slavery entrepreneurs. They were among those who, with money from their reviled business, built this shrine to their own glory, at a cost of $1.5 million ($45 million today).[2]

Each day, these men congregated in the vast rotunda at two o'clock, a swirl of black hats and silk vests, a visual concentration of the nation's slavery affluence and power, indulging in further speculations and schemes. Thousands of corporations were represented under the dome. Among the throng were members of the boards of Aetna Insurance and Nautilus Insurance, writing policies on the lives of enslaved people, paying premiums on Black men killed in mines; along with dozens of directors of Fulton Bank, the Mechanics Bank, and City Bank of New York, their vaults heavy, and growing, from transacting the business of southern plantations, the so-called Southern trade. Also congregating there were the heads of the nation's shipping industry, presidents of the thriving Liverpool lines.

There had been no cotton ships of which to speak when Benjamin Marshall had arrived in this harbor half a century earlier. Now, outside the rotunda, just steps away, such ships crowded the piers of the East River abutting Wall Street, in historically greater numbers than ever; up the Hudson River, as well, they clogged the waterfront in chaotic lines, "a forest of masts," wrote one observer, "extending far toward Harlem on either side of the town."[3] The ships carried the sugar harvests of James Brown to the city, and officers at Brown Brothers & Co. could be found almost every day at the Exchange, arranging shipments and extending credit lines. The ships carried also the plantation yields of Stephen Duncan, Francis Surget, and other Mississippi Nabobs. Charles Leverich, their banker at the Bank of New York, then carefully orchestrated the proceeds through the stock exchange.

Under the dome of the Merchants' Exchange, these men constituted the corporate body of America, indeed, the earliest manifestation of corporate America itself. With untold riches from Black people's enslavement, they were creating more corporations than had ever existed in the country, or anywhere else in the world. And within the dizzying emporium of their business activities, lurking behind its illustrious facade, the corporate directors of Wall Street were all the while busy with something else: laundering the ill-gotten gains of global human bondage through New York, washing vast sums of money clean and organizing it into the foundations of America's industrial revolution, a sweeping phase of modernization deeply connected to, though seemingly untouched by, slavery's chain. The unparalleled expansion of corporate industrial power and wealth these men oversaw became a hinge for national prosperity, a bridge through which the riches produced by enslaved peoples were transferred across geographical borders, epochs, and time.

Moses Taylor was a leader among these corporate magnates. On Wall Street, they called him "the Dean of Banking." By the 1850s, Taylor's business dealings, corporate partnerships, and flow of contracts seemed to touch nearly every investor and industrialist of consequence in the United States. This included politicians, for Taylor was a well-regarded fundraiser and organizer for the Democratic Party, one of New York's so-called Democratic friends of Free Trade.[4] A centrifuge of money and power, the Dean could be seen each morning leaving the marble portico of his four-story home on Seventeenth Street and Fifth Avenue, heading south to his office at 52 Wall, a "side-whiskered autocrat" with a ruddy complexion and thin lips, as he was described.[5]

Taylor was the most prominent director in the history of City Bank, famously ornery, determined, and terse. The bank, then sitting on a stretch of Wall Street that was little more than a narrow sidewalk, with a plain front of hewn stone, had a flight of steps leading up to the main open corridor. Inside, on the building's expansive banking floor, lit by rear windows and encircled in mahogany railing, Taylor sat each day on a platform at the center of the room, "surveying his kingdom," a lord indeed.[6]

Ten years before the Civil War, he had almost single-handedly built City Bank into one of the most important financial institutions on Wall Street. He did it by conducting a thriving business with both southern enslavers and the leading enslavers of Cuba, commingling their funds, harvests, and barbaric practices with those of his private accounts and City Bank's. The global scale of Taylor's slavery ties, and the riches he derived from forced labor, would prove greater even than James Brown's. It was those lucrative connections to worldwide bondage that Taylor brought with him into City Bank; it was those operations that the bank's liquidity and services, in turn, amplified even more. And the result was that City Bank prospered spectacularly from global slavery, and Moses Taylor did too.

By 1850, the success of Taylor's slavery operations and the success of the bank were one and the same. "City Bank had no identity of its own," wrote Harold van B. Cleveland and Thomas Huertas, in their official history of the bank. "It functioned as a treasury for the many firms that constituted Taylor's personal business empire."[7]

That empire, tied by a hundred spokes to the leading corporations of his day, was an instrument through which the foundations of America's industrial revolution and the foundations of institutional white supremacy would eventually fuse into one—a singular vision of white progress achieved by extinguishing the possibility of Black equality. Taylor drew into his orbit a formidable network of the country's leading cotton brokers, plantation owners, and merchants of raw materials like sugar and metal, men positioned at the center of the country's exploding wealth, poised to invest the proceeds of slavery into a new financial age.

————

THE SURVIVING BUSINESS records of Moses Taylor—326 boxes of leather-bound ledgers, letters, and notes, most handwritten on brittle paper in a looping cursive script—are housed today in the rare collections room of the New York Public Library. For decades, they had sat forgotten in the basement of the library's main branch, covered in dust, until Roland T. Ely, then a young doctoral student at Harvard, set out to catalogue them in the 1950s. (Ely, while sifting through the collection, often wore a special face mask, due to the dust, a story he later recounted to the *New York Times*.)[8] Today, the Moses Taylor collection, accessible only by special appointment at the library, constitutes a one-of-a-kind window into the nexus binding slavery to Wall Street, telling an illuminating story about a man who, though still relatively unknown today, was a principal architect in channeling stolen Black wealth as he organized his business alliances against Black freedom. Through the figure of this most eminent of City Bank directors and an analysis of the records he left behind, we encounter an unusually perfect metaphor of his age.

City Bank's success as a powerhouse of lucre hadn't been assured. Quite the contrary. Taylor had joined the ranks in 1837, when the bank's fortunes, like those of many others, were nearly in ashes. "In all probability," wrote Cleveland and Huertas, the "bank stood on the brink of failure."[9] Taylor wasn't who initially saved it. Rather, a bailout came from one of his trusted friends: John Jacob Astor, then seventy-four years old, a wizened patron and arguably the country's richest man.

Records are scanty, but Astor appears to have kept a City Bank account. Among his sprawling business holdings had been a sizable real estate empire managed by a man named Jacob B. Taylor—Moses Taylor's father, with some histories describing Taylor's father as Astor's rent collector.[10] His son was therefore trusted by Astor as well. And so when the illustrious tycoon bought a majority ownership in City Bank, forestalling its collapse, he personally tapped Moses Taylor as a director.

Taylor was just thirty-one years old but already an eminence of his own, helming a thriving shipping, loaning, and importing empire. He'd risen by taking a different tack than the cotton magnates around him, escaping their road to ruin. For the roots of his business, though tightly bound to slavery, were diversified far beyond southern plantations alone. His deepest connections were to enslaved labor throughout the Caribbean, hauling on his ships thousands of pounds of Cuban sugar to New York each year. He also loaned money on handsome terms to the finca enslavers, Cuban plantation runners—money with which they purchased more and more enslaved people, and more equipment, expanding the most lethal plantations in the world. Through these Cuban connections, Taylor was entangled in a web of murky yet wildly profitable cartels run by white merchants (many of them based in New York), and these cartels kept alive, despite its having long been outlawed, the transatlantic slave trade. They loaded thousands of stolen African men and women into battered, flagless barks each year, shipping them to the markets of Cuba and Brazil.

As far back as the 1830s, his letters show, Taylor had been aggressively pursuing the leading cotton merchants of the South for business, proffering both his services and ships. His marketeering paid off. Not long after he became director of City Bank, his fleet was carrying thousands of pounds of cotton, rice, sugar, and tobacco from plantations in Savannah, Charleston, and beyond. His account books reflect that in the year 1842 he shipped $80,000 worth of rice alone, or $2.7 million today. (Taylor took the standard fee of up to 2.5 percent on these cargoes.)[11] He did so year after year.

What is revealing about these shipments isn't merely their scale but their destination: Taylor sailed much of this slavery-produced rice to the plantations of Cuba, where the island's most notorious enslavers paid for it on their accounts. These included the Drake brothers, Anglo-Spanish traders whose sprawling sugar estates, together enslaving more than four hundred men, women, and children, accounted for up to two-thirds of all sugar exported from Cuba.[12] Taylor, in other words, wasn't merely a high-volume trader with southern enslavers and Cuban enslavers. His business records show he was a critical node *between* them, an interface through which southern slavery and its rice output literally nourished the Cuban slavery system. Plantation owners used the rice produced by enslaved people in South Carolina to feed the enslaved people trapped on Cuba's cane fields.

Rice wasn't all Taylor supplied. He was also one of the principal sources of financing for Cuba's enslavers over a period of several decades. Finca owners like the Drakes subjected enslaved people to such brutally harsh conditions—physical abuse, disease, heat, exhaustion—that many died, on average, within just seven years of arriving to the island. Enslavers, needing constantly to replenish these ravaged labor supplies, turned to Taylor for ready credit and cash. The Drake brothers, Taylor's primary partners in Cuba, drew on Taylor's funds like a personal bank.

John Harris, author of *The Last Slave Ships*, illustrates one example of how this worked: Among Taylor's records is a letter documenting how the Drake brothers needed to pay a known Portuguese slave trader in Cuba, José Lima Vianna. The Drakes issued two credit notes to Vianna, for a sum of $12,000 or roughly $400,000 today. Vianna later brought the notes to Taylor's office near Wall Street, where one of his partners paid out the slave trader in cash. Vianna had "no business in Cuba except the slave trade," Harris writes, so we can presume that slavery was the basis of this transaction.[13]

Several other enslavers also kept personal credit lines with Taylor, including Lorenzo Jay, who held $322,435 on account, or almost $5.7 million today. And even those not on personal terms with Taylor ended up using his money. They turned to merchant bankers in Havana, and those merchants, in turn, were borrowing large sums from Taylor's private office, at 44 South Street. "Since Cuba possessed no 'legitimate banking system,' the merchant had to draw 'on his foreign credit' with such houses as Moses Taylor & Co. in New York," described Roland T. Ely, adding that without such credit, they would not be able to "obtain food and clothing for their labor force; to purchase Negro slaves in a rising market...to acquire land...machinery."[14]

Another historian, Maeve Glass, traced that Taylor's financial and shipping network came to encompass twenty-three Cuban plantations, "worked at any one time by as many as 6,000 and perhaps many more enslaved men and women."[15]

Moses Taylor proves a chief architect tying the Cuban system together. For simultaneous to fertilizing the island's labor camps with cash and grain, Taylor carried each year aboard his ships thousands of pounds of Cuba's ill-gotten sugar, which he then stored in his warehouses in New York to be sold later at auction to merchants and refiners. From there, Taylor's brown and white Havana sugars helped feed the burgeoning middle-class appetites of a city and nation growing addictively attached to the saccharine pleasures of confections, cakes, and sweetened coffee. Taylor recycled portions of the profit back into Cuba, arranging for enslavers to make purchases of US equipment and industrial machinery, including steam engines. Because of the constant revolving order of Taylor's involvement, the Cuban slavery economy grew exponentially through the 1840s and '50s, becoming the most mechanized sugar production zone in the world. Thus, its sugar exports also became the largest in the world, while the number of enslaved people trapped on the island swelled to half a million, up from 180,000 in the 1830s, when Taylor first began doing business there.

US newspapers in the 1850s recurrently highlighted the horrors of the system Taylor was underwriting. "This scheme of Slavery…sickens the traveler in Cuba at every turn," wrote the *New York Daily Times* in 1856, depicting enslaved people "driven to the field or the mill, like cattle, retained at work with the lash, and whipped cruelly for idleness or insubordination."[16]

Papers also reported how numerous American vessels, their ownership cloaked through false paperwork and other subterfuge, were delivering enslaved Africans at the rate of roughly six thousand a year to the markets of Havana, and for a profit of $365 per man, woman, and child, on average. The trade in Cuban slavery, in other words, was netting profits of $2.2 million, or $73 million today; it would later rise to $11 million per year, or roughly $366 million today, a stunning amount.[17] Newspapers repeatedly pointed out, without ever naming names, that it was New York businessmen, operating from the shadows, who secretly ran these slavery expeditions, and that "the immense profits derived from this business have proved too strong a temptation for many of our wealthy men." [18]

US Navy documents attested to the same, detailing in diplomatic correspondence the names of vessels that, engaged in the trade, were captured off the coast of Africa after sailing from New York, though their true owners always escaped censure, let alone prosecution.[19] "In the year 1852," states one such report, "an American captain, then demanding of his employers a certain amount of 'hush money,' stated to an American officer, that, not only American vessels had been extensively engaged in the slave trade, but American merchants in New York and elsewhere, had embarked a large amount of capital in the traffic."[20]

Was Moses Taylor one of these merchants? In addition to loaning money, and paying off traffickers for the Drakes, did he have a deeper hand in this detestable trade, contracting out his ships for runs to the Congo and elsewhere in Africa, taking a cut of the enormous profits? He was never so directly accused, either in news accounts or official diplomatic dossiers. But this fact, that Moses Taylor managed to straddle such worlds—at once blatantly enabling the viciousness of Cuban slavery yet avoiding all public critique for doing so—only reinforces that he was a deeply inscrutable, opaque figure, with one foot in the shadows and one foot in the light. It seems not far-fetched to question whether such a man, openly supportive of slavery and unabashedly engaged in extracting its profits, might also have been one of the unnamed merchants who, operating from behind the skein of respectability, took a direct yet hidden role in the selling of human beings. Evidence further suggestive of this fact would emerge over time.

————

It isn't clear how much money Moses Taylor ultimately poured into Cuba's slavery system, though certainly it would have been a tremendous amount. Clearer is what Taylor, and City Bank, got out of it: a wash of enormous profits, from sales of sugar, but also returns on loans to Cuban plantations. By 1842, Ely calculated, Taylor's overall wealth stood at $350,000, or $11 million today. Of that, he took $200,000 in profits from the Cuban sugar trade, or $6.2 million, and reorganized his personal business into an investment company.[21] One of the most significant things Taylor did with these funds, money inextricably linked to slavery, was invest $11,738 ($403,000 today) in City Bank stock, taking a large ownership stake in the bank. It was a trend that would continue: by the time he died, Taylor owned one-third of the bank.[22]

City Bank also prospered. It is important to recall that "Taylor, his business associates, and the companies they controlled supplied most of the bank's deposits," writes Hazel J. Johnson in her study of antebellum banking, *Banking Alliances*.[23] Thus, the substantial sums Taylor was extracting from enslavement, both in the South and in Cuba, formed an important core of City Bank's growing deposits. Add Cleveland and Huertas: "As Taylor's business empire grew, so did City Bank." The bank's total assets increased from $1.7 million in 1837, when Taylor became a director, to $2.1 million by 1844, when he organized his investment company, and to $3.3 million by 1858.[24]

It's said that Taylor rose early and arrived at the bank each morning by nine. His letters are a barrage of opportunity and engagement, reflecting a frightfully busy man—overseeing ships, taking cargoes, buying shares, sending favors to Cuban enslavers, and remitting money, evidently, through circuitous means, to slave traffickers themselves. Taylor's business book was a huge vortex, nearly incomprehensibly so. And it was by seaming together these various revenue streams, in a helix braiding the southern and Cuban slavery zones, integrated with the finances of Wall Street, that he then began channeling his money into something even more lucrative and lasting for himself, City Bank, and the country: Moses Taylor & Co. began funneling wealth into mines, iron, and railroads, enterprises critical to the modernization of the United States.

Taylor's investing was promiscuous, driven by opportunity. He became a director of the Manhattan Gas Light Company, then took shares in its rival, the New York Gas Light Company. (Taylor would later oversee the merger of the two, forming what became Consolidated Edison.) He bought shares in southern rail lines and, meanwhile, helped build railways that opened the coalfields of Pennsylvania, including the Cayuga and Susquehanna Railroad, a critical transport hub for the country's coal producers. In 1848, he organized yet another investment firm, capitalized at $123,000 ($4 million today), with a partner named Percy Pyne, later his son-in-law. In 1851, Taylor incorporated the Chestnut Hill Iron Ore Company in Pennsylvania, its furnace and rolling mills remaining in operation until 1901.

His partners included William Havemeyer, a sugar baron with extensive ties to enslavement, and August Belmont, the New York cotton buyer for the famed Rothschild bankers of France.[25] In 1852, Taylor financed the coal investments of the brothers George and Selden Scranton, took a one-third share in their operations, and eventually became a leading stockholder in their Lackawanna Iron and Coal Company. As these corporations proliferated under Taylor's hand, dozens of new corporate directors took their place in the Merchants' Exchange rotunda, swelling the ranks under the Merchants' dome.

By 1855, Taylor had become one of the nation's leading coal producers. At the same time, he was also handling sales of Cuban sugar worth a staggering $2.5 million a year, or $76 million today; he netted an average profit of $200,000 per annum, or $6 million, according to Ely. His star kept rising. Taylor became in 1856 City Bank's single largest shareholder. He was also elected its president that year, a position he would hold for almost three decades. At the height of America's great sectional crisis over slavery, City Bank and Moses Taylor—fulcrum of Cuban bondage, banker to southern plantations, fierce antagonist to abolitionists—were effectively one and the same.

It's not just that Taylor made industrial investments with his own money; his firm, using the facilities of City Bank, also invested and organized the riches of enslavers, both in the South and in Cuba. Among them was Tomás Terry, one of Cuba's leading financiers of enslaved labor. Terry, according to multiple accounts, got his start running slave ships from Africa. In 1851, he began investing his own slavery wealth with Moses Taylor, buying, from his large estate on Cuba's southern coast, a vast book of American securities. Among his first purchases, Terry bought $10,688 ($391,000) worth of stock in Taylor's Forest Improvement Company.

This one investment alone invites pause. It crystallizes the unexpected mobility and stunning afterlife of the funds that are the subject of this book: how profits sourced from Black people's subjugation, hundreds of miles away, ultimately made possible investments as seemingly disconnected from slavery as Pennsylvania coal, which was crucial to the industrial revolution. Because of Taylor, Terry became in fact a major corporate investor, his portfolio of American securities worth over $6 million by 1875, or $153 million today. According to the scholar Daniel Hodas, Taylor by 1872 had invested at least $3 million (nearly $69 million today) "of Cuban planter profits…in the American economy."[26]

Taylor remained a unique and towering presence in this epoch of capital transfer. Few matched his commercial connections, his affluence, or the sheer range of his enterprises. Yet he was but part of a proliferation of similar types, other New York magnates passing wealth derived from plantations into the foundations of a new industrial order. Many were loosely tied to Taylor through commercial association or social acquaintance; others were more directly tied to the orbit of his empire.

James Brown, for one, had for many years been investing his family's slavery capital in stocks and government bonds, and by 1845 Brown Brothers had acquired 407 shares of City Bank itself, at a value then of $30,525, or $1.13 million now.[27] Slavery was cross-pollinating and fertilizing the corporate dominance of Wall Street and, meanwhile, financing large-scale infrastructure projects, such as a consortium of railroads. As far back as 1843, James Brown had been elected vice president of the Erie Railroad, and Brown Brothers & Co. continued infusing the railroad with funds throughout the 1850s.[28] Investing in the Erie Railroad put Brown on the same board as Anson G. Phelps.[29]

Phelps and his son-in-law, William Dodge, had, like Taylor, also been investors in the operations of the Scranton brothers and their railroad lines. Through that association, Phelps and Dodge became business partners with Moses Taylor directly, buying shares in the Cayuga and Susquehanna Railroad, which he controlled.[30]

Throngs of others congregated under the Merchants' dome, including the Minturns and the Grinnells, John Beers, and John Delafield, who sat on the board of Phoenix Bank, to name but a few. They invested in steamships, gas lighting, the first telegraph systems, and new incarnations of steel, not to mention canals, turnpikes, and roads.

So destructive did industry become to Black people's lives that southern mine and iron company owners, hoping to protect their "assets," began taking out insurance policies on enslaved workers. The policies became an industry unto themselves, and insurance companies, many headquartered on Wall Street, profited extensively from this lurid business. In one such example, Nautilus Insurance, later to become New York Life Insurance, found itself compelled to pay out premiums when several Black laborers were killed at the Mid-Lothian Coal Mining Company of Virginia. It was an incident that greatly vexed Nautilus's board, which was made up of many prominent New York slavery merchants, including James Brown himself.

Moses Taylor, James Brown, William Dodge...such men fertilized the industrial underpinnings of the nation with the proceeds of the labor stolen now from nearly four million enslaved Black people. Stout enough was the source of that power and wealth. But it was redoubled by something else, made everlasting by another dynamic: with this wealth pouring from unfree labor, the men under the Merchants' dome, and across the North, were building empires of corporations—immortal empires as it would turn out.

Men in the North—men of Wall Street—had driven a steady expansion of incorporation since the 1820s, when the Merchants' Exchange was first built. But it had accelerated during the 1840s, when six states passed laws for general incorporation, meaning that white men could found enterprises more easily without strict legislative intervention. By the end of the 1850s, fifteen additional states did so. The result was an explosion of corporations in the United States: between 1830 and 1860, men in northern states formed 11,574 new enterprises, nearly a 400 percent increase from the period of 1790–1830.[31] "The United States thus became what might be called the first *corporation nation*," observe Ralph Gomory and Richard Sylla in their essay "The American Corporation." They also say, "One of the less appreciated reasons for the rapid rise of the U.S. economy in the nineteenth century in comparison to other nations was the relative ease of obtaining a corporate charter in America."[32]

The result was that the use of the corporate form, granting limited liability and other protections, encouraged entrepreneurs to speculate in large-scale commercial and industrial enterprises like railroads and coal. These were enterprises requiring extensive infusions of cash and many investors. Because they took years to complete, such enterprises reaped profit over a long horizon of time. These were precisely the kind of speculative ventures that men like Moses Taylor, William Aspinwall, and James Brown, flush with the epochal, record-producing windfalls from enslavement, increasingly turned to in the latter half of the nineteenth century. The cotton, tobacco, and rice exchanged for sterling abroad, the sterling exchanged for dollars upon return, not to mention a circuit of credit and wealth flowing from plantations to Wall Street, seeded a diffusion of corporate seed capital.

The proceeds of slavery didn't drive America's corporate expansion alone, but it's hardly a coincidence that as the wealth of slavery rose, the concentrated power and riches of corporations grew, and the US economy expanded too—three dynamics which, though perhaps not dependent, were certainly intertwined. It was the chain of corporations these men built, and the profits from slavery invested in them, that would survive after emancipation, after the institution of slavery, and these men themselves were long gone.

Ironically, as the South and the North became ever more physically attached, interlaced literally by railroads and steam navigation financed by slavery wealth, the union was never more acrimoniously divided, fast dissolving politically and soon to fall apart. Not even the resources of the wealth of slavery would stop that.

CHAPTER 10

"THE UNION MUST PERISH"

In the decade leading up to the Civil War, when it became clear that mounting political strife could destroy the business of slavery and its vast production of wealth, an alignment arose under the Merchants' dome between bigotry and profit-making that was unprecedented in US history. This alignment has shaped the legacy of racial inequality up until this day, as the goals of the leading corporations in the United States and violent white supremacy became explicitly intertwined. The country's strategic vision of industrial development, as a result, became indistinguishable from the strategic violent denial of Black people's rights.

This wasn't a vision driven by southern enslavers and politicians but by northern corporate leaders, the founding fathers of Wall Street and corporate America, and what was unprecedented in this alignment of bigotry and capital was not merely its intensity of purpose; perhaps most unprecedented was its clarity. The early men of slavery profiteering—Benjamin Marshall, Jeremiah Thompson, and Archibald Gracie—had been pious hypocrites, donating to supposed causes for Black amelioration, but doing so with the riches they stole from Black people; they meanwhile publicly demurred on the issue. Even the colonizationists had professed an altruistic cause. By 1850, however, this had changed.

It wasn't enough, in other words, for these men and their corporations to grow rich from the exploitation of Black labor and turn a blind eye to its miseries; when abolitionists threatened their livelihood and their cause, they became increasingly bent on protecting the segregation of the nation and the privileges of whiteness. They grew determined, above all, to destroy the abolitionist movement and fight for slavery and for the supremacy of the white race if and when the cataclysm of civil war should come—a cataclysm that their own agitation and violence helped produce. In the process, the wealth of slavery itself, mobilized by the full might and resources of corporate America, became a treasury to fund the preservation of the nation's business of slavery and to prepare the ground for race war against Black people.

———

IN 1850, THE *New-York Daily Tribune* printed a white writer's account of traveling to Virginia and encountering there enslaved people being sold off at an auction. His passage, as it appeared to the public that morning in May, is quoted in full:

> Here they were subjected to a most particular examination. It was curious to see the manner of the speculators in examining their teeth. They would order them to open their mouth, then press back their lips with their two thumbs, just as a jockey would examine a horse. On a window-sill lay a large pile of manacles; some were constructed of a large rod of iron with handcuffs on each side, so as to form a row. The first lot sold was the white woman and her two children, that I before spoke of [he is referring to an enslaved woman with fair skin]. The auctioneer extolled her qualities by representing her to be a first-rate seamstress, etc. She was struck down at $1,105.
>
> The lackey of the place (himself a slave) then leads up a man about 25. "Unharness yourself, old boy," says he. The man, trembling like a leaf all the while, strips himself, with the assistance of the lackey, in full view of the street and of the female slaves. The lackey asks him what he is shaking for, as he is not going to be hurt. The auctioneer announces no scars on his back of any consequence, and the sale proceeds: sold at $455. Next comes a little girl of 13, about half white; then two twin

brothers of about 14, sold to different masters, one, I was told, to a South-ern trader; and so on to the end of the sale, when the gentlemen were thanked for their attention, and their attendance requested to-morrow, when they would be shown something nice. During the sale my atten-tion was called to the door by a string of slaves going past, chained together, probably on their way to some Southern plantation.

Altogether, this was the most heart-sickening sight I ever saw. I involuntarily exclaimed: "Is it possible that this is permitted in my own native country—the country I have loved so well, and whose institutions I have exultingly pointed to as an example for the world?"

I am confident that the most effective way for Abolitionists to gain converts to their cause is to send Northerners as far South as this place, and let them attend one of these slave auctions. Hard, indeed, must be the heart of one who could look upon such a scene and not blush for his country's shame. I remonstrated with some of the inhabitants for per-mitting such a thing among them. They all have the Bible and Christi-anity at their tongue's end, and are ready to point out passages to justify it, and show that it is a God-ordained institution. "If this is Christianity," I replied, "don't call me a Christian."[1]

Over a period of sixty or more years, white wealth taken from Black enslavement had underwritten steamships, iron, coal, machinery, and manufacturing. Profits from slavery formed the basis of a banking and credit system, not to mention a global transportation and shipping logistics regime. Slavery made possible international trade treaties, corporate part-nerships, and Fifth Avenue mansions. It furnished the very sugar urban elites swirled in their coffee, the cotton napkins with which they dabbed their mouths. Slavery had grown so entwined with America's prosperity, so much of the country's complexity and progress, that its vile origins in racial brutalization were strategically forgotten, easily erased. Yet here, in the newspaper, was all that complexity and progress stripped down to its cruel essence: the manacles of the auction and its iron rods, and the daily traumatization of more than four million Black people in the labor zones of the South.

New York, the financial center of the country, like the nation itself, existed in a divided, self-delusive state over this reality. On one hand, the cruelties of slavery were better documented and more widely broadcast in mainstream papers, therefore harder to deny. Yet on the other hand, the corporate directors of the nation, turning the pages of their papers in the morning, perusing the cotton prices before heading to the Merchants' Exchange, more willfully avoided the subject. The prevalence of news reports like the one in the *Tribune* highlights that for the magnates of Wall Street, a critical ingredient in their continuing success was a deeper commitment to the barbarism that made their businesses and private riches possible. Hard, indeed, must have been their hearts, as we will see.

In 1836, there were so few abolitionists that Theodore S. Wright, the reverend, warned when addressing them: "The whole land has been raised up against you, because you have labored to convince the oppressor, that he should no longer oppress. You have had to contend with a world in arms. Talent, power, wealth, the Government and the Church have all been roused against you."[2] Abolition had been a showdown between David and Goliath, David Walker versus the Goliath of colonization and its monied bank directors, aligned with southern enslavers. Now, however, the battlefield wasn't so stark, and Reverend Wright had occasion to reflect during another speech just a year later: "What gratitude is called for on our part, when we contrast the state of things…with the dark period when we could number the abolitionists, when they were few and far between? Now a thousand societies exist, and there are hundreds of thousands of members."[3]

Abolition's energy had crumbled old alliances, causing a dizzying array of new ones to burst forth. There were political parties organized around abolition (the Liberty Party), and abolitionists lodged in mainstream political parties (the Barnburners faction of the otherwise pro-slavery Democratic Party). The Liberty Party had broken from the Anti-Slavery Society, seeking reform within the electoral sphere, an idea William Lloyd Garrison abhorred. But then many broke from Liberty, forming a more mainstream party, Free Soil, which opposed slavery's further expansion but not its abolition altogether. In time, committed abolitionists then broke from Free Soil, and Liberty as well, and, joined by Barnburners, evolved into something new: the Republican Party.

"The highest offices of the U.S. government, Senators, and Representatives of Congress and of State Legislatures, politicians, pro-slavery clergymen and pro-slavery presses—all—all agree that the abolitionists are an enemy to be feared and respected," one observer wrote. "There is not a man in the nation, that any party would dare nominate for president, without *first* asking how he can conciliate the abolitionists."[4] Abolition had turned US politics into a frothing sea of white men's ambitions and concerns, their myriad private and conflicting agendas. Because, of course, Black people themselves, as well as white women, couldn't contest any of the elections these white men hoped to win.

In the meantime, the day-to-day dangerous work of abolition continued—a struggle from the pulpit, a struggle of community organizing, sheltering, and legal aid, a struggle that sometimes culminated in physical tussles on the street. Reverend Wright at that time lived in a house at the corner of White Street and West Broadway, a house that still stands today. Not only was he the first Black person to graduate from Princeton's Theological Seminary and one of the founding members, with the Tappan brothers, of the Anti-Slavery Society, but he was moreover the head of the New York Committee of Vigilance, first established in 1835 by a firebrand of freedom, David Ruggles. It meant that, among other things, Reverend Wright was a conductor in the Underground Railroad, assisting self-emancipated Black people to flee the horrors of slavery, providing them safe houses and secretive contacts to make their way north to cities like New York. Other men like Wright then aided them further in establishing new lives. (The Underground Railroad helped as many as one hundred thousand Black people escape the South, including an estimated forty thousand who made their way over the border into Canada.)

By the late 1840s, Wright and the vigilance committee were conducting several hundred Black people each year on the railroad, thus striking at the yoke of slavery. The committee provided transportation, succor, and safe passage; it paid lawyers to prosecute for Black people's freedom, both in southern courts but also in New York's; and its operations protected Black people against a wider reign of violence.

There weren't only the white bounty hunters, scouring northern cities to find and imprison those who'd escaped. There were also organized criminal gangs, principally in New York but throughout the North as well, including some with ties to the police. They were kidnapping Black people from the streets, under the pretext of their being runaways, so-called fugitives, and they were selling free people into slavery. "Children have been carried off from their play-grounds, while on errands, or in the darkness of night," the Anti-Slavery Society reported.[5] Such a kidnapping is what Solomon Northup, a Black violinist, captured in his famous memoir, *Twelve Years a Slave*, later made into the Academy Award–winning film of the same name. Northup was drugged and kidnapped from the streets of Washington, DC, by the same slaver trader, James H. Birch, who'd tried to sell Dorcas Allen.

Multiplying the terrors, authorities in New York and Boston, in constant and ever-disturbing rotation, were seizing dozens of merchant ships at port. The ships, it was divulged in arraignments, were those sailing to the African coast, kidnapping men, women, and children there and selling them into bondage in Cuba and Brazil. It was affirmed by no less than US naval authorities that New York was in fact the secret financial headquarters of this still-existing global slave trade. And the trade was run, moreover, by powerful businessmen, legitimate New York businessmen, who, though they could no longer traffic African people to the United States to sell them—the offense was punishable by death—had found a way to do it elsewhere, shrouding their involvement all the while. The New York Committee of Vigilance took aim at this trade as well, working to expose its evils but also to sue for the emancipation of its victims. In 1840, in fact, the vigilance committee, through financial and legal support, helped bring a case to the US Supreme Court, winning the freedom of Africans who escaped from slavery in Cuba. They had arrived off the coast of Long Island, in the now-famous ship called *Amistad*.[6]

Abolitionists, in other words, were no longer just *calling for* emancipation; they were *cementing* hundreds of Black people's emancipation. They were no longer *hypothetically* disintegrating the slavery system and its spoils. They were *actively* helping disintegrate it. Their actions were on a condensed scale to be sure, but their victories had a larger symbolic resonance, for the lawsuits they filed were argued on the grounds of habeas corpus, that Black people, whether trafficked illegally to Cuba, falsely accused of "running away" from the South, or self-emancipated, had a constitutional right, through jury trial, to prove that their enslavement was unlawful, because all humans were inherently born free.

In some cases, they won, winning protection from state courts, thereby setting precedents. (In 1840, both Vermont and New York granted the right to jury trial to self-emancipated people.) For Wright and the committee, plucking the spoils of the wicked while restituting Black people's natural-born rights was righteousness at work.

For the beneficiaries of slavery, both in the North and the South, the vigilance committee was bleeding their treasury, depleting their bane investment in human capital—plucking their spoils indeed. According to its own tabulations, the vigilance committee had conducted more than thirty-five hundred Black people to freedom by 1850. It meant that, because white enslavers valued each of these Black women, men, and children at $600 apiece on average, abolitionists had wiped nearly $2 million worth of slavery wealth from the earth, or something on the order of $65 million today. (According to one southern politician, the loss to the South, caused by self-emancipation, was at least $150,000 a year, or more than $5 million today.)[7]

So embittered was he by these losses that James Murray Mason of Virginia, during a session of the US Senate in January 1850, put the problem starkly in financial terms: "The property held by that part of the United States valued at hundreds of millions of dollars is the subject of wanton depredation by the people of the non-slaveholding States."[8] Senator Mason was railing against the Underground Railroad. The US census that very year documented him as the enslaver of at least fifteen Black people, roughly half of whom were children. Mason, in other words, was speaking from naked self-interest. Protecting this "property," including his own, was tantamount to ensuring the integrity not just of southern institutions, he argued, but "the fundamental laws of this government." As the Constitution had enshrined in its Fugitive Slave Act of 1793, he continued, the right of enslavers to recover all so-called fugitives from labor, the harboring of self-emancipated people, in open violation of this act, had "inflicted a wound upon the Constitution" itself. Emancipating slaves, attacking the Constitution, and attacking the nation were one and the same, in Mason's mind; they were essentially an act of war.

By 1850, many dominoes were falling that enraged the arbiters of slavery—the proposed abolition of slavery in the District of Columbia, for one. Violence hovered over the country, over the question of slavery's expansion into new territories, in this case California, Utah, and New

Mexico. Gridlock in government, coupled with agitation by abolitionists, promoted talk of the nation's dissolution. But, as Mason's speech crystallized, nothing rankled enslavers like the abolitionists' flagrant rebuke of this old Fugitive Slave Act; it not only bled their money but fertilized the expectant dream of slavery's downfall. "In our opinion, the open violation of this supreme law of the land, by Northern people, and Legislatures, and Courts, is the greatest wrong perpetrated by the North against the South," fumed the *Fayetteville Observer* of North Carolina. It added: "The Southern people cannot and will not stand this robbery."[9]

When Senator Mason took the step of proposing a new bill "to provide for the more effective execution of the stipulation in the Constitution relative to the recapture of fugitive slaves" the South rallied around the call, evoking the cause of retribution and defense. They did so in the blood-soaked language of near holy war, of a soldier carrying his banner across "an ensanguined battle-plain," armed against the forces "urging us onward to the brink of dismemberment."[10] Mason's new fugitive slave law, enjoining all citizens, not just legal authorities, to assist in renditioning Black people back to their enslavers, also proposed a fine of $1,000, plus possible criminal prosecution, for any person who refused to assist such proceedings whether in free or slaveholding states.[11] All citizens were expected, in other words, to conspire in manacling Black people.

Mason and his supporters, anticipating northern abolitionist resistance to the new law, warned of its dire consequences. "When such attempts are made," a southern editorial inveighed, "the whole South will present one unbroken phalanx, ready for any contingency other than an invasion of their constitutional rights."

In the North, the call to slavery's defense was also heard and received, in banking offices clustered along Wall Street, and under the dome of the Merchants' Exchange—received, stirringly, as a choice, as an ultimatum. How was it, after all, that New York's corporate directors could sit indifferently yet comfortably in their mansions, surrounded by riches, unmoved by the injustices of slavery on the one hand and unperturbed by southern saber-rattling on the other? The answer is they didn't sit passively indifferent to slavery at all. Corporate America would prove fanatically supportive of the injustices daily perpetrated on Black people through slavery, because peace and freedom for Black people would cost them tens of billions of dollars a year, the accumulation of riches they had built over a lifetime for themselves and their sons.

The building pressure of sectional conflict, the rising power of the abolitionists, and the practical threats to slavery's wealth that the Underground Railroad had achieved brought out their true colors now. And so northern industrialists, capitalists, bankers, and leading merchants like Moses Taylor, already tightly interlinked through financial partnerships, began to mobilize their networks, along with their capital, to prepare for war: a war at first to be fought in the streets against the abolitionists, but eventually a campaign against Black people seeking any life other than enslavement, a war to protect the white race.

———

ON MAY 15, 1850, the vigilance committee held its fifteenth-anniversary gathering at Shiloh Presbyterian Church on Prince Street, near what is today Lafayette. Samuel Cornish had founded the original church, then known as the First Colored Presbyterian Church, in 1822, and it also served as a stop on the Underground Railroad. The gathering, part of an annual abolitionist convention organized all that week in the city, had drawn a large, racially mixed crowd, among whom were many leaders of the abolition movement, including luminaries like Samuel Ringgold Ward, who became head of the vigilance committee when Theodore S. Wright died in 1847. That evening in the church, a treasurer spoke first, detailing for the crowd that the vigilance committee had already helped 151 Black people that year to escape to freedom. They were raising funds, the treasurer added, to help even more.

It was when the financial statements had been dispensed with and Reverend Ward took the pulpit to speak, that a gang of white men, who had blended into the crowd, began shouting, interrupting the reverend and taunting him. "I am an American," Ward was saying, when suddenly the rioters shouted, "A Black one!" Jeers and laughter rose from various corners of the crowd. "Yes, a Black American!" Ward replied. "The son of a father who fought in the Revolution!" A reporter for the *New York Tribune*, present at the gathering, recorded that supporters then began to cheer on Reverend Ward. "A Black citizen of New York!" he continued;

the crowd applauded. "A Black American am I—gloriously Black!"[12] At that, there were several more disturbances and yells, pushing in the galleys, and booing. Though several policemen were present, they did little to stop the interruptions.

The growing tension in the church had all the echoes of an earlier time, when rich merchants, aligned to colonization, whipped up mobs in the 1830s, mobs that had attacked the abolitionists in the streets for days and lit Arthur Tappan's furniture on fire. As in that time, here again, the leaders of Wall Street had been meeting for months in their mansions, devising all manner of schemes to crush the abolitionist cause—by fair means or foul, as they had warned. Historian Philip S. Foner, in his book *Business and Slavery*, traces that in February 1850, they had assembled at the home of Morris Ketchum to devise one such scheme. (Ketchum, one of the city's oldest cotton brokers, had invested his money from enslavement into machinery and locomotives.) The meeting pledged $10,000 ($358,000 today) to form a new pro-slavery newspaper, called the *Albany State Register*, to counteract abolition publications and their call. William B. Astor, John Jacob Astor's son, contributed $1,000 on the spot, Foner reports.[13]

In subsequent days, other corporate managers met and raised money to endorse pro-slavery politicians, including Senator Henry Clay and the Massachusetts senator Daniel Webster, both of whom were rallying support for the South's proposed new Fugitive Slave Law. Merchants also paid to print and disseminate those men's speeches.

As in the past, these slavery entrepreneurs also utilized the city's leading newspapers to whip up public outcry against abolitionists. For days leading up to the vigilance committee's anniversary, the papers had called upon the men of the city, as a dispensation of their Christian and patriotic duty to protect slavery, to confront the abolitionists in the churches where they gathered. "These abolitionists should not be allowed to misrepresent New York," wrote the *New York Herald*. "Here is where all political factions can unite. All who are opposed to having our city disgraced should go there, speak their views, and prevent it."[14]

The *New York Globe*, in raging capital letters, went further, singling out for attack a noted personality: Frederick Douglass, who was scheduled to attend these events. "One of the heralded orators for this Anniversary is the black Douglass, who at a public meeting, in Syracuse, on the 15th of January 1850, uttered the following infamous exclamation: LET THE UNION BE DISSOLVED. I WISH TO SEE IT DISSOLVED AT ONCE," the *Globe* professed. It called for retribution, bloody mob justice against Douglass. "If this Douglass shall re-proclaim his Syracuse treason here, and any man shall arrest him in his diabolical career, and not injure him, thousands will exclaim in language of patriotic love for the Constitution and the rights of the south, 'DID HE NOT STRIKE THE VILLAIN DEAD?'"[15] To lay hands on Douglass, and not kill him, the paper exclaimed, would be treason.

Whig and Democrat business leaders in the North, using the might of newspapers, had been violently intimidating the abolitionists for nearly two decades. But now the tenor had changed. Now the threat of local violence was amplified by the threat of violence on a national scale. That threat emanated as well from the nation's capital, after Henry Clay proposed his divisive compromise: a package of laws that would abolish slavery in Washington, DC, on the one hand, but grant the South its stronger Fugitive Slave Law on the other; that would admit California to the nation as a free state, but allow Utah and New Mexico to decide the fate of slavery themselves. The compromise, though designed to avert conflict, in fact paralyzed the workings of the legislature and instead occasioned daily talk of civil war. As Clay and others continued championing the compromise for months, hundreds of New York's corporate directors rallied to their side.

In early 1850, they gathered in New York to organize themselves into something they hadn't before: a political coalition dedicated to upholding all parts of the compromise, and especially to upholding slavery. They called themselves the Union Committee. Moses Taylor was among this new organization's vice chairs.

As one of their first acts, in March 1850, Taylor and his associates staged a pro-slavery rally that, attended by as many as ten thousand people, was unprecedented in the city's history ("We stand pledged, by our sacred honor and oaths, that whenever any slave escapes from service, and his master claims and proves property in him, we should yield him up," one of the speakers proclaimed.)[16] Taylor was presiding, flanked by thronging crowds, when the nation, its wealth, and its laws, was reconsecrated, in their eyes, as an order of white masters and Black slaves.

In the days that followed, these pro-slavery Unionists—at that time not a contradiction in terms—enjoined the city's able-bodied men, including its teeming wards of white Irish immigrants, proven and hardened loyalists, to protect their Constitution, since it had been "openly and shamefully violated in relation to fugitive slaves." "The time had come to vindicate the rights of the South," the newspapers and the Unionists bade.[17]

And so when the abolitionists' week of anniversary events arrived, the mobs obeyed, fanning across the city to attack. They were led through the streets by a man named Captain Isaiah Rynders, a former US marshal, noted thug, and underworld don rising through the Democratic Party. (In 1845, President Polk had in fact invited Rynders to the White House, thanking him for helping to deliver Polk's victory at the polls.)[18] Rynders was known to be involved in hunting Black people on the streets, grabbing both runaways but also free Black people to sell them into slavery. For years, his power had germinated in a demimonde of political back-office meetings, violent intimidation, and hired muscle; now the Democrats unleashed their most vicious instrument.

On May 15, 1850, his mob struck its first blow, disrupting an abolitionist gathering on Broadway. There, Rynders, the viper, had jumped onstage, where he came face-to-face, in a tense and singular moment, with two of the great luminaries in the abolitionist movement: William Lloyd Garrison and Frederick Douglass. ("A lean and wiry-looking man," Douglass described Rynders, of "a hoarse and thundering tone.")[19]

Just two months earlier, Rynders had appeared before a judge, charged with brutally assaulting a man at a hotel. Months before that, he had been tried, though acquitted, for setting the Astor Opera House on fire during a riot. In 1823, he'd killed a man in a knife fight in Natchez, Mississippi. It wasn't impossible that Rynders, often armed with a blade or a firearm, could have killed either Garrison or Douglass, or permanently wounded them both. He was there on the stage, as the *Globe* had inveighed, in a position to "arrest [Douglass] in his diabolical career."

Did he not strike the villain dead? In fact, when Douglass stepped forward to confront Rynders, Rynders, unmoved neither by Douglass's imposing physical stature nor his imposing stature as a man of international fame, threatened to knock Douglass down and then abused him with the N-word. Amid great shouting, a man in the crowd lunged with a pistol and looked to be about to fire on Rynders, but he was held off by the crowd. Rynders then tried to start a fistfight, according to witnesses, with William Lloyd Garrison, but Garrison refused, challenging him to an intellectual duel instead. Somehow, by the narrowest of the threads, the proceedings avoided descending into utter chaos.[20]

The altercations made clear the perilous stakes now converging in the battle between the powerful interests protecting the wealth of slavery and those fighting for freedom and equality for Black people. When the meeting eventually adjourned, moving to another location, Rynders and his men broke that up as well, and the police were called in.

The following day was Reverend Ward's speech at Shiloh Presbyterian. It was Rynders and his men who were again disrupting the meeting, shouting and booing. Their voices intensified as Ward came to the most pointed passage of his speech. The vigilance committee's work to help Black people flee from slavery, Ward expounded, wasn't a violation of the Constitution. "Ward understood the plight of fugitives since his entire family had been slaves on Maryland's eastern shore," the scholar Jamila Shabazz Brathwaite has pointed out. "[They had] escaped slavery and eventually settled in New York State."[21] Ward avowed that assisting self-emancipated people was an act of revolution, in fact—an act of revolution sanctified by both the Founding Fathers' document and the Bible itself.

At that, Rynders's men erupted in full frenzy, and "a general attempt was made by the rowdies to break up the meeting," records the *Tribune*.[22] "Fire!" yelled someone among the rioters, spreading panic through the church, and a woman in the crowd fainted. Other rioters surrounded and threatened a police officer who made to throw them out. In the meantime, Rynders, again rushing the stage, shouted down and threatened those who demanded he leave.

The heckling droned on, until at last, Ward and the others were unable to hear or be heard. "At times there were fights going on in different parts of the hall; threats to throw the abolitionists out of the windows, to set fire, and to tear down the building, were frequently made," observed a newspaper report, adding, "We consider the triumph of mob law as now fully established in New York."[23]

Other papers decried the riots as being among New York City's worst disgraces, a travesty of police misconduct (the police arrested no one) and a vicious attack on freedom of speech. "If men like Rynders are to become the properest exponents of national patriotism and national dignity," the *Liberator* railed, "Heaven save the Republic!"[24]

Nothing overtly linked Moses Taylor to these acts. The Dean was no doubt safely in his home. Yet as the pinnacle of New York's financial order and one of the chief organizers of its slavery Unionists, he was implicitly present, ambiently responsible, though unseen. Certainly, in the minds of the abolitionists, the link between Rynders and Taylor's elite financiers was abundantly clear. Frederick Douglass, writing days later about the riots, said of the instigators: "They have appealed to the mob, in the name of self-interest, as New Yorkers, commercially connected with the South."[25]

Moses Taylor and Isaiah Rynders occupied very different stratifications of the Democratic Party—the former, the highest rung, the latter, the lowest—and yet it was one ecosystem of racist, pro-slavery precepts, an ecosystem that would in fact bring the two men directly together over time. Until then, it was the privilege of Moses Taylor, Morris Ketchum, and other financiers not to show up for these brawls in the war being waged on the ground against abolition; it was their privilege merely to inspire them, to pay for the grandstanding that fanned the flames of tension. They controlled the tempests and the atmosphere of violence.

That violence flared again greatly when Congress, just months later, finally passed Henry Clay's compromise in September 1850. It remained a question whether individual states would popularly endorse and protect the measures. The South made clear its position: many enslavers hated the compromise, thinking it not stringent enough; they pushed state delegates to vote against it. In the North, abolitionists denounced the fugitive law as draconian, vowing to defy it. Another battle was to ensue, and Taylor and his coterie began organizing new measures to ensure that Black subjugation remained the basis of their wealth and power. What had started with Rynders, and dozens of rioters denouncing Black freedom, would grow into crowds of thousands, a national movement to protect the avowed supremacy of the white race and the industrial order it was building. "The land rocks with AGITATION…to smother the warm and generous sympathies of the people for three millions of men in bondage," decried the *Emancipator and Republican*. "In the name of the 'Union' slavery was defended and freedom denounced."[26]

These industrialists were building more than a new world. What drew them together, in tighter association under the Merchants' dome, wasn't merely the imperative of so-called progress. What drew them together was the imperative of defense: defense of the privileges they afforded to themselves as white people; defense of the privilege to profit from Black people's subjugation; defense of the notion that such subjugation was sanctioned by a Christian God; defense of the purity of the white race and the white purity of America. Simultaneous to building a new industrial order, Moses Taylor and the circle around him worked to institutionalize the racial segregation of the United States.

White men of their commercial class, being born into privilege, had long worked to reinforce their social advantages, and particularly white men of southern extraction. But never before had the northern merchants tied to slavery felt their privileges under such threat—threatened as they were by the rising power of the abolitionist movement and the growing notion of disunity through war. Nor had they marshaled so many organizational and financial resources to protect them. As historian Peter James Hudson has written: "These men of business understood that the protection of their economic interests was tied to the protection of their interests as white men. Race and capital were intertwined."[27] Another historian, Iver Bernstein, has called this order "free trade and white supremacy."[28]

The primary expression of this order, financed and managed by the corporate directors of Wall Street, became hatred: hatred for the notion of Black people's freedom; hatred for the possibility of Black people's equality; hatred for those who worked toward such goals. Moses Taylor and his circle set as their primary goal, almost in equal measure to their pursuit of profit and industry, the destruction of the abolitionist cause in order to save slavery and the nation. And if slavery couldn't be saved, then, they believed, it was incumbent upon white leaders like themselves to destroy the Black race through cataclysmic war, in this way fulfilling the divine destiny God had bestowed on the United States. It was men of the greatest slavery fortunes, men driving the country's financial evolution from their mansions on Fifth Avenue, their corporations hailed for advancing American progress and contributing to the country's legacy of financial excellence who became in this period the most active white nationalists of their era, or of any era, in the history of the United States.

———

Moses Taylor had never been a great orator, nor even much of a public figure. He was a man who, living for business, and for making money, was otherwise socially reclusive, in fact famously terse. "He fixed on me his keen eye, as if he would look through me: and then, sitting down, he listened to me for nearly an hour without saying a word," a close associate of his once said.[29] The causes Taylor passionately engaged he did so from the sidelines, as a shadow organizer—a convener and bankroller of more visible men; for good reason, he was called the Dean. In Cuba, he chose not to be an enslaver like the Drake brothers themselves; he chose to enable them with money from behind the curtain. That is why, for the next ten years, in pivotal moments that brought the Union Committee into full clash with abolitionists, clashes that helped pave the nation's path to civil war, we find the handiwork of Moses Taylor woven throughout the background, recurrently inscribed, like a thread. Taylor was outspoken not in words, but through other means.

In October 1850, the Union Committee called a huge rally in New York. "Never has there been a more imposing public meeting in our city... in moral force, intellectual weight, and dignity, and real power," reported the *New York Express*.[30] Thousands thronged in fanatical support of slavery. They filled a building near the battery called Castle Garden and spilled out into the surrounding avenues from its circular hall. The meeting's energies, drawing from the street and deposits of white bitterness, brought forth two new figures who, like Captain Rynders before them, gave violent new shape to the vocabulary of white supremacy and its aims. They were James T. Brady and Charles O'Conor, both lawyers, both northerners, both hardened proponents of the southern cause. Moses Taylor was presiding as, banners fluttering with the motto of "Union," Brady and O'Conor stoked the hostilities of the Garden's all-white crowd.

"I hate the abolition party," Brady fumed, and had earlier said, "They are addicted to any color, and any reform except that of the race to which they belong."[31] The Union Committee, through the figure of Brady that night, and for years thereafter, reduced patriotism to the starkest of binary choices, choices incumbent upon all white men as demanded by their race, literally white versus Black. "The enemies of our Union base all their wicked efforts on an affected love for the blacks,"[32] Brady said. In other words, one could love the nation or love Black people, but not both. O'Conor echoed similarly stark choices: the union could have continued white prosperity, predicated on Black subjugation, or it could have war. "Let us not jeopard these prospects by dissensions about the African," he told the crowd.[33]

O'Conor was a man who, proudly advocating no existence for Black people other than enslavement, grew in power from that night, rising through the ranks of the Democratic Party and the echelons of government, where he worked to ingrain his bigotry as policy until the outbreak of the Civil War. "Whatever may be thought of the negro's capacity for improvement," he said, "it is not wise, benevolent or patriotic, by a doubtful experiment in that direction, to hazard the prosperity of the countless millions of white men for whom Providence has appointed this continent an asylum and an abode."[34] Such was O'Conor's clarion call.

Both he and Brady closed that evening with an evocation of approaching racial war. "If that struggle should ever occur," said Brady, "I know that I speak your sentiments, in declaring, that whatever may befall, we will stand by our own race, and aid it in the fulfillment of the glorious mission for which it was unquestionably designed."[35] It was a showdown likely, the Union Committee believed, to result in the extermination of Black people, and northern white men were called upon to fight not for liberty or the union as much as their own race.

The Union Committee was already a powerful body, boasting thousands of the North's richest men, among them the core of Wall Street magnates bound to southern slavery—"cotton operators," as the press called them. That evening, the committee sought to concentrate its power and activities even more. With O'Conor officiating, it appointed fifty men to the vice presidency of a new group, a kind of corporate council pledged to disseminate racially divisive views, uphold Henry Clay's compromise, and protect the right of enslavers, particularly their right to capture so-called fugitive slaves. This new council they called the Union Safety Committee.

Its title was chosen to connote existential perils and threats—the threat, above all, of Black freedom and equality, which would end the privileges of racial supremacy to which the white men assembled at Castle Garden had grown all too dear. ("Where slavery is abolished the slaves must be put on an equality with the whites," George Wood, the committee's president, had professed that night, to which the crowd voiced: "Never.")[36]

Moses Taylor was among the fifty men appointed vice president. Also appointed was a man named John H. Brower. He was a fellow City Bank director whose business, centered on advancing credit to plantations in Texas, tied him directly to Black people's enslavement.[37] Presidents of insurance companies, directors of shipping lines, and directors of multiple banks, not to mention other corporate officials, stocked this enterprise of white supremacy, braided together with its prominent lawyers and financiers at the top, and the street power of Captain Rynders and his legions at the bottom. Several thousand of New York's corporate ranks officially endorsed the Garden's proceedings in a publication disseminated after that night. Among them were William Dodge, and Brown Brothers & Co.[38]

The Union Safety Committee, working to disintegrate the possibility of abolition, put in place a kind of infrastructure—legal, financial, operational, and political—of white supremacy that operated for the next ten years, and even beyond. It showered the equivalent of millions of dollars on its enterprises. It began by targeting the church, by turning preachers against abolition, and raised $25,000 ($914,000 today) to do so. According to historian Philip S. Foner, Brown Brothers & Co. topped the list of patrons, with $1,000 in this effort ($36,600 today).[39] Its money helped produce a pamphlet, written by a pastor in Buffalo, John C. Lord, that justified the capture and rendition of so-called runaway slaves. Lord did so with the doctrine of Christian theology: "The forms of freedom are of little consequence to him who is made by color and caste a 'hewer of wood and drawer of water,'" he wrote.[40]

The hundreds of thousands of copies of Lord's sermon that Taylor and his circle disseminated across the country, including in the halls of Congress, had its desired effect. The pulpit became an organ of support for the Fugitive Slave Law across the North. In Boston, Rev. W. M. Rogers told his congregation: "When the slave asks me to stand between him and his master, what does he ask? He asks me to *murder a nation's life*; and I will not do it because I have a conscience—because there is a God."[41]

A nation's life was on the line in the war over slavery—its commercial and financial life, above all. And so the Union Safety Committee arrayed not only preachers to rail against self-emancipation; it organized a team of lawyers. The lawyers fought in court to ensure that captured "runaways" were remanded to their enslavers in the South. The committee underwrote these legal actions as much to safeguard the South's "property" as to send a message to Black people that slavery was where they belonged.

This included one of the earliest and most famous of such cases, involving Henry Long, a Black man from Richmond, Virginia, who sought his freedom in New York. Long was arrested by marshals and thrown in jail. His enslaver back in Virginia was John T. Smith of Russell County. The Union Safety Committee arranged for George Wood, its president, to represent Smith at court, and it raised in the effort $500 to remand Henry Long back to slavery. Wood and the Union Safety Committee prevailed.

In January 1851, when Long was escorted under a fading sun by two hundred New York policemen to the docks, where a steamboat waited to take him back to Richmond, a crowd of five thousand men, supporters of the committee, were on hand to witness the "justice" of slavery done and the supremacy of white people ensured. At their head stood Daniel Webster, now US secretary of state, whose efforts had contributed to the passage of the fugitive law. Standing next to Webster, with a rifle slung across his shoulders, was Captain Rynders. Rynders and his gang were present once again, acting as muscle for the committee's corporate powers.[42] When Henry Long reached Virginia, John T. Smith auctioned him off just days later for the price of $750.[43]

The power of the Union Safety Committee turned New York, Boston, Philadelphia, and Buffalo into centers of such renditions throughout the 1850s and, consequently, into centers of strife as well. Legal proceedings became battlegrounds as Black abolitionists, taking matters more directly in hand, organized to break into courtrooms and jails, spiriting self-emancipated people to freedom. A newspaper in 1853 reported that abolitionists had assisted two thousand formerly enslaved people that year to escape to freedom through Cleveland and Canada; the paper lamented that the Underground Railroad had thereby eroded $2 million of slaveholders' wealth, or $72 million today.[44]

These flashpoints further divided the nation, put the legality of the Fugitive Slave Law to the test, and hardened northern resistance to that law, certainly among abolitionists but also among the general citizenry and at the level of state government. "There is nothing, I think, that has come so near to making an impassable gulf between the South and the North as this Fugitive Slave Law," opined white abolitionist Henry Ward Beecher.[45]

Senator James Murray Mason had proposed the law; Senator Henry Clay had made it a reality; but it was the Union Safety Committee and Wall Street that made it a weapon. And so resistance to it, as it grew, did so in direct response to the money and corporate directors of Wall Street, to Moses Taylor and the Union Safety Committee, "an association," Frederick Douglass reprovingly called them, "of great merchants, bankers, capitalists, and hack politicians."[46]

Resistance would in time give rise to more emboldened efforts to stop the renditions of Black people, including the northern states' passage of personal liberty laws, which, among other things, forbade state authorities to act on enslavers' fugitive claims. It was those laws that South Carolina, when it became the first state to secede, cited as a cause. A line of money flowed through Wall Street and Black suppression to civil war.

A New York newspaper in 1856 presented a widely circulated special report about the "merchant princes" of Manhattan and how lavishly they lived, in mansions "rivaling in magnificence almost any of the royal palaces of Europe." Among the eminences it highlighted was Moses Taylor. It detailed that Taylor had spent $54,000, or $1.8 million today, furnishing just four of the five sections of his mansion (the massive dwelling took up the entire block of Seventeenth Street), and up to $30,000 ($1 million now) on one section alone.[47] Striding from such opulence down to City Bank each morning, Moses Taylor spent the day building the foundations of American industrial prowess, but his evenings shoring up systems of oppression based on white supremacy. He used the power of his office to literally build railroads for a growing white middle class and to figuratively destroy the Underground Railroad in the more northern outposts where it stopped.

Taylor's biographers always stressed his work ethic, his industriousness. What we can stress here is his callousness, how diligently he worked to normalize the brutalization of Black families as part of his bourgeois routine. He spent hours at balls and fundraisers, conferences, and committee meetings; seated with southern enslavers at the fashionable Niblo's

Saloon, at the corner of Broadway and Prince; and otherwise scheming and partaking in conversation about the talk of the day: that those assisting Black people toward liberty were "levying war against the United States... nothing less than treason."[48] It remained Taylor's privilege not to trouble himself with the moral and legal questions surrounding the Fugitive Slave Law's oppression (jurists like Charles O'Conor did), nor the dirty work of its enforcement (that was Rynders's job). Rather, it was the true mark of his station that he wrote checks, sat on stages, and gave of his time; he endorsed, organized, and hobnobbed to enshrine bigotry and bondage.

It is telling that Taylor did all this while president of City Bank. To overlook this role is to miss the point of what Taylor, capitalism, and City Bank in that era had become: overlapping presidiums in the expanding sphere of white empire and supremacy."[49]

In 1856, Taylor and the Union Safety Committee arranged for the former governor of Virginia, John B. Floyd, to speak from the grounds of the Merchants' Exchange, the North's temple of commerce. Floyd, born on a plantation and an enslaver himself, was then a presidential elector for James Buchanan, the Democratic Party's presidential nominee that year. Taylor and his coterie had long circled their wagons around Buchanan, funding his electoral bid, and some among them, including August Belmont, one of the city's wealthiest financiers, had pledged $10,000 to found a newspaper, the Morning Star, in support of Buchanan, though it never got off the ground.[50] A special dais was erected at the Exchange's imposing entrance that afternoon, and again thousands congregated on Wall Street to listen. John H. Brower, Taylor's codirector at City Bank, presided, speaking of portentous questions before the nation, of the need to preserve sectional accord.

By the late 1850s, here at this crossroads of national destiny, as momentous events headed toward them, the corporate directors of the Merchants' dome, their power concentrated in the council of Moses Taylor and the Union Safety Committee, knew all too well what they stood to lose. It was precisely that which Governor Floyd had come to highlight, and to remind them of their covenant with southern slavery. "What fund supplies the United States with European exchange?" Floyd asked the roiling crowd. "It is almost exclusively the product of the Southern States—cotton, rice, tobacco, turpentine. These exchanges constitute the foundation stone upon which rests the whole structure of the banks—and upon the banks again cluster and rest all the mercantile and mechanical prosperity of this city—indeed, of the whole North." For Wall Street directors to stand by and let this system of wealth-making be destroyed, Floyd remonstrated, was madness. "Take away from New York the exchange which Southern States give to her, and every interest and every pursuit here would be thrown into chaos." Floyd then asked the crowd, goadingly, if they were willing to give it all up, all their entitlements as white men and merchants of consequence, because of enmity and dissension that abolitionists and Black people had sown. "Are you prepared for it, fellow citizens?" The crowd cried "No!" At that moment someone among the spectators shouted for all to hear, "We will have a strife with them first." It was Captain Rynders, mingling in the crowd, like a malignant refrain embedded in these histories, ever ready to ignite a tempest. "Three cheers for the Captain!" the men around him replied.[51]

For many more years, we find the Union Safety Committee and its powerful interests rallying thousands of men up and down the Atlantic Seaboard in the name of white supremacy. In 1857, we find Moses Taylor and Captain Rynders, together onstage at Tammany Hall, officiating a monster rally in honor of President Buchanan.[52] We find the same corporate powers busy organizing the New York Democratic Vigilant Association in 1859 (Taylor sat on the executive committee) to counteract the rising power of William H. Seward, the New York senator who, having joined the recently formed Republican Party, helped turn that party into a platform for pro-abolitionist views. We find Taylor and his circle, after the violence of Harpers Ferry, quickly and widely condemning abolitionist John Brown, who led the raid there, and funding an investigation—"do[ing] the dirty work of their Southern Task-masters,"[53] as one northern newspaper observed—to uncover northern sympathizers who aided his cause. The resulting booklet Taylor's Democrats financed, impugning Seward and the abolitionists for conspiring with Brown, served to project onto those parties the blame for inciting a "war of the races" that the members of the committee themselves seemed to hunger for.[54] "We have displayed to you an abyss, in which, without your aid, not only the prosperity, but the very existence of this Union may be engulfed," the booklet said.[55] It was Taylor and his network who spent years, and the equivalent of millions of dollars,

on such conflict and agitation, pouring fuel on the fire of white nationalism, pushing the union closer to collapse.

What was the sum effect of all their organizing, all their fomenting to
save the nation and slavery? Demonstrably, it was not to forestall war. Nor
did the Union Committee prevent the eventual triumph of abolitionism
and the emancipation of enslaved Black people. In fact, by encouraging
support for abolition, by inspiring northern legislative efforts to obstruct
the Fugitive Slave Law, it only widened divisions in the nation it purport-
edly hoped to forestall. The white supremacists of the Union Committee
seem to have foreseen this, to have been fatally resigned to the reality that
they could save slavery or the union, but they couldn't do both.

In 1859, Charles O'Conor, ever the rabid racist, had written a letter to a
committee of merchants in which he said as much, and many other things
of note as well. It might be that O'Conor gave voice here to sentiments that
more genteel circles perhaps would not. Perhaps he summated the hope-
lessness of white supremacists all around him, confronting with clear-eyed
despair that their abysmal economic experiment, rooted in racial caste, a
system of spoils and privileges based on the suffering of Black people, was
destined to collapse:

> Our negro bondmen can neither be exterminated nor transported to
> Africa. They are too numerous for either process, and either, if practi-
> cable, would involve a violation of humanity. If they were emancipated,
> they would relapse into barbarism, or a set of negro States would arise in
> our midst, possessing political equality, and entitled to social equality.
> The division of parties would soon make the negro members a powerful
> body in Congress—would place some of them in high political stations,
> and occasionally let one into the Executive chair.
>
> It is in vain to say that this could be endured; it is simply impossible.
> What then remains to be discussed?
>
> The negro race is upon us. With a Constitution which held them in
> bondage, our Federal Union might be preserved; but if so holding them
> in bondage be a thing forbidden by God and Nature, we cannot lawfully
> so hold them, and the Union must perish.
>
> This is the inevitable result of that conflict which has now reached
> its climax.[56]

What is significant is that Wall Street's drive to save slavery may ironically have helped to destroy it, using the profits of enslavement itself no
less, by enabling the calls for secession and insurrection that precipitated
civil war. And no wonder, when in the 1860s Taylor and his circle, now
stylizing themselves the Union Club, encouraged and coddled the idea
of rebellion, sponsoring massive gatherings in New York City for leading southern proponents. They trumpeted the ideas of men like General
Leslie Combs of Kentucky, a vociferous opponent of Abraham Lincoln's,
and William L. Yancey, "the most active representative of Secessionism at
the South."[57] Yancey, spewing racist barbs, and goading violence—"If this
question means by the integrity of the Union the preservation of an administration that shall trample on any portion of the rights of the South…
I will aid my State in resisting it to blood"—delivered his harangue from
a new public space in Manhattan, paid for by the richest merchants and
known from then as the Cooper Institute.[58]

The very breakup of the union was sponsored by the Union Club. Fernando Wood, the mayor of New York, even propounded as much, saying
the city should itself secede, the better to be an independent commercial
zone, free from federal tyranny and handmaiden to the South's slavery
wealth. "When Disunion has become a fixed and certain fact, why may
not New York disrupt the bands which bind her to a venal and corrupt
master?"[59]

From the fiery speeches of Yancey and Combs in October 1860, it
was but mere months more to South Carolina's actual secession, and
from there, a short distance more to the firing on Fort Sumter and the full
onslaught of war.

———

WE LEARN SOMETHING revealing from the firing of those shots in April
1861. We learn where the loyalties of Moses Taylor and his circle ultimately lay. We learn about the depth of Wall Street's commitments to
upholding slavery and that, despite the astonishing profits involved, there
was a limit to the risks these men were willing to take. Civil war clari-
fied those limits; the shots at Fort Sumter crystallized the risk. When it
became clear, after the outbreak of hostilities, that the price of supporting

slavery would mean supporting full-fledged rebellion, not merely as cant, broadcast from Union Square, but as aid to those taking up arms treasonously against the government, Taylor and nearly all those of his commercial class—all the financiers and corporate directors whose businesses were steeped for decades in Black enslavement, all of them essentially to a man—did a remarkable about-face. Their commitments, when put to the hardened test, turned out not to have been based on deeply rooted principle or loyalty. Not surprisingly, they were rooted in the cold pursuit of profit and calculated risk, much as any other business choice. In the space of mere weeks, the corporate directors of the Merchants' dome abandoned the southern cause, abandoned their southern partners, and abandoned, above all, the idea that slavery as a foundation for their wealth and their world could be saved.

The Union Safety Committee, through an evolution of astounding speed, became the Union Defense Committee, the nucleus of the most important fundraising entity for the North at the outbreak of war, as historian Philip S. Foner meticulously traced. Suddenly, the Dodges, the Howlands, and the Grinnells, merchants of slavery capital who yesterday had rallied to destroy abolition in service of the South, today raised funds to underwrite subscriptions for the stock of the United States, a war fund against the Confederacy. Foner traced that by early 1861 this newly christened committee set about raising $8 million to this effect. There followed what appeared to be a wholly paradoxical effect: portions of wealth that had underwritten Black people's bondage and been reaped from that bondage, now flowed into the Union's coffers, soon to underwrite Black people's freedom.

What is remarkable is not that these northern merchants so quickly and resolutely mobilized their resources into the new business of the Union's war effort. What is remarkable is that they faced virtually no resistance in doing so. Their once stalwart support for enslavement resulted in no public condemnation nor political ostracization, and their profiting from slavery even less so. On the contrary, they were welcomed, and their former positions strategically overlooked. The absence of any censure, as we will see—this silence that instantly reigned over their actions, and that continued to do so for years—would set off powerful aftereffects of history we still grapple with to this day.

The clearest manifestation of these startling alterations was the fact that Lincoln, now president, when convening a committee charged with raising credit and administering loans in the Union's new war effort, selected as its chair none other than Moses Taylor himself. In the space of just months, the figure of Taylor on the axis of southern support dramatically shifted. From rallying thousands in support of enslavers' rights, Taylor now oversaw the dispensation of $200 million in funds and securities to suppress the uprising of the very same people.

City Bank, as a result, also played a prominent role, and it is reported that under Taylor's leadership the bank advanced funds to the US Treasury at the favorable rate of 7.3 percent.[60] Taylor's political prowess ascended accordingly, his financial acumen, at this critical time of war, practically a vindication to his former Confederate support. "He was offered at one time, by President Lincoln," it was reported, "the Assistant Secretaryship of the Treasury, but after mature consideration decided to decline it."[61]

What did it mean that Moses Taylor, a man so central to the story of slavery, a man so personally enriched by its rise, was now intimately and instantly folded by President Lincoln into the story of its destruction? Something seemingly upside down, upon closer look, helps put many things right side up—a stroke of clarity to rationalize otherwise perplexing actions and their designs. Among other things, it meant that for Lincoln and his administration, as no doubt for much of the nation, the prevailing notion that had enabled slavery and its production of wealth endured: that is, it was not deemed immoral or objectionable, but entirely acceptable, for northern men to have amassed their wealth from this system of subjugating Black people. What was immoral, in this view, was only the South's rebellion.

That sitting among Lincoln's most trusted council of financiers were men enriched by the reviled business of destroying freedom—and this included not only Taylor but also August Belmont, Pelatiah Perit, and too many other men to name—crystallized all the more that the wealth of slavery was certainly neither the target of nor the impetus for Lincoln's war, and further, that the conflict was conceived as neither a corrective to, nor a referendum on, the horrid basis through which prosperity had been achieved in the United States.

Taylor's prominent role contradicts the idea that Lincoln's commitment to conflict and his pursuit of emancipation were somehow driven by a desire to save Black people. His actions, as scholars like Ibram X. Kendi have argued, were driven by a calculation to save the nation, not by the anti-slavery cause itself.[62] As wrote Africano, the pen name of an anonymous Black soldier in the Fifth Massachusetts Cavalry Regiment: "Mr. Lincoln's policy in regard to the elevation and inseparability of the negro race has always been one of a fickle-minded man—one who, holding anti-slavery principles in one hand and colonization in the other, always gave concessions to slavery when the Union could be preserved without touching the peculiar institution."[63] Lincoln was as much a calculating pragmatist as the driven merchants he saw fit to put on his council. He continued to develop schemes for banishing Black people from the United States, and in 1862 alone, the US House of Representatives' Select Committee on Emancipation and Colonization authorized $600,000 for the president's colony proposals.[64]

Like Lincoln, Taylor was no sudden convert to the principles of anti-slavery. His newfound orientation as Lincoln's advisor is somewhat difficult, on the one hand, to fully suss out, forming yet another layer of opacity around an already shadowy and troubling man. There is every reason to believe that his about-face was effected rather reluctantly, as a last resort, and for that reason he has been aptly described as an "ambivalent war Democrat."[65] And yet, though motives here remain difficult to fathom, the president of City Bank's decisions appear wholly consistent with his corporate ethos, reinforcing the notion that, where business was concerned, he was a coldly calculating realist—a rationalist and opportunist of the most cutting and amoral kind. So long as the suffering and dehumanization of Black people in the United States could be mined for profits, Moses Taylor, like the corporate leaders around him, supported that business and supported its underlying southern cause. When those profits, and the system furnishing them, became utterly unviable, they abandoned all ties; they cut and ran. Their business, in the end, was to survive, and they chose now the more viable course of the Union. Taylor himself captured this calculus in a phrase he is reported to have repeated throughout the war: "If our Government be not sustained, what are our properties, or our institutions worth?"[66] Wealth from southern slavery was all good and well, he counseled, but not if it meant losing the country.

Taylor could afford by then to cut and run. He had already made millions financing enslavement and transporting its wares; he had a multiplicity of other business lines, seeded with the millions he had sapped from slavery. By rational calculation, he could afford to give the business up, as he had comprehensively invested and laundered his ill earnings into other things. War, however, proved excellent business, as it always does, and Taylor profited handsomely again. One of his companies, Mount Hope Iron, almost single-handedly sourced huge orders of iron ore for the Union army, undergirding the war effort and making Taylor extravagant riches. Moreover, he leased his fleet of ships to the US Navy in lucrative contracts. The war against slavery now magnified his riches as much as protecting the business of slavery once had.

"We are a hypocritical race," exclaimed the Republican statesman William M. Evarts in a noted speech, "that we are fond of money above every other thing, and trample, for gain-sake, our principles under our feet; that we fit out slave-traders; that our merchants furnish the means, the credit, and the insurance; and they say: 'Look now at the North, which professes to be opposed to Slavery, and yet furnishes the means for this abominable traffic.'"[67]

To dismiss the actions of these northern men as being hypocritical alone is perhaps not quite right. Hypocritical certainly they were, and certainly in the eyes of their former allies in the South, who seethed with indignation now, livid over abandonment and treachery. ("Of all the execrable spots on the American continent, the city of New York bears off the palm," exhorted the *Richmond Dispatch*.)[68] Yet from another standpoint, the directors of Wall Street were wholly consistent with themselves, and, what's more, they were loyal to the ruthless principles of capitalism they had been forging. Precisely by cleaving so readily with old southern alliances, forsaking sentiment for business sense, they purified the lode of their capitalistic ideals and set the system on the stages to what it was to become, including what it has become today. To have retarded or misshaped those ideals in some way, through feeling and loyalties, would not have been their sort of capitalism at all. And so the calculus of profit that had always guided them into the deepest stages of slavery now guided them to break with it. Such actions from morally bankrupt men on Wall Street—men who donated to Black manumission here with funds sourced from robbing freedom there; who spoke of temperance while indulging limitless greed; who achieved success through more willful blindness to Black human suffering; who built the ramparts of civilization with the proceeds of selling Black children from their parents—from such men, such actions during the great conflict really come as no surprise.

Their new stance, it is important to note, did not end their racism, did not end their desire for racial segregation, their hatred for the idea of Black equality, or their commitment to white supremacy. It wasn't an ideological transformation, or a transformation of conscience these men underwent, only a change in business strategy, an acceptance of the inevitability of Black emancipation. "They were prepared to accept the fact that the war emancipated Blacks, made them citizens and put the personal and property rights of all citizens on the basis of equality. However, they were not willing to indulge the freedmen in full political participation," scholar Paul R. Migliore states in "The Business of Union: The New York Business Community and the Civil War."[69]

These men continued to pursue "solutions" to the "problem" of free Black people, including exiling them through colonization, a scheme which, though manifestly futile in its aims, they keenly supported nonetheless. William Dodge, when he rose to the rank of vice president of the American Colonization Society after the war, remained outspokenly against Black suffrage, stating: "I feel that we are now in great peril, and ought not to look simply to the immediate enfranchisement of the negro race, overlooking all the other great interests of the country which are dependent upon the legislation we may adopt."[70] The *Merchants' Magazine*, a mouthpiece for Taylor and Dodge among others, would later insist on a compromise when the Fifteenth Amendment was debated, whereby Black men would have to pass a literacy test, show that they owned $250 in assets, or show evidence of service in the Union army—standards designed to impede their voting rights, not facilitate them. Men of the Merchants' dome, using the power of their corporate wealth and position, continued organizing against Black equality throughout the war and well past Reconstruction.

All through those years, Moses Taylor, war Democrat and Dean of Banking, didn't cease to profit from the enslavement of African people and their descendants. He merely ceased doing so in the United States. His extensive finance and transportation operations in Cuba continued throughout the conflict, and for several more decades, in fact—decades during which he scoured from the sugar plantations of that island, and from people bound and enslaved there, the equivalent today of millions of dollars more. He did so because he could, and for as long as it made business sense. Taylor remained a murky figure, deeply implicated in that trade, until he died, and further hints have bubbled to the surface over time suggesting that his involvement wasn't limited to financing alone.

One such passing glimpse came in official British correspondence with the US Navy, where it was revealed that a British warship stationed off Sierra Leone in 1858 had captured a suspicious American bark "fully equipped to receive a cargo of slaves." British authorities questioned the ship's captain, a known slave trader named Antonio Huerta, operating out of Cuba, and he told them the name of his bark was the *Amanda and Maria*.[71] A British admiral then relayed this information to the US consul general in Havana, who, checking it against records and ship manifests, grew confused. The US consul general could find no trace of any such ship, except one owned by Moses Taylor. And so, confounded, he volunteered the following, perhaps implausible explanation: "The American barque 'Amanda,'…belonging to the House of Moses Taylor, New York, cleared from this port for New York with a cargo of produce on the 24th February last. She is at this moment in Havana from New York; the respectability of her owner [meaning Moses Taylor] leaving no room for a suspicion of her having been engaged in Slave Trade, and no other 'Amanda' has been here during the last twelve months, so that Don Antonio Huerta must have invented a name for the captured bark, probably to prevent the captors from examining the vessel more minutely, and discovering her real name, and the place she came from."[72]

The name *Amanda* was not the same as the *Amanda and Maria*, the name given by Huerta, but they were so alike, and there existed evidently no other American ship with such a name operating out of Cuba, that the consul general felt compelled at once to draw a comparison, and then to dispel it just as quickly, given Taylor's respectability. And yet such seemingly impenetrable esteem had long operated in this way, breeding the unthinkable, precisely to shield businessmen of the highest order operating within the trade.

Were authorities correct that Huerta fabricated entirely this name for his ship to avoid detection? (It's not clear from existing documents what ultimately became of Huerta or his ship.) Or is the likeness in names not to be overlooked? It is possible that Huerta, rattled and afraid under interrogation, merely spoke the truth? It seems entirely plausible that the coincidence of this slaving ship being practically identical in name and description to a bark owned by Moses Taylor was no coincidence at all, that the two ships were one and the same. Perhaps this encounter serves as further proof that the president of City Bank, using the very respectability of his stature as cover, was deeply involved in the still-operating and wildly lucrative transatlantic slave trade.

————

IN 1865, THE brutality that men like Benjamin Marshall had organized into a business, the business that men like Daniel Hillman Jr. had organized into an industry, and the enslavement industry that men like Moses Taylor had organized into modern capitalism was at last destroyed with the passing of the Thirteenth Amendment. With the stroke of his pen, President Lincoln effected the demise of this evil institution, but the battle for liberation was won—hard won, against the crushing hands of capital and bigotry—by the dream spire of organized Black thought and effort. And Black resistance prevailed, despite the most privileged white men at the greatest corporations in the world using all their schemes, ships, and resources to forestall it. Freedom wrestled through blood, from the sacrifice of unnamed millions, slipped through the hourglass of American days spent, over a road of centuries, until it was pulled at last from the wilderness of empty words into "the broad sunlight of our Republican civilization," as the Black abolitionist H. Ford Douglas wrote in a heart-skipping letter to Frederick Douglass, at the time of the Emancipation Proclamation. There Ford Douglas added: "The slaves are free! How can I write these precious words?"[73]

There were new hopes and dreams to attend to in an exploded world where the business of putting a price on human beings, whose freedom was priceless, was left smoldering in the cinder fires of white resentment. Elvira Garrett, a woman formerly enslaved in Louisiana, when later interviewed at her home in Los Angeles by the Works Progress Administration, recalled the disorienting, giddy pleasure of gazing with new eyes upon such a world: "It was a funny sight to see the mistresses in the doorways raging with madness as the slaves passed by singing. With nothing but freedom, but that was a fortune in itself."[74]

For nearly 250 years, first in the colonies, then in the life of the republic before the war, millions of enslaved Black people in the United States gave and lost everything to build the greatest expression of national wealth in the history of the world. The white men of Moses Taylor's circle, in sharp contrast, lost nothing, in war or peace, in name or position, in wealth or time. All that they built, all they took and gained, would go on, and, as we'll see, much of it remains. The rapacious form of capitalism they pioneered, though no longer overtly based on coercing the labor of Black people for no pay, entered a new stage of development, still endowed with the riches that the system of slavery had made: "A key triumph for American capitalism," observes the catalogue accompanying Moses Taylor's papers at the New York Public Library. "It was a coup."[75] A coup staged, in the coming years, as much through memory and the rendering of official history, as through the building of enduring institutions of financial power.

CHAPTER 11

"THE MANTLE OF OBLIVION"

To begin a new life, Mayer Lehman, founder of the now infamous Lehman Brothers Bank, barely had to shed his old one. His journey of reinvention began when he left his former home in Montgomery, Alabama, and reached New York City in late 1867, traversing the broken landscapes of Southern defeat in between.[1] It was two years since the end of the war. Two years since the outpouring of death; two years since Appomattox and Robert E. Lee's surrender. Two years since Lincoln's assassination by John Wilkes Booth; two years since four million formerly enslaved Black people in the United States were at last free. It seemed, after two such titanic years, that much in the nation had irrevocably changed. And yet Mayer Lehman, moving his belongings into his new home in Manhattan, a stately four-story brownstone on West Twentieth Street, embodied how much had not.[2]

Lehman arrived flush to the Empire City, where his brother was waiting, with his fortune and his sterling reputation intact, a fortune reaped from slavery, a fortune amplified by being a Confederate banker, one of Jefferson Davis's most trusted treasurers. The Lehman brothers, all through the war, had avidly financed treason, in the cause of white supremacy. Yet no magistrate was coming to arrest Mayer Lehman, nor his brother Emanuel, on a Manhattan street. Quite the opposite. The

Lehman brothers, and thousands of merchant enslavers like them—those who had fought for secession—had by now been pardoned by President Andrew Johnson.[3] And so they were free to prosper again, with the spoils stolen from Black people's lives. And in the case of the Lehman brothers, the spoils amounted to many millions—millions they were plowing into their Wall Street bank.

The same was true for the thousands of slavery merchants in the North, those who had sided with the Union, but only after first fighting for white supremacy—the corporate directors under the Merchants' dome: Moses Taylor, James Brown, and the rest. They too were free to prosper, their spoils from slavery still intact, though the institution itself was now destroyed. Those men of the North, however, needed no official pardon. Their role in building, fortifying, and protecting America's business of slavery faded like a whisper or a wind, little spoken of on Wall Street or at the Exchange. It was the business of America now to forget such deeds. In New York City, its streets bursting with more than one million lives, Mayer Lehman and Moses Taylor, once enemies upon opposite sides, were now effectively one and the same amid the burgeoning crowds. Unchastised, unaccountable, they remained an unbroken circuit of wealth and privilege, their power coursing together through Wall Street, soon to interlink across one another's corporate boards.

As he climbed the stairs to his new home, Mayer Lehman, then thirty-seven, was accompanied by his wife and four children. It is said that he was a man of circumspect qualities, demure and intensely focused—a man then ascending to his prime. He was the son of a Bavarian cattle herder, but a man reinvented in the United States through the riches that slavery made—a man now reinventing himself again. It is recorded also that with Lehman that day were a Black man and a Black woman, whose names we don't know. They were two of the seven Black people that Lehman had, in Alabama, formerly enslaved.[4] Though emancipated, they would continue serving Mayer Lehman in New York, now as butlers and attendants. Eventually, they would help raise Lehman's children in settings of ever-greater affluence and exclusive privilege, a dynasty infused with nearly interminable riches. So much had been lost and fought over, and yet so much in the way of racial caste and privilege in the country remained unchanged.

THERE IS A tapestry of myths in the United States that tells how the South was rendered destitute during the Civil War, and what these myths want to suggest is that the sin of slavery, through this imagined financial cataclysm, was somehow stamped out and erased. One of these myths tells that when Jefferson Davis fled Richmond, Virginia, he loaded the Confederacy's gold onto a train, hoping to save what wealth of the slave-abiding treasonous cause remained, but that it was looted at Irwinville, Georgia, plucked by Union soldiers, and spirited away, the South's slavery fortune lost forever, never to be found. Yet even now, people hunt for it, and the History Channel makes documentaries about their quests.

It's a soothing, self-deluding myth for some to think that the fortune of slavery, all the incalculable wealth that white people reaped for generations from enslaved Black people, from decimated families and stolen children, could be loaded onto one train and that it could vanish into thin air. It would mean that nothing from slavery had been gained in the end, as if the "whole thing had never happened"; that the moral ledger had therefore been set to zero; that sin had been recompensed by some higher form of justice (reversal or collapse); and that any sense of white guilt and culpability could vanish too. It is the same myth at play in the wildly popular image of Scarlett O'Hara, stalking a smoldering landscape in *Gone with the Wind*. The sins of O'Hara's enslaving family are erased because she is broken and destitute after the war, meaning a white audience can feel sympathy and heartbreak, as much for O'Hara as for itself, instead of guilt.

The same myth holds up a cornerstone of Civil War history, positing that the war obliterated the southern aristocracy, and that "no ruling class of our history ever found itself so completely stripped of its economic foundations as did that of the South in this period."[5] Those are the words of C. Vann Woodward, a giant of postwar history, and though extrapolated from a single survey, conducted in 1920, no less, using a sample of just 254 southern industrialists, they have defined our view of history for generations. It is a false history, spelling out false white hope, through the evisceration of slavery's wealth.

The myths white America tells itself about the wealth Black people created in enslavement are legion, defying logic. They are ultimately dangerous to the fabric and well-being of American life. Among other things, these myths sustain the popularly held misunderstanding, widely spread online today, that slavery didn't enrich America, because most of that stolen wealth was destroyed during the Civil War. A case in point illustrates this disturbingly well. On the conservative website The Unz Review, hundreds of people have posted comments since June 2020 in reply to the question: "Where Are the Great Slave Fortunes?"[6] The Unz Review was founded by Ronald Keeva Unz, a former Republican senatorial candidate for California and former publisher of the *American Conservative* magazine. While it attracts some commentary from left-leaning observers, its adherents tend to be extremely right-leaning. The site has been described as a breeding ground for antisemitism.

Most of those commenting use handles, as anonymity encourages them to speak without fear of consequences. And so while some make observations in the spirit of open debate—"Cotton plantations weren't where the money was at. You need to look up North to the men who owned the shipping lines"—most answers devolve quickly into debased racist and antisemitic smears. The smears posit that the Civil War wiped out any wealth from slavery (wealth that Jewish people supposedly made most of), and that therefore the country need not consider any debt to Black people because there's no wealth left. The forum shows clearly how misconceptions about slavery's profits, fomenting in the ecosystem of online conspiracy, became a basis for magnifying hatred toward Black and Jewish people.

The most sanitized of these comments might be: "Weren't the slave fortunes generally destroyed during the Civil War?" To which another person replied: "Correct. The main asset of wealthy slaveowners were the slaves themselves. The war caused a complete loss of that main asset." Another commentator, referencing Scarlett O'Hara directly, underscores the point: "As Scarlett said, [the slave fortunes] are 'gone with the wind that swept through' the South."

There's no doubt that the Thirteenth Amendment, by formally abolishing slavery through emancipation, destroyed the overt basis for monetizing Black people's lives, though less overt ways persisted. And there's no doubt that, because the market for collateralizing, bartering, and selling

Black people as property evaporated, the dollar value of those who were formerly enslaved also evaporated. As a result, some enslavers—and probably quite a lot of them—naturally lost a sizable portion of their ill-gotten assets. And yet we know from history, data, and recent scholarship that vast portions of the wealth created by slavery survived.

The Lehman brothers are demonstrable proof. The Lehman family together enslaved several dozen Black people between the 1850s and the 1860s, including many children. The brothers themselves, in their households, enslaved at least ten people, including a fourteen-year-old girl, presumably to work as domestic servants. The Lehman Brothers firm, separately, enslaved nineteen, according to a disclosure the firm itself made back in 2003. The bank's disclosure seems not to have accounted for yet additional information, housed at Columbia University, showing that the Lehman brothers purchased in 1863 ten enslaved people from Augusta, Georgia, for the price of $5,400.[7] This would appear to bring the total to thirty-nine; because records are scanty, there may have been more.

The Lehmans were, in other words, significant enslavers. What's more, they became institutional pillars of the slavery system itself in Montgomery: they served as cotton factors, brokering a large volume of cotton sales; they financed plantations through loans, and thus the buying and selling of Black people; they often took cotton as payment, and, in one instance, they were compensated for a debt through the sale of a young Black woman named Betsey and her child. Merchandising the stolen time of Black people and abetting their systemic abuse was the centerpiece of the family's fabulous wealth. They made that wealth spectacularly quickly, moreover, for Mayer Lehman didn't arrive to the United States until 1850, and already, within a decade, they were profoundly rich.

According to the logic of the myths just cited, from conservative and more mainstream viewpoints alike, the Lehmans should have been ruined after the Civil War. By 1865, however, after the Black people they had enslaved had been emancipated and after the entire economic system around them in Alabama, much of it based on enslavement, was disrupted, even then the Lehmans weren't financially ruined. Why? The reason is that they had invested their slavery money into other instruments and other places outside of the southern slavery system.

Almost a decade earlier, in 1858, before the war had even begun, they had opened an office in New York, on Liberty Street, where Emanuel Lehman's job was to convert their earnings and letters of credit into securities and other assets. "For the cotton sold," conveys one history of the Lehmans, "the firm received drafts on New York banks or bills on London, which Emanuel exchanged for cash in New York."[8] The Lehmans presided over a diversified emporium. Even as Mayer stayed in Alabama, fighting for and financing the Confederate cause, Emanuel, in the enemy territory of New York, was leveraging their vast business book into southern railroads, northern and international bonds, and corporate stock.

So rich were the Lehmans *after* the Civil War that the state of Alabama itself borrowed at least $623,672 ($17.3 million) from the Lehman firm (known then as Lehman, Durr & Co.) to service its debts and avoid insolvency, as court records and Alabama fiscal documents show.[9] And this is not even to mention, as we know, that the Lehman Brothers Bank, after the war, grew to become the fourth-largest investment bank in the United States.

The Lehmans are but one family illustrating this fallacy of lost wealth. If it were true that emancipation destroyed the totality of enslavement wealth, none would have been more devastated than Mississippi plantation owner Stephen Duncan, given the twenty-two hundred Black people he and his family enslaved. These women, men, and children carried a value of roughly $1.3 million at that time, and so, certainly, Duncan's holdings were diminished by their emancipation. And yet Duncan was hardly devastated; on the contrary, he, too, had diversified his plantation earnings. We read in the work of historian Morton Rothstein: "Duncan, like several other leading Southern planters, held investments in northern land and during the 1850's was constantly changing his portfolio of securities in northern and southern state and municipal bonds and in railroad stocks."[10] By 1860, Duncan's portfolio was worth more than $500,000, or $16 million today, an amount roughly equivalent to the capital of many of the nation's banks at that time. (On average, the capital of banks in Philadelphia was $600,000, points out another historian, William Kauffman Scarborough.)

Duncan was lavishly rich. In 1863, amid the conflict, he permanently quit the South and relocated to New York, to a fashionable town house he had purchased near Washington Square Park.[11] Flush with his investments, he ably prospered after the war, like the Lehman brothers, and like so many others, including the Mississippi Nabobs of Duncan's circle: the Surgets, the Minors, the Marshalls. Many of them also settled in sumptuous mansions in New York or its environs, living off sizable investments in northern corporations. They remained very rich men indeed. Theirs are but a few stories in a continuum, several strands among countless thousands, bridging the slavery of the past and the wealth of the present.

The point is not that all southern enslavers emerged from the Civil War completely unscathed. Of course, it is true that parts of the South burned: That during his famous march to the sea, Union general William Sherman confiscated four hundred thousand acres of land, destroyed three hundred miles of rail and bridge, and caused $2 billion worth of damage in today's dollars. That in Vicksburg, Mississippi, fine houses were reduced to ash. That in Montgomery, Alabama, cotton stores worth more than $50 million today were put to flame. That many families, having lost their land and those they enslaved, became destitute or fought for years in courts to retrieve assets confiscated or otherwise lost. But the larger point is that the vast portion of southern wealth generated by enslavement did not go up in smoke.

A groundbreaking academic study published in 2019 by the National Bureau of Economic Research in Cambridge, Massachusetts, amplifies this point. Remarkably, the team of scholars behind it, using census data, identified hundreds of enslaving families in the South, and then followed hundreds of thousands of their descendants between 1860 and 1940. They traced these descendants' levels of income and other economic metrics (including education levels). While the researchers certainly noted a temporary decline in family assets due to emancipation, overall, their work reveals that, within just one generation, these white families had dramatically reinvented themselves and recovered their wealth, redirecting their capital into the modern economy. "We find that white slaveholding families in the South quickly recovered from the loss of material resources due to emancipation, relative to comparably wealthy Southern households with fewer or no slaves," they reported.[12]

The team hypothesized that many families, though experiencing a "wealth shock" after the war, nonetheless capitalized on the most precious asset they retained: their personal networks and social standing, social capital that allowed them to rebuild, through jobs and financial partnerships, but also, importantly, through marriages. Their loss of hard capital, in other words, was a mere setback quickly offset by a much more valuable asset, namely their membership in a monied white elite. "These close social ties facilitated investments in nascent manufacturing ventures and merchant activities even though slaveholders as a group lost wealth," the team wrote. They went on to say that more research on the subject is necessary. But already their findings have helped debunk an enduring myth: that southern enslavers, as a class, were rendered destitute after the Civil War.

Our discussion, so far, has intentionally indulged a larger fallacious logic: that in talking about the wealth of slavery, we are talking about something that only happened to, or in, the South. We will address that in a moment. But first, it must be pointed out that the notion that America's wealth derived from slavery was inconsequential proliferates not only among a segment of the public writing anonymously on unregulated forums. A version of these views is also prevalent among well-regarded academics at institutions of higher learning.

Some academics have concluded that the role of Black people's labor in shaping America's prosperity was minimal, perhaps even meaningless, and they have done so, tellingly, by basing their argument on the prevalence of cotton. "Slavery was of course appalling, a plain theft of labor," writes Deirdre Nansen McCloskey, a professor emerita at the University of Illinois at Chicago, in a 2018 article for *Reason* magazine entitled "Slavery Did Not Make America Rich."[13] She goes on to say: "The enrichment of the modern world did not depend on cotton textiles…prosperity did not depend on slavery. The United States and the United Kingdom and the rest would have become just as rich without the 250 years of unrequited toil." McCloskey, recognized as a leading scholar on the history of economic liberalism, articulates a commonly held belief among many academics and policy makers. There is a lot to unpack in her argument, so let us take it one piece at a time.

Certainly, there is truth to what McCloskey writes, to the extent that cotton, produced by enslaved people, did not alone drive US economic growth, as we've already seen. But why is cotton's role alone in driving, or not driving, the *entirety* of US economic growth the sole criteria for assessing the scale of the wealth it created? We are missing the forest through the trees. Affirming that cotton did not drive growth does not negate a resolutely salient fact: that enslaved people, toiling endlessly and excruciatingly over cotton in the life of the republic, *did* produce a mind-boggling amount of enrichment in the United States, the equivalent, as we've seen, of billions of dollars each year. Even if cotton dollars did not constitute the totality of American prosperity, clearly they contributed to that prosperity at a time that the nation was modernizing. Why should we negate this? What purpose does this negation serve?

Bearing that in mind, there are two additional problems with McCloskey's argument that prove illuminating. The first is her phrasing: "The United States and the United Kingdom...would have become just as rich without 250 years of unrequited toil." How can she possibly know this? To understand her concept would require us to decouple in our minds known historical facts; we would need to imagine an alternative reality in which the enrichment of America took place without 250 years of slavery. Note the absurd mental gymnastics some would resort to rather than face a demonstrable truth: In the past that concretely happened, there *were* 250 years in which British and American white people enslaved Black people for the purposes of making riches. In those 250 years, as enslavement generated prodigious wealth, the United States, not surprisingly or coincidently, *did become rich*.

But look even closer: McCloskey posits that "the enrichment of the modern world did not *depend on cotton textiles*" (italics added). We can take issue here again: Why should America's long, tormenting business of enslaving Black people for profit be reduced to cotton alone? The vast labor camps of enslavement—fifty million acres or more on which Black people produced not only cotton, but sugar, tobacco, rice, corn, whiskey, gin, hemp, turpentine, lumber, iron, and coal—furnished many, many products and services of exceeding value. Available statistics document the amount of this wealth in excess of $240 million a year, or more than $8.5 billion a year now.

Recent studies have reinforced that wealth produced by enslaved people, while it may not have solely driven growth, was more important to US economic development than has previously been understood. Sven

Beckert, a professor of history at Harvard University, testified to this fact in April 2022, before a congressional hearing on slavery's economic legacy. "Initial findings of an ongoing research project have shown that during the 1840s and 1850s, between 10 and 14 percent of the U.S. gross national product (GNP) was derived directly from the labor of enslaved people," he said.[14]

This fact should not, and cannot, be minimized; it is worth a lot. It matters little whether prosperity "depended" on these billions; these billions of dollars *were* prosperity, a whole lot of prosperity. As Beckert adds: "Unpaid labor mattered greatly to the American economy. We can see this clearly if we compare it with contemporary industries. In 2021, all manufacturing activities in the United States combined contributed 11 percent to the nation's economic output, which is roughly the same share that the labor of enslaved people contributed during the Antebellum years."

Is it the position of scholars such as Deirdre Nansen McCloskey that this trove of money did not significantly contribute to America's becoming rich? Or is it the position of scholars like McCloskey that this money simply disappeared at some point, and therefore no longer counts in the ledger of current US wealth? Does its negation serve to erase and excuse the way this money was made, thus pardoning the crime of its procurement? And how did it disappear? In the Civil War? We have seen that argument used; we have seen that is not true. So where did this money go, then? How do McCloskey and scholars of her view answer this question? For that *is* a question worth asking, and as the path to its answer is the most illuminating of all, let us turn to it now.

Exploring this avenue of inquiry causes us to stumble upon the most significant fallacy of all: the notion that slavery's vast production of wealth was strictly a southern phenomenon, and strictly an *antebellum* southern phenomenon at that, limited to that place and to that time. This is among the most misleading and enduring of our national misconceptions about enslavement. (Note how popular learning tools reinforce this idea, like this entry from the website Encyclopedia.com: "The North, which had an economy based on business and manufacturing, was not dependent on slave labor and did not support the institution. Meanwhile, the South, which was agricultural, depended heavily on slave labor.")[15] Let us not indulge this fallacy by focusing on southern enslavers exclusively, nor through the lens of their "property" alone. Clearly, the value of enslaved people themselves—their bodies as property—wasn't the only wealth that enslaved people engendered. More importantly, southern enslavers, those managing enslaved labor forces, were not the only ones who profited.

As we've seen, over the period from 1790 to 1865 alone, and longer from colonial times, white people broadly extracted immense volumes of wealth from enslaved people's unpaid labor, including commodities, merchandise, and other transferable assets, and invested the proceeds into yet other forms of wealth. This began as far back as the time of Archibald Gracie (indeed, earlier), when slavery merchants converted their profits into the earliest corporate shares. Anson G. Phelps, even as his fleet of Charleston and Liverpool packets trundled slavery's cotton across the world, used that wealth to finance, among many other things, fashionable housing tracts on Second Avenue in Manhattan, as well as the terrace of elegant row houses on East Fourth Street known as Albion Place.[16] Stephen Girard, in Philadelphia, and Stephen Whitney, in New York—two of the richest men in the antebellum period, men for whom Black people's enslavement was foundational to their wealth—did the same.

How many more men, flush with the proceeds of Black bondage, followed their path, such that the foundations of New York and its landmarks, not to mention Philadelphia and the Atlantic cities, truly are monuments not only to the crime of exploiting Black people's labor but to the additional crime of laundering the proceeds? Again, real estate is but one example. By the time of emancipation, white men such as Moses Taylor, Tomás Terry, and Charles Leverich had channeled such immense sums of slavery wealth into other investable funds, securities, and commercial entities, filling the vaults of the banking streets of New York, Boston, and Baltimore, that this wealth was ironclad in its security and stability, ably insulated from the disruptions of the Civil War.

To see this process of laundering, whereby financiers converted wealth derived from slavery into other forms, and to cease believing that the wealth of slavery was thus limited in geography, limited to southern people and places, is also to begin to appreciate that it was not limited in time to the antebellum period. White people's enslavement of Black people, being a wealth-generating system, unleashed a chain reaction of flowing wealth—wealth that flowed geographically, but also across time, epochs, and generations. Wealth, as we know, circulates through reinvestment and transfer. It is preserved through corporate vehicles, through wills, through monetary instruments. It is passed down. Wealth that cannot be preserved and moved across ages is no wealth at all. And so the question is not whether white people grew immensely rich from slavery; obviously, they did. The more penetrating question to ask is: What became of this transferable wealth *after* the Civil War? Where did this wealth go? What life, so to speak, did it go on to lead? In exploring the answer, and following the money even further, we come stumbling upon another popular misconception that it is also critical to address.

This misconception can again be found on The Unz Review website, deeper down the forum chain. There a poster writes: "Slave holder and slave trading fortunes probably simply couldn't keep pace with the huge new fortunes created by the massive economic value added by industrial revolution."[17] The writer adds for emphasis: "The wealth created and accumulated by those engaged in the new industrial economy... probably rapidly eclipsed the modest old-time slave fortunes." In this person's rendering, the advent of the industrial revolution, its fabulous outpouring of new wealth, somehow eclipsed the fortunes that white men acquired through Black people's enslavement.

Leaving aside why that would even be so, it underscores the prevalent notion at play: that wealth reaped from slavery, on the one hand, and wealth generated during the industrial revolution, on the other, were two entirely different things, two distinct financial stages, two distinct financial streams, which never intersected or interacted.

This disconnection happens because the writer, it seems, believes that only southern enslavers made fortunes from Black people's coerced labor, and evidently, that they never invested it. But the construction tells us something also in a larger sense: The commentator cannot conceive that the white men who made fortunes from Black enslavement, whether in the North or the South, might have been the *very same people driving the industrial revolution*. That those same men who invested significantly in the nation's industrial base in the mid-1800s—men like Mayer Lehman, like Moses Taylor, like Anson G. Phelps, like Daniel Hillman Jr.—did so with the very funds they derived from enslavement and from the profits of slave commodities.

It is worth pausing over this fact. It begs many questions. Why is it that predominant US history separates the epoch of Black enslavement from the industrial revolution? Why is it that slavery's profits, though building over some many decades, yet, in the national mind, seem unconnected to—indeed, decoupled from—anything that comes afterward? It is almost as if a gap, an epistemological void, has been inserted into the sequence of historical events, creating a mental block, a kind of amnesia.

This peculiar mental block, by the way, is a wholly modern construction, it should be pointed out. As we've seen, Thomas Prentice Kettell, writing in the nineteenth century, and meticulously tracking the flow of enslavement riches to the North, never suffered from that misapprehension. On the contrary, he was keenly aware, in 1860, of how these riches underwrote US industrial development. Southerners generally were also keenly aware, in that time, of this fact. It rankled them, as we've seen, that so much of northern wealth was derived from the "Southern trade," and that it was fertilizing the industrial advancement—the manufacturing, the machinery, the factories—of cities like New York and Boston. Likewise, the mass of northern corporate directors under the Merchants' dome, staking all to protect slavery and its emoluments, were clearly aware of, and vocal about, this link. And so this is a recent mental block, resulting in a lost sense of continuum that's prevalent only now, in our time. Why?

Part of the reason is this: The elite men who formed the living link between enslavement and industry, who acted as the conduit for the funds flowing one to the other, men whose character and actions have been the concern of this book, are still virtually unknown today, despite their destructive impact. Or they are known only in the narrowest sense—that is, they are barely studied as relates to their role in enslavement. Remember that not a single lecture delivered under the auspices of the Anson G. Phelps Lectures at New York University has ever looked at Anson G. Phelps himself. Note, too, that in all the Hillman Library at the University of Pittsburgh, endowed with that family's riches, there is not a single document nor plaque attesting to Daniel Hillman Jr.'s role in the forced Black labor of the iron industry.

The resulting chasm of knowledge, barely bridged for more than 150 years, has been blinding and debilitating and deep. Let us imagine, for a second, its opposite. Imagine if more were known about men like

Benjamin Bailey and Moses Taylor, about the ties linking enslavement to the directors of Bank of America and New York Life, or the explosion of corporations such men oversaw in antebellum times. Imagine what is to be learned, about the institutionalization of Black bondage, the furnishing of its riches, and the throng of connections to modern American prosperity, by further excavating the lives of these men and the web of their corporate linkages.

Such men, and the history of the corporations they founded, it should be added, are not unknown because it is impossible to know them, because all trace of them has been lost—all their records, letters, and documents somehow burned up, like the imagined disappearance of their wealth. On the contrary, a thousand biographies of this kind are slumbering—their business ledgers intact, their letters organized in folders—at major libraries and universities in Boston, Philadelphia, New Jersey, and Baltimore, not just in New York and New Orleans. The problem is not possibility; the problem is that we've barely begun to look.

But why is *that*? Why are these men, and the history of the firms they built, as if covered in a blanket of oblivion so thick that it has allowed them to avoid censure, scrutiny, and full accountability of their actions, still in *our time*? Part of the answer rests in the myths we've discussed, and in the fact that predominant history privileges those myths over the facts. Those myths have served as the imposing door to the mausoleum these men built for themselves long ago, shutting us out, turning us away. But why those myths in the first place? Where did they come from? How did they start?

To find an answer, perhaps we must look to the nature of accountability in *that time*, which is to say, to that critical turning point in history involving the near-effortless rehabilitation, the second act, so to speak, of slavery profiteers like Moses Taylor and Mayer Lehman. Predominant history tends not to dwell on their second act. It tends not to dwell on how so many of these white men, untold thousands of financiers, and corporate directors, rich from the proceeds of slavery—and still rich *through* the enslavement of Black people, *though* enslavement was legally ended—prospered for thirty more years after the war, and their corporations for even longer; how they prospered not only financially, but free from reputational blight. We must ask ourselves: How was it that these men, despite abetting a system brutalizing Black people for money, a system over which the nation went to war, took their places so easily once again under the Merchants' dome, no sooner was the great traumatizing rebellion over? What accounting did these white men have to face for their hand in brutalization?

The answer is clarifying. It has something critical to teach us about the power of oblivion, about the breeding ground for myths, about how history is built not only on what a society, predominantly, chooses to memorialize, but what it chooses, willfully, and collectively, to forget. To understand the operating scheme of such willful forgetting requires us first, not surprisingly, to remember. We must remember, if we are to grasp these men and the hordes of wealth they derived from Black people's labors—not to mention the path this wealth would later take—that in the society supposedly reborn after the war, a society yet still championing the supremacy of white people, these men were all *pardoned*, officially or otherwise. They were pardoned through one of the most sweeping, comprehensive, and national enterprises of constructed consciousness in the history of the nation, such that all their vast transgressions in abusing Black people for profit were politically, almost instantly, absolved.

Among other things, it meant that, as the mass of fortunes reaped from Black people's forced labor—fortunes intact and magnifying—were pushed forward in time by elite white industrialists and financiers, this wealth itself was decoupled in the national mind from its detestable origins, from its abominable source, and the knowledge of the history of this connection was knowingly discarded, as if thrown into an abyss. With the end of the Civil War, white society closed its eyes and blinked, and the memory was gone. So began the process of laundering memory, so that the stolen wealth of slavery could be washed clean.

———

THE PROCESS OF laundering memory began almost immediately after Abraham Lincoln was dead and Andrew Johnson, fresh in the president's chair, began rehearsing the language of retribution. Johnson called for Confederate traitors to be hanged; he signaled he would confiscate their assets and redistribute their wealth. Johnson's pronouncements seemed to contemplate vengeance and justice on a breathtaking scale. "After making treason odious, every Union man and the Government should be remunerated out of the pockets of those who have inflicted this great suffering upon the country," were his words.[18] But they were empty words, as it turns out, in more ways than one.

Johnson, though born poor in North Carolina and a tailor by profession, had used what wealth he had accumulated to enslave at least five Black people throughout his public career, some as young as thirteen.[19] "Every Union man," in his worldview, did not include African Americans, even those who spilled blood for the Union. Johnson overruled General Sherman's order, stunning in its time, that each freed Black family was to be given, as a form of reparations for slavery, forty acres of land.[20] On the issue of Black people's equal suffrage—an issue the Republican Party generally agreed upon, and Black people and white abolitionists increasingly lobbied for—Johnson also notably waivered, paying lip service, but little more. ("Mr. Johnson has pinched and withered the fairest bud of promise put forth by the Republican party," wrote the N.Y. *Independent*, "the present prospect of Equal Suffrage.")[21] Johnson turned out to have been grandstanding.

By May 1865, all his promises had evaporated. Instead of accountability, he presided over a season of clemency and a betrayal of Black patriotism. "Johnson's program swung swiftly into its stride," W. E. B. Du Bois wrote.[22] His amnesty proclamation, as sweeping and immediate as it was, restored all rights and property to those who had fought and murdered to continue Black people's enslavement. There were multiple exceptions. But, in the main, these meant only that the wealthiest enslaving families (those with taxable property over $20,000, or roughly $340,000 today), instead of being automatically restored, had to apply for pardons.

They did so in droves. Already by September 1865, Johnson had pardoned more than one hundred prominent Confederates, and another twenty-five thousand had petitioned.[23] Prominent New York bankers and merchants sometimes came to their aid. Moses Taylor, for one, petitioned Johnson to pardon Robert Mills, the wealthiest cotton and sugar planter in all of Texas, whose holdings included more than twenty-one thousand acres and three hundred enslaved people.[24] Johnson granted the pardon on October 6, 1865.[25]

Treason wasn't made odious, nor suffering remunerated with wealth that slavery had stolen. On the contrary, those restored returned to lives of privilege and political power in the South: Stacking state legislatures, they mobilized to deny Black people's right to vote. They passed the discriminatory "Black codes," restricting how Black people worked, migrated, and acquired property. "The war does not appear to us to be ended, nor the rebellion suppressed," affirmed Philip A. Bell, the Black editor of the California-based newspaper the *Elevator*.[26]

By October, so many hundreds of southern white men and women were beseeching the president each day, swarming his very desk, that his staff were compelled to shut down the White House gates.[27] The speed of Johnson's forgiveness, the speed of his forgetting southern treason, caused universal alarm. Quipped the *Boston Traveller*: "The Pardon Mill is in full operation, and daily hundreds of rebels, red as Union blood can make them, are ground over it, coming out white as snow. President Johnson has kindly had a stamp made, with which he signs pardons swiftly. He should have it 'go by steam,' in order that the work may be the more speedily done."[28]

What were all these white men and women pardoned for exactly? Not the injustice of enslaving Black people. They were pardoned for the crime of rebellion. What does the nuance tell us? It signifies travesty. An executive pardon, by absolving the guilty party of the legal consequences of their crime, recognizes, at a minimum, that a crime took place. But here—despite a nation sundered and a million people perished in enmity over the system of enslavement and its profits, "our great national transgression"[29]—the crime recognized and absolved wasn't the abhorrent subjugation of Black people. *That* wasn't even recognized as a crime to be pardoned, let alone one to be prosecuted, legally or otherwise. Slavery, or profit therefrom, was not a transgression for which any white person would be tried.

Worse still, in the great national project of forgiveness just then beginning, in the vast discourses unfolding in Congress about healing and conciliation, the root cause of which was white people's barbarism toward Black people, enslavement wasn't reckoned with but shunted aside. Elite white society was in the stages of leaving the history of slavery behind, for the purposes of their own "healing."

It is important to remember this break. It helps to show how this epoch of mass clemency, "the most monstrous insult to justice and liberty in the annals of our country," wrote the African American newspaper the *Christian Recorder*, was a critical turning point in the construction of national memory.[30] Why does predominant American society today lumber as if in amnesia of its own past? Because a cornerstone of Reconstruction policy, built upon ever since, was to willfully forget. By and by, the bloodstains of history were covered in whitewash.

The betrayal to Black people was stunning. So captured Samuel Childress, formerly enslaved in Nashville, in a searing letter of 1865: "Our race has tilled this land for ages so whatever wealth has been accumulated in the South has been gained mainly by our labour," he wrote to the *Anglo-African Magazine*. His words, heavy with the consciousness of history, make clear that Black people, broadly speaking, weren't in the process of losing their memory willfully, as white people were, over slavery, over the illicit wealth for white people it had bade. "It cannot be denied that the coloured race has earned nearly all of this property," Childress wrote. "Justice requires that it should be paid over to the coloured race who have been robbed of it. But what did they do with it? It has gone back into the hands that are dripping with the blood of murdered prisoners, and whose cruelties cry to heaven for vengeance."[31]

Men rich from enslavement were born again, enriched again with money gone back into the hands of cruelty. In Alabama, two enslaving brothers, having evidently applied for pardons, received them from President Johnson by October 1865. Thus, we read in the *Cincinnati Gazette*, from a correspondent visiting Montgomery at that time, how the Lehman brothers were pardoned.[32] The Lehmans had proved not only loyal but essential to the South's secessionist cause. While Emanuel traveled to London, entrusted with selling Confederate bonds, Mayer, deputized by Jefferson Davis, journeyed behind enemy lines, his mission to negotiate for the release of Confederate soldiers (unsuccessfully, it turns out). All the while, the brothers had grown spectacularly wealthy selling Confederate cotton at a time when its price, due to Union blockades, soared from 10 cents to $1.20 a pound. The brothers "amassed a fortune," in that time, reports an official history commissioned by the Lehman Brothers Bank.[33]

If, after the war, the Lehmans faced no financial disruption, it was partly because they faced no reckoning for rebellion, let alone for destroying Black people's freedom. A second chance is what they freely got. What the nation cared about now, what Johnson carried about, were oaths of allegiance, loyalty to the republic, so that the nation might move on. But a republic loyal to what and to whom? Not Black people; not equality; still the supremacy of white men. "This country was formed for the white, not for the black man," wrote John Wilkes Booth, the assassin, in that eerie letter he penned premeditating Lincoln's death. Lincoln's supposed crime, upon Lee's surrender, was to speak of Black suffrage, to contemplate racial integration. How much had been fought for and lost, only to see the manifesto of white supremacy enacted by President Johnson.[34] The assassin's bullet had made it so.

Stephen Duncan, perhaps the single largest enslaver of Black people in the history of the United States, also sought clemency. After settling in New York, he expended great amounts of energy, according to historian Martha Jane Brazy, lobbying for pardons both for himself and his son, a noted Confederate. The pardons were granted. Duncan thereafter found almost everlasting peace.[35] It is recorded in Bacon's *Abridgment*, a canonical text on English common law, that a pardon frees a person not just from punishment, but "clears the party from infamy...for the pardon makes him as it were a new man."[36] Duncan, too, was reborn, decoupled from gross misdeeds. "Dr. Duncan was beloved by all who knew him, and he leaves not, we think, an enemy behind," the *New York Express* eulogized upon his death in 1867.[37]

For nearly 150 years after the Civil War, hardly a word of opprobrium was printed against this most odious of enslavers. It wasn't until the 1990s, in fact, that scholarship began critically dissecting his legacy. Until then, his reputation slumbered comfortably under history. Some two hundred thousand men like him were pardoned, together by Johnson and Lincoln, restored to honor, mobility, and wealth...a legion of "new men."[38] Perhaps history has forgotten their crimes, those of Duncan and Lehman, Hillman Jr. and so many others, because they were never made infamous or odious through trial or public rebuke.

In 1868, not long after Mayer Lehman reunited with his brother in Manhattan, President Johnson issued the final stroke of conciliation, this time a complete and total amnesty for all Southerners, including Jefferson Davis, formerly on trial for treason. The silencing of justice was comprehensive. "It throws a complete mantle of oblivion over the past," the *Charleston Tri-Weekly Courier* lauded, using an apt phrasing. "Its effect not only wipes out the alleged offense, as if it never existed, but also carries with it a restoration of all rights, privileges and immunities under the Constitution of the United States."[39]

Here, then, in this momentous act, was a wellspring of American historical amnesia, the breeding ground for our myths: "as if it never existed." The writer had been referring to the offense of rebellion—rebellion in pursuit of protecting slavery. But he may as well have been talking about America's history of enslavement itself. The president, with the input of white majorities, and availing the power of "executive grace," waved a wand and erased the past, fabricating an altered social memory. In Congress and in the papers, they spoke thereafter of a new policy, a keystone of hope and future progress, the fundament of which was this: the "nation's pledge of forgetfulness."[40] America had to forget in order to live.

To be clear: What was it the nation was pledging to forget exactly? Again, not only rebellion, the crimes of the Confederacy, and the blood spilled for secession, but the crimes and bloodshed antecedent to that conflict: the crimes white people, both North and South, committed against Black people in the pursuit of supremacy and prosperity. All now were as if they had never existed.

An extraordinary exercise that was: a nation's white elite pledging together, without input from those actually aggrieved, to forget its colossal breach with morality, to erase its very past. So extraordinary it was, in fact, that it warrants a moment more of attention. Imagine the German chancellor, after the Holocaust, calling for the nation's pledge of forgetfulness, an act of oblivion to erase from social memory the heinous crimes Germany's people committed against the Jewish population, and decided to do so without asking for the input of representatives of Jewish people themselves. Of course, that is what many German people did anyway—forget and suppress—though they did so in the absence of a national policy, in what the Germans would call *Wiedergutmachung*, the discourse of avoidance.

Avoidance, denial, burial: such have been the tools used by victorious nations, peoples, and empires, architects of genocide and ethnic destruction throughout time—Japan, the Romans, the Spanish, the Turks—to suppress parts of history in the pursuit of inventing new ones. Here, in the United States, such oblivion was mandated by executive decree, through a nation's pledge. Black people, perversely, were expected to forget too. And so the mantle was thrown as much over insurrection as over the proceeds of slavery and over the men who made possible its output of wealth and privileges, from the mansions of Mississippi to the marble palaces of Broadway.

What becomes of a nation pledged in forgetfulness to the crimes of its past? One answer is found in the story of Mayer Lehman.

Endowed with new immunities, the Lehmans' ascent in restoration was swift, like the ascent of the men around them. They lived in a sense of continuum unbroken by justice. Note that the Lehmans continued to enrich themselves through cotton after the war, and that they continued exploiting Black people to do so. A trade directory lists Lehman, Durr, the southern arm of their firm, as running six cotton mills in Montgomery as of 1869.[41] According to a legal deposition, taken from a manager of the firm, the mills were supplied by sixteen plantations that Lehman, Durr controlled. Black people mostly worked on these plantations, one of the few jobs available under the Black codes. The Lehman brothers, we learn, almost never paid them, however, except in supplies. "It is very seldom that they get anything," testified the manager, Frederick Wolffe, describing a system of near plantation slavery and exploitation even after emancipation. "At the end of the year, in almost every instance, [Black workers] come out behind," Wolffe said.[42]

By 1870, no doubt thanks to his strong position in cotton production, Mayer Lehman was elected to the board of managers of the New York Cotton Exchange.[43] That same year, he bought a new house at 190 East Forty-Sixth Street, for the equivalent of $600,000 today.[44] His corporate linkages at the center of American financial power grew, as did his social standing. Up and up he rose.

The stages of his rehabilitation—building upon his legacy of Black enslavement while increasingly divorced from recrimination over it—reflected not just the evolution of an individual life; they mirrored the stages of the nation's financial evolutions, writes Sarah Churchwell,

professor of American literature at the University of London.[45] And we are
still living within the consequences of its transformation.

Churchwell's words themselves reflect that fact. She wrote them
in reaction to a disturbing cultural phenomenon, a highly revealing one. In 2019, when the National Theatre in London staged a play
about the Lehman brothers—*The Lehman Trilogy*, written by the Ital-
ian playwright Stefano Massini and adapted by the film director Sam
Mendes—critics lauded it as a virtuoso performance, a stirring allegory
on the decline of capitalism and the collapse of the American dream.
The play's subsequent run in New York was also a smash hit. But there
was a glaring problem, as Churchwell, and several other writers, strove
to point out: Massini's play never mentions that the Lehman brothers
were enslavers, that their origins were steeped in the merchandising of
human beings, their foundational wealth extracted from Black people's
brutal exploitation.

Staging scenes of the brothers' origins in Montgomery, the play erases
any depiction of the slavery system that in reality defined that world. In
fact, the Lehmans, as any cursory researching of their lives will show, lived
directly across the street from Montgomery's largest slave market, there on
Court Square, one of the most significant slave markets in all the South.
The daily agonies for Black people, the torments to Black children, the
breaking apart of families and the shattering of lives, were the sadistic
backdrop to the Lehmans' upper-middle-class life and, worse, the bread
and butter of their business. These furies are all stage-silenced by Massini,
edited out for an eager audience watching from the dark.

The allegory of the play becomes an allegory of troubling omission,
one still pertinent to our time. "The erasure of slavery from the play matters," Churchwell wrote for the *New York Review of Books*. "It distorts the
history of Lehman Brothers' beginnings in the antebellum South, allowing the play to evade the question of whether making money out of money
is really more reprehensible than making money out of slaves. That erasure is, ironically enough, perhaps the most allegorical aspect of the entire
story: a history of American capitalism that disavows the central role slavery played in that history."

Here again, we witness the distorted myth of slavery wealth returned,
invested with new energy, propelled forward to a new generation. Histories

conceived in historical oblivion naturally perpetuate that oblivion. And not only in plays. The facts of the Lehman brothers' ties to slavery are omitted or minimized in accounts of the family posted on the website of Columbia University, where the family has endowed chairs and donated money; on the website of Harvard University's Baker Library, which, despite housing an extensive archive of the Lehman Brothers business records, mentions only in passing the family's deep ties to enslavement; in the official congressional biography of Mayer's son, Herbert H. Lehman, who served as senator for New York, which contains not even a passing trace about his family's wealth being derived from slavery; likewise his biography in *The Encyclopedia of New York State*, which, while celebrating his four terms as governor, never acknowledges the tainted privilege in which he was raised.[46]

Predominant white society still cannot look at this history. The pledge of forgetfulness holds.

If Mayer Lehman escaped accountability, we can well imagine that Moses Taylor, opportunistic war Democrat, sugar baron, and Dean of Banking, did too. Taylor emerged from the Civil War a hero of the capitalist class. As early as 1864, the lionization of his reputation had already begun. That year, Hunt's *Merchants' Magazine and Commercial Review*, in a sprawling ten-page profile, full of flattery and praise, celebrated "a man who, in many respects, stands foremost among the active and intelligent business men of this community."[47] What the magazine admired above all was Taylor's incomparable affluence. Not mentioned was his zealous support for southern slavery, nor how that support itself had tipped the country toward war; the energies he engaged, politically and otherwise, in denying equality for Black people in the United States; nor his unbroken and central role, while president of City Bank, in financing the enslavement of African peoples on the island of Cuba.

The oblivious, unquestioning, uncritical mythification of Moses Taylor continued for one hundred years or more, at least well into the 1960s, particularly after Roland T. Ely, then a student at Harvard, discovered the tycoon's business papers. Ely's doctoral thesis, as well as his subsequent articles, were the first to capture the scale of Taylor's financial linkages in Cuba. Yet Ely did so with conspicuous disregard, blind to the linkages to slavery—casting Taylor, once again, as an exceptionally astute businessman, to be admired for his operational rectitude, rather than held accountable for his reprehensibly destructive pursuits.

Through Ely, Taylor was reclaimed in the twentieth century from oblivion, but as a commercial paragon, not a moral pariah. But as the Spanish scholar Claudia Varella wrote: "We question the official image of immaculate honesty that Ely conveyed of Taylor." (Since the late 2000s, a host of critical new scholarship, beginning with historian Alan Singer, and later, John Harris and Varella, among others, has brought vital accountability to bear on Taylor's legacy.)[48] Varella likewise points out that Daniel Hodas, author of the only biography ever written about Taylor (it was published in 1977), never mentions "Taylor's economic relations with the great names of the illegal slave trade to Cuba. He represents him at all times as someone scrupulously ethical, principled; a patriotic entrepreneur, incapable, yes, of offending his clients."

What happens to a nation pledged to forgetfulness? It elevates to near mythical status, in the void of memory, men like Mayer Lehman and Moses Taylor, pedestaling them as models of entrepreneurial success. It cheers and embellishes, even long after their deaths, their hand in shaping not only the course of industrial development, but the ethos of racial exploitation that drove it. "Scrupulously ethical": scholarship, histories, commentaries, and culture have for decades said the same of James Brown, of Stephen Duncan, of Daniel Hillman Jr., of Anson Phelps and Benjamin Marshall, and many others. Undoubtedly, by celebrating the so-called scrupulousness, the so-called principledness, of these men for 150 years, men who flourished within the most unscrupulous and vile business in the history of the world, the national culture makes it easier for itself to perpetuate the ethos of racial exploitation they pioneered.

Had men like Mayer Lehman and Moses Taylor been held to account 150 years ago, made infamous and odious for their transgressions, rather than rehabilitated as idols to imitate, how might capitalism today have its roots in a different ethical basis? It is a question we must consider, given that James Brown and Moses Taylor, through their creation of the first investment banks and industrial conglomerates, instilled the foundations of big business. Their generation of slavery capitalists set the mode of exploitative monopolies that continues to this day.

A nation pledged to forgetfulness institutionalizes its collective amnesia in the face of slavery and its wealth. It was in the vacuum of memory created by Reconstruction that the myth of the Lost Cause emerged, a new mythology about the Old South, painting enslavers as noblemen, their actions motivated by a code of honor, not by dehumanizing greed. Henry Louis Gates Jr. has called the campaign to posit this myth "our country's first culture war,"[49] giving the example of Mildred Lewis Rutherford, who, styling herself the "historian general" of the United Daughters of the Confederacy, fought to remove all negative portrayals of the South from popular textbooks. "Reject a book that says the South fought to hold her slaves," Rutherford wrote in her 1919 book *A Measuring Rod to Test Text Books*. "Reject a book that speaks of the slaveholder of the South as cruel and unjust to his slaves."[50] Her extraordinarily popular work— peddling falsehoods that the experience of Black people during enslavement wasn't so harsh, that the South seceded to protect states' rights, not to protect slavery—not only galvanized conservatives throughout the 1920s to ban textbooks exploring the economic underpinnings of slavery. These deeply erroneous beliefs have overshadowed generations, embedding false notions of history that persist today.[51]

What happens to a nation pledged to forgetfulness? Its history remains hostage, even now, to revisionists seeking to stylize an unblemished, untroubling past, of which white people should feel no guilt, and which they can, almost pathologically, long to return to…the ideological pathway to Donald Trump's campaign slogan Make America Great Again. Amnesia emboldens men like Senator Tom Cotton of Arkansas and former US secretary of state Mike Pompeo, prominent conservatives who have argued, in an attempt to discredit the 1619 Project of Nikole Hannah-Jones, that America's history of capitalism is not indebted to slavery, and that saying otherwise is to sow a false and "dark vision of America's birth."[52]

Such a nation remains pledged to burying knowledge, and pledged to banning books that explore how racism is embedded in our institutions, as we see happening all around the country now. It becomes a nation where Republican lawmakers, in their ongoing crusade against "critical race theory," have now introduced bills or other measures in an astounding forty-four states to limit how teachers are allowed to discuss the history of race in the United States, as *Education Week* has reported.[53] Eighteen states have already imposed such bans.

In a nation reconstructed out of mental oblivion, committed to mental oblivion, the proponents of culture war, seeking to up the stakes, apply downward pressure on an ever-growing roster of targets, as Governor Ron DeSantis has done in Florida, banning the teaching of an Advanced Placement class in African American studies merely because it examines the transatlantic slave trade, the Black Lives Matter movement, and the roots of the growing call for slavery reparations. Such pundits, seeking to suppress the country's legacy of oppression, are creating a new cycle in that very legacy of suppression. In a nation pledged to amnesia, history is a loop, condemned to repeat itself.

The links binding modern corporations to this history are all around us, though still hidden, actively denied, and obscured. Against the prevalent tendency to forget and erase, the pioneering work of Black activists since the late 1990s has increasingly pulled these links up from the ground, examining how the foundations of corporate wealth and power in the United States—representing billions of dollars today—are rooted in the bedrock of enslavement. Their efforts, by winding back the motion of history, and reverse-engineering the link from modern corporations to slavery, have resulted in pioneering litigation and the establishment of new laws, and have shown how many of the world's most prestigious and influential brands, everyday corporate names, are—despite those brands' concerted efforts to silence history—the living vessel of wealth derived from the enslaved.

That story began, fittingly, when the unexpected excavation in New York of a forgotten world, lost beneath the sediments of the city and the buildup of metropolitan life, led one Black woman on a quest to follow that trail.

CHAPTER 12

"THE BODIES AND THE BONE"

In an alley in lower Manhattan, on a workday afternoon in 1991, a construction crew on a dig punched its backhoe through the street, ripping open a hole and breaking the seal to a world not seen for nearly two hundred years. They saw coffins in the dark below, hexagonal in shape, and they were resting side by side in a crumbling catacomb. The excavation was supposed to lay the foundation for a $275 million federal skyscraper; instead, it uncovered an anchor of history that has recentered America's story of slavery in New York ever since. The wood of the coffins, the workers could see, had almost completely perished, revealing skeletal remains inside—remains that were, in most cases, fully intact; they appeared never to have been touched or moved. It was a sacred resting place, its origins unknown but clearly of portentous historical value. The construction crew immediately brought the excavation to a halt.

The team of specialists and archaeologists called in afterward spent weeks exploring down in the tombs. They discovered dozens more skeletons in the dark and discovered also that each had been carefully wrapped in winding sheets. In many cases, the sheets had disintegrated, but the metal pins fastening them had not. They were buried with buttons, shells,

and beads. Their deaths, in other words, had been attended to with lov-
ing care. Pieces of history had endured, the first clues found resting with
the dead, to speak of those who had lived: a community of Africans and
African Americans, generations that had labored, lived, and loved in New
York, building its colonial foundations, some as free people but most
enslaved.

Records dating back to the 1750s had spoken of this place, a burial
ground for Black people, on what was then the margins of the city, just
past City Hall. The records told that the cemetery had been laid in 1712;
that it had closed around 1794; that in between it had expanded to an
enormous size, encompassing nearly seven acres, reaching, according
to some colonial accounts, as far as Washington Square. Experts in the
modern era came to believe that as many as twenty thousand Black people were interred there, an astonishing testament to the Black lives that
shaped Manhattan, and a truly powerful piece of US history. Yet no one
alive had ever seen it, or knew what, if anything, might remain.

That all changed with the dig. Rev. Herbert Daughtry, called to the
site to speak of its discovery, said: "Had it not been for the bodies and
the bone, the body and the labor of those people who rest yonder—our
ancestors—there would not have been a United States of America."[1]

The excavation team eventually brought 417 skeletons to the surface.
At Howard University, researchers later determined that almost half were
children under the age of fifteen, their bones recording a life of harsh
physical toil, malnutrition, and disease. "The burial ground revealed the
centrality of daily slave labor to New York City's black population but also
African Americans' hopes for a life beyond slavery," writes historian Leslie
M. Harris, in *In the Shadow of Slavery*.[2] There were signs of harrowing
brutality and resistance, but signs, too, of triumph: in one coffin reposed
a Black Revolutionary War hero, buried with his uniform, a burial of
distinction.

As excavation of the site continued, tensions over its fate rose. The US
General Services Administration, the builder of the skyscraper, pressed
to go ahead with the project, meaning that it would remove the skeletons
and desecrate the burial ground. Activists and Black community leaders,
including members of an African Burial Ground steering committee
appointed by Congress, vehemently opposed.

When they began staging events to draw attention to the issue in 1993, more and more people converged on the site. And among them was a woman named Deadria Farmer-Paellmann, then twenty-seven years old. Her indelible impact in helping launch the reparations movement in the United States proceeded from that night. Farmer-Paellmann was then a press officer for the New York City Department of Health, but she was also a musician; she'd been invited by a coalition of activists to stage a drum vigil as part of the publicity. While there, a close friend, who was passionate about the history of the site, extended to her an invitation she hadn't expected: Did she want to go down into the dig? And so, donning a hard hat and descending into the catacomb, Farmer-Paellmann stumbled upon an experience that forever changed her, she says.

"What I saw down in the burial ground were first-generation Africans," Farmer-Paellmann described to me, in a recent video call from her home in New Jersey.[3] Today, she is the executive director of the Restitution Study Group, which advocates for slavery reparations. "Some of the remains had etchings on their teeth, carved. There were beads that had been worn by enslaved women, who managed to hold on to them even during their enslavement. And there were some mass burials." The visit stirred and terrified her in equal measure. "One [skeleton] in particular struck me," she said. "The head was turned, and the jaw was wide open. It looked like the person had been screaming. It was really a scary experience for me."

Farmer-Paellmann found that, down amid this sacred link to the past, so many questions raced to the surface of her mind: "Where did these people come from? How did they find them?" As they walked, her friend explained that nothing had ever been built on this part of the cemetery, and so the remains, miraculously, had never been touched. And then he said something more: he explained that in the world of colonial-era and antebellum New York, enslaved Black people "were the stock on Wall Street," traded and used by white people as commodities.

Something about that struck a nerve for Farmer-Paellmann. It tapped into a reservoir of harrowing memories, a lingering sense of injustice—memories of her childhood in Bensonhurst, Brooklyn, a place where white children routinely called her the N-word and attacked Black children in her school, and where gangs of young white men beat and harassed Black people on the streets. This included the mob of white men who, in 1989, brutally murdered Yusuf Hawkins, a sixteen-year-old Black teenager. His death was a visceral memory for Farmer-Paellmann.

"It was a very racially charged upbringing," she said, "and I became really conscious of a lot of things, injustices, I had to endure, as if we lived in the South, the old stories of the South. And I was very clear: These were the vestiges of slavery. This kind of violence that we had to duck on a daily basis—we were still living with it." She already wanted to become a lawyer because of that, to address the intolerable racism and violence she had experienced in her upbringing. That plus the recurrent conversations she had with her grandfather ("They never gave us our forty acres and a mule," he had often said) evoked the sense that to Black people something vital by America was owed. Her visit to the burial ground, suggesting the injustices connecting Wall Street to slavery, the present to the past, gave greater shape and focus to Deadria Farmer-Paellmann's blooming ambition.

"I understood that there was something there that we needed to pay close attention to," she said. "So I actually applied to law school, and I was bold enough to tell them that I wanted to build a case for slavery reparations. I wanted to be an architect for that case, an architect for justice." As children, Farmer-Paellmann and her five sisters had shared one room. "We were really broke growing up," she said. No one in her family had ever gone to law school. She was accepted by and enrolled at New England Law in Boston.

With every course Farmer-Paellmann took, she applied what she learned to build her reparations case. One legal precedent she studied helped hone her strategy, by suggesting what would probably *not* work: *Cato v. United States*, in which a class of Black plaintiffs sued the federal government for reparations based on the history of enslavement. The case, filed in California, was eventually dismissed by the Ninth Circuit Court of Appeals, and the takeaway for Farmer-Paellmann was that it was dismissed because the government has sovereign immunity, which means it can't be sued for its role in slavery. "So I said: Okay, I'm not going to sue the federal government. Let's see who else is out there. Let's see who else can be held liable," Farmer-Paellmann said. "So I started looking at private estates. Individual estates that might still be around. I started looking at the richest people in America. And from there, I started to look at corporate entities and the law of restitution."

Over hours at the Boston Public Library, she tracked down every link that she could find between slavery and companies still existing today. The evidence overwhelmed her. "I realized: this is the bottom line," she said, "the foundation, really, for slavery in America."

Certainly, others before Deadria Farmer-Paellmann had advocated for reparations to address the atrocities committed against African Americans during enslavement. As far back as 1989, when Congressman John Conyers, representative of Michigan's Thirteenth District, introduced a bill seeking to establish a commission to study the issue, the push for reparations at a federal level had grown. But no one had ever sued a modern corporation seeking reparations for slavery before. The mechanism of Farmer-Paellmann's groundbreaking litigation fell into place.

———

BY THE DAWN of the twentieth century, nearly all the men responsible for institutionalizing the business of slavery, for anchoring it as a font of American wealth, were dead. Mayer Lehman died in 1897; Daniel Hillman Jr., in 1885; Moses Taylor, in 1882; and James Brown, in 1877, to name but a few. They were buried, each of them, with great pomp and publicity, their remains committed to large marble sarcophagi or buried under elaborate slabs, in grounds considered the most fashionable burial plots of their age—graves never to be lost nor buried over.

The press were keenly interested to observe, meanwhile, not merely what these men had accomplished in life, but more importantly, what they would leave behind in death. Their wills and other instruments, the newspapers attentively speculated, would no doubt pass down great fortunes to children, wives, and heirs—a cascade of riches ensuring that familial dynasties and merchant houses would survive for generations to come. ("This will," wrote the *Independent Statesman* of New Hampshire when James Brown died at the age of eighty-six, "adds to the number of enormous estates which have so recently gone through the surrogates' hands.")[4]

The public unveiling of these bequests put to rest any lingering mystery or doubts: these were among the richest capitalists and industrialists in the history of the United States, some with truly staggering estates. (Moses Taylor bequeathed $25 million, or nearly $700 million today, to five of his heirs.) The attention that then swirled around these fortunes, in private chambers and public gatherings throughout the nation, crystallized an important fact: the money itself had become a character all its own, quite apart from the men, such that though their individual lives had ended, another story about their wealth was just beginning, a new chapter in the history of America's commercial evolution and continuing prosperity.

Deeply entwined within that story weren't just the private estates of the deceased; what they left to their heirs, in other words, was not all that would live on. For each of these men (not to mention dozens, if not hundreds, of others like them) had also created corporations, as we've seen—a bevy of corporations, many of them financed and capitalized for years with funds appropriated from Black people's stolen labor. Collectively, this network of interlacing corporations constituted a kind of living dynasty all its own.

Traces of it were what Deadria Farmer-Paellmann was uncovering in her ongoing research. At the library, she tracked down older and rarer books, books that weren't on the shelves. "What I discovered is: really, really juicy books, you have to make a request," she said. There, Farmer-Paellmann came across northern names like the Browns and the DeWolfs, prominent families of Providence, Rhode Island. They were maritime dynasties in the early 1800s, a time when the transatlantic slave trade had yet to be outlawed. They grew superlatively rich; some of the earliest and finest homes ever built in Providence and Newport they erected with this wealth. Their vessels, they sailed across the Atlantic for the African coast, buying men, women, and children, trading them for sugar in the Caribbean, then sailing the sugar back to Rhode Island, where their distilleries processed the sugar into rum. The wealth the Browns amassed from slave runs, they funneled into a variety of enterprises, some of which they later incorporated.

"I started looking at old money," explained Farmer-Paellmann, "and realized these people are connected to companies." One of the Browns' corporations, Farmer-Paellmann traced through records, evolved, in stages, into the Providence Bank of Rhode Island. The link would become a foundation of her legal argument, a model of how wealth created from slavery flowed into corporations.

What makes it possible for a corporation founded more than two hundred years ago to still live on, such that there is any basis for saying it is the same? To answer that question, it helps to consider another one first: Why did white men in the eighteenth and nineteenth century, a time that marked the full blossoming of incorporation in the history of the United States, choose to form corporations at all? The most obvious answer—they wished to generate profit, and, through the legal particularities of the corporate form, to protect themselves and their shareholders from liability and risk—isn't the most illuminating for this discussion. For there's an added benefit to the process of incorporation, truly a priceless and rare one at that, and it's also for this reason, at a time of exploding wealth in the antebellum period, that white men incorporated enterprises at a rate unprecedented in the history of the nation. Corporations, unlike people sheaved in their mortal bodies, don't have to die, at least not a natural death. Though the men who created a corporation may perish, and though all the original shareholders of the corporation so formed in that time may perish, we do not, according to US law and convention, say that the corporation has perished.

If we did, corporations in the United States would enjoy drastically short life spans, with the result that almost every year, corporations would be dying and the US economy would perpetually be on the brink of collapse. Our earliest laws, however, stipulated quite the opposite, that a corporation could live on from its founders, through perpetual successions, indefinitely, in fact, so long as its board of directors wanted it to, and this allowed for continuity. A corporation, then, is a very peculiar and unnatural thing, its form chosen, specifically, for this particular reason: it is eternal. "Among the most important [objects for which corporations are created] are immortality and, if the expression may be allowed, individuality." So observed John Marshall, the fourth and longest-running chief justice of the United States, in a famous legal opinion of 1819.[5]

Accruing within such immortality isn't merely the corporation's name, but its agency. US courts from an early period recognized this agency, that corporations are a repository for men's moral decisions, including their moral failures, as the scholarship of W. Robert Thomas, lecturer at Harvard Law School, traces. Thomas cites, among other examples, how the highest court in Alaska in 1901 concluded: "If...the invisible, intangible essence of air which we term a corporation can level mountains, fill up valleys, lay down iron tracks, and run railroad cars on them, it can also intend to do those acts, and can act therein as well viciously as virtuously."[6] A corporation is the sum total of its actions, taken over time.

Immortality is the reason that City Bank, founded in 1812, and then revitalized by Moses Taylor in 1837, can be said to still exist today. In that time, its name has evolved from City Bank of New York to National City Bank, and from there to Citibank and now Citi, but it is, for all intents and purposes, the same entity. This is reaffirmed by the firm's own logic and statements. Citi doesn't say, and in fact, has never said, that it is today an altogether different company from the firm that Benjamin Bailey, John Swartwout, and other slavery profiteers formed more than two centuries ago. It doesn't say that it's a wholly reinvented company from the one Moses Taylor built. Instead, the company claims, proudly, an unbroken continuum and connection with that past—indeed, with those people—though, tellingly, it does so while utterly occluding the part about slavery: "With more than 210 years of experience making a positive financial and social impact, we are proud of our past contributions and excited about our future," reads the "Heritage" section of Citi's website. "Many of the bank's early leaders were significant figures in the New York merchant economy. Quaker merchant Isaac Wright, a one-time board director and bank president, was a leading importer of British textiles. He founded the Black Ball Line, which was believed to be the first regular packet line service between New York and Liverpool. Benjamin Marshall, his partner in the shipping line, joined the board as well."[7]

This unbroken chain of historical connection is, in large part, the basis of Citi's prestige, the value of its brand, and as a result, that brand is worth a tremendous amount. And if it is true that Citi's claims of being connected, through history and time, to its original founders, are both legitimate and acceptable, that its identity has, in a sense, evolved yet never changed, making the company what it is today—if all this is true, then it stands to reason that Citi today is also legitimately connected by that chain to something else, something that has also endured and evolved over time, something without which the company would not be what it is today. And that is its foundational wealth—its slavery wealth.

Men of the nineteenth century utilized the corporate form not only to sheath the reputation, the operations, the brand, and the expertise of a firm in perpetuity. They utilized the corporate form to shield the corporation's profits and assets in perpetuity as well. Corporations were invented, among other things, to be a vessel of financial immortality, something unprecedented in the history of the world, where wealth was passed along familial lineages, so long as such lineages endured, but not among collections of investors. Because they do not die like people, corporations have no need of wills; they do not bequeath their wealth to heirs after a certain time. Rather, the wealth of a corporation, like the span of the corporate charter itself, lives on.

That is what corporations, after all, do: they oversee the continuity of "durable wealth," of long-term profit, and by turning one form of wealth into another, by marshaling various instruments (stocks, bonds, loans, products, services) to amplify their assets, they cause the wealth at their core to evolve over long periods of time. Sometimes, that evolution means the corporation is acquired by and absorbed into another one, still in essence living on.

It can be said that this evolution of wealth, the path it takes over time, *is* the corporation. For while the people who work there may live and die (though they leave their impress) and the headquarters may change, it is the wealth of a corporation, alongside the name and the brand, that truly remains.

Citi exemplifies this fact. In the days preceding its famous move in 1908, the bank exchanged as much of the silver and gold in its vault for paper notes as it could. In the days to follow, it would convert tens of millions more, changing coin to cash, the currency of the nineteenth century to the currency of the twentieth. And so it washed away any physical trace of how the institutionalization of Black enslavement had wrought that wealth in between. All this treasure the bank then placed into the centerpiece of its new home: a vault of steel, twenty feet high, twenty-four feet long, and fifteen feet wide. It weighed six hundred thousand pounds, clad in armor a foot and a half thick, including eight inches of railroad iron.

The new building that City Bank moved into at 55 Wall Street, though called the Custom House, had earlier been known by a different name: it was the Merchants' Exchange Building, its dome the very one under which so many of the country's slavery capitalists had gathered, causing so much of the country's sectional strife.

The specific gold coins and dollar notes from City Bank's original time in slavery no longer existed, but neither, as we've seen, did the firm's founders or the original furniture. This doesn't mean that the corporation no longer endures, merely that its wealth and assets have evolved as must happen for survival. Arie de Geus, a former Shell executive, has argued that corporations are, in fact, in no other business than the business of evolving and surviving. [8]

If we accept this, while also knowing that City Bank's directors, not to mention its many clients, deposited the profits of Black enslavement into the bank, week after week for a period of fifty years or more, from 1812 to 1865, thus building a significant portion of the bank's original corporate wealth…if we understand this, how can we not say that Citi is today what it is because of its origins in slavery? Was every single penny of the bank's profits derived from slavery? Of course not. But was the portion derived from slavery so sizable and so interconnected with the bank's capital as to make slavery integral and indelible to Citi's overall fortunes? Certainly.

To deny so is to deny the rudiments of history. This is like discovering one day that in New York City, hidden below a forgotten layer of time, there rests a lost burial ground of the enslaved. Certainly, New York is many things, many layers, many stories. But uncovering such a burial ground, can we reasonably say that this foundational layer of history, con-noting a community of Africans and African Americans—twenty thousand people who triumphed, lost, and lived—had no bearing on what form the life of the city takes now?

On the contrary, such a discovery, as in fact it has, would dramatically alter our understanding of New York, of how it came to be. Reasonable minds would be compelled to conceive, in fact, that it is only *because* of this history of slavery that New York City is the place we experience today. Slavery, and the city's evolution, are integrally, and eternally, linked. So too with Citi, and the many, many corporations existing today that prospered with profits reaped from Black bondage. The corporate form fared spectacularly well in granting immortality to that wealth.

Though Moses Taylor died, the corporations he founded never did, and nor did the profits from slavery that he placed in them. His earliest

investments in start-up gas and lighting companies, seeded with the profits he channeled from slavery, profits arriving aboard his ships each year
from the plantations of Cuba and the labor camps of the South, evolved
over time into something lasting, that still remains: the Consolidated Gas
Company. It was Taylor's son-in-law, Percy Pyne, succeeding Taylor as
president of City Bank, who oversaw the ultimate creation, through mergers and consolidation, of this vast enterprise by the late 1880s. Today the
company is known as Con Edison, a firm generating more than $10 bil-
lion in annual revenue. It is but one company among dozens that Taylor
incubated.

The corporations that Anson G. Phelps created didn't perish when
his body perished, nor did they perish when William Dodge died. Phelps
Dodge, a firm rooted in the global exchange of slavery-produced commodities for precious metals, a firm that helped channel the stolen labor of
Black people into modern industry, evolved, under a succession of corporate leaders, into higher and higher stages throughout the twentieth century, until it became one of the largest mining companies in the world. (It
did so by using its network of railroads, and copper enterprises throughout
Arizona and New Mexico, to produce cables and metal wire, at a time
when those products were essential to the industrial revolution.)

The firm's banker during this evolution was City Bank; Moses Taylor
passed on his relationship with Phelps and William Dodge to Pyne, his
son-in-law. Throughout the 1900s, Phelps Dodge came to acquire mines
in Peru, Iraq, and the Congo. By turns, through the effect of fate, will, and
time, as happens in the history of such enterprises, where success builds
upon success, it became a multibillion-dollar conglomerate. In 2007, the
mining company Freeport-McMoRan acquired Phelps Dodge for nearly
$26 billion.

It is an immutable law of time and history, is it not, that there was only
a corporation for Freeport-McMoRan to acquire in the first place because
Anson G. Phelps, standing on the deck of a four-hundred-ton bark, so many
years before, specialized in sourcing cotton from labor camps worked by
the enslaved. The same can be said of Alexander Brown and the Brown
brothers, their corporations having evolved into two multibillion-dollar
investment firms today, Brown Brothers Harriman, headquartered in New
York, and Alex. Brown, headquartered in Baltimore. These are firms that,

by gladly promoting the unbroken lineage to their original founders, bind themselves to a family of slavery financiers, and the ill-gotten gains that Black people's forced labor afforded them.

It is erroneous to think that this metamorphosis, by which slavery-steeped enterprises become global multinationals, is rare or unlikely, or even complicated, as we may have tended to think. Recall that survival, continuity, and evolution are precisely the functions that corporations were invented to ensure. Dozens, and perhaps even hundreds, of US corporations evolved like this, flowing like a current, or a river, from actions and decisions rooted in monetizing the brutalization of Black people. What is untimely and vexed is not this process, but the willingness to see it so.

This corporate lineage is a central core of the history of American capitalism, "leaving slavery behind but banking its profits," as Sarah Churchwell has written.[9] We must imagine what volumes of wealth from slavery—handled by men like Taylor, Lehman, Phelps, and Pyne—such corporations ingested and preserved, compounding and turning these material riches into other things. It is impossible to know, of course, in any exact figure, yet an exact figure does not prevent us from reasonably inferring that we are conceiving of hundreds of billions of dollars. Many corporations now surviving fulfill the seed of promise, the pursuit of long-term profit, planted so long ago by men seeking a vessel of immortality to sheath the gains they pilfered from slavery like lesser gods. This cascade of wealth has now spilled over into our time. And Deadria Farmer-Paellmann's lawsuit helped illuminate the path of this cascade in more detail than ever before.

It had been while standing amid the ruins of the Black cemetery, encircled by skyscrapers just blocks from Wall Street, and then later during her research, that she had perceived these facts: That many of our corporations, still existing all around us, exist only because they had been able to pilfer through slavery. And yet none of them, the heirs to fortunes stolen from the enslaved, had ever been held to account. Why? The fact that a crime so monstrous had taken place so long ago did not make it any less monstrous. What's more, the very story linking these corporations to slavery, Farmer-Paellmann also perceived, though abundantly detailed in documents she continued to find in Boston, was nonetheless woefully unexplored in scholarship or otherwise, and particularly unexplored by the corporations themselves. How, like the lost cemetery, could we let this history remain so buried, covered over by so-called progress and the march of time? Farmer-Paellmann hoped that at minimum, through her research, these details would be brought to light.

By the year 2000, she was making headway to that effect. Her efforts were focused on a corporation called Aetna Inc., an insurance giant based in Hartford, Connecticut. (Founded in 1853, the company is owned by CVS Health, with nearly fifty thousand employees and revenue in 2022 of more than $80 billion.)[10] Farmer-Paellmann had uncovered a 1906 history of Aetna detailing that "among the first 1,000 policies issued, 339 were upon the lives of negro slaves in Maryland and Virginia."[11] She wrote to Aetna with these facts, insisting that the company apologize and pay restitution, something no one had ever done before.

In response, Aetna went back into its archives; it found at least four policies, dating from the 1850s, showing that Farmer-Paellmann was right.[12] The company refused to consider the idea of restitution, however, maintaining that a public apology was sufficient. Its standoff with Farmer-Paellmann, morphing quickly into a flashpoint, was covered by dozens of news outlets, but much of the reportage, it must be said, was acrid, skeptical and often sneering about her efforts. Suddenly, what began as the work of a lone activist, labeled as out of tune, had set off a nationwide debate, focused on how major corporations—indeed, the country—needed to address the harrowing atrocities of slavery and the past. "How long are we going to stay asleep on this?" Farmer-Paellmann said in an interview with Robin Finn of the *New York Times*. Finn's biting profile attempted to cast doubts not just on Farmer-Paellmann's legal efforts, but on her integrity, questioning, for one, why a Black woman seeking reparations for slavery would choose to live in a building with a doorman. "I don't mind starting this alone," Farmer-Paellmann replied. "I'm the wake-up call."[13]

When at last it was filed, Farmer-Paellmann's lawsuit would set in motion a chain of events that continued that momentum, helping found a movement and further piercing the long veil of corporate silence, a mantle of oblivion all its own. The tangle of controversies leading up to this, involving several of the largest banks in the world, proved, once again, that her theory and her research were right.

CHAPTER 13

"THE UNIVERSE OF PREDECESSORS"

The evidence was all there, in old leather-bound volumes. Most were breaking down and tucked away in New Orleans, the pages brittle, and scrawled with the careful penmanship of a bygone age. These were the official meeting minutes of Citizens Bank of Louisiana, a bank that, though founded in the nineteenth century, today is part of the global conglomerate JPMorgan Chase. The ledger minutes detailed how Citizens' board of directors, all well-to-do white men, would routinely meet around a table to discuss, openly and indifferently, transactions in which clients seeking to secure mortgages and other loans, to build new destinies for themselves and their children, did so by wagering away as collateral the lives and fates of enslaved Black people. "The terror of the mundane and quotidian" was one of the many brutalities of enslavement that Saidiya V. Hartman, professor of English at Columbia University, explores in the celebrated book *Scenes of Subjection*.[1] That terror was fully at work here: bank approval, home ownership, the American dream, transacted each week by prolonging the nightmare for Black families. The clients seeking such loans included upwardly mobile townspeople, widows, and farmers.

There was also a rakish card shark, the ledgers revealed, an inveterate gambler and notorious aristocrat of French origin, Bernard de Marigny. He owned a large plantation with dozens of enslaved people. The more he lost at cards, the more he sought loans from the bank's directors; the more loans they approved, the more the directors took enslaved people as surety. The terms of such deals stipulated that, should any clients default, the bank itself would possess the Black people so bonded, to be disposed of as the directors saw fit. De Marigny, for one, lost all he had in the 1850s, and sixty-two Black people's lives were thrown into the coffers of the bank. He wasn't the only one. The bank, the ledgers would one day show, profited spectacularly from this reviled business.

The story tracing how these transactions tie back to JPMorgan Chase—a twisting history of acquisition, commercial evolution, and perpetual existence—almost never came to light, buried as it was under time, nearly forgotten and lost. But then, in 2002, Deadria Farmer-Paellmann filed her lawsuit, and unexpected events leading to that history began springing into place.

Farmer-Paellmann filed her case in New York. The feeling for her was utter elation, she said, the fulfillment of accomplishing something she had set out to do, something vital, something never done. In her suit, she cited the African Burial Ground, as supporting proof that slavery, even outside of the South, "fueled the prosperity of the young nation."[2] She also tied corporations to the enormous wealth gap that afflicts African Americans today, arguing that the stolen Black labor that made corporations rich was wealth deprived to Black people and their descendants for generations, leaving them to confront far greater economic challenges than white people across the board. Her suit sought financial restitution ("disgorgement of illicit profits" was the technical term) from three named defendants around whom her research all those years had coalesced: FleetBoston Financial, the predecessor to Providence Bank; Aetna Inc.; and the railroad company CSX, whose expansion was driven by enslaved labor.

JPMorgan wasn't among these defendants. But by a twist of fate, another legal team, filing a similar reparations lawsuit around the same time, did name JPMorgan, and in that way the company was pulled into the spotlight. In fact, three legal teams filed reparations lawsuits that year, seeking billions in forfeited profits and naming as defendants a total of eighteen companies, including Brown Brothers Harriman, Lehman Brothers, and New York Life Insurance. The spotlight quickly grew and grew.

The news coverage that ensued, as wide as it was incredulous (the story was picked up in England), reflected sharply how the issue of slavery reparations, at that moment in time, wasn't an issue the white majority of Americans had much heard of and certainly wasn't one they were disposed to hear. Deadria Farmer-Paellmann appeared on CNN, where anchor Paula Zahn asked her: "What do you say to the people out there this morning who are saying, 'Hey, wait a minute. It is time to move on'?"

Farmer-Paellmann replied: "I say to them that these are corporations that benefited from stealing people, from stealing labor, from forced breeding, from torture, from committing numerous horrendous acts, and there's no reason why they should be able to hold on to assets they acquired through such horrendous acts."

Perhaps never on American television had the horrors of Black enslavement been so incisively linked to the profits of corporations still in business. Farmer-Paellmann's lawyer, seated next to her, added: "Why they should be accountable today is that they are the beneficiaries of a crime, that they are the beneficiaries of monies that were ill-gotten, monies that came from stolen labor."[3]

The case, after that, took on a life of its own, edging closer to the forgotten ledgers of Citizens Bank, seemingly a world away. One of the reasons was that in Chicago, Dorothy Tillman was watching. Tillman was one of the longest-serving aldermen on the Chicago City Council. Born in Montgomery, Alabama, she had been an activist from her earliest days, marching in Selma with Martin Luther King Jr. She was larger than life, intrepid, unflinching toward foes, and famous for wearing large, magnificent hats.

Tillman had long been exploring avenues for slavery reparations, and she was already aware of a novel California law that, enacted in 2000, required insurance companies doing business in that state to disclose any past ties to slavery. As a result, several large companies—including New York Life Insurance—had, in fact, come forward, revealing such connections. It showed that it could be done, that a law could force a corporation's hand. With the timing of those disclosures, and now the reparations law-suits, Dorothy Tillman moved the Chicago City Council to enact a similar ordinance of its own, and she did so in part to aid the litigation that Farmer-Paellmann and others had filed. "We want to know what was your role in slavery, what did you do, was your company built off the backs of slaves," Tillman said at the time.[4]

By October 2002, the Chicago City Council overwhelmingly approved the ordinance, calling it the Slavery Era Disclosure Ordinance. Today, a dozen other states have enacted slavery-era ordinances of a similar kind, with the power to compel corporations to reveal their past. At the time, however, the Chicago law was unprecedented. It required not just insurance companies but any entity seeking to do business with the city to scour its records and disclose any past connections to slavery it may have had, no matter how loose. (The term *connection* was kept exceedingly broad.) Corporations found to have been untruthful in their filings, Tillman made clear, could have their contracts voided. Billions of dollars were at stake. More than two thousand corporations quickly filed disclosures.[5] Most said they had no ties to slavery. But in another unexpected twist, one company admitted that it did. It was Lehman Brothers Bank.

Back in 1950, in an official history the Lehman Brothers Bank self-published to mark its one hundredth anniversary, the firm had made no mention whatsoever of slavery, and hardly any even of cotton. Not in any of its literature or any statement at all had the firm ever disclosed its founders as being enslavers, nor that their business had originally been tied to the business of coercing free labor from enslaved people. The Chicago disclosure was unprecedented, not just for the company, but for the country. What Farmer-Paellmann had achieved once before, and what Tillman had helped make law, was coming true again: a major corporation, compelled to search back through its own records, to confront its own past, had found that, yes, it had benefited from enslaving Black people, including children.

Lehman Brothers, at the time one of the most influential institutions on Wall Street, made these facts known in a press conference in November 2003. It did so, however, in a decidedly halfhearted manner. Henry Lehman, Mayer's older brother (he died in 1855), had purchased, for the fee of $900, a fourteen-year-old girl named Martha in 1854, a company spokesman told reporters. Yet he added, with strange vagueness, that the Lehman brothers "may have personally owned other slaves." He didn't elaborate.[6]

The company hoped the matter would end there. But Dorothy Tillman, sensing that Lehman Brothers was withholding, threatened, unless the firm did a more thorough review, to void its contracts with the city. (Lehman Brothers was then pursuing a stake in a $1 billion bond deal to expand Chicago's O'Hare International Airport.) She would turn out to be right.

Another twist was unfolding in the meantime. JPMorgan Chase had also submitted its disclosure to the Chicago City Council. The bank, already a defendant in one of the reparations lawsuits, was in the process of acquiring the Chicago-based Bank One Corporation; if it were found to be unforthcoming, that deal could fall apart. Unlike Lehman, JPMorgan Chase stated in its official filing that it had had no connection whatsoever to slavery. It said so publicly as well, reaffirming its position. "Since the allegation has surfaced, we've undergone a search of our records and have used an outside archivist to see if we can find any truth to it and we can find none," a company spokesman, Tom Johnson, told the press in late 2003. "We believe the allegations are not true."[7] Ironically, by acquiring Bank One, JPMorgan was about to deepen its past ties to slavery.

The ledgers in Louisiana, sitting and waiting to be found, told that story, and soon that story would be told publicly as well. For now, Dorothy Tillman didn't even know about those ledgers. But she was already in possession of different information, thanks to her daughter, Ebony, suggesting that JPMorgan wasn't being forthright. There followed more twists and unexpected turns. Ebony Tillman, conducting her own research, had uncovered, at the Library of Congress, historical records showing that the earliest corporate foundation of JPMorgan Chase—Peabody, Morgan & Co., founded in 1854—had two partners: Junius S. Morgan (father of John Pierpont Morgan) and George Peabody.

Peabody (his name is still connected today to a famous philanthropic organization) was a man cut from the same cloth as Alexander Brown: a merchant who grew rich sourcing and marketing slavery-produced tobacco and cotton; who funneled his profits from slave commodities into loans and credits; and who later moved to London to work in sterling exchange, turning the riches of enslavement into the foundations of Atlantic trade. At the time of the Chicago controversy, JPMorgan's website appeared to claim Peabody as one of its own, detailing that, when he opened his London bank in 1838, this set about "establishing the roots of the House of Morgan."[8] Yet to the City Council and the press, JPMorgan Chase insisted the firm wasn't a predecessor.

The bank's dealings with the city were as tense as they were confusing. It nonetheless offered to amend its filings, attesting that, yes, J. P. Morgan and George Peabody had, in fact, done business together, but that it was of an entirely unclear nature, and that any ties to enslavement were even more uncertain.

Dorothy Tillman wasn't convinced. She accused the company of perjury, threatening to void $400 million in city funds and contracts. She demanded that they, like Lehman Brothers, go back and do a more thorough search of their records. Dorothy Tillman would turn out, once again, to be right.

Then came another twist. By this time, Deadria Farmer-Paellmann's reparations lawsuit, consolidated now with a total of nine others, had been transferred to the jurisdiction of a federal court in Chicago. In January 2004, those cases, unprecedented not only as litigation but also for the global awareness they had generated, were, after long advancing through their proceedings, at last ruled upon by US District Court Judge Charles R. Norgle. He dismissed the consolidated reparations lawsuits, but "without prejudice," meaning that, because he saw merit in some of the plaintiffs' arguments, he left open the possibility that they could file an amended complaint.

Norgle highlighted the "historic injustices" of slavery but found that the plaintiffs lacked standing, both because they'd filed suit long after slavery had ended and because they'd failed to draw a direct connection between specific victims of slavery and the liability of the corporations so sued. In his ruling, he made a point of saying that the atrocities of slavery were an open wound needing to be addressed, and that the judiciary, by declining to address that wound, was not acting out of callousness. "To suggest that the lions have won again and that the court is impervious to human suffering at the core of this case would be absurd," Norgle said. Rather, he argued, because the issue of reparations was a political one, it wasn't for the courts to decide the matter based on technical merits; Congress or the president were the proper authorities to do so.[9]

Deadria Farmer-Paellmann has since referred to this as a defeat of the litigation but not of the issue, which by sheer number of the plaintiffs involved, the number of activists drawn to the call for reparations, and the sustained and growing news coverage over several years, had created a new kind of consciousness that remains. "Today it's like the baseline for young people," she told me. "They have grown up knowing, 'Of course we know who the companies are, what slavery in America built.' They have no idea there's a Black woman behind that research. But it's okay, as long as they know it. That's the reward of all of the work."

Other litigation and research has since revealed that the number of corporations with roots in slavery is vast. In 2004, Bob Brown, codirector of an activist group called Pan-African Roots, filed a lawsuit in Chicago, based on the Slavery Era Disclosure Ordinance, which ultimately named 102 corporations, including Caterpillar and Novistar Equipment, as historically tied to Black people's enslavement.[10] "I deliberately chose 102 to represent the different industries and to create a corporate genealogy," Brown told me in a phone interview. "No, they didn't all exist during slavery, but they used the money."[11] Brown's suit, which didn't seek damages but aimed to compel corporate defendants to release internal records showing their links to enslavement, was also dismissed.[12]

———

SOME YEARS BEFORE these legal proceedings, in 2000, Eric Foner, the noted professor of history at Columbia University, had published an op-ed in the New York Times—a highly prescient one. In it, he crystallized themes playing out in his time, themes that would eventually play out in Chicago, themes that are still, more than twenty years later, playing out now. Foner had written his editorial, interestingly enough, in response to breaking news: Deadria Farmer-Paellmann had elicited an apology from Aetna. The apology "remind[s] us of the usually glossed-over participation of the North in America's slave system," Foner attested, and added: "In the

North, too, textile factories relied on slave-grown cotton, shipping interests carried cotton to England, and banks and merchants financed cotton production." Corporations apologizing for slavery was both vital and merely the tip of a bigger iceberg, Foner insisted. The larger failure, of museums, schools, and popular histories to disseminate these facts, he said, was the reason that our history, befuddled and befogged, keeps us in a perpetual state of forgetting—trapping our understanding, impeding our progress. Foner lamented particularly that "New York should more candidly acknowledge that much of its early prosperity rested on slave labor," further suggesting that "the city should have a permanent exhibition—perhaps even an independent museum—depicting the history of slavery and New York's connection with it."[13]

As Foner wrote those words, the African Burial Ground, the sacred link that had started Farmer-Paellmann's journey—a journey resulting in Foner's very editorial, was still mired in controversy and infighting. In 2000, the federal government had at last earmarked $1.6 million to construct a memorial commemorating the cemetery, to honor the twenty thousand African Americans who had helped build New York, but the announcement had come nine long years after the cemetery's discovery. "All that stems from fundamental disrespect, specifically for the African-American ancestors that are here, but then for this whole process," Howard Dodson, then director of the Schomburg Center for Research in Black Culture, told the press at the time, decrying the delay in establishing a museum.[14] It wouldn't be until 2007 that the African Burial Ground museum at last opened to the public.

The discovery of that burial ground; Farmer-Paellmann's letter to Aetna and the resulting debate; Foner's editorial; the dismissal of the reparations lawsuits; Chicago's Slavery Era Disclosure Ordinance; the halfhearted, shallow response from Lehman Brothers and now JPMorgan Chase: each seemed like rings of a concentric circle in which the truth, though resounding, still remained trapped within the box cage of American understanding, condemned to spin perpetually in place. These connected events, though playing out in different times, underscored not only how poorly and shallowly mainstream America has explored the history connecting our national wealth to slavery, but what an abundance there is to find when at last we dare to look.

The resolution of Chicago's dealings with JPMorgan Chase and Lehman Brothers epitomized this yet again. For while the dismissal of Farmer-Paellmann's lawsuit meant the banks would not be compelled to pay reparations, the facts of their ties to the profits of slavery remained intact, and, by dint of the law in Chicago, those details continued to be revealed.

———

BY MID-2004, JPMORGAN Chase had entered what might be called a more earnest phase of searching. The man it hired to lead this effort is named James Lide, and he was working at that time for History Associates, a private research firm based in Maryland. Lide, a trained scholar, had a team at his disposal, including corporate executives at JPMorgan, to help him cull documents from around the country and seek out clues. Together, he and his team had spent months looking for ties to slavery (it appears Lide is the outside archivist whom JPMorgan referenced in 2003) but had essentially come up empty-handed. Then, Lide told me, they had a breakthrough.[15]

For years prior to the JPMorgan case, one of Lide's main projects had been tracking down lost assets connecting major corporations to the Holocaust. Much of that work had centered on banks and the flow of tainted Nazi money in Europe. Lide understood, because of that work, that as corporate entities evolve over time, through a succession of acquisitions or mergers, tracing their historical lineage is the painstaking stuff of sifting through what he calls "the universe of predecessors." He explained: "JPMorgan Chase was the amalgamation of probably fifty or sixty banks over the years, some of which go all the way back—the Canal Bank goes back to the 1700s."

So vast and convoluted can this universe become, Lide detailed in a video call from Washington, DC, where he is now based, that a corporation itself no longer knows its own lineage. It took Lide's team months just to map out all of JPMorgan's predecessors ("Nobody there at the company had a firm idea of all the potential connections," he said), and then several more months to sift through the Manhattan entities alone, like Manhattan Bank and Leather Manufacturers' Bank.

JPMorgan wasn't the only bank overwhelmed by its own history.

As the work progressed, several other major banks, also seeking to avoid violating Chicago's ordinance, contacted History Associates. They, too, wanted help understanding their historical connections to slavery—connections they either didn't know or didn't understand. In all, Lide has estimated, as many as twenty banks retained him and his team to plumb their own records; these included Lehman Brothers, Morgan Stanley, ABM AMRO, and Citizens Financial Group. That twenty major US banks, compelled no less under pain of losing contracts, spent months in the early aughts engaged in this enterprise—interrogating their own linkages to Black people's enslavement (interrogations with varying outcomes, as we'll see)—constitutes a high-water mark achieved by activists and lawmakers in compelling corporate America to confront its slavery past, and one that has never taken place since.

The increased scale of the project got Lide and his team thinking deeply about what a bank's "connection" to slavery might mean. "We started to think about it as a spectrum," he said. "And it moved across from about as direct a connection as you think of: There were banks that owned slaves. Part of the bank's assets and collateral were slaves. Typically, a bank would foreclose on a mortgage, take over a plantation. So that's a direct connection. There are founders of banks who owned slaves. There are founders of banks who made their money from moving slaves and slave trading, particularly some of the New England banks. Then you move along the spectrum: There are banks that had clients who owned slaves, both north and south. You've got connections where banks may have been loaning money or financing projects that use slave labor in some way."

Lide found a spectrum of connections to slavery in all the banks that hired his team. But sometimes, records couldn't be traced to flesh out this spectrum. "There were many cases where we had banks that knew there was a predecessor, but we just couldn't find any record of it," he said.

Some banks let the effort die there. "Some were more eager to look at this than others," Lide said. "Some were more willing to put in the work than others." Ultimately, it meant that many of the banks had grounds to say, in their official filings with Chicago, that they could find no records linking their past to slavery.

This wasn't the case for JPMorgan Chase. "One of the things that made the JPMorgan case unusual was we had access to very, very detailed records," Lide said. This included records of JPMorgan's New York banks themselves, which, though yielding few direct clues, nonetheless suggested an important association. "As we were doing this lineage work, we came across references to two Louisiana banks, Canal Bank and Citizens Bank."

The universe of predecessors showed that JPMorgan Chase, in acquiring Bank One, was, in turn acquiring another bank that Bank One had acquired seventy years earlier (the First National Bank of Commerce in New Orleans), and that that bank had acquired Canal Bank and Citizens Bank.[16] And so, by swallowing up the one, JPMorgan had subsumed within itself, through a corporate chain of custody, these others. They had become the bank, the bank had become them, and the resulting fusion meant their lineages, their assets, and—as Deadria Farmer-Paellmann and many others were arguing—their liabilities had become one.

The link to Canal and Citizens was the breakthrough. After that, Lide and his team began focusing on getting all the records they could out of Louisiana. They called up Tulane University in New Orleans and discovered, with not a little satisfaction, that the university had among its archives the meeting minutes of the board of directors of the Citizens Bank of Louisiana: the forgotten ledgers. From that discovery, the pieces fell—not quickly, but steadily and painstakingly—into place.

———

OVER THE COURSE of the next few weeks, Lide himself flew back and forth to Louisiana multiple times. At Tulane, he interrogated the handwritten minutes, trawling page by page. Though the text was dense and the handwriting at times excruciating to decipher, the minutes, he realized, were a trove of the names of the bank's many borrowers. "We started to find all these references that the bank made loans to planters," he said, "who secured those loans with their plantation."

He also realized that, as such, the minutes were not the terminus of his search, but merely another doorway, another threshold to cross. To connect these borrowers to enslaved people, and thus the bank to slavery, his team would have to correlate the bank ledgers to official mortgage documents—in other words, deeds at the time they were deeded. The ledger minutes contained hundreds of names, which meant a correlation to a multiple of even more deeds. (Some borrowers took out multiple loans or renewed them multiple times.) The documents, like the ledgers, would also be more than 150 years old, but unlike the bank ledgers, they would be scattered all over Louisiana, in an untold number of offices, archives, and parishes. It would be a massive undertaking.

To keep the data together, Lide began compiling a spreadsheet, a list of names of the borrowers of both Citizens Bank and Canal Bank. Then he dispatched his team across the state to find the mortgage records. (At the investigation's height, he said, he had more than a dozen people working on it.) Sometimes they found them discarded on shelves, sometimes stuffed in closets, sometimes neatly packed in boxes. In one parish, the mortgage deeds were housed in the cells of an old county jail. Hours and days and months ensued, months during which Dorothy Tillman and the Chicago City Council were waiting.

"We went through every single [mortgage]," said Lide. "Those mortgage books would often include the name of the banks, the name of the person, the name of the plantation." Sometimes, the deeds were written in French, sometimes in English; either way, they were once again, because of the handwriting, excruciating for the team to decipher. But almost always the deeds contained the name of the bank who had made the loan and, more importantly, a list of the enslaved people whom the borrower had put up as collateral. There was the connection at last.

What Lide's team was holding in their hands was evidence of what abolitionists after the Panic of 1837 had decried: the kind of defaults that had made James Brown and the Brown brothers enslavers themselves; and what a lone Black scholar, often dismissed as foolhardy and misguided, had originally shown, through her pioneering research, with Aetna Insurance—proof that the bedrock of the US financial system was built with profits from the industry of Black enslaved labor. As his team correlated more of these names to the mortgages, James Lide entered the data into his spreadsheet.

In early 2005, after six months of this work, History Associates presented its findings to the executives of JPMorgan Chase. The bank, Lide said, had all the while approved his every move, never exerting any pushback. (JPMorgan Chase declined repeated requests to speak about this and other matters.)

Lide's spreadsheet showed that Canal Bank and Citizens Bank, both of which now form JPMorgan Chase, had taken about thirteen thousand Black people as collateral in loans of various kinds between 1831 and 1865, each signed off by the board of directors.[17] It means that, using an average market price for the value white buyers then put on an enslaved Black person—$600—these loans were collateralized with roughly $7.8 million then, or between $230 million and $262 million now—quite an extraordinary book of business, in other words. Because of borrowers who defaulted, Lide tabulated, Canal Bank and Citizens Bank took as possession, directly as assets on their own books, more than 1,250 enslaved people, valued at roughly $750,000 then, or between $23 million and $25 million today.

What ultimately became of these 1,250 people is not known. Lide pointed out, moreover, that the thirteen thousand enslaved people captured in his spreadsheet are just those whom we can see, the collateral of just two banks in Louisiana, two banks among dozens. We are left to imagine the hundreds of thousands of additional enslaved people, collateralized by banks not just in Louisiana, but across the country, whose stolen lives made possible the very inhumane foundations of America's racial caste system of wealth—not just banking, but home ownership, affluence, American aspiration for white people.

Lide had been hired to find a connection to slavery, and certainly his team had found it. "The argument is that the banks benefited from that because their loans that they made were secured," he reflected. "They were in a better position to profit from those loans because of all the assets that had been provided as collateral—that includes slavery."

JPMorgan Chase, he said, was not happy; it was not what they had wanted to hear. But they accepted it. They amended their disclosure to the city of Chicago and issued a public apology on January 20, 2005. "Its admission [that] predecessor institutions owned slaves," one news report observed at the time, "is unprecedented in modern U.S. business history."[18] JPMorgan also announced that it had earmarked $5 million, to be paid out over five years, to pay full tuition for Black students from Louisiana to attend college. The bank was, and remains, the only modern corporation in the history of the United States to offer restitution of any kind for profiting from the enslavement of Black people.

Back then, when such a disclosure, let alone a reparations payment, was entirely unheard of, the bank's scholarship announcement had the effect of telescoping its contrition into something monumental. Certainly, it was not nothing: the country had gone from complete silence about corporate America's role in slavery, and no acknowledgments from corporations themselves, to $5 million in reparations. (JPMorgan's payment "confirms that the corporations can be held accountable for their roles in slavery," Deadria Farmer-Paellmann told the *New York Sun* at the time. "They've been brought to realize that they owe something.)[19] And yet the amount of JPMorgan's payment was clearly paltry compared to how much the bank had derived from the mortgaging of enslaved people; it was grossly minuscule relative to JPMorgan's overall fortunes in 2005, which amounted to $54 billion in revenue and roughly $8.5 billion in profit.[20]

The $5 million was a token amount, Bob Brown of Pan-African Roots told me. It actually functioned to make the problem go away, he said, part of a tactic based on the idea that "You admit a little bit of the truth but you hide the rest." If so, it seems to have worked, for the bank's controversial standoff with Chicago ended there.

Eight months later, Lehman Brothers, having also hired Lide's team, came forward with what their renewed search had found: As the firm itself had earlier insinuated, its founders had enslaved not just Martha, the fourteen-year-old girl purchased in 1854. The business had enslaved three Black people in 1852, two in 1858, three in 1859, two in 1860, four in 1861, and five in 1865, bringing the total to twenty. (This does not include the nine other enslaved Black people, detailed in census records, that Mayer, Henry, and Emanuel Lehman enslaved, nor the ten additional Black people Lehman Brothers purchased in 1863.)[21] "There would be no Lehman Brothers if there were not a slave trade," Dorothy Tillman told the press.

The firm apologized and said it would amend its disclosure form. "We are not denying that in all likelihood that the company profited from slavery," the firm's general counsel, Joseph Polizzotto, said. "It is virtually inconceivable that the company didn't profit in some way, shape, or form."[22] Lehman Brothers did not offer to earmark any money for restitution.

———

Today, James Lide works as a creative director for a commercial design firm. (One of its recent projects was designing a historical exhibit highlighting how enslaved people built the White House.) Even now, his time scouring the slavery-era records of Fortune 500 companies, though some two decades past, has left a lasting impression on him—an impression, among other things, that for corporations, the task of confronting their own history is not unreasonably difficult, but a question of will.

The JPMorgan case had been complex, a path of twists and turns, but the Lehman case had not. These two contrasting examples showed that unearthing this history can be done. "I mean, it's work, and you have to spend a long time reading, and it's effort," Lide told me. "It's not like it's technically hard to do. You just have to sit down and do the research."

JPMorgan Chase hadn't even known what banks, with what links to the brutalization of Black people for profit, existed in its family. The pieces of this network, the vestiges of this wealth, are everywhere, and the liability is spread out too. "What this tells me," Lide said, "is that the practice of slavery was deeply engrained as a major pillar of America's social and economic system up through the end of the Civil War. Those connections are not limited to the states where slavery was legal. The divide that many people make between northern-owned or northern areas and southern slavery is not quite as clear as many people would imagine."

At the heart of her litigation, Deadria Farmer-Paellmann had argued that such companies still retained the benefits of, and were therefore beneficiaries of, wealth derived from enslaved people's labor. "The shipping and railroad industry benefited and profited from the transportation of the slaves," she had argued in her legal filing. "The railroad industry utilized slave labor in the construction of rail lines. These transportation industries were dependent upon the manufacturing and raw materials industry to utilize the slaves they shipped. The cotton, tobacco, rice and sugar industries thrived on profits generated from their use of slave labor, and relied upon financial and insurance industries to finance and insure the slaves that they utilized and owned. All industries: raw market, retail, financial, insurance, and transportation, benefited from the reduced costs of slave-produced goods." [23]

"People are not conscious of this," Farmer-Paellmann told me, "but the litigation was successful not just in exposing corporate complicity, but we actually created precedent that made it clear that these companies can be held liable in court if they lie about their role in slavery." She added that the lawsuits of that era created the groundwork, including the growing pressure that has lasted until today. "The litigation we did, exposing the companies, played a huge role in that. It didn't just happen overnight that education institutions…church institutions—it didn't happen overnight that they said, 'Oh, it's time for us to pay reparations.' It was this litigation that we did."

The result today is that a wider and wider array of institutions across the United States, from city governments and major universities, are now committed to divulging their ties to enslavement, and paying reparations to Black Americans as a means to atone.

And yet, still conspicuously absent among this chorus of voices calling for reparatory justice, now even two decades later, is one institution above all: the major corporations in the United States that are the living repository of slavery's wealth.

CHAPTER 14

AFTERMATH: THE UNRAVELING TO COME

In June 2020, Lloyd's of London, one of the world's premier insurance institutions, made a major public announcement. Lloyd's is a company more than three hundred years old. From its earliest days, having insured the British Crown's greatest ships, it made possible the very commerce of Atlantic trade, the exploitative practices of empire, and helped forge the basis of British prosperity itself. The company's profits in 2021 were close to $2.78 billion.[1] In its public statement, Lloyd's acknowledged for the first time that, intermingled with its known revenue streams, there was another it had worked hard to downplay, a kind of open secret: As white merchants transported more than three million African people into slavery, Lloyd's had insured, over a period of more than a century, a substantial number of those ships as well, indemnifying cargoes of enslaved people as "perishable goods." At least one of the company's founding members had enslaved 162 African people himself.[2] Lloyd's had made slavery possible, slavery had made Lloyd's possible, and together they made Great Britain into what it is.

Lloyd's admitted to being not only complicit in slavery but complicit in silence—a silence equating to cowardice. "As the world's specialist insurance market for more than 330 years," the company said, "we often say that Lloyd's has helped to create a braver world. But our market's historic participation in the transatlantic slave trade, and our early failings to fully acknowledge this history, were anything but brave."[3] Lloyd's added that, as a form of reparations, it would make payments to charities and other institutions "promoting opportunity and inclusion for black and minority ethnic groups," though not to Black or minority groups directly. Lloyd's full apology, now hosted on a dedicated section of the firm's website, has since spawned a collaborative research project, in conjunction with Johns Hopkins University, to study the depths of the company's involvement in the transatlantic slave trade.

Notably, it was not the passing of a new city ordinance, nor the threat of litigation, that prompted Lloyd's disclosure. The company opted to make these statements at a time of its own choosing, though certainly there is an important note to be made about that timing: Lloyd's did so as public outcry over racial injustice had erupted in the summer of 2020, following the police murder of forty-six-year-old George Floyd in Minneapolis. With the release of harrowing videos showing Derek Chauvin, a white officer, killing Floyd by crushing his knee against Floyd's neck for more than eight minutes, outrage exploded in cities throughout England as well, and Floyd's last words—"I can't breathe"—became a rallying cry against racism and police brutality around the world.

No sooner had a crowd of anti-racism protesters, converging in a public park in Bristol, torn down and thrown into the sea a statue of Edward Colston, a notorious seventeenth-century slave trader and director of the Royal African Company, then Lloyd's came clean about its history—a history it no doubt could have disclosed long ago but did not. Evidently, the company worried that it too would become the object of spreading public rebuke. It cited "recent events" that "unleashed difficult conversations that were long overdue."[4] The company's self-disclosure looks a lot like saving face, rather than dynamic, emboldened leadership. And considering that it did "the right thing" only in reaction to grievous wrongdoing, Lloyd's hardly merits sweeping praise. Be that as it may, the company did disclose, and its disclosure, because of Lloyd's pedigree and institutional weight, made international headlines. And that quickly set off a trend.

Not a day later, Greene King, the corporate owner of a chain of bars and breweries in the United Kingdom, disclosed that its original founder,

Benjamin Greene, had, in the nineteenth century, enslaved more than two hundred Black people on plantations in the Caribbean. Greene King also said it would "make a substantial investment" in Black and minority communities, though it would not say how much it intended to pay.[5] A day after that, the Bank of England, the country's central financial institution, also apologized, lamenting its historic role in profiting from the sale and enslavement of African people. (According to University College London's Legacies of British Slave-Ownership project, at least forty-three of the bank's governors and directors were enslavers or linked to slave trading.)[6] The Bank of England, too, promised to pay reparations for its role, again to increase opportunities within Black and minority communities, though it also did not say how much.

Whether any of these companies will ultimately fulfill their pledges, and how, remains an open question in England. In the meantime, there are several noteworthy elements here worth pausing over. Consider first the fact that Lloyd's and others were able to identify their historical links to slavery so quickly and easily, suggesting that the companies had this information stored in accessible archives somewhere, ready to be disclosed at a moment's notice. It meant that companies like Lloyd's were sitting on this information, closing it up as if it were in a vault, and choosing not to divulge it. And they did so collectively, forming a wall of silence. They could have done the right thing at any time, but they didn't. Yet when one broke ranks, many others followed, and the chain of disclosures ensued.

Equally interesting is this: Recall that British corporations made these disclosures in reaction to the murder of George Floyd, a case of police brutality so horrific that it became a touchstone for global racial reckoning; that what they disclosed about their own role in slavery was seemingly disconnected from that convulsion, but that their disclosures made clear how the two were in fact inextricably linked. It remains striking that, more than two hundred years after slavery was outlawed in the United Kingdom, major corporations in that country for the first time recognized, in that moment, their own role as the institutional foundation of the very racism and racial injustice roiling the world today. That is, their revelations, however self-interested, nonetheless firmly posited that, as a baseline for addressing racial injustice and inequality, we must first acknowledge the historical root cause: slavery, and more particularly the role that corporations played in organizing the enslavement of Black people into a business, and played in organizing their profits therefrom into the basis of British wealth, prosperity, and class. Coming clean in the United Kingdom consisted of coming clean about all of it, from the beginning. It was about fundamental history.

These developments are certainly notable in their own right, but they are even more striking because of a contrast they provide—a contrast to what is happening in the United States. Here, too, of course, major corporations, also reacting to the historic protests sparked by the murder of George Floyd, made many statements in the aftermath of that unprecedented summer. Apple, Johnson & Johnson, and Facebook, to name but a few, swiftly pledged investments, and other actions, such as diversity hiring, as part of a sweeping program for societal change.

One by one, these companies followed each other, as if falling in line—a domino effect, as in the United Kingdom—and they tended to pledge very much the same things. Collectively, fifty of the largest public companies in the United States earmarked nearly $50 billion to address racial inequality, as an analysis and accompanying database compiled by the *Washington Post* points out.[7] That same analysis revealed, incidentally, that 90 percent of those pledges were in the form of loans or other investments from which the companies themselves stood to profit. How and if these companies will make good on such pledges remains an open question (many have not yet released their funds), just as in the United Kingdom. But there was a remarkable difference in the content of the resulting discourse and its outcome. Here in the United States, not a single big bank or chain acknowledged its ties to slavery. There were no self-disclosures that corporate founders had profited from the business of enslaving Black people or been enslavers themselves.

Why such a striking difference from the United Kingdom? Are we to believe that corporations here, unlike in England, lack company archives and records detailing their role in enslavement? This hardly seems the case. The epoch of Deadria Farmer-Paellmann and James Lide, as we saw, proved that such records exist, and that corporations, when compelled to look, can find them; it is the will to look that is missing. We can venture a guess that corporations in the United States sat on this information during the summer of George Floyd's murder, and that they continue to sit on it now, even though some are in possession of such information and are able to disclose it.

In the sweeping statements that corporations made with ready fervor during that summer, not even one mentioned that, to address systemic racism and injustice in the United States today, they themselves must reckon with their own role in the country's long history of enslaving Black people for profit. That long history was met, on the contrary, with almost total corporate silence. There was one notable exception: Ben & Jerry's. The avowedly progressive ice cream company, a company not known to have any ties itself to slavery, issued a statement saying: "As we've worked with our partners to grow and support a movement to transform the criminal justice system, we've come to realize that the most important thing we can do to achieve equity across the system and across the entire country is to reckon honestly and openly with slavery.

"Why? Because slavery isn't some long-ago evil that we've dealt with and moved on from—its legacy lives on today in the systemic racism that affects every aspect of contemporary American life."[8]

Unlike Lloyd's of London, Ben & Jerry's announcement set off no trend of other disclosures, and perhaps for obvious reasons: the ice cream company, certainly not a peer to big banks or insurance companies, lacks the institutional weight to do so. And so corporate America, in the aftermath of the police murder of George Floyd and the unprecedented public outcry that followed, presided over a discourse of silence, a discourse of avoidance. Juxtaposed to the corporate response in the United Kingdom, that silence served to project the idea that among the many vital things necessary to grapple with during one of the greatest convulsions over racial injustice in the nation's history, the history of slavery didn't matter. The mantle of oblivion, in other words, still holds.

It has been holding for a long time. As it stands as of this book's writing, in mid-2023, precisely four corporations in the history of the United States have ever admitted to and apologized for their ties to slavery, and two only did so, as we've seen, after initial obfuscation, the threat of litigation, and considerable public outcry. Since those events, not a single US corporation in the last twenty years has ever acknowledged any complicity in profiting from Black people's enslavement, let alone issued a public apology, or, more still, considered reparations. JPMorgan Chase remains the only company ever to have paid out funds to Black people as restitution for enslavement.

Taking the full measure of this response, we are led to no other conclusion than the obvious one: in the twenty-first century, corporations in the United States remain wholly uncommitted to acknowledging the basic truth of their long role in abetting and profiting from the heinous atrocities committed against Black people. In part, this is because they face virtually no pressure to do so, internal, societal, or otherwise. But it is also because, manifestly, they do not care; the issue of accountability is not a priority within their business operations, rather an issue they take pains to avoid. Resultantly, corporations also remain uncommitted to exploring ways in which, from their vast concentrations of corporate wealth, they might voluntarily make monetary repairs for their role in this horrific history.

CORPORATE AMERICA'S SILENCE around slavery is conspicuous not only when contrasted to the United Kingdom's, but even more so when placed in contrast to something else: the actions of other institutions in the United States. Consider the fact that, in recent years, dozens of American universities, religious organizations, and nonprofit endowments have widely publicized their complicity in enslaving Black people, generating a groundswell of attention, discussion, and support for the idea of reparations. In the United States, unlike in the United Kingdom, this is happening despite the resistance of corporate actors, not with their input, and thanks, of course, to the pressing, unceasing efforts of reparations proponents, beginning with Deadria Farmer-Paellmann and others, and now including a vast array of organizations, activists, and political leaders.

The stirring essay on reparations that Ta-Nehisi Coates published in the *Atlantic*,[9] and Nikole Hannah-Jones's groundbreaking 1619 Project for the *New York Times*,[10] have reinvigorated those efforts more recently. The staggering range of actors now committing to paying reparations—an individual Episcopal church in Baltimore, the Catholic Church as a whole, the Virginia Theological Seminary, and Harvard University—also includes a growing number of municipal and state authorities. The city of Evanston, Illinois, has proposed a Restorative Housing Program as part of the city's reparations committee; Oak Park, Illinois, is exploring ways to use a marijuana tax to fund reparations; and the state of California, which has a reparations task force, is exploring a mechanism to, as one task force member has said, "reverse the harms of chattel slavery," through individual payments, but also through programs to address the health, education, and incarceration disparities that Black people face.[11]

The fruits of the efforts of Rep. John Conyers, the Democrat from Michigan who introduced the first federal reparations bill back in 1989, H.R. 40, have blossomed, with the House Judiciary Committee voting for the first time, in April 2021, to advance the bill to the House floor for a vote. (The bill, still limited for now to establishing a commission to study reparations, doesn't propose any particular payment structure or method of redress.) On its website, Human Rights Watch highlights that 215 members of Congress have committed to voting yes, and that should the bill advance, it would likely pass, though its fate in the Senate, given divisions there, remains difficult to forecast.[12]

We are living, it seems clear, through an unprecedented period of institutional soul-baring around slavery in the United States. And yet, this trend is not mirrored, as we'll have occasion to see, in growing public support for reparations; quite the contrary.

The trend toward institutional transparency began as far back as 2003, starting with Brown University. But it culminated in 2016, after Georgetown University famously disclosed that its founders, having sold 272 enslaved Black people in 1838, used the profits to fund the institution's survival and expansion.[13] Georgetown has since committed to paying reparations to the descendants of the people the university enslaved.

Many universities followed Georgetown's lead. In 2017, Princeton, for example, also began to unearth the channels through which profits from slavery had enriched and benefited the university, employing a team of more than forty scholars to do so. At the center of one of their investigations? Moses Taylor.

Princeton scholars traced how, after Moses Taylor died in 1882, he left one-fifth of his estate to his grandson, Moses Taylor Pyne, a graduate of Princeton in the class of 1877. Endowed with a fortune made from the commerce of slavery, Pyne became an important benefactor to his alma mater, joining its board of trustees. He then wrote checks equivalent to millions of dollars today, including a sum worth $14 million, just to expand the university's library, according to legal historian Maeve Glass, then an academic fellow at Columbia Law School who oversaw the Taylor investigation.

"Pyne's financial contributions subsidized not only the new library, but also the construction of two undergraduate dormitories on Nassau Street, a slew of new faculty and graduate housing, and endowments for initiatives ranging from a history seminar to a professorship," Glass wrote. "Today, the Pyne family name graces some of the most iconic buildings on campus, as well as the résumés of celebrated graduates who have received the Pyne Prize, Princeton's highest undergraduate honor." It was funds from Moses Taylor's trove of slavery earnings, Glass concludes, that helped "transform a small college in New Jersey into one of the world's leading universities."[14]

These and other findings, including that several Princeton University presidents enslaved Black people themselves, were later unveiled as part of the Princeton & Slavery Project, now a dedicated section on the university's website.[15]

Princeton's commitment to interrogating this past, its marshaling of energy, resources, and forthrightness, stands in sharp relief to the inaction of major US corporations, broadly speaking, but to one corporation in particular: Citi. Princeton has grappled with the legacy of Moses Taylor, and with the legacy of enslavers from whom the university benefited more broadly. Citi never has. Princeton did the work of transparency, tracing how its "finances were shored up with slave money," in its own words, including funds that passed through Taylor and his heirs. Most corporations have not.

Until July 2023, Citi, the banking giant, had also avoided any acknowledgment of its ties to enslavement, including the prominent role of Moses Taylor. On its website, Citi for a long time celebrated Moses Taylor's success as a director and president yet airbrushed out that Black people's enslavement was crucial to that success. "[Taylor] set up his own firm to import sugar from Cuba in 1832," a historical timeline on the bank's website had earlier reported, adding the additional anodyne statement: "It soon expanded into trading other commodities, such as pineapples, limes, and tobacco, and invested in ships to carry cargo between Havana and other Latin American ports."[16] The bank, however, removed this description and issued, following a review of its historic business records, a new assessment of their formerly most celebrated president: "[G]iven that a significant portion of Taylor's business was connected to the trade of sugar and its derivatives from Cuban plantations that used enslaved labor, City Bank of New York likely profited indirectly from enslaved labor in Cuba by engaging in transactions with Taylor and his businesses," the bank said.[17] Citi has at least tempered its statements on Taylor, statements that were, especially today, easily shown to be distortions and falsehoods, given how voluminously Taylor's involvement in the commerce of slavery is documented in the business records Taylor himself left behind, in Princeton's investigation, in the studies of Daniel Hodas and Roland T. Ely, and in the work of scholars like Alan Singer, John Harris, and Claudia Varella, among others.

Citi's historic records review concludes, for the first time in the bank's more than two-hundred-year history, the following: "Citi predecessors likely profited from financial transactions and relationships with individuals and entities located or operating in slaveholding states in the United States before 1866 that owned enslaved persons, relied on the labor of enslaved persons, or otherwise were involved in or connected to the US slave trade."[18] The acknowledgment is certainly unprecedented, but what is truly significant in Citi's newfound acknowledgment is what it did *not* cover, the things it did *not* say: the words "We are sorry" or "We apologize" appear nowhere in the bank's statement. Also unaddressed is how Citi plans to make repair for the vast role it played in abetting the devastation that enslavement caused to Black people's lives. On that issue, Citi continues to be conspicuously silent. And that silence is telling because it directly contradicts the bank's own stated commitments to addressing structural racism—commitments it announced, in fact, in the months after police killed George Floyd. That September, Citibank vowed to take a leading role in addressing the country's racial wealth gap and said that, by pledging $1 billion to initiatives focused "on antiracist practices in the financial services industry," it would help build a fairer and more inclusive world. "Words are not enough," Citi's chief financial officer, Mark Mason, even said. "We need awareness, education, and action that drives results." These are words to remember.

The bank published an accompanying report at the time, entitled

"Closing the Racial Inequality Gaps," and, interestingly, Citibank made only the briefest remarks there about slavery, calling it a root cause of continuing discrimination today: "The 400 years of enslavement of Black populations in the Americas has residual effects that persist to this day despite tomes of legislation providing equal access to various aspects of American life under the law." The report says nothing about a societal or corporate need to address the history of slavery, and nothing about Citibank's own role in that history. In this silence, the company pointedly contradicts its own commitments, and more importantly, ignores its own advice—advice that is spelled out in its own report under the section "What Can Companies Do?" The answer, the bank says, is for corporations committed to anti-racism to engage in corporate social responsibility and "conscientious reform." The section says little else (it is short and rather vague), but it does say: "Firms can also consider public actions to accelerate policies and legal measures to protect and support vulnerable populations."[19]

It is stating the obvious to say that a critical and foundational public action that Citibank can take today, to prove its leadership role in conscientious reform, in building awareness and education that drives results and accelerating policies to protect vulnerable populations, is, at a minimum, to issue a public apology, as the prelude to outlining a course of meaningful repair, including the payment of reparations.

Instead, at the crux of the bank's unprecedented acknowledgment is a duplicitously calculated moral distortion. "[W]e did not find records providing evidence of any direct involvement [in enslavement]," the bank says. It reiterates this several times, outlining that the bank itself never directly sold or held enslaved people. It is on this basis that Citi seems to feel itself justified in withholding any real apology.

The bank is grotesquely splitting hairs. Are we to accept the terms, conveniently laid out by Citi itself, that the bank's involvement in enslavement can be reduced to whether records exist showing that the bank *itself* directly held or sold enslaved people? What does "itself" even mean here? For even if the bank "itself" did not engage in these activities, its directors most certainly did, profiting in myriad ways from the exploitation of enslaved people; and as we know from Citi's own official history, the commercial activities of the bank's directors and the activities of the bank were one and the same.

When we consider that twelve of City Bank's directors enslaved Black people themselves, and that at least seven of these directors did so while serving at the bank;[20] when we consider that City Bank participated in organizing the Black Ball Line, the primary transportation infrastructure that transformed cotton into a global commodity, and slavery into an industry, and that two of the principal architects of Black Ball, Isaac Wright and Benjamin Marshall, were later elected City Bank directors themselves; when we consider that the City Bank directors Daniel Parish, James Magee, and John Brower were deeply involved in financing plantations, and thus Black people's enslavement, and that their profits no doubt built the bank's deposits, as the bank likewise enabled their slavery-tied trades; when we consider the historically unparalleled role that Moses Taylor played, while director and president of City Bank, in channeling profits from southern and Cuban slavery into industry, even as his financing and loan operations expanded Cuba's slavery system itself; when we consider the long list of City Bank clients whose profits were directly dependent on Black people's enslavement—the enslavers Robert and John Oliver, Anson G. Phelps, and Charles Stillman, the powerhouse Texas cotton broker whose son, James Stillman, later became president of the bank—when we consider these facts in their totality, we are left to conclude that few corporations in the history of the United States were more active in, and crucial to, the institutionalization of slavery as a business, to the global disbursement of its products, and to the laundering and investment of its tainted profits, than City Bank of New York.

No, City Bank wasn't the only corporation historically to do so. But as it played an outsized role in the system of slavery that, as the bank itself says, has left residual effects in structural racism and inequality; and as the bank wants to project itself now as a corporate leader in addressing those inequalities, Citi has an opportunity, it seems clear, to play a leading role in atonement for slavery as well. It could be a leader in confronting this discomfiting truth, and by doing so, would commit to an unprecedented public act of corporate social responsibility, a historic moment of conscientious reform.

That is a leadership role that Citi, so far, refuses to play. That's because the firm, like every company confronting slavery, is afraid, says Amanda Yogendran, cofounder of the creative agency All Good Things, which advises corporations on issues of purpose and advocacy. The bank, she says, is afraid not just of backlash, but afraid that, were it to play such a role, tracing and revealing its roots in enslavement, it would find itself thrust down a deeper well of accountability, compelled to commit to a cascade of further actions and internal changes, not just talk. And it would be compelled to do so in order to maintain its integrity and relevance as a brand.

"I think that the accountability piece is huge. You can't look into something and then be, like, 'Well, that was fun. Thanks a lot. We're going to get back to what we were doing before,'" Yogendran told me in a telephone interview.[21]

It's a sound argument, but to be fair, wasn't that precisely what JPMorgan and Lehman Brothers, more or less, did back in 2005? They looked into their historical links to slavery; made an apology; in the case of JPMorgan, paid out $5 million; and then went back to what they were doing, business as usual.

Yes, but times are different now, Yogendran stresses. That was the era of corporate social responsibility 1.0, as she describes it, referring to the self-regulation whereby corporations pledge to contribute to societal improvement. Back in 2005, corporate social responsibility looked like this, she says: "It was the Citibanks giving a certain philanthropic donation. It was companies putting aside money, having a kind of siloed approach: 'Okay, we'll give this x amount, or we'll help our employees volunteer,' and it was very separate from everything else. It was kind of an afterthought, like a box check."

It's almost twenty years later now, and Yogendran argues that the tenets and commitments of corporate social responsibility have changed. Just a few years ago, millennials helped charge up corporate social responsibility version 2.0, certainly as consumers but also as employees of corporations themselves. The result: "Those kinds of values of community and philanthropy started to be more embedded in the brand and marketing and communication functioning of companies." Now we're in version 3.0, Yogendran says, and it's driven by Gen Z: "Where we're headed, it's way more. You can't just talk about it. You can't just put it in your communications. You have to live and breathe it as a company. There's a new expectation for brands to not just be a vessel for getting me my products, but to be a badge of identity. They said Black Lives Matter. Now is their time to prove it."

Yogendran added one more thought-provoking thing when she was talking about powerful brands potentially confronting their own history in slavery. She said: "Once you start, there's an unraveling process."

It's, of course, impossible to know whether not apologizing for slavery and not committing to reparations would ultimately harm Citi's reputation and its brand. Certainly, its silence, so far, has not diminished the company's market value: $90 billion, as of 2023.[22] Yogendran's assertion, though, is an occasion to wonder: What exactly would an unraveling process look like, both for a company like Citi, but also the wider society in which it operates? And relatedly, what are corporations so afraid of that they seem to have avoided such an unraveling at all costs for so many years?

Perhaps we can get to an answer by way of comparison once again, contrasting side by side the different approaches taken by corporations, on the one hand, and universities, on the other, around these issues. It comes as no surprise, there, that major universities like Georgetown and Princeton, being institutions dedicated to critical inquiry and examination, have done the work of transparency willfully and willingly, while corporations, being dedicated to profiting their shareholders, have not. Strictly speaking the one exists to examine the world, the other does not. But a related question we might entertain is: Is there a difference in the quality of the revelation when a university examines these ties to slavery and discloses them versus when a corporation does? This seems a vitally important question to ask, given that so few corporations in the United States, and certainly not recently, have spoken of these ties and this truth, while many universities have. What might we be missing, so to speak, from the public discourse?

The real purpose of asking such a question is to explore another one: Would it make a difference if corporations in the United States, as they have in the United Kingdom, exposed themselves as being complicit in slavery? Would corporate disclosures by large banks or other corporate institutions change our perception of and our national discourse around slavery? Would it change the very story the nation tells itself about this history and its legacy? The scenario in England suggests that, yes, it would, in several seemingly subtle yet profound and groundbreaking ways.

To understand why, we might look at the statements that universities in the United States have made when disclosing their role in slavery, and then contrast these to what banks and large corporations in England have said. In the nuance lies a critical difference with imposing aftereffects. Here is Princeton University (all italics in the following quotes have been added): "Princeton University, founded...in 1746, exemplifies the central paradox *of American history.* From the very start, liberty and slavery were intertwined."[23] Brown University states: "Brown's early endowment benefited from contributions made by slaveowners and slave traders."[24] Brown elsewhere says: "Our primary task was to examine the *University's historical entanglement* with slavery and the slave trade and to report our findings openly and truthfully."[25] In their examinations and resulting reports, what the universities reveal, in other words, is largely the impact of slavery on *themselves,* that is, the benefits the university accrued from Black people's enslavement, and, to some extent, how the university shaped the country's views on enslavement more broadly. These are revelations mainly historical in nature, and, of course, they are critically important as such.

But note how they differ from the statements made by Lloyd's and other corporations in the United Kingdom (again, italics have been added). Here is the Bank of England talking about the impact of its role in enslavement: "We cannot retrace the lives of those enslaved, but it is important to reflect on *how the wealth they created shaped the development of Britain.*"[26] In a museum exhibition related to its findings, the Bank of England describes how its examination "looks at the Bank's place in *the wider financial system* at a time where enslavement was considered a legitimate trade."[27] Here is Lloyd's of London: "The rise of Lloyd's... coincided with *the emergence of Britain in the 18th century* as the largest slave-trading power and the development of the British transatlantic colonies as a major slave-system....*The slave-economy was clearly a principal feature in the British financial construct* and by extension also significant to its marine insurers."[28]

In their examinations and resulting reports, what these British corporations revealed is the impact of slavery on the financial development of their nation overall and the development of a global financial system as a whole. Their revelations pointed to systemic wealth—wealth for the whole country that arose throughout centuries of British history. It is wealth so entangled in the "British financial construct," even now, that everyone, the entire nation, has been touched by this larger system of benefits, and continues to be so. Major corporate institutions had never made such statements in the history of the United Kingdom. The tone, scale, and nature of these statements suggests, as we'll see, that were corporations in the United States to make similar disclosures, the impact would be singular and transformative in ways that differ significantly from the disclosures that have been made thus far by many of our leading universities.

Which leads us back to our questions: What would actually happen if multibillion-dollar institutions in the United States began acknowledging their complicity in slavery, and what scenario would it create that corporations here seem so keen to avoid? To find out, we can look once again at what is happening in England.

A groundswell is taking place there, something unprecedented—an unraveling process, as Yogendran suggested. It is not just that more and more corporations have come forward since 2020, as have educational and religious institutions, funding further internal reviews and reports. It is that because of these disclosures, corporations, many partnering with major universities, are rewriting their own histories, and, as a result, helping to rewrite the history of Great Britain itself.

For one thing, the Bank of England, after commissioning an in-depth study back in 2020, disclosed new information in 2022: that its directors took as collateral, after a client defaulted, 599 enslaved people beginning in the late 1770s.[29] The study also revealed seminal evidence showing that not only the bank, but England's banking system itself, profited directly from enslavement, and that has led to even more calls to study how widely and deeply such linkages within the country's financial system go.

A host of museum exhibits across the country, some stemming from these findings, have already explored slavery's deep impact on the nation's overall development, and this, coupled with university-driven research initiatives, is disrupting the financial order itself, with greater quakes and tremors likely to follow. The *Times* reported that Barclays, HSBC, and NatWest Group are conducting similar reviews.[30] Meanwhile, the Church of England in January 2023, having divulged in a report for the first time its links and investments in the transatlantic slave trade, has pledged £100 million in funding to "address past wrongs."[31]

The ripple effect has even reached outside the United Kingdom. In the Netherlands, ABN AMRO, a major international bank, came forward in April 2022, apologizing that its predecessor companies were "actively involved in the day-to-day business of plantations."[32]

Today, the story of what Great Britain is, of how it came to be, has already been fundamentally altered, changing how England presents and perceives itself. The very basis of the country's wealth has been exposed as tainted by crimes against humanity. Hard questions, painful questions, relating to entitlements and class, are being asked by the public and in Parliament, a discourse that, not surprisingly, has also fueled a backlash from conservative elements, who, much as they do in the United States, seek to downplay both the horrors and the existing impact of enslavement. Despite that backlash, however, vaults of hidden information are opening for the first time, exposing all that these companies and the British government haven't been saying, all that they have been working to hide—in other words, exposing their lies. The most repressed secrets in the sordid history of British slavery are now being ferreted out and irretrievably tied to British wealth. And, in what is truly significant, corporations themselves are the ones opening the vaults. It is not a perfect process—certainly no panacea—but the result is a profound transformation, in fact a new kind of cultural shift, and that is a very powerful thing in itself.

"I think where companies and brands have the most power are not the great structural changes, because at the end of the day they're just functions of capitalism, and ultimately they are there to make money," Amanda Yogendran said, adding: "I think brands are at their best as culture shapers."

Perhaps one lasting result of the unraveling of slavery's lies that is taking place in England is the possibility of a new kind of enlightenment, shaping a new culture of revelation and accountability—one beset with its own problems, to be sure, but in which the resulting discourse over wealth and slavery is far more revealing and remarkable, its impact greater, than what is currently achievable in the United States. It is all the more remarkable because the largest corporate financial institutions in the United Kingdom, the living repositories of the wealth created by slavery, are involved in the divulgence, corroborating, with their documents and records, this discourse on wealth.

This is not meant to credit corporations unduly for creating or driving the process, a process that activists, organizers, and academics in Britain began years ago, much as in the United States. The point is to highlight that in the United Kingdom, companies like Lloyd's are not obstacles to this flow of information—indifferent or hostile to its findings—as they are in the United States. And because those very institutions that built the system of slavery, that built the financial order of the nation itself, are saying: "We did this. We institutionalized slavery, and we institutionalized its abominable wealth as the basis of our development and prosperity," the argument that slavery had no impact on national wealth; that corporations in this history had no role to play, and therefore have no reparative payments to pay; and that this history has no impact now—all those arguments become much harder to make. They wither more easily in an environment of growing facts, and the chances for a culture of accountability grows.

Paradoxically, creating such a cultural shift is both the sort of "conscientious reform," the kind of public action, that Citi has made such a display of caring about and, at the same time, the basis for the very unraveling the bank seems so keen to avoid. But if we look to England as precedent—the only precedent we currently have—are we not justified in asking if this unraveling is really something Citi and other corporations need to fear? Is it not the case in England that neither Lloyd's nor the Bank of England has, as far as anyone can tell, crumbled to the ground through insolvency or been wracked by reputational strife to the point of irrelevancy or ruin? What is unraveling within these firms, and all around them, is antiquated modes of thinking, stale lies, old fears. Can it not be argued that what is happening there is a kind of innovation, and that these corporations, by honestly confronting their past, are becoming something new, something even more successful?

Corporate success today requires dealing with the past, including the past of slavery, write Sarah Federman, a professor of conflict resolution at the University of San Diego who has studied the Lloyd's case, and Judith Schrempf-Stirling, an associate professor in responsible management at the Geneva School of Economics and Management at the University of Geneva. They conclude that firms "who try to avoid historical issues… risk the company's reputation and sometimes more." The authors counsel that, "in the age of information, digitalization, and social media, it is impossible to hide from public exposure," that it's better for companies to choose "to address the past proactively rather than hide in vain until being called out."[33]

———

THE GROUNDBREAKING LAWSUITS that Deadria Farmer-Paellmann and others filed in the early 2000s, and which have not been taken up since, showed that it is unlikely that the US legal system, based on existing precedent and the political question doctrine, can compel private corporations in the United States to acknowledge their ties to slavery and make payments in repair. For now, as a matter of settled law, corporate reparations—and all slavery reparations, for that matter—would appear to be "beyond the province of judicial determination," as the parlance goes. Congress and the president, in direct consultation with the descendants of enslaved people themselves, must decide this most consequential of issues facing the nation, including who would receive reparations, how much, and when.

The issue is likely to meet public opposition for the foreseeable future. White adults in the United States, as well as most Latinos and Asian Americans, do not believe that living Black descendants of the enslaved deserve recompense, according to research undertaken by Tatishe Nteta, a political science professor at the University of Massachusetts Amherst, as NPR recently reported.[34] Polling by the Pew Research Center found similar opposition: that about seven out of ten US adults believe that descendants of the enslaved should not be compensated.[35]

And yet, as many observers have pointed out, such public resistance need not be an insurmountable hurdle. After all, Congress, back in the 1980s, passed a bill authorizing reparations payments to Japanese Americans who were incarcerated in camps during World War II, or their heirs. That reparations program, too, faced stiff public opposition. But when Congress held a series of groundbreaking public hearings, providing searing testimony from families who'd been incarcerated, it changed public perceptions, particularly among members of Congress, and amplified support for the idea of reparations for Japanese Americans. Beginning in 1988, about eighty-two thousand people received a payment of $20,000 each.

It was a year after those payments began that Rep. John Conyers first tabled his slavery reparations bill. The foundational agenda of that bill, H.R. 40, which still exists today, is to hold a series of similar public hearings. The hope there, too, is that through testimony and expert opinion, more Americans can be persuaded that atoning for the atrocities committed against Black people, still living with the damaging aftereffects of enslavement and racial discrimination, is part of our national destiny and our national interest.

There can be little doubt that major corporate actors committing to reparations would significantly sway public support. Corporate reparations may not be enforceable by law, but they are a choice in this time—a shifting time, a time when a growing number of universities, families, foundations, cities, states, religious organizations, and others have committed to reparations—a choice that corporations can choose to make. The reputational risks, while they avoid making this choice, are growing, Sarah Federman argues, "as large portions of society push for what they see as an overdue reckoning. Schools are being renamed, mascots are being discarded, and statues of historical figures that only a few years ago barely drew a glance are being toppled. Businesses face scrutiny over the origins of wealth and how they may have exploited people to enable their current profitability."[36]

Citi's net income in 2021 was $22 billion.[37] It is a financial powerhouse that, bearing even more institutional weight than Lloyd's of London, was also instrumental to the financial construct of enslavement, and for that reason, a potential culture shaper. What's more, Citi has its own library, a library the public knows little about, but which the bank's biographers, Harold van B. Cleveland and Thomas Huertas, had access to when researching and writing their book. The library appears to contain, among other documents and records that Cleveland and Huertas consulted, the official meeting minutes of the board of directors of City Bank throughout its antebellum years. Much like Lloyd's own library, this is a trove of information, almost certainly pertinent to the bank's investments and profits in global slavery, that Citi could make available to scholars for groundbreaking facts of great public interest—facts, it must be added, that the firm could have been mining all these years, but chose not to, much like Lloyd's. But Citi could choose to now, and it could, like Lloyd's, through a public apology and commitment to reparations, help revolutionize its country's discourse about slavery, by using its own archival material to corroborate how the country's financial system is indebted to Black people's labor. These facts would be all the more difficult to refute if they were to come from one of the institutions that built the very institution through which slavery produced the nation's wealth.

A larger unraveling of deceits could follow, a domino effect applying pressure on other corporate institutions to do the same. By divulging their own role in enslavement, companies like Citi, many of which are rooted in Wall Street, in the North, would help erode the notion that slavery, and its wealth, was something that benefited only the South. Their disclosures would underscore that enslavement, by robbing Black people of their own wealth and enriching corporations, contributed to gross disparities that have affected Black Americans ever since. This could help build public support for reparations, and awareness over why such payments, given the historical roots of the Black-white wealth gap, are just. It would compel us to reset popular notions of commercial virtue, by showing that these notions are rooted in antebellum industries of enslavement and theft; a new, ethical definition for success could grow in the wake of where these notions are shorn away. By revealing how enslavement built not only their own wealth, but that of the entire financial system, major corporations would show how the country as a whole benefited, meaning the nation collectively bears responsibility, not a particular region, class, or people. A new culture of revelation and accountability would be possible.

"When a company like Citibank stands up and says 'We're going to take ownership of this' [meaning its ties to slavery], that's a signal for policy and that's a signal for structural change," Amanda Yogendran argues. "That decision in itself won't change the world, but that's a cultural tipping point."

Is it not within the interests of Citi to make an apology, to be a leader of cultural corporate change that honors the lives and loss of African Americans who shaped this country and its wealth, rather than clinging to distortions and falsehoods?

"The healthier response," says Deadria Farmer-Paellmann, "that would be more healing for everyone is to say, 'Wow, this is a horrible history. But we're not that company today. In fact, we are paying restitution or reparations. We want to repair the injuries.' It's just a normal thing to do. That's how the world works today. You hit someone with your car, and you pay something to repair that person. And people can heal that way."

Corporations throughout the United States, given their embedded history in enslavement, and the wealth they retain because of that brutal oppression, have a unique role to play in repairing those harms through the payment of reparations. A special congressional hearing in April 2022, convening a panel of experts and advocates on the subject, highlighted this fact. "[Slavery] was a horrific crime against humanity that demands redress, a crime which cannot be whitewashed with a solution of ignoble ignorance," Rep. Al Green, then chair of the House Subcommittee on Oversight and Investigations said in the hearing's opening address. "Consequently, it becomes important for banks, insurance companies, and other financial institutions with historic ties to slavery to atone."[38]

How much should US corporations be prepared or willing to pay? In other words, how much of the total reparations bill would major companies be expected to foot? Such questions and their answers, while meaningfully important, should not overshadow a much more central concern, suggested William Darity, a professor of public policy, African American studies, and economics at Duke University, who was a witness for the 2022 congressional hearing. Darity, whose pioneering work has helped show that meaningful reparations to Black Americans would require trillions of dollars, highlighted that the corporate role in reparations would be vital, as would be the contribution of private institutions and individuals overall, whomever they might be.

He affirmed, however, that it is primarily the federal government who is both responsible for and capable of paying the tremendous tab for reparations in the United States. He outlined: "The minimum sum needed to close the Black-White chasm in wealth is $14 trillion. Only the Federal Government has the capacity to fund such an amount. If private individuals and institutions paid $1 billion a month into a 'reparations' fund, it would take a millennium for the fund to reach $14 trillion." His conclusion was not, he added, a "recipe for paralysis," meaning that corporations have no role to play; he meant only that their role cannot substitute for the federal government's responsibilities, that any corporate payments should supplement the federal government's total amount.[39]

Deadria Farmer-Paellmann argues that corporations should be paying millions into a trust fund that is administered by Black communities themselves. "I'm willing to accept from each of these companies $20 million a year," she says. "And that is a drop in the bucket. Individual CEOs are making $20 million. I say give us annually what you give the CEO. Put it into the trust fund every year."

She and many others emphasize that corporations will have to work directly with Black communities and leaders, and that those communities and leaders themselves will have to set the terms, not the other way around. She pointed to Lloyd's of London, and the company's pledge to make donations to charities and other payments, all on its own terms, as raising a red flag. "We don't know what they're doing," she says. "They have dictated what they're doing, and that's the mistake. I try to convey to all the young people out there on the streets, all of the activists in the boardrooms, all the opportunists sitting in the boardrooms, to understand: don't let them dictate what they will do." Small corporate actions, or token gestures, made without involving Black communities themselves, activists and observers caution, cannot possibly address the scope of enslavement and repair the damages.

Federman and Schrempf-Stirling have offered the same counsel to corporations themselves. "While it's tempting to tiptoe around an issue by, say, adding a brief statement to the corporate website or placing a memorial plaque, we find it's best to develop a comprehensive approach in conjunction with harmed communities," they write in MIT *Sloan Management Review*.[40]

Such consultation is a cornerstone of the growing practice of restorative justice, a legal theory based on the notion that crimes not only break the law but cause injury to victims and communities. Corporations in the United States, in fact, have done precisely this sort of consultation with victims in innumerable examples before. After the Deepwater Horizon oil spill in the Gulf of Mexico, an environmental disaster of unparalleled proportions, a federal court mandated, as part of a criminal settlement, that the major corporations involved, including the oil company BP, work directly with communities in the affected zone to devise a $20 billion victim compensation fund.[41] Those payments, which were paid on top of $4 billion in criminal fines, were designated as a means of healing social wounds.[42]

What is noteworthy about the Deepwater Horizon case, and many others like it, is that corporations devised reparative payments in consultation with affected groups, even when direct victims couldn't be identified. The US Department of Justice, and US courts in general, have experience in arranging such payments, for instance payments connected to violations of environmental law and white-collar crime cases like overseas corporate bribery. Such cases underline that even if corporations like Citi are unable to directly identify the descendants of Black people whom their directors enslaved (though this certainly seems possible in some cases), that does not mean corporations cannot devise ways to make reparations to Black communities and Black families as a means of social repair.

One thing is certain: major corporations like Citi, Alex. Brown, Brown Brothers Harriman, and CSX, to name just a few, can afford it. If the Jesuit Order of Catholic priests can pledge to raise $100 million in reparations for Black people, and the Church of England can pledge £100 million, major blue-chip corporations can too. They can afford, indeed, to make *multibillion-dollar* pledges, over a period of time, and it would barely be noticed on their bottom line.

So can multibillion-dollar private foundations and trust funds, such as the one that the Hillman family of Pittsburgh, the descendants of the enslaving iron baron Daniel Hillman Jr., controls. Hillman Family Foundations, whose annual budget in 2019 was $1.5 billion, supports eighteen philanthropic entities dedicated to "improving the quality of life," the "health and healing for society and the planet," and supporting programs "with the goal of creating a better world for all," as its website says.[43] Amid all this philanthropy, neither the family nor its foundation has ever acknowledged the origins of the family's wealth in enslavement, nor explicitly sought, through donations or other programs, to make repair. A program of reparations for Black Americans, it is clear, would be among the most important efforts ever made by the Hillman family in its demonstrated commitment to civic values. It is an opportunity for the family to engage in essential societal healing and improvement, one in direct alignment with its history of such efforts. (Hillman Family Foundations did not respond to repeated requests for comment.)

Is such an investment not one that corporations, philanthropies, and foundations indebted to enslavement should want to make? Would these payments not be, as the scholar Olúfẹ́mi O. Táíwò has suggested, "an opportunity to construct the just world, or at least to rebuild the world in the direction of justice"—the very thing that many of these entities claim to want to do?[44]

———

It is often argued that because no one alive today was involved in the slavery of the past, and, conversely, that because the people who profited from slavery are now all dead, there's no one, and nothing, any longer to hold to account. Underlying this argument is the premise that only living individuals directly responsible for slavery can be held accountable today, and that as no such individuals exist, being all dead, any accountability, by extension, would unfairly impugn innocent people alive. ("None of us currently living are responsible," is how Senator Mitch McConnell, whose own forebears enslaved Black people,[45] has dismissed the call for reparations.)[46]

And yet it is well established in political practice, in social theory, and even in law, that the culpability of individuals, whether living or dead, isn't the only basis for the redress of past crimes. Societies, institutions, corporations, and, indeed, governments, being collectives made up of many individuals, can be held to account for wrongdoings.

The legal scholars Susan S. Kuo and Benjamin Means recently published a cogent argument in favor of reparations with this very idea in mind. Their thesis is that the United States of America, in our collective connection to the crimes committed against Black people through enslavement, is a lot like another entity at the center of this discussion: a corporation itself. Under established law, it's not necessary for every single individual in a company to have committed a crime for the company to be guilty. A corporation can be held liable for the collective misconduct of its employees, quite apart from whether certain individual employees are prosecuted or otherwise deemed responsible. "In a corporation," they wrote, "individual innocence is irrelevant because the responsible person is the entity itself."[47]

Kuo and Means's point is that the United States, like a corporation, is a strange, unique legal entity, at once made up of, and in service to, its individual citizens, and yet distinct from them, and thus responsible for its own wrongdoings, including those committed long ago—much as a corporation, also a unique legal entity, is distinct from its shareholders and responsible for its own wrongdoing. Kuo and Means employ this analogy to help us see how even though no one alive today is guilty of slavery, that doesn't mean that the United States is innocent. "Seeking reparations from the United States," they say, "does not turn on the guilt of its citizens any more than prosecuting a corporation turns on the guilt of its shareholders." As a nation, the United States was enriched by the stolen labor of Black people, much as a corporation might be enriched by corruption or another crime; we all have benefited from that enrichment, though none of us alive today is directly guilty ourselves, much as all the shareholders of a corrupt company, though not participating in that activity, are nonetheless enriched by the crime.

"The payment of restitution," Kuo and Means write, "does not require any finding that individuals alive today are responsible for past transgressions; only that they have benefited from them and that it would be unjust for them to retain the benefit." Kuo and Means, it is important to say, are making a moral argument, not a legal one, since they recognize that courts are unlikely to be the instrument through which reparations in the United States are determined. And that is perhaps as it should be. Reparations are a choice that the United States overall, like the corporations that built and benefited from the nation's business of Black enslavement, should opt to make.

Kuo and Means see such a choice as a commitment to America of the highest degree. "If patriotism is love of country, therefore, patriotism should take as its object the country that actually exists," they say. "Rather than jettisoning the nation's history in favor of a sanitized, mythological version, those who are patriots should embrace the work necessary to perfect the nation they love. That task cannot be accomplished without dealing with the legacy of slavery and Jim Crow. In this sense, reparations can be seen as a kind of patriotism: a nation willing to hold itself to a higher moral standard is one worth celebrating." American exceptionalism can be this moral commitment to addressing our most immoral chapter. If we claim to be leaders in the world, let us perform having such courage and conscience.

It is to see the trail that binds us all, our history collectively inscribed in the cycle of ships that sailed from the coast of Africa to the South, and from the South to New York, laden with the spoils of calculated exploitation, the bounty of crimes. To see that a trove rose from this compassionless pilfering of Black people's time, a pilfering not contained by geography, but flowing South to North, and North to South, building the prosperity of the whole nation—prosperity passed through generations, preserved through institutions, over time, of which no one living may be guilty, but in which all today share. That is the privilege, the burden, and the responsibility of our citizenship.

We live in a time when the wealth of slavery is all around us, yet conservative lawmakers are actively disappearing, more and more each day, the story of how it came to be. A time when our cities, though living monuments to the labors that Black people gave, reign with power and privilege as silent witnesses to these facts; when our corporations, vessels to enslavement's wealth, remain sealed vaults to their founders' role in that pain and disgrace. These were the white architects who built the financial, industrial, and commercial foundations of our lives, not to mention much of its politics. Willfully forgetting and obscuring what these men did, what they built through slavery, what they took through slavery, makes it easier to dismiss what's owed to Black people and what's in need of repair.

An acknowledgment, an apology, and a commitment to reparations would constitute an arc of restoration in a meaningful and cultural sweep. It requires that much within individual corporations and the surrounding financial system will have to be uprooted and looked at, painfully torn into, held up in the light. Ideas and false notions will have to be pulled down—corporate ones, public ones, personal ones, political ones—before new and emboldened commitments to equity, restoration, and virtue can be built up. We don't even know all that this would consist of, all that it would entail, all that would follow, because it hasn't happened yet—and never has, in this country's history. The unraveling of lies and amnesia, oblivion, and deceit, has yet to come, but it can no longer wait.

ACKNOWLEDGMENTS

This book came to be, foremost, because of my wife, Mehr. While out walking one day, she mentioned reading in the news that Lloyd's of London had disclosed its ties to enslavement. She suggested I look into it. Her suggesting so was a precious gift. Her encouragement from that day, and all her amazing support throughout, reading drafts and offering insights, and her love in general, sustained me and this book.

My fantastic agents, Larry Weissman and Sascha Alper, saw the promise of this work and helped it come to life. I am ever grateful for their support in refining the early concept of the book and finding it such a wonderful home. My deepest gratitude to you both.

It was a stroke of absolute fortune to work with Krishan Trotman. She saw not only the potential of this book but pushed it beyond its original boundaries, making it a much more consequential work as a result. I am so thankful she did that, and equally thankful for the insights and support she brought to this project. I feel extremely lucky to have worked with her team at Legacy Lit.

Clarence Haynes was such a joy to work with throughout the editing phase, offering much-needed suggestions, streamlining the prose, and keeping the whole process moving so seamlessly as to make it seem effortless.

Deadria Farmer-Paellmann was the first person I called when setting out to research this book. She was a font of hope and knowledge and support. Her generous spirit and incredible dedication to this issue was an inspiration. It was Deadria who suggested I seek out and call up Bob Brown, who, as luck would have it, ended up calling me. I drew such great encouragement throughout this journey from Bob's warm support. His voice on the line, through hours of conversation and exploration, was truly a comfort throughout the construction of this book. I will forever be grateful for his encyclopedic knowledge, his wit, and his support. His presence has been nourishment.

The research behind this book was only possible because of the generous support of the Fund for Investigative Journalism. I have the deepest admiration for the work that they do. They are a critical lifeline for projects of this kind, and I am honored to have been a recipient of one of their grants.

I want to thank the wonderful staff at the New York Public Library's Brooke Russell Astor Reading Room, where I spent many an afternoon in those splendid surroundings, digging through old ledger books and manuscripts. It was a joy to be there and among them.

I am grateful for the support of friends and family. Daniel Mirsky so generously read through a critical chapter, pushed and encouraged its refinement, and marked up the pages so enthusiastically that I only hope I did justice to his efforts. That support means so much. As does the warm companionship of the Pittsburgh fire circle, whose mirth sustained my and Mehr's spirit throughout the long, uncertain days of the pandemic. I am truly thankful for that friendship.

Finally, to the Monteros. My brothers, Michael and Gabriel, encouraged this book's beginnings, and I'm touched by their support, as I am by that of my father, and my sister, Olivia, who encouraged me enthusiastically all the while. All my love to them; theirs means everything to me.

NOTES

INTRODUCTION

1   "Bank's Big Capital: National City May Increase Stock to Ten Millions," *Philadelphia Inquirer*, December 3, 1899.
2   All dollar conversions have been calculated using the Purchasing Power Calculator at Measuring Worth, www.measuringworth.com, to derive a relative value, with 2022 used as the conversion date.
3   Eric Foner, "Slavery's Fellow Travelers," *New York Times*, July 13, 2000, https://www .nytimes.com/2000/07/13/opinion/slavery-s-fellow-travelers.html.
4   Statement of Sven Beckert, "An Enduring Legacy: The Role of Financial Institutions in the Horrors of Slavery and the Need for Atonement," hybrid hearing before the Subcommittee on Oversight and Investigations of the Committee on Financial Services, US House of Representatives, 117th Cong., 2nd session, April 5, 2022, https:// www.govinfo.gov/content/pkg/CHRG-117hhrg47476/html/CHRG-117hhrg47476 .htm.

CHAPTER 1

1   The scholar Alexey Krichtal, using shipping records, detailed that the top twenty New York importers of cotton received 4.7 million pounds' worth of cotton between 1808 and 1810. Using average pricing at the time, the value of this cotton would have fallen between $500,000 and $700,000. Alexey Krichtal, "Liverpool and the Raw Cotton Trade: A Study of the Port and Its Merchant Community, 1770–1815" (master's thesis, submitted at Victoria University of Wellington, 2013), 73.
2   Robert G. Albion, *Square-Riggers on Schedule: The New York Sailing Packets to England, France, and the Cotton Ports* (Princeton, NJ: Princeton University Press, 1938), 52.
3   "Tobacco Trade," National Museum of American History, Smithsonian, https:// americanhistory.si.edu/on-the-water/living-atlantic-world/new-tastes-new-trades /tobacco-trade.

4   Douglass C. North, *The Economic Growth of the United States 1790–1860* (New York: W. W. Norton, 1966), 43.

5   Joseph Alfred Scoville, *The Old Merchants of New York City*, 2nd series (New York: Carleton, 1863), 5.

6   Advertisement placed by Archibald Gracie, *Independent Journal*, May 19, 1784.

7   David Thurston and the American and Foreign Anti-Slavery Society, *An Address to the Anti-Slavery Christians of the United States* (New York: J. Gray, 1852), 12.

8   Toni Morrison, *Playing in the Dark: Whiteness and the Literary Imagination* (New York: Vintage Books, 1992), 38.

9   Cited in *American State Papers 02, Foreign Relations*, vol. 2, 440–58, 7th Cong., 1st session, April 20, 1802, publication no. 173, 451. Other references to Gracie's cargo are made in *Message from the President of the United States, Transmitting a Report and Sundry Documents*, from the secretary of state, of the depredations committed on the commerce of the United States, since the first of October, 1796; in pursuance of a resolution of the House, of the tenth instant. June 22, 1797. Ordered to lie on the table. Published by order of the House of Representatives.

10 The New York City Census of 1800 lists Archibald Gracie as enslaving five Black people in his household.

11 Elihu Hubbard Smith, *A Discourse, Delivered April 11, 1798: At the Request Of and Before the New-York Society for Promoting the Manumission of Slaves, and Protecting Such of Them as Have Been or May Be Liberated* (New York: T & J Swords, 1798), 3.

12 David N. Gellman, *Liberty's Chain: Slavery, Abolition, and the Jay Family of New York* (Ithaca, NY: Cornell University Press, 2022), 108.

13 John L. Rury, "Philanthropy, Self Help, and Social Control: The New York Manumission Society and Free Blacks, 1785–1810," *Phylon (1960–)* 46, no. 3 (1985): 233.

14 Jennifer Schuessler, "Alexander Hamilton, Enslaver? New Research Says Yes," *New York Times*, November 9, 2020, https://www.nytimes.com/2020/11/09/arts/alexander-hamilton-enslaver-research.html.

15 Jessie Serfilippi, "'As Odious and Immoral a Thing': Alexander Hamilton's Hidden History as an Enslaver," Schuyler Mansion State Historic Site, New York State Office of Parks, Recreation, and Historic Preservation, https://parks.ny.gov/documents/historic-sites/SchuylerMansionAlexanderHamiltonsHiddenHistoryasanEnslaver.pdf.

16 Harry B. Yoshpe, "Record of Slave Manumissions in New York during the Colonial and Early National Periods," *Journal of Negro History* 26, no. 1 (1941). A copy of the order by which Gracie manumitted Abram, Sarah, and Charles Short is reproduced in "A Visit to Gracie Mansion, the People's House, A Resource Guide for Teachers," pg. 35. Available at: www.graciemansion.org/wp-content/uploads/2018/11/gmc_tour_curriculum_2017.pdf.

17 *The Journals of Washington Irving*, ed. by William P. Trent and George S. Hellman, vol. 2, 96, https://www.loc.gov/resource/lhbtn.1680c/?sp=1&st=slideshow.

18 *New-York Evening Post*, April 2, 1802.

19 Nichol Turnbull, letter to the *Georgia Gazette*, November 28, 1799, reprinted in "The Beginning of Cotton Cultivation in Georgia," *Georgia Historical Quarterly* 1, no. 1 (March 1917): 42.

20 Morris R. Chew, *History of the Kingdom of Cotton and Cotton Statistics of the World* (New Orleans: W. B. Stansbury, 1884), 37.

21 François Alexandre Frédéric, Duke de la Rochefoucault Liancourt, *Travels Through the United States of America*, vol. 1 (London: R. Phillips, 1799), 605.

22 "The Beginning of Cotton Cultivation," *Georgia Historical Quarterly*, 42–43.
23 The Beginning of Cotton Cultivation," 42.
24 *The Cotton Plant: Its History, Botany, Chemistry, Culture, Enemies, and Uses* (Washington, DC: US Department of Agriculture, Office of Experiment Stations 1896), 35.
25 Eric Williams, *Capitalism and Slavery* (Chapel Hill: University of North Carolina Press, 1944), 128.
26 *The Cotton Plant*, USDA, 36.
27 *The Cotton Plant*, USDA, 35.
28 W. E. B. Du Bois, *Black Reconstruction in America 1860–1880* (New York: Free Press, 1935), 5.
29 Williams, *Capitalism and Slavery*, 128.
30 Williams, *Capitalism and Slavery*, 102.
31 Walter Johnson, "To Remake the World: Slavery, Racial Capitalism, and Justice, *Boston Review*, February 20, 2018, https://www.bostonreview.net/forum/walter-johnson-to-remake-the-world.
32 Nichol Turnbull's will accessed at Ancestry.com: Georgia, U.S., Wills and Probate Records, 1742–1992, Chatham, Georgia, November 1, 1824.
33 Duke de la Rochefoucault Liancourt, *Travels Through the United States of America*, vol. 1, 564.
34 Advertisement placed by Nichol Turnbull, *Georgia Gazette*, November 28, 1799.
35 Oxford African American Studies Center, *1800 to 1899*, accessed at https://oxfordaasc.com/page/2637; U.S. Census, 1800, *Return of the Whole Number of Persons within the Several Districts of the United States*, accessed at https://www.census.gov/library/publications/1801/dec/return.html.
36 Charles F. Kovacik and Robert E. Mason, "Changes in the South Carolina Sea Island Cotton Industry," *Southeastern Geographer* 25, no. 2 (November 1985): 83.
37 Douglas C. North, *The Economic Growth of the United States 1790–1860* (New York: W. W. Norton, 1966), 46–53.
38 Richard Sylla and Robert E. Wright, "Corporation Formation in the Antebellum United States in Comparative Context," *Business History* 55, no. 4 (2013): 650–66.
39 Du Bois, *Black Reconstruction in America 1860–1880*, 11.
40 William E. Dodd, *The Cotton Kingdom: A Chronicle of the Old South* (New Haven, CT: Yale University Press, 1919), 29–30.
41 Nichol Turnbull, *Georgia Gazette*, November 20, 1801.

CHAPTER 2

1 François Alexandre Frédéric, Duke de la Rochefoucault Liancourt, *Travels Through the United States of America*, 2nd ed., vol. 4 (London: R. Phillips, 1800), 229.
2 Alexander Ramsay, "Observations on the Yellow-Fever in New York in 1803," included in *The Edinburgh Medical and Surgical Journal*, 1812, vol. 8, 2nd ed. (Edinburgh: George Ramsay, 1815), 422–24.
3 Morrison, *Playing in the Dark*, 44–45.
4 Albion, *Square-Riggers on Schedule*, 100.
5 *New-York Commercial Advertiser*, July 3, 1811.
6 *Mercantile Advertiser*, New York, October 20, 1813.
7 A. W. Ferrin, "The Great Banks of New York," *Moody's Magazine*, vol. 17, January–December 1914 (New York: Moody Magazine and Book Company, 1914), 251.

8   John M'Cready, A *Review of the Trade and Commerce of New-York from 1815 to the Present Time: With an Inquiry into the Causes of the Present Distress and the Means of Obviating It* (New York: C. S. Van Winkle, 1820), 32.

9   Advertisement placed by Benjamin Bailey, *New York Gazette*, March 3, 1815.

10 New York Manumission Society records show that Bailey freed Dolly Clark on November 12, 1812, and Joseph Clark on December 14, 1817. See Yoshpe, "Record of Slave Manumissions in New York during the Colonial and Early National Periods," *Journal of Negro History* 26, no. 1 (1941), 93. Bailey's enslavement of Hannah is recorded in manumission records at the Office of the Register, New York County, and cited by Yoshpe, 78.

11 J. S. Gibbons, *The Banks of New-York, Their Dealers, the Clearing House, and the Panic of 1857: With a Financial Chart* (New York: D. Appleton, 1858), 21.

12 Swartwout's enslavement of Jenny is documented in records kept by The New York Historical Society, namely two certificates written by Swartwout upon the birth of Jenny's daughters Susan in 1802 and Harriet in 1804. See: "Birth certificate of a certain female child named Harriet," Slavery Collection, Series VII: Legal Documents, 1709-1858, Subseries 1. Birth Certificates 1800-1818. Digital copy of Susan's birth certificate available at: https://nyheritage.contentdm.oclc.org/digital/collection/p15052coll5/id/24977/rec/1. Digital copy of Harriet's birth certificate available at: https://nyheritage.contentdm.oclc.org/digital/collection/p15052coll5/id/24978/rec/2.

13 Harold van B. Cleveland and Thomas F. Huertas, *Citibank 1812–1970* (Cambridge, MA: Harvard University Press, 1985), 8.

14 Cleveland and Huertas, *Citibank*, 9.

15 Cleveland and Huertas, *Citibank*, 9.

16 Magee's position as one of New York's top twenty cotton exporters is detailed in the master's thesis of Alexey Krichtal, "Liverpool and the Raw Cotton Trade," 73.

17 See Boisgerard's advertisements, for example from the *Mercantile Advertiser*, December 7, 1812; the *National Advocate*, January 1, 1813; and the *New York Gazette*, "For Charleston," August 30, 1815, detailing the *Ann*.

18 See Desobry's advertisements from the *Mercantile Advertiser*, March 6, 1818, and the *National Advocate*, June 12, 1818.

19 George W. Sheldon, "Old Shipping Merchants of New York," *Harper's New Monthly Magazine* 84 (February 1892): 463.

20 Henry Wysham Lanier, A *Century of Banking in New York, 1822–1922* (New York: Gilliss Press, 1922), 125–27.

21 Steven H. Jaffe and Jessica Lautin, *Capital of Capital: Money, Banking, and Power in New York City, 1784–2012* (New York: Columbia University Press, 2014), 27.

22 M'Cready, A *Review of the Trade and Commerce of New-York from 1815 to the Present Time: With an Inquiry into the Causes of the Present Distress and the Means of Obviating It*, 35.

23 Thomas Prentice Kettell, *Southern Wealth and Northern Profits, as Exhibited in Statistical Facts and Official Figures: Showing the Necessity of Union to the Future Prosperity and Welfare of the Republic* (New York: George W. & John A. Wood, 1860), 71–72.

24 John Livingston, *Portraits of Eminent Americans Now Living; Including President Pierce and His Cabinet: With Biographical and Historical Memoirs of Their Lives and Actions*, vol. 3 (New York: R. Craighead, 1854), 448.

25   Robert G. Albion, *The Rise of the New York Port, 1815–1860* (New York: Charles Scribner's Sons, 1939), 39.

26   Robert G. Albion, "Planning the Black Ball Line, 1817," *Business History Review* 41, no. 1 (Spring 1967): 104–07.

27   Grant Thorburn, *Fifty Years' Reminiscences of New York; or Flowers from the Garden of Laurie Todd* (New York: Daniel Fanshaw, 1845), 136.

28   "Direct Trade with the South; Navigation of the Atlantic—Packet Ships of New York—Their Influence over the Commerce of the United States—and Their Effects on American Naval Architecture," *Southern Literary Messenger* 5, no. 1 (January 1, 1839): 7.

29   The figure for the number of vessels built is compiled from Kettell's statistics, Kettell, *Southern Wealth and Northern Profits*, 80.

30   George McHenry, *The Cotton Trade: Its Bearing upon the Prosperity of Great Britain and Commerce of the American Republics Considered in Connection with the System of Negro Slavery in the Confederate States* (London: Saunders & Otley, 1863), 180.

31   Figures cited from Emily Buchnea, "Transatlantic Transformations: Visualizing Change Over Time in the Liverpool–New York Trade Network, 1763–1833," *Enterprise and Society* 15, no. 4 (December 2014): 711. Buchnea cites cotton imports in bales, which have been converted by the author to pounds, using an average weight of four hundred pounds per bale.

32   E. J. Donnell, *Chronological and Statistical History of Cotton* (New York: James Sutton, 1872), 105.

33   McHenry, *The Cotton Trade*, 109.

34   Grant Thorton, "Communications: The Last of the Knickerbockers," *Home Journal*, September 14, 1850.

35   "Celebrating the 125th Anniversary of the National City Bank of New York," *New York Times*, June 14, 1937.

36   Advertisement placed by Jeremiah Thompson, *New York Gazette*, May 8, 1826.

37   Frank Thistlethwaite, "Atlantic Partnership," *Economic History Review* 7, no. 1 (1954): 5.

38   John R. Killick, "Risk, Specialization and Profit in the Mercantile Sector of the Nineteenth Century Cotton Trade: Alexander Brown and Sons 1820–1880, *Business History* 16, no. 1 (January 1974): 9.

39   "Direct Trade with the South," *Southern Literary Messenger*, 12.

40   "Direct Trade with the South," 4.

41   Williams, *Capitalism and Slavery*, 43.

42   Cited in *Minutes of the Proceedings of the Thirteenth American Convention for Promoting the Abolition of Slavery, and Improving the Condition of the African Race* (Philadelphia: John Bouvier, 1812): "From the credentials produced, it appeared that Samuel Hicks, Thomas Collins, Willet Robbins, Jeremiah Thompson, Gilbert Shotwell, Mordecai Lewis, Thomas Tucker, Willet Seaman, Sylvanus F. Jenkins, and Joshua Underhill, had been appointed to represent the Manumission Society of New York."

43   *American Convention for Promoting the Abolition of Slavery and Improving the Condition of the African Race: Minutes, Constitution, Addresses, Memorials, Resolutions, Reports, Committees and Anti-Slavery Tracts*, vol. 2 (New York: Bergman Publishers, 1969), 91.

44   From a statement made by Benjamin F. Porter (Alabama House of Representatives, 1832 to 1834) in a report to the Legislature of Alabama and reprinted in

James D. B. De Bow, *Commercial Review of the South and West*, vol. 4 (New Orleans: J. D. B. De Bow, 1846–1850), 340.

CHAPTER 3

1   William Armstrong Fairburn, *Merchant Sail*, vol. 2 (Lovell, Maine: Fairburn Marine Educational Foundation, 1955), 51.
2   James Kent, *Commentaries on American Law, II* (New York: O. Halstead, 1827), 220.
3   Edward Pessen, "The Egalitarian Myth and the American Social Reality: Wealth, Mobility, and Equality in the 'Era of the Common Man,'" *American Historical Review* 76, no. 4 (October 1971): 1023.
4   Advertisement, *Mercantile Advertiser*, New York, March 7, 1818.
5   Harry B. Yoshpe, "Record of Slave Manumissions in New York during the Colonial and Early National Periods," *Journal of Negro History* 26, no. 1 (1941). Yoshpe excerpts portions of the Instruments of Manumission on Record in the Office of the Register, New York County, and details Abraham Bloodgood's name.
6   The Slave Trade: The Act Prohibiting the Importation of Slaves," enacted March 1807 and in effect as of January 1, 1808, National Archives, https://www.archives.gov/education/lessons/slave-trade.html.
7   *Further Papers Relating to The Slave Trade, Viz., Copy of the Report of the House of Representatives of the United States of America, in Their Last Session of Congress, Relative to the Manual Exercise of the Right of Search, by Great Britain and America, with a View to the Suppression of the Slave Trade* (London: Houses of Commons, 1822), 4–8.
8   John Quincy Adams, *Memoirs of John Quincy Adams, Comprising Portions of His Diary from 1795 to 1848*, ed. Charles Francis Adams, vol. 4 (Philadelphia: J. B. Lippincott, 1875), 524.
9   Theodore Parker, *An Address Delivered by the Rev. Theodore Parker, Before the New York City Anti-Slavery Society: At Its First Anniversary, Held at the Broadway Tabernacle, May 12, 1854* (New York: American Anti-Slavery Society, 1854), 18.
10 Kettell, *Southern Wealth and Northern Profits*, 80.
11 Tabulated from "Corporation Formation in the Antebellum United States in Comparative Context," Richard Sylla and Robert E. Wright, 6.
12 Gavin Wright, "The Antebellum US Economy," in *Handbook of Cliometrics*, eds. Claude Diebolt and Michael Haupert (Berlin: Springer, 2015), citing a 1966 study by Robert E. Gallman.
13 Alan L. Olmstead and Paul W. Rhode, "Cotton, Slavery, and the New History of Capitalism," *Explorations in Economic History* 67 (2018): 1–17.
14 Statistics from the US Treasury quoted in Mathew Carey, *A Warning Voice to the Cotton and Tobacco Planters, Farmers and Merchants of the United States: On the Pernicious Consequences to Their Respective Interests of the Existing Policy of the Country* (Philadelphia: H. C. Carey & I. Lea, 1824), 58.
15 Williams, *Capitalism and Slavery*, 105.
16 Du Bois, *Black Reconstruction in America*, 5.
17 William Crawford to Tombecke Bank, St. Stephen's, October 16, 1819, included in *American State Papers: Documents, Legislative And Executive, of the Congress of the United States*, vol. 4, class III (Washington, DC: Gales and Seaton, 1858), 736.
18 Du Bois, *Black Reconstruction*, 5.

19 Thomas Hart Benton, in an address entitled "Public Lands," December 27, 1827, reprinted in *Register of Debates in Congress*, vol. 4 (Washington, DC: Gales and Seaton, 1828), 26.

20 The first house was lit by gas in New York City in 1825. It was No. 7 Cherry Lane, the house of Samuel F. Leggett, president of the Gas Company. From John Cox Jr., "Quakerism in New York 1657–1930" (New York: privately printed, 1930), 136.

21 Frederick Douglass, *Narrative of the Life of Frederick Douglass, an American Slave* (Boston: Anti-Slavery Society, 1845), 113.

22 Hall Gleason, *Old Ships and Ship-Building Days of Medford, 1630–1873* (West Medford, MA, 1936), 55–56. Accessed at https://www.medfordhistorical.org/wp-content/uploads/2021/07/Gleason_Ship-Building-Days-of-Medford-1630-to-1873.pdf.

23 Tax assessments are taken from a variety of sources, including Henry Wysham Lanier, *A Century of Banking in New York, Minutes of the Common Council of the City of New York, 1784–1831*, vol. 13, 194.

24 Pessen, "The Egalitarian Myth," 995.

25 Figures from Robert A. Margo, *Wages and Labor Markets in the United States, 1820–1860* (Chicago: University of Chicago Press, 2000), 11; and US Department of Labor, Bureau of Labor Statistics, *Monthly Labor Review* 30, no. 1 (January 1930): 13, https://babel.hathitrust.org/cgi/pt?id=umn.31951d029289565&view=1up&seq=21&skin=2021.

26 William Hillhouse, *The Crisis, No. 2, or Thoughts on Slavery, Occasioned by the Missouri Question* (New Haven, CT: A. H. Maltby, 1820), 4.

27 Works Progress Administration, interview with Rufus Houston, John B. Cade Slave Narrative Collection, Date 1844-01-15, Box 1, Folder Number 006, Archives, Manuscripts and Rare Books Department, John B. Cade Library, Southern University and A&M College.

28 Works Progress Administration, interview with Jennie Haggens, John B. Cade Slave Narrative Collection, Date 1935-03-23, Box 1, Folder Number 005, Archives and Manuscripts Department, John B. Cade Library, Southern University and A&M College.

29 James K. Paulding, *Letters from the South, Written during an Excursion in the Summer of 1816*, vol. I, letter XI (New York: 1817, 117), reprinted in William Jay, *A View of the Action of the Federal Government, in Behalf of Slavery* (New York: J. S. Taylor, 1839), 66.

30 Julie Winch, "The Making and Meaning of James Forten's *Letters from a Man of Colour*," *William and Mary Quarterly* 64, no. 1 (January 2007): 130.

31 James Forten, *Letters from a Man of Colour, on a Late Bill Before the Senate of Pennsylvania* (Philadelphia, 1813).

32 Christopher J. Bryant, "Without Representation, No Taxation: Free Blacks, Taxes, and Tax Exemptions Between the Revolutionary and Civil Wars," *Michigan Journal of Race and Law* 15 (2015): 93.

33 Bryant, "Without Representation, No Taxation."

34 Yohuru Williams, "Why Thomas Jefferson's Anti-Slavery Passage Was Removed from the Declaration of Independence," June 29, 2020, History.com, https://www.history.com/news/declaration-of-independence-deleted-anti-slavery-clause-jefferson.

35 Williams, "Why Thomas Jefferson's Anti-Slavery Passage Was Removed from the Declaration of Independence."

36 William Cooper Nell and Harriet Beecher Stowe, *The Colored Patriots of the American Revolution: With Sketches of Several Distinguished Colored Persons: To Which Is Added a Brief Survey of the Condition and Prospects of Colored Americans* (Boston: Robert F. Wallcut, 1855), 178.

37 "Resolutions Passed by the Colored Inhabitants of Philadelphia," the *National Advocate*, issue 1444, vol. V, August 14, 1817, 2.

38 Edwin Clifford Holland, *A Refutation of the Calumnies Circulated Against the Southern & Western States: Respecting the Institution and Existence of Slavery among Them, to Which Is Added a Minute and Particular Account of the Actual State and Condition of their Negro Population Together with Historical Notices of All the Insurrections That Have Taken Place Since the Settlement of the Country* (Charleston, SC: A. E. Miller, 1822), 36.

39 Holland, *A Refutation of the Calumnies*, 36.

40 Holland, *A Refutation of the Calumnies*, 37.

41 Whitemarsh B. Seabrook, *A Concise View of the Critical Situation, and Future Prospects of the Slave-Holding States, in Relation to Their Coloured Population* (Charleston, SC: A. E. Miller, 1825), 3.

42 Thomas Jefferson in a letter to John Holmes, April 22, 1820, reproduced in *The Writings of Thomas Jefferson: Being his Autobiography, Correspondence, Reports, Messages, Addresses, and Other Writings, Official and Private*, ed. Henry Augustine Washington (Washington, DC: Taylor & Maury, 1853–1854), 159.

43 James Madison, "Memorandum on an African Colony for Freed Slaves," October 20, 1789, from *The Founders' Constitution*, vol. 1, chapter 15, document 43 (Chicago: University of Chicago Press), https://press-pubs.uchicago.edu/founders/documents/v1ch15s43.html.

44 John Parrish, *Remarks on the Slavery of the Black People; Addressed to the Citizens of the United States, Particularly to Those Who Are in Legislative or Executive Stations in the General or State Governments; and Also to Such Individuals as Hold Them in Bondage* (Philadelphia: Kimber, Conrad, 1806), 41.

45 Hillhouse, *The Crisis, No. 2*, 14.

46 William Hillhouse, *The Crisis, No. 1-2, or, Thoughts on Slavery, Occasioned by the Missouri Question* (New Haven, CT: A. H. Maltby, 1820), 9–14.

47 "Resolution concerning emancipation and colonization" submitted for consideration in the US Senate, February 18, 1825, by Rufus King, cited in "Great Scheme for Carrying on Colonization," *African Repository and Colonial Journal* 26, no. 5 (May 1850).

48 Brandon Mills, *The World Colonization Made: The Racial Geography of Early American Empire* (Philadelphia: University of Pennsylvania Press, 2020), 32.

49 American Anti-Slavery Society, *Fourth Annual Report of the American Anti-Slavery Society, with the Speeches Delivered at the Anniversary Meeting Held in the City of New York on the 9th May, 1837* (New York: William S. Dorr, 1837), 56.

CHAPTER 4

1 Letter from Mr. Samuel A. Crozer to E. B. Caldwell, Esq., secretary of the American Colonization Society, March 31, 1820, reprinted in *Address of the Board of Managers of the American Colonization Society to the Auxiliary Societies and the People of the United States* (Washington, DC: Davis and Force, 1820), 13.

2   Ebenezer Burgess and the American Colonization Society, *Address to the American Society for Colonizing the Free People of Colour of the United States* (Washington, DC: Davis & Force, 1818), 56.

3   John Hanson Thomas McPherson, *The History of Liberia* (Baltimore: Johns Hopkins Press: 1891); *The Seventh Annual Report of the American Society for Colonizing the Free People of Colour of the United States: With an Appendix* (Washington, DC: Davis & Force, 1824), 160.

4   Sarah Tuttle, *Claims of the Africans, or the History of the American Colonization Society* (Boston: Massachusetts Sabbath School Union, 1832), 66.

5   Jehudi Ashmun, *Memoir of the Life and Character of the Rev. Samuel Bacon, A. M.* (Washington, DC: J. Gideon Jr., 1822), 245.

6   John Pendleton Kennedy, *Report of Mr. Kennedy, of Maryland, from the Committee on Commerce of the House of Representatives of the United States, on the Memorial of the Friends of African Colonization, Assembled in Convention in the City of Washington, May, 1842*, House and Senate Reports, no. 283, 33.

7   The American Colonization Society quoted this statement, from a January 1811 letter written by Jefferson, in several of its publications, including *Fifth Annual Report of the Colonization Society, of the City of New-York: with the Constitution of the Society* (New York: Mercein & Post's Press, 1837), 5.

8   Jeffrey A. Fortin, "Little Short of National Murder: Forced Migration and the Making of Diasporas in the Atlantic World, 1745–1865" (PhD diss., University of New Hampshire, fall 2006), 160, https://scholars.unh.edu/cgi/viewcontent.cgi?article=1335&context=dissertation.

9   Abraham Lincoln, "Peoria Speech, October 16, 1854," Lincoln's Writings, Dickinson University, https://housedivided.dickinson.edu/sites/lincoln/peoria-speech-october-16-1854.

10 Henry Clay credited Caldwell in a speech made in Washington in 1827. Quoted in Epes Sargent, *The Life and Public Services of Henry Clay, Down to 1848*, ed. Horace Greeley (New York: C. M. Saxton, 1858), 132.

11 Robert Finley in a letter to John P. Mumford, February 14, 1816, quoted in Isaac V. Brown, *Biography of the Rev. Finley, D.D., of Basking Ridge, N.J.: With an Account of His Agency as the Author of the American Colonization Society; Also a Sketch of the Slave Trade; a View of Our National Policy and That of Great Britain Towards Liberia and Africa*, 2nd ed. (Philadelphia: John W. Moore, 1857), 99.

12 See, for example, the society's newspaper, the *African Repository*, which reported on the will of one Timothy Rogers, of Bedford County, Virginia, who emancipated thirty of the Black people he enslaved "on condition of their roval to Liberia." *African Repository and Colonial Journal* 26, no. 6 (June 1, 1850): 2 ; see also "The Last Will and Testament of John McDonogh, Late of MacDonoghville, State of Louisiana," as well as his memoranda of instructions to his executors, relative to the management of his estate (cited in "Land, Slaves, and Bonds, Trust and Probate in the Pre-Civil War Shenandoah Valley," Alfred L. Brophy, West Virginia University, *Research Repository* 119, no. 1 (September 2016): 385.

13 Rhondda R. Thomas, "Exodus and Colonization: Charting the Journey in the Journals of Daniel Coker, a Descendant of Africa," *African American Review* 41, no. 3 (Fall 2007): 507, 517.

14 *The Third Annual Report of the American Society for Colonizing the Free People of Colour of the United States: With an Appendix* (Washington, DC: Davis and Force, 1820), 33.

15 James Forten, "A Voice From Philadelphia," January 1817, in William Lloyd Garrison, *Thoughts on African Colonization: Or an Impartial Exhibition of the Doctrines, Principles and Purposes of the American Colonization Society* (Boston: Garrison and Knapp, 1832), 173.

16 Calvin Cotton, *The Last Seven Years of the Life of Henry Clay* (New York: A. S. Barnes, 1856), 76. The American Anti-Slavery Society stated that Henry Clay "considers the Society the best scheme ever devised for effecting an entire separation of the two races," American Anti-Slavery Society, *St. Domingo* (date of publication unknown), 61.

17 *The Twelfth Annual Report of the American Society for Colonizing the Free People of Colour of the United States* (Washington, DC: James C. Dunn, 1829), 6.

18 Officially, the act was entitled "An Act in Addition to the Acts Prohibiting the Slave Trade," and was passed on March 3, 1819, https://www.history.navy.mil/research /library/online-reading-room/title-list-alphabetically/a/secnav-reports/annual -report-secretary-navy-1830.html.

19 "An Act in Addition to the Acts Prohibiting the Slave Trade."

20 Annual Report of the Secretary of Navy, Showing the Condition of the Navy in the Year 1830, 21st Cong., 2nd session, December 6, 1830, https://www.history.navy.mil /research/library/online-reading-room/title-list-alphabetically/a/secnav-reports /annual-report-secretary-navy-1830.html.

21 Samantha Seeley, "Beyond the American Colonization Society," *History Compass* 14, no. 3 (March 2016).

22 Reported in *Abstract of a Journal Kept by E. Bacon, United States Assistant Agent for the Reception of Recaptured Negroes on the Western Coast of Africa: Containing an Account of the First Negotiations for the Purchase of Lands for the American Colony* (Philadelphia: Clark & Raser, 1824), 4.

23 *African Repository and Colonial Journal*, vol. 3, American Colonization Society (Washington, DC: James C. Dunn, 1828), 180.

24 Jay, *A View of the Action of the Federal Government, in Behalf of Slavery*, 105.

25 Samuel John Bayard, *A Sketch of the Life of Com. Robert F. Stockton; with an Appendix, Comprising His Correspondence with the Navy Department Respecting His Conquest of California; and Extracts from the Defence of Col. J. C. Fremont, in Relation to the Same Subject; Together with His Speeches in the Senate of the United States, and His Political Letters* (New York: Derby & Jackson, 1856), 49.

26 George Lewis Prentiss, *A Sermon, Preached in the Mercer-Street Church, on the Occasion of the Death of Anson G. Phelps, on Sabbath Morning, December 11, 1853* (New York: John A. Gray, 1854), 56.

27 Excerpts from Phelps's diary printed in Prentiss, *A Sermon, Preached in the Mercer-Street Church*, 43.

28 A microfilm facsimile of Phelps's diary for the years 1808–1863 is kept at the Library of Congress, Manuscript Division (Madison), Washington, DC.

29 This was the claim of Henry B. Smith, made in Henry B. Smith, *A Memorial of Anson G. Phelps* (New York: Charles Scribner, 1860), 33.

30 The others were John Jacob Astor, Stephen Van Rensselaer, Stephen Whitney, Peter G. Stuyvesant, and Peter Lorillard. From the book by Frank R. Kent, *The Story of Alexander Brown & Sons, Issued on the One Hundred and Twenty-Fifth Anniversary of the Foundation of the House, December 19, 1800* (Baltimore: Norman T. A. Munder, 1925), 20.

31 A Phelps Dodge shipping receipt, detailing the passage of R. R. Gurley from "New York to Washington City," is included in *Debates over Slavery and Abolition*, American Missionary Association Archives, 1839–82, 133.

32 Richard Lowitt, *A Merchant Prince of the Nineteenth Century: William E. Dodge* (New York: Columbia University Press, 1954), 196–97.

33 Prentiss, *A Sermon, Preached in the Mercer-Street Church*, 58.

34 "Liberia: This Country, Originally Comprising a Tract of Land," *North Star*, March 2, 1849. The editorial is signed M. R. D., indicating it was written by Martin Robison Delany.

35 Lowitt, *A Merchant Prince of the Nineteenth Century*, 197.

36 Burgess and the American Colonization Society, *Address to the American Society*, 42.

37 Grove Wright's position as treasurer is detailed in *First Report of the New York Colonization Society* (New York: J. Seymour, 1823); Thomas, "Exodus and Colonization."

38 Hayden Waters, "An Address to the Gentlemen and Ladies of the County of Otsego, NY, September 30th, 1830," in Garrison, *Thoughts on African Colonization*, 226.

39 "American Colonization Society Address," *Religious Intelligencer* 18, no. 21 (October 19, 1833): 330.

40 "American Colonization Society," *Niles' Weekly Register* 45, no. 112 (October 19, 1833), 122.

41 *African Repository and Colonial Journal*, vol. 6 (Washington, DC: James C. Dunn, 1830–31), 347.

42 "American Colonization Society," *Niles' Weekly Register* 45, no. 112 (October 19, 1833), 122.

43 "Donations Recently Made in Aid of the Colonization Society," *Pittsfield Sun*, October 24, 1833.

44 New York University Alumni Association, 1894, "Officers and Members of the Council of the University of the City of New York, 226. https://www.google.com/books/edition /Biographical_Catalogue_of_the_Chancellor/yDpMAAAAMAAJ?hl=en&gbpv=0.

45 As mentioned on the official website of NYU's Department of History: https://as.nyu .edu/content/nyu-as/as/departments/history/graduate/phd-program/history-of-the -atlantic-world.html.

46 Adams, *Memoirs of John Quincy Adams*, vol. 4, 292.

47 Adams, *Memoirs of John Quincy Adams*, vol. 2, 437.

48 *Minutes of the Proceedings of a Special Meeting of the Fifteenth American Convention for Promoting the Abolition of Slavery at Philadelphia, on the Tenth Day of December, 1818, and Continued by Adjournments until the Fifteenth of the Same Month, Inclusive* (Philadelphia: Hall & Atkinson, 1818), 49.

49 *Minutes of the Proceedings of a Special Meeting of the Fifteenth American Convention for Promoting the Abolition of Slavery*, 49.

50 Telephone interview with Rhondda Thomas, January 24, 2023.

51 Carlos Martyn, *William E. Dodge, The Christian Merchant* (New York: Funk & Wagnalls, 1890), 178.

52 In the year 1840, for example, the society's revenue was $51,617, according to *Twenty-Third Annual Report of the American Colonization Society* (Washington, DC: J. Etter, 1840), 37. In 1841, the revenue was $62,526, according to *Twenty-Fourth Annual Report of the American Colonization Society* (Washington, DC: J. Etter, 1841), 28.

53 James Forten to Paul Cuffe, January 25, 1817, reproduced in *Classical Black Nationalism: From the American Revolution to Marcus Garvey*, ed. Wilson J. Moses (New York: New York University Press, 1996), 51.

54 Anti-Slavery Society, "Colonization," *Anti-Slavery Record* 3, no. 2 (February 1837): 7.

55 Theodore S. Wright, "Address of the Rev. Theodore S. Wright, Before the Convention of the New-York State Anti-Slavery Society, on the Acceptance of the Annual Report, Held at Utica, Sept. 20," *Colored American* 1, no. 41 (October 14, 1837).

56 Wright, "Address of the Rev. Theodore S. Wright, Before the Convention of the New-York State Anti-Slavery Society."

57 Jacqueline Bacon, "The History of *Freedom's Journal*: A Study in Empowerment and Community," *Journal of African American History* 88, no. 1 (Winter 2003): 3–4.

58 David Walker, *Walker's Appeal, with a Brief Sketch of His Life by Henry Highland Garnet* (New York: J. H. Tobitt, 1848), 66.

59 Walker, *Walker's Appeal*, 76.

60 Walker, *Walker's Appeal*, vi.

61 Walker, 5.

62 Lori Leavell, "'Not Intended Exclusively for the Slave States': Antebellum Recirculation of David Walker's 'Appeal,'" *Callaloo* 38, no. 3 (Summer 2015): 1–17.

63 In the collected edition of the *Liberator* (Boston: Directors of the Old South Work, 1897), 24.

64 Gene Andrew Jarrett, "'To Refute Mr. Jefferson's Arguments Respecting Us': Thomas Jefferson, David Walker, and the Politics of Early African American Literature," *Early American Literature* 46, no. 2 (Spring 2011), 297.

65 Walker, 65.

66 Mathew Carey, *A Warning Voice to the Cotton and Tobacco Planters, Farmers and Merchants of the United States*, 65.

67 Fortin, "Little Short of National Murder," 156.

68 The quote is from a speech given by William S. Archer, Representative of Virginia, at the fifteenth annual meeting of the Society and reprinted in The Fifteenth Annual Report of the American Society for Colonizing the Free People of Colour of the United States (Washington, DC, 1832), xxvi.

69 Maria Stewart, "An Address: Delivered at the African Masonic Hall, Boston, February 27, 1833," from *Meditations from the Pen of Mrs. Maria W. Stewart (Widow of the Late James W. Stewart), Now Matron of the Freedman's Hospital, and Presented in 1832 to the First African Baptist Church and Society of Boston, Mass.* (Washington, DC: Garrison & Knapp, 1879), 73.

70 Stewart, *Meditations*, 70.

71 *The Twelfth Annual Report of the American Society for Colonizing the Free People of Colour of the United States* (1829), 26.

72 *The Twelfth Annual Report of the American Society for Colonizing the Free People of Colour*, 32.

73 One of the earliest reports of the American Colonization Society showing its balance of funds appears to be from 1820. Total subscriptions, donations, and other revenue are listed at $14,031.50, according to *Address of the Board of Managers of the American Colonization Society: to the Auxiliary Societies and the People of the United States* (Washington, DC: Davis and Force, 1820), 20.

74 *Twenty-Fourth Annual Report of the American Colonization Society: With the Abridged Proceedings of the Annual Meeting, and of the Board of Directors, at Washington, January 19, 1841* (Washington, DC: J. Etter, 1841), 32.

75 The American Anti-Slavery Society, *4th Annual Report* (New York, 1837), 29; *Annual Report: Presented to the American Anti-Slavery Society by the Executive Committee, at the Annual Meeting held in New York, May 9, 1855* (New York, 1855), 121.

76 Stewart, *Meditations*, 71.

77 *Annual Report of the Secretary of the Navy, Showing the Condition of the Navy in the Year 1830*, https://www.history.navy.mil/research/library/online-reading-room /title-list-alphabetically/a/secnav-reports/annual-report-secretary-navy-1830.html: "The whole number of negroes transported to Africa by the government since the passage of the act of 1819, is, according to the best information I can collect, less than 260. The appropriations for their support in the United States, transportation to Africa, and superintendence there, have amounted to $264,710."

78 The figure of five thousand is taken from Colonization Society figures presented by William Wilcocks Sleigh in *Abolitionism Exposed!: Proving That the Principles of Abolitionism Are Injurious to the Slaves Themselves, Destructive to This Nation, and Contrary to the Express Commands of God: With Strong Evidence That Some of the Principal Champions of Abolitionism Are Inveterate Enemies to This Country, and Are Taking Advantage of the "Antislavery War-Whoop" to Dissever, and Break Up, the Union* (Philadelphia: D. Schneck, 1838), 83. The figure of one thousand formerly enslaved people being removed to Liberia is taken from *The Colonizationist and Journal of Freedom* (Boston: George W. Light, 1834), 122.

79 Telephone interview with Rhondda Thomas, January 24, 2023.

80 *Annual Report of the American Anti-Slavery Society: With the Speeches Delivered at the Anniversary Meeting* (New York: Dorr & Butterfield, 1840), 17.

81 Jay, *A View of The Action of the Federal Government, in Behalf of Slavery*, 63.

CHAPTER 5

1   Joseph Alfred Scoville, *The Old Merchants of New York City*, 1st series (New York: Carleton, 1864), 95.

2   "The Architects and Architecture of New York," *Brother Jonathan* 5, no. 3 (New York: Wilson, 1843), 92.

3   "An Address to the Anti-Slavery Christians of the United States," *The Annual Report of the American and Foreign Anti-Slavery Society: Presented at New-York, May 11, 1852*, 261.

4   Scoville, *Old Merchants of New York City*, vol. 1, 186.

5   "The Obituary of Alexander Brown," *Baltimore Patriot and Mercantile Advertiser*, April 8, 1834.

6   "Obituary: James Brown, of Brown Brothers, Bankers," *New York Times*, November 2, 1877.

7   Alexis de Tocqueville, Henry Reeve, and John Canfield Spencer, *The Republic of the United States of America and Its Political Institutions, Reviewed and Examined*, vol. 1 (New York: A. S. Barnes, 1855), 192.

8   "Wall Street," The New-York Mirror, Vol. IX No. 2, January 21, 1832.

9   Joseph Alfred Scoville, The Old Merchants of New York City, Volume 3, Part 1 (New York: M. Doolady, 1870), 272.

10 William Worthington Fowler, *Ten Years in Wall Street; or, Revelations of Inside Life and Experience on 'Change* (Hartford, CT: Worthington, Dustin, 1870), 25.

11 De Bow, *Commercial Review of the South and West*, vol. 4, 351.

12 John Thomas Scharf, *History of Baltimore City and County from the Earliest Period to the Present Day: Including Biographical Sketches of Their Representative Men* (Philadelphia: Louis H. Everts, 1881), 543.

13 "Belle Mina," Society of Architectural Historians, https://sah-archipedia.org/buildings
     /AL-01-083-0037.

14 Alexander Brown letter to William Brown, March 22, 1820, Alexander Brown & Sons
     Papers (Manuscript Division, Library of Congress, Washington, DC), cited by John
     R. Killick, "The Cotton Operations of Alexander Brown and Sons in the Deep South,
     1820–1860," *The Journal of Southern History* 43, no. 2 (May 1977): 176.

15 The episode is related by Scoville in *The Old Merchants of New York City*, 3rd series
     (New York: Carleton, 1865), 204.

16 Nolte discusses the credit of $50,000 in his memoir, *Fifty Years in Both Hemispheres:
     Or Reminiscences of the Life of a Former Merchant* (New York: Redfield, 1854), 326.

17 Nigel Hall, "'A Quaker Confederation'? The Great Liverpool Cotton Speculation
     of 1825 Reconsidered," Historic Society of Lancashire & Cheshire, https://www.hslc
     .org.uk/wp-content/uploads/2017/10/151-2-Hall.pdf.

18 "Money Making," *Niles' Weekly Register* 6, no. 24 (July 29, 1826): 377.

19 Eric Hilt, "Rogue Finance: The Life and Fire Insurance Company and the Panic of
     1826," *Business History Review* (Spring 2009): 99.

20 "The Late Crisis in the Money Market Impartially Considered," *Museum of Foreign
     Literature & Science* 9, no. 53 (November 1, 1826): 415.

21 "The Devil Among the Quakers," *Cobbett's Weekly Political Register* (London,
     England), October 13, 1827.

22 Robert Lenox to Nicholas Biddle, November 8, 1825, cited by Eric Hilt, "Wall Street's
     First Corporate Governance Crisis: The Conspiracy Trials of 1826," National Bureau
     of Economic Research, April 2009, Working Paper 14892, 10 (see note 35). Accessed
     at: http://www.nber.org/papers/w14892.

23 Scoville, *The Old Merchants of New York City*, vol. 1, 1863, 306.

24 David R. Meyer, *The Roots of American Industrialization* (Baltimore: Johns Hopkins
     Press, 2003), 262.

25 Elizabeth Gilman Brown, *Outline History of Utica and Vicinity* (Utica, NY: L. C.
     Childs and Son, 1900), 35.

26 Vincent Nolte, *Fifty Years in Both Hemispheres; or, Reminiscences of the Life of a
     Former Merchant* (New York: Redfield, 1854); Peter Evans Austin, "Baring Brothers
     and the Panic of 1837" (PhD diss., University of Texas, Austin, 1999).

27 "Jeremiah Thompson," *Newport Mercury*, November 24, 1827.

28 "Summary," *Hallowell Gazette* (Hallowell, ME), December 5, 1827.

29 Sheldon, "Old Shipping Merchants," *Harper's*, 462.

30 "Money Making," *Niles' Weekly Register*, reprinted *New-Hampshire Patriot & State
     Gazette*, August 7, 1826.

31 *The Life & Fire Insurance Company of New York v. Christopher Adams*, 34 U.S. 573,
     US Supreme Court, February 24, 1835.

32 Robert Hayne, "Bankruptcy Bill," May 1, 1826, *Register of Debate in Congress*, vol. 2
     (Washington, DC: Gales & Seaton, 1826), 327.

33 Sharon Ann Murphy, "The Financialization of Slavery by the First and Second Banks
     of the United States," *Journal of Southern History* 87, no. 3 (August 1, 2021): 385–426.

34 Robert Hayne, "Bankruptcy Bill," May 1, 1826, *Register of Debate in Congress*, vol. 2
     (Washington, DC: Gales & Seaton, 1826), 327.

35 Killick, "Risk, Specialization and Profit," 8.

CHAPTER 6

1   William Lloyd Garrison, *A Brief Sketch of the Trial of William Lloyd Garrison, for an Alleged Libel on Francis Todd, of Newburyport, Mass.* (Boston: Garrison and Knapp, 1834), 15.

2   William Lloyd Garrison, *A Brief Sketch of the Trial of William Lloyd Garrison*, 17.

3   William Lloyd Garrison, "Walker's Appeal," *Liberator*, January 8, 1831.

4   Lewis Tappan, *The Life of Arthur Tappan* (New York: Hurd and Houghton, 1870), 164.

5   "James Forten to William Lloyd Garrison, December 31, 1830," Anti-Slavery Collection, Boston Public Library, Boston, MA, published by courtesy of the Trustees of the Boston Public Library, accessed through ProQuest: Black Abolitionist Papers.

6   William Cooper Nell, *The Colored Patriots of the American Revolution, with Sketches of Several Distinguished Colored Persons: To Which Is Added a Brief Survey of the Condition and Prospects of Colored Americans*, with introduction by Harriet Beecher Stowe (Boston: Robert F. Wallcut, 1855), 344.

7   Ibram X. Kendi, *Stamped From the Beginning: The Definitive History of Racist Ideas in America* (New York: Bold Type Books, 2016), 173.

8   Thomas Roderick Dew, *Review of the Debate in the Virginia Legislature of 1831 and 1832* (Richmond: T. W. White, 1832), 4.

9   "We Cannot Say That This Meeting Resulted Exactly as We Had Anticipated," *New York Journal of Commerce*, reprinted from *Liberator* 3, no. 41 (October 12, 1833).

10 John Jay Chapman, *William Lloyd Garrison* (Boston: Atlantic Monthly Press, 1921), 212.

11 Lewis Tappan, *The Life of Arthur Tappan* (New York: Hurd and Houghton, 1870), 170.

12 "An Inquiry into the Character and Tendency of the American Colonization, and American Anti-Slavery Societies," excerpted in *New York Spectator*, March 26, 1835.

13 These details are taken from an account provided on November 1, 1833, by the *Abolitionist, or Record of the New England Anti-Slavery Society*, in an article entitled "Riot in New York."

14 "The Anti-Slavery Meeting," *New York Spectator*, October 7, 1833.

15 "The Anti-Slavery Meeting," *National Intelligencer*, vol. 21, issue 6446, October 7, 1833.

16 Douglas A. Jones Jr., "Black Politics but Not Black People: Rethinking the Social and 'Racial' History of Early Minstrelsy," Routes of Blackface: Special Issue, *TDR* 57, no. 2 (Summer 2013): 22.

17 Tappan, *The Life of Arthur Tappan*, 171.

18 William Jay, *An Inquiry into the Character and Tendency of the American Colonization and American Anti-Slavery Societies*, 3rd ed. (New York: Leavitt, Lord, 1835), 117.

19 Garrison, *A Brief Sketch of the Trial of William Lloyd Garrison*, 4.

20 George Weiss, *America's Maritime Progress*, 460.

21 Kent, *Story of Alexander Brown and Sons*, 20.

22 Details of James Brown's loans to various enslavers are derived from various court filings, including: *Pickersgill & Co. v. Brown*, 7 La. Ann. 297, 1852 La. LEXIS 159 (Supreme Court of Louisiana, New Orleans May, 1852, Decided; *Brown v. Routh*, 4 La. Ann. 270, 1849 La. LEXIS 162 (Supreme Court of Louisiana, New Orleans April,

1849, Decided; US Supreme Court, No. 104, 1850, *Bennett v. Butterworth: Admis' Adm'rs v. Butterworth: Hunt v. Butterworth*, 53 U.S. 367.

23 John R. Killick, "The Cotton Operations of Alexander Brown and Sons in the Deep South, 1820–1860," *The Journal of Southern History* 43, no. 2 (May 1977): 179.

24 Kent, *Story of Alexander Brown and Sons*, 129.

25 Philip Hone, *Diary of Philip Hone 1828–1851*, vol. 1 (New York: Dodd, Mead, 1889), 364.

26 The figure of 250,000 enslaved people being moved into the lower states by 1836 was widely discussed in national newspapers. See "Connection of Slavery with the Present Money Pressure," *Ohio Observer*, July 6, 1837; "Multiple News Items," *Arkansas State Gazette*, March 21, 1837.

27 These figures were printed in *The Liberty Almanac, Magnitude of the American Slave Trade* (New York: American & Foreign Anti-Slavery Society, 1849), 29. Also discussed in William Goodell, *Slavery and Anti-slavery: a History of the Great Struggle in Both Hemispheres: with a View of the Slavery Question in the United States* (New York: W. Harned, 1852), 248.

28 "The Financial Power of Slavery," *Emancipator*, October 22, 1840, quoting the *United States Gazette* of February 1, 1840.

29 Brown Brothers and Company, *Experiences of a Century 1818–1918* (privately printed, Brown Brothers, 1919), 8.

30 James Silk Buckingham, *The Slave States of America* (London: Fisher, 1842), 593.

31 "National City Passes Milestone: New York Institution Founded One Hundred and Twenty-Five Years Ago This June Founding of the Bank First Meeting of the Board Affiliation with The Farmers' Loan and Trust Company One of the World's Great Banks," *Bankers Magazine* 134, no. 6 (June 1937).

32 Henry Clarke Wright, "A Nation Crushed in the Embraces of Slavery," *Liberator*, June 2, 1837.

33 *Philanthropist*, May 19, 1837, reprinted in Thomas Price, *Slavery in America: with Notices of the Present State of Slavery and the Slave Trade Throughout the World* (London: G. Wightman, 1837), 310.

34 Many of the details about Dorcas Allen's case are derived from the fascinating doctoral dissertation of Alison T. Mann, "Slavery Exacts an Impossible Price: John Quincy Adams and the Dorcas Allen Case, Washington, DC" (PhD diss., University of New Hampshire, Durham, September 2010), https://scholars.unh.edu/dissertation/531.

35 *The Memoirs of John Quincy Adams*, vol. 9, 417–28.

36 American Anti-Slavery Society, *Fourth Annual Report of the American Anti-Slavery Society, with the Speeches Delivered at the Anniversary Meeting Held in the City of New York on the 9th May, 1837* (New York: William S. Dorr, 1837), 52.

37 Killick, "The Cotton Operations of Alexander Brown and Sons in the Deep South, 1820–1860," 176.

38 Hone, *Diary of Philip Hone*, 337, 354–55.

39 *Pickersgill & Co. v. Brown*, 7 La. Ann. 297, 1852 La. LEXIS 159 (Supreme Court of Louisiana, New Orleans, May, 1852, Decided.

40 Killick, "The Cotton Operations of Alexander Brown and Sons in the Deep South, 1820–1860," 190. See Table 4.

41 "More Gold," *Public Ledger* (Philadelphia), August 13, 1836.

42 Kent, *Story of Alexander Brown and Sons*, 111.

43 Kent, *Story of Alexander Brown and Sons*, 141.

44 James Brown, letter, April 14, 1838 to his brother William, New York Historical Society, Brown Brothers Collection, Box 3: Historical Files 1837–1840.

45 Killick, "The Cotton Operations of Alexander Brown and Sons in the Deep South, 1820–1860," 186-87 (see especially Table 3).

46 Works Progress Administration, interview with James Lucas, "Mississippi Narratives," *Slave Narratives*, accessed through the MSGENWEb Slave Narrative Project: http://msgw.org/slaves/lucas-xslave.htm.

47 *Religious Intelligencer*, vol. 19 (January 1835), ed. Nathan Whiting, 526.

48 Kathryn Boodry, "August Belmont and the World the Slaves Made," in *Slavery's Capitalism: A New History of American Economic Development*, ed. Sven Beckert and Seth Rockman (Philadelphia: University of Pennsylvania Press, 2016), 174.

49 *St. Domingo: Compiled, Chiefly, from Recent Publications* (New York: American Anti-Slavery Society: date unknown), 183.

50 "Public Sale of Negroes," William Trapp advertisement in the Alabama Beacon, December 13, 1838, reprinted in "Northern Dealers in Slaves," *Emancipator*, January 10, 1839.

51 "Northern Dealers in Slaves," *Emancipator*, January 10, 1839, reprinted in *Pennsylvania Freeman*, January 17, 1839.

52 "Northern Dealers in Slaves," *Emancipator*, January 10, 1839.

53 *Northern Dealers in Slaves* (New York: American Anti-Slavery Society, 1839), 2.

54 "Northern Dealers in Slaves," *Emancipator*, January 10, 1839.

55 "Execution of U.S. Laws," *Emancipator*, August 30, 1838.

56 *The Parish Will Case, a Litigation Pending in the Courts of the State of New York…*, in six volumes (New York: John F. Trow, 1864), 338.

57 *Northern Dealers in Slaves*, 11.

58 William Wells Brown, *William Wells Brown: A Reader*, ed. Ezra Greenspan (Athens: University of Georgia Press, 2008), 118–19.

59 *An Appeal to the Women of the Nominally Free States, Issued by an Anti-Slavery Convention of American Women: Held by Adjournments from the 9th to the 12th of May, 1837*, 2nd ed. (Boston: Isaac Knapp, 1838), 24.

60 Fowler, *Ten Years in Wall Street*, 176.

61 See for example The Quarterly Anti-Slavery Magazine, Vol 2. Issue VIII, 23: "Northern merchants, anxious to partake the rich plunder, have offered their aid to the whip-wielding power. They have furnished the capital for the extension of slave labor, and have been permitted to reap great profit from the carrying trade."

62 Chapman, *William Lloyd Garrison*, 32.

CHAPTER 7

1 W. E. B. Du Bois, *The Suppression of the African Slave-Trade: 1638-1870*, ed. Henry Louis Gates Jr. (Oxford: Oxford University Press, 2007), 107.

2 John P. Parker, *His Promised Land: The Autobiography of John P. Parker, Former Slave and Conductor on the Underground Railroad*, ed. Stuart Seely Sprague (New York: W. W. Norton, 1996), 137.

3 Louis Hughes, excerpts from *Thirty Years a Slave: From Bondage to Freedom*, in *National Humanities Center Resource Toolbox: The Making of African American Identity*, vol. 1, 1500–1865, http://nationalhumanitiescenter.org/pds/maai/enslavement/text3/plantationhughes.pdf.

4   Emilie Connolly, "Panic, State Power, and Chickasaw Dispossession," *Journal of the Early Republic* 40, no. 4 (2020): 683–89, https://doi.org/ 10.1353/jer.2020.0096.

5   McHenry, *The Cotton Trade*, 19.

6   *Voices of the Old South: Eyewitness Accounts, 1528–1861*, ed. Alan Gallay (Athens: University of Georgia Press, 1994), 144.

7   "Pine Forests of Georgia," *Hunt's Merchants' Magazine and Commercial Review*, October 1860, vol. 43, issue 4, 448.

8   Charles Post, *The American Road to Capitalism: Studies in Class-Structure, Economic Development and Political Conflict, 1620–1877* (Boston: Brill, 2011), 140–41.

9   Arlen M. Hanson, *"Troubled Voices: Choctaws in Mass Deportation and Ethnic Cleansing"* (PhD diss., University of North Carolina at Greensboro, 2021), 369, quoting from Peter Pitchlynn to "Brother," September 23, 1846, Peter Perkins Pitchlynn Collection, Box 1, Folder, 109, University of Oklahoma.

10 Solomon Northup, *Twelve Years a Slave: Narrative of Solomon Northup, a Citizen of New-York, Kidnapped in Washington City in 1841, and Rescued in 1853, from a Cotton Plantation Near the Red River, in Louisiana* (Auburn, NY: Derby and Miller, 1853), 156.

11 *The Yearbook of Agriculture, 1958*, 85th Cong., 2nd session, House document No. 280, 409.

12 Kettell, *Southern Wealth and Northern Profits*, 131.

13 James D. B. De Bow, *The Industrial Resources, Etc., of the Southern and Western States*, vol. I (New Orleans: De Bow's Review, 1852–53): 229.

14 Michael Williams, "Clearing the United States Forests: Pivotal Years 1810–1860," *Journal of Historical Geography* 8, no. 1 (1982).

15 Mart A. Stewart, "From King Cane to King Cotton: Razing Cane in the Old South," *Environmental History* 12, no. 1 (January 2007): 59–79.

16 Fortescue Cuming, *Sketches of a tour to the western country: through the states of Ohio and Kentucky, a voyage down the Ohio and Mississippi rivers, and a trip through the Mississippi territory, and part of West Florida, commenced at Philadelphia in the winter of 1807, and concluded in 1809* (Pittsburgh: Cramer, Spear & Eichbaum, 1810), 157. Cuming is quoting the recollection of one Captain Waller.

17 Stewart, "From King Cane to King Cotton: Razing Cane in the Old South," 62.

18 *The Yearbook of Agriculture, 1958*, 409.

19 John Bezis-Selfa, "Forging a New Order: Slavery, Free Labor, and Sectional Differentiation in the Mid-Atlantic Charcoal Iron Industry, 1715–1840" (PhD diss., University of Pennsylvania, 1995), 64, https://repository.upenn.edu/dissertations/AAI9543050.

20 James R. Bennett and Karen R. Utz, *Iron and Steel: A Driving Guide to the Birmingham Industrial Heritage* (Tuscaloosa: University of Alabama Press, 2010), 3–4.

21 H. W. Hillman, *Ancestral Chronological Record of the Hillman Family, 1550–1905* (Scotia, NY: The Walsh Press, 1905).

22 Anne Kelly Knowles, *Mastering Iron: The Struggle to Modernize an American Industry* (Chicago: University of Chicago Press, 2013), 4.

23 Robert S. Starobin, "Industrial Slavery in the Old South, 1790–1861: A Study in Political Economy" (PhD diss., University of California, Berkeley, 1969), ii.

24 De Bow, *The Industrial Resources, Etc., of the Southern and Western States*, vol. III, 37.

25 "Statement of Furnaces, Forges, and Rolling Mills on Cumberland River, Now In Operation with Names of Proprietors, Estimate of Capital," *Merchants' Magazine* 28, no. 5 (May 1853): 645.

26 Abram Stevens Hewitt, *On the Statistics and Geography of the Production of Iron: A Paper Read Before the American Geographical and Statistical Society, on the 21st February, A.D., 1856* (New York: W. C. Bryant, 1856), 2.

27 Samuel D. Smith, Charles P. Stripling, and James M. Brannon, *Tennessee's Western Highland Rim Iron Industry: A Cultural Resource Survey* (Nashville: Tennessee Division of Archaeology, Department of Conservation, 1988), 83.

28 "Slavery by an Eye-Witness," reprinted in *Anti-Slavery Monthly Reporter* 2, no. 7 (July 1, 1854), under the sanction of the British and Foreign Anti-Slavery Society.

29 Boston Female Anti-Slavery Society, *Report of the Boston Female Anti-Slavery Society; with a Concise Statement of Events, Previous and Subsequent to the Annual Meeting of 1835* (Boston: Boston Female Anti-Slavery Society, 1836), 4.

30 Starobin, "Industrial Slavery," 43.

31 Starobin, "Industrial Slavery," 45.

32 The story comes from the TNGenWeb Project, a volunteer-based genealogical site based in Tennessee. The story about Pole Marable and the card game is attributed to "notes transcribed from the notes of Dr. John Hartwell Marable, IV, entitled 'My Family and Their Traditions.'" Author could not trace the said "My Family and Their Traditions." Accessible at: https://www.tngenweb.org/montgomery/obit-3.html #POLE_MARABLE.

33 Ethel Armes, *The Story of Coal and Iron in Alabama* (Tuscaloosa: University of Alabama Press, 2011), 286.

34 "Killed by a Train," *Daily Tobacco Leaf Chronicle* (Clarksville, TN), August 31, 1892.

35 According to Kentucky land grant records, accessed through Ancestry.com, Hillman acquired 3,934 acres in Caldwell County on January 29, 1845, and 3,600 acres in Trigg County on July 5, 1845.

36 "The River," *Times Picayune*, June 23, 1893.

37 *Campbell v. Hillman*, Court of Appeals of Kentucky, December 1854.

38 James R. Bennett, *Images of America: Tannehill Ironworks* (Charleston, SC: Arcadia, 2011), 11.

39 "Statement of Furnaces, Forges, and Rolling Mills on Cumberland River, Now In Operation with Names of Proprietors, Estimate of Capital," *Merchants' Magazine* 28, no. 5 (May 1853), 645.

40 "Hillman, Gustavus," U.S. Civil War Pension Index: General Index to Pension Files, 1861–1934, August 1, 1890, accessed through Ancestry.com.

41 John L. Smith, "History-Incrusted Junk of Pioneer Iron Mills Coming to Louisville," *Courier-Journal*, August 20, 1911.

42 *Reports of Cases at Law and in Chancery argued and determined in the Supreme Court of Illinois, 1899*, vol. 180, 262.

43 File for enslaver Shouse, James H., Slaveholders of Boone County, Boone County Public Library, https://omekas.bcplhistory.org/s/cbc/item/9925.

44 "Military Records: Partial Index to Slave Compensation Records for Kentucky," compiled by Danville Boyle County African American Historical Society, Danville, KY, https://sites.rootsweb.com/~kydaahs/The%20Past/Other-recs/Military-recs/military .htm.

45 R. Bruce Council, Nicholas Honerkamp, and M. Elizabeth Will, *Industry and Technology in Antebellum Tennessee: The Archaeology of Bluff Furnace* (Knoxville: University of Tennessee Press, 1992), 57.

46 "Better Days Loom," *Paducah Sun*, June 21, 1963.

47 Kentucky, US, Death Records, 1852–1965 Film 994056: Todd, Trigg, Trimble, Union. Accessed through Ancestry.com.
48 Interview of Emanuel Elmore, son of Emanuel Elmore, Federal Writers' Project: Slave Narratives Project, vol. 14, South Carolina, Part 2, https://www.loc.gov/resource/mesn.142/?sp=10&st=text.
49 Knowles, *Mastering Iron*, 187–88.
50 Hewitt, *On the Statistics and Geography of the Production of Iron*, 21.
51 Hewitt, *Production of Iron*, 31.
52 Hewitt, *Production of Iron*, 4.
53 W. David Lewis, "The Emergence of Birmingham as a Case Study of Continuity between the Antebellum Planter Class and Industrialization in the 'New South,'" *Agricultural History* 68, no. 2 (Spring 1994): 65.
54 John Witherspoon DuBose, *Jefferson County and Birmingham, Alabama* (Birmingham, AL: Teeple & Smith, 1887), 588.
55 Alfred L. Brophy, "Land, Slaves, and Bonds: Trust and Probate in the Pre-Civil War Shenandoah Valley," *Research Repository* 119, no. 1 (September 2016): 346.

CHAPTER 8

1 "Message from the President of the United States to the two Houses of Congress at the commencement of the second session of the Thirtieth Congress, December 5, 1848," (Washington, DC, 1848), 35.
2 Lina Mann, "The Enslaved Households of President James K. Polk," White House Historical Association, January 3, 2020, https://www.whitehousehistory.org/the-enslaved-households-of-james-k-polk.
3 US loans included $500,000 from Citibank and a reported $1 million from Stephen Girard. (Girard, a Philadelphia banker, had for decades transported cargoes of slavery-produced goods from Haiti and the Caribbean, making him one of the richest men in the world.)
4 The figure of $32 million in duties is taken from an article by Ellwood Fisher in the *National Era* on June 7, 1849, entitled "The North and the South." The figure of $100 million paid down in foreign debt is from economist Douglass C. North.
5 G. S. Callender, "The Early Transportation and Banking Enterprises of the States in Relation to the Growth of Corporations," *Quarterly Journal of Economics* 17, no. 11 (1902): 111.
6 Referenced in *Report of the Secretary of the Treasury on the State of the Finances for the Year Ending June 30, 1856*, 34th Cong., 3rd session, ex. doc. no. 2 (Washington, DC: Cornelius Wendell, 1856), 35.
7 *Report of the Secretary of the Treasury*, 426.
8 Israel De Wolf Andrews and US Department of the Treasury, *Communication from the Secretary of the Treasury, Transmitting, in Compliance with a Resolution of the Senate of March 8, 1851, the Report of Israel D. Andrews, Consul of the United States for Canada and New Brunswick, on the Trade and Commerce of the British North American Colonies, and upon the Trade of the Great Lakes and Rivers; Also, Notices of the Internal Improvements in Each State, of the Gulf of Mexico and Straits of Florida, and a Paper on the Cotton Crop of the United States* (Washington, DC: Robert Armstrong, 1853), 389.
9 Andrews and US Treasury Department, *Communication from the Secretary of the Treasury*, 835.

10 Report of the Secretary of Treasury, 188.

11 Statistics tabulated from US Department of Agriculture, Bureau of Statistics, Rice Crop of the United States 1712–1911, George K. Holmes, Circular No. 34 (1912), 7–10; Kettell; De Bow.

12 Statistics tabulated by the US Treasury and quoted in Mathew Carey, *A Warning Voice to the Cotton and Tobacco Planters, Farmers and Merchants of the United States* (Philadelphia: H. C. Carey & I. Lea, 1824).

13 Theodore Parker, *An Address Delivered by the Rev. Theodore Parker, before the New York City Anti-Slavery Society, at Its First Anniversary, Held at the Broadway Taberna-cle, May 12, 1854* (New York: American Anti-Slavery Society, 1854), 30.

14 "Thomas Jefferson to Patrick Gibson, 26 April 1817," Founders Online, National Archives, https://founders.archives.gov/documents/Jefferson/03-11-02-0249.

15 "To Thomas Jefferson from Bayard & Co. LeRoy, 10 July 1822," Founders Online, National Archives, https://founders.archives.gov/documents/Jefferson/98-01-02-2945.

16 "Memorandum Books, 1818," Founders Online, National Archives, https://founders.archives.gov/documents/Jefferson/02-02-02-0028. [Original source: *The Papers of Thomas Jefferson*, 2nd series, *Jefferson's Memorandum Books*, vol. 2, ed. James A. Bear Jr. and Lucia C. Stanton (Princeton, NJ: Princeton University Press, 1997), 1340–50.]

17 De Bow, Commercial Review, vol. 4, 340.

18 Ulrich Bonnell Phillips, *American Negro Slavery* (New York: Peter Smith, 1952), 391. Quoted in Yasukichi Yasuba, "The Profitability and Viability of Plantation Slavery in the United States," *Economic Studies Quarterly* 12, no. 1 (1961): 60.

19 Carina Schauland, "The Economics of Slavery: The Effect of the Plantation's Size and its Capital Utilization on the Viability of Slavery as an Economic System" (bachelor's thesis, Tilburg University, Netherlands, 2011), http://arno.uvt.nl/show.cgi?fid=129502.

20 Martha Jane Brazy, "An American Planter: Slavery, Entrepreneurship and Identity in the Life of Stephen Duncan, 1787–1867" (PhD diss., Duke University, 1998), 429.

21 William Kauffman Scarborough, *Masters of the Big House: Elite Slaveholders of the Mid-Nineteenth-Century South* (Baton Rouge, LA: LSU Press, 2006.

22 Dodd, *The Cotton Kingdom*, 24.

23 Kettell, *Southern Wealth and Northern Profits*, 90, 98.

24 Stephen Colwell, *The Five Cotton States and New York; or, Remarks upon the Social and Economical Aspects of the Southern Political Crisis* (Philadelphia: publisher unknown, 1861), 27.

25 Ricky-Dale Calhoun, "Seeds of Destruction: The Globalization of Cotton as a Result of the American Civil War" (PhD diss. Kansas State University, 2012). Calhoun cites as a source Albion's *The Rise of the New York Port*, wherein Albion details more than two thousand ships carrying goods from the South.

26 *Insurance Monitor and Wall Street Review*, vol. VIII (December 1860), 227, quoted in Eli Goldschmidt, "Northern Businessmen and the Sectional Crisis" (PhD diss., New York University, October 1972), 82.

27 Dodd, *The Cotton Kingdom*, 29.

28 Kettell, *Southern Wealth and Northern Profits*, 98.

29 By 1860, William H. Leverich's total reported wealth, according to the 1860 Census Report of Real Estate, was $200,000 ($6.2 million today), Henry S. Leverich's wealth was $120,000 ($3.7 million today), and Charles P. Leverich's was $23,000 ($720,000 today). From Alana K. Bevan, "'We Are the Same People': The Leverich Family of

New York and Their Antebellum American Inter-Regional Network of Elites" (PhD diss., Johns Hopkins University, 2009), 104.

30 On the 1860 Census Report, Levin Marshall listed his real estate value at $35,000 and his personal estate value at $186,000. 1860 Census Report accessed through Ancestry .com.

31 Bevan, "'We Are the Same People,'" 46.

32 Bevan, "'We Are the Same People,'" 65.

33 Paul Wallace Gates, "Southern Investments in Northern Lands Before the Civil War," *Journal of Southern History* 5, no. 2 (May 1939): 155–85.

34 Bevan, "'We Are the Same People,'" 18.

35 Martha Jane Brazy, *An American Planter: Stephen Duncan of Antebellum Natchez and New York* (Baton Rouge, Louisiana State University Press, 2006), 2.

CHAPTER 9

1   John MacGregor, *Commercial Statistics: A Digest of the Productive Resources, Commercial Legislation, Customs Tariffs, Navigation, Port, and Quarantine Laws, and Charges, Shipping, Imports and Exports, and the Monies, Weights, and Measures of all Nations Including All British Commercial Treaties with Foreign States*, vol. 3 (London: C. Knight, 1847), 170.

2   "Pillars for the New York Exchange," *Colored American*, August 24, 1839.

3   *New York Sun*, reprinted in the *Philadelphia Gazette*, February 10, 1842.

4   "Public Dinner to Honor D.H. Lewis," *Montgomery Daily Advertiser*, July 15, 1847.

5   "Masters of Capital in America, the City Bank," *McClure's Magazine*, May 1911.

6   John K. Winkler, *The First Billion: The Stillmans and the National City Bank* (New York: Vanguard Press, 1934), 35. The description of City Bank comes from A. T. Goodrich, *The Picture of New-York and Stranger's Guide to the Commercial Metropolis of the United States* (New York: A. T. Goodrich, 1828), 253.

7   Cleveland and Huertas, *Citibank, 1812–1970*, 16.

8   Meyer Berger, "About New York: Masked Scholar of Library Subcellar Toils 4 Years Over Rich Eccentric's Files," *New York Times*, December 6, 1954.

9   Cleveland and Huertas, *Citibank*, 15.

10 Elizabeth L. Gebhard, *The Life and Ventures of the Original John Jacob Astor* (New York: Bryan Printing, 1915), 280.

11 New York Public Library, Moses Taylor Collection, Sales Books 1842 August–1846 December, vol. 165; Accounts Current 1841 October 15–1844 August 29, vo. 212; Receipt Books September 1843–December 1847, vol. 295.

12 Maeve Glass, "Moses Taylor Pyne and the Sugar Trade," *Princeton University Library Chronicle* 77, no. 1–2 (Winter 2016), 104.

13 John A. E. Harris, "Circuits of Wealth, Circuits of Sorrow: Financing the Illegal Transatlantic Slave Trade in the Age of Suppression, 1850–66," *Journal of Global History* 11, no. 3, 409–29, https://doi.org/10.1017/S1740022816000218; New York Public Library, Moses Taylor Collection, Box 220, Folder 2, R. Drake to H. Coit, 14 January 1854.

14 Roland T. Ely, "The Old Cuba Trade: Highlights and Case Studies of Cuban-American Interdependence during the Nineteenth Century," *Business History Review* 38, no 4. (Winter 1964): 469–71.

15 Glass, "Moses Taylor Pyne and the Sugar Trade," 103–06.

16 "Commerce in Coolies," *New York Daily Times*, April 8, 1856.

17 "The African Slave Trade," *New York Herald*, August 15, 1859.

18 Ibid.

19 *Slave and Coolie Trade, Message from the President of the United States Communicating Information in Regard to the Slave and Coolie Trade*, 1856, 34th Cong., 1st session, ex. doc. no. 105.

20 Andrew Hull Foote, *The African Squadron: Ashburton Treaty: Consular Sea Letters* (Philadelphia: William F. Geddes, 1855), 13.

21 Ely, "The Old Cuba Trade," 459.

22 Daniel Hodas, "The Business Career of Moses Taylor: Merchant, Finance Capitalist and Industrialist" (PhD diss., New York University, 1974), 18.

23 Hazel J. Johnson, *Banking Alliances* (Hackensack, NJ: World Scientific Publishing, 2000), 48.

24 Cleveland and Huertas, *Citibank*, 29, 319.

25 Cited in John Ward Willson Loose, *Anthracite Iron Blast Furnaces in Lancaster County 1840–1900*, https://collections.lancasterhistory.org/media/library/docs/edit_vol86no3pp78_117.pdf.

26 Hodas, "Business Career of Moses Taylor," 74.

27 Brown Brothers & Co., "Stocks and State Bonds Belonging to William & James Brown: Value 29 May 1845," lists 407 shares of City Bank at $30,525. Brown Brothers Collection, New York Historical Society, Historical Files, Box 4, Folder 1.

28 Brown Brothers & Co. also bought $200,000 worth of Central Railroad bonds and an additional $200,000 in stocks and bonds of the Canandaigua & Niagara Falls Railroad and the Lake Ontario Railroad. They also acquired a significant stake in the Chicago & Mississippi Railroad. Detailed in a publication prepared by Brown Brothers Harriman & Co., "Building America's Railroads: A Conversation with Peter Gilbertson, Founder and CEO of Anacostia & Pacific, 2016, 7; Financial and Commercial," *Weekly Herald*, August 12, 1854.

29 "Money Market," *New York Herald*, October 12, 1843.

30 Daniel Hodas, "Moses Taylor—New York Merchant American Industrialist and Finance Capitalist: A Case Study in Success," *Proceedings of the Business History Conference*, 2nd series, vol. 2 (1974), 26, 95–131. A balance sheet from 1856 shows Dodge holding 1,033 shares, and Phelps, 577.

31 Richard Sylla and Robert E. Wright, "Corporate Formation in the Antebellum United States in Comparative Context," *Business History* 55, no. 4 (2013), figures tabulated from Table 3: Number of Special Incorporations by Region and Decade, 1790–1860, 654.

32 Ralph Edward Gomory and Richard E. Sylla, "The American Corporation," *Daedalus* (Spring 2013), https://www.amacad.org/publication/american-corporation.

CHAPTER 10

1 "Southern Slavery, by an Eye-Witness," *New-York Daily Tribune*, May 30, 1850.

2 Speech of Theodore S. Wright, "Proceedings of the New England Anti-slavery Convention: held in Boston, May 24, 25, 26, 1836" (Boston: I. Knapp, 1836), 21.

3 "Address of the Rev. Theodore S. Wright, Before The Convention of the New-York State Anti-Slavery Society, on the Acceptance of the Annual Report, held at Utica, Sept. 20," *The Colored American*, October 14, 1837.

4 Anonymous newspaper article written by "A New York Merchant," entitled "The Late Anson G. Phelps—His Great Benevolence," *North Star*, December 23, 1853.

5   *The Annual Report of the American and Foreign Anti-Slavery Society, Presented at New-York, May 6, 1851* (New York: American and Foreign Anti-Slavery Society, 1851), 52.

6   "The New York Slave Trade," *Leeds Mercury*, August 7, 1856.

7   This was the view of Senator William Butler Jr., of South Carolina. Quoted in "Doings in Congress," *North Star*, February 1, 1850.

8   "Speech of Mr. Mason, of Virginia, on the Bill for the Recovery of Fugitive Slaves," *National Intelligencer*, January 30, 1850.

9   "Fugitive Slaves," *Fayetteville Observer*, January 29, 1850.

10   "The Union of the States," *Semi-Weekly Raleigh Register*, January 2, 1850.

11   "By Magnetic Telegraph, for the North American and U.S. Gazette," *North American, Philadelphia*, January 4, 1850.

12   "The New York State Vigilance Committee," *North Star*, May 16, 1850, quoting a report from the *New York Tribune*.

13   Philip S. Foner, *Business and Slavery: The New York Merchants and the Irrepressible Conflict* (Chapel Hill: University of North Carolina Press, 1941), 25.

14   *New York Herald* article reprinted in "Refuge of Oppression," *Liberator*, May 10, 1850.

15   "The Anniversary," *New York Globe*, reprinted in *National Anti-Slavery Standard*, May 9, 1850.

16   "The Voice of New York on the Union," *National Anti-Slavery Standard*, March 7, 1850.

17   "Great Anti-Proviso Meeting of the Democrats of New York," *Missouri Courier*, March 21, 1850.

18   "The Washington Correspondent of One of Our Exchange Papers Says," *Semi-Weekly Raleigh Register*, January 7, 1845.

19   Frederick Douglass, "Letter from the Editor," *North Star*, May 16, 1850.

20   "Disunion," *Liberator*, March 15, 1850.

21   Jamila Shabazz Brathwaite, "The Black Vigilance Movement in Nineteenth Century New York City" (master's thesis, CUNY City College, New York, 2011), 43.

22   "The New York State Vigilance Committee," *North Star*, May 16, 1850, quoting a report from the *New York Tribune*.

23   "Row in New York-Garrison and Rynders," *Atlas*, May 10, 1850.

24   "Refuge of Oppression," *Liberator*, May 24, 1850.

25   Frederick Douglass, "Anniversary of the American and Foreign Anti-Slavery Society," *North Star*, May 16, 1850.

26   "Slavery Agitation," *Emancipator and Republican*, November 7, 1850.

27   Peter James Hudson, "The Racist Dawn of Capitalism: Unearthing the Economy of Bondage," *Boston Review*, March 14, 2016, https://www.bostonreview.net/articles/peter-james-hudson-slavery-capitalism.

28   Iver Bernstein, *The New York City Draft Riots: Their Significance for American Society and Politics in the Age of the Civil War* (New York: Oxford University Press, 1990), 143.

29   Henry M. Field, *History of the Atlantic Telegraph* (New York: Charles Scribner, 1867), 39.

30   *The Proceedings of the Union Meeting, Held at Castle Garden, October 30, 1850* (New York: Union Safety Committee), 4.

31   *The Proceedings of the Union Meeting, Held at Castle Garden*, 37, 35.

32   *The Proceedings of the Union Meeting, Held at Castle Garden*, 37.

33 *The Proceedings of the Union Meeting, Held at Castle Garden,* 19.

34 Ibid.

35 *The Proceedings of the Union Meeting, Held at Castle Garden,* 37.

36 *The Proceedings of the Union Meeting, Held at Castle Garden,* 8.

37 Brower, while a director at Citi Bank, loaned credit for cotton to the partnership of John Adriance and Morgan L. Smith, who together owned the Waldeck Plantation in Texas. For more on Brower's relationship with Adriance and Smith, see Abigail Curlee Holbrook, "Cotton Marketing in Antebellum Texas," *Southwestern Historical Quarterly* 73, no. 4 (April 1970): 431–55.

38 See *The Proceedings of the Union Meeting, Held at Castle Garden,* 39-53.

39 Foner, *Business and Slavery,* 57.

40 John C. Lord, *"The Higher Law," in Its Application to the Fugitive Slave Bill: A Sermon on the Duties Men Owe to God and to Governments: Delivered at the Central Presbyterian Church, Buffalo, on Thanksgiving-Day* (New York: Union Safety Committee, 1851), 14.

41 *Annual Report of the American and Foreign Anti-Slavery Society, Presented at New York, May 6, 1851,* 35.

42 "Long Sent Back," *National Anti-Slavery Standard,* January 16, 1851.

43 "Henry Long at Auction," *New York Tribune,* January 21, 1851.

44 *Fayetteville Observer,* quoting "The Fugitive Slave Law and Its Working," N.Y. *Express,* December 15, 1853.

45 Henry Ward Beecher, "Speech before the American and Foreign Anti-Slavery Society: New York, May 6, 1851," from *Patriotic Addresses in America and England, from 1850 to 1885, on Slavery, the Civil War, and the Development of Civil Liberty in the United States,* ed., John R. Howard (New York: Fords, Howard & Hulbert, 1888), 190.

46 Frederick Douglass, "Cotton Divinity-Presbyterian General Assembly," *North Star,* July 18, 1852.

47 "Splendid Houses in New York," *Journal of Commerce,* excerpted in *National Intelligencer,* November 6, 1856.

48 "The Dinner at Niblo's Saloon," *New York Weekly Herald,* March 1, 1851.

49 *Proceedings of an Union Meeting, Held in New York: An Appeal to the South* (New York: John H. Duyckinck, 1860), 14.

50 Foner, *Business and Slavery,* 82–83.

51 "Gov. Floyd's Speech in Wall Street," *New York Herald,* October 3, 1856.

52 "The Grand Rally at Tammany," *New York Herald,* December 24, 1857.

53 "The Brotherhood of Spies," *Cleveland Daily Herald,* October 28, 1859.

54 "The Brotherhood of Spies," *Cleveland Daily Herald,* October 28, 1859.

55 The New York Democratic Vigilant Association, *Rise and Progress of the Bloody Outbreak at Harper's Ferry* (New York: John F. Trow, 1859), 23.

56 Charles O'Conor, "The Real Question Stated; Letter from Charles O'Conor to a Committee of Merchants," December 20, 1859. Reprinted in William Henry Seward, *The Irrepressible Conflict* (Albany, NY: Evening Journal, 1859), 14.

57 "Mr. Yancey in New-York," *New York Times,* October 11, 1860.

58 "The Impending Crisis: Great Speech of William L. Yancey," *New York Herald,* October 11, 1860.

59 Fernando Wood, "Mayor Wood's Recommendation of the Secession of New York City," January 6, 1861, Teaching American History, https://teachingamericanhistory .org/document/mayor-woods-recommendation-of-the-secession-of-new-york-city.

60 A. W. Ferrin, "The National City Bank," *Moody's Magazine* 17 (January–December 1914), 54.

61 "The Late Moses Taylor," *Frank Leslie's Illustrated Newspaper*, June 3, 1882, 13.

62 Kendi, *Stamped from the Beginning*, 217.

63 Africano, "Letter from 'Africano' to Robert Hamilton, 18 July 1864," *Weekly Anglo-African*, August 6, 1864.

64 James D. Lockett, "Abraham Lincoln and Colonization: An Episode That Ends in Tragedy at L'Ile à Vache, Haiti, 1863–1864," *Journal of Black Studies* 21, no. 4 (1991): 431, http://www.jstor.org/stable/2784687.

65 See accompanying Collection Overview notes to Moses Taylor papers, Manuscripts and Archives Division, The New York Public Library, accessible at: https://archives.nypl.org/mss/29.

66 "The Late Moses Taylor, *"Frank Leslie's Illustrated Newspaper*, June 3, 1882.

67 "Speech of William M. Evarts, Esq.," *New York Times*, October 19, 1860, https://www.nytimes.com/1860/10/19/archives/speech-of-william-m-evarts-esq-what-the-republicans-intend-doing.html.

68 Reprinted in *National Anti-Slavery Standard*, "Movement of the Rebels," May 4, 1861.

69 Paul Renard Migliore, "The Business of Union: The New York Business Community and the Civil War" (PhD diss., Columbia University, 1975), 352. Migliore cites, in his statement, David Montgomery's *Beyond Equality: Labor and the Radical Republicans, 1862–1872* (New York: Alfred A. Knopf, 1967).

70 Bernstein, *The New York City Draft Riots*, 218.

71 *Class A. Correspondence with the British Commissioners at Sierra Leone, Havana, the Cape of Good Hope, and Loanda; and Reports from British Vice-Admiralty Courts, and from British Naval Officers, Relating to the Slave Trade from April 1, 1859, to March 31, 1860*, vol. 2 (London: Harrison and Sons, 1860), 263, 294–95.

72 "Consul-General Crawford to Lord J. Russell, October 3, 1859," in *Class B. Correspondence with the British Ministers and Agents in Foreign Countries, and with Foreign Ministers in England, Relating to the Slave Trade, from April 1, 1859, to March 31, 1860*, vol. 14 (London: Harrison and Sons, 1860), 349.

73 H. Ford Douglas, "'Letter to Frederick Douglass,' January 8, 1863," *Douglass' Monthly*, February 1863.

74 Works Progress Administration, interview with Elvira Garrett, John B. Cade Slave Narrative Collection; Date (unknown); Box 1; and Folder Number 042; Archives and Manuscripts Department, John B. Cade Library, Southern University.

75 "Moses Taylor Papers, 1793–1906," New York Public Library Archives & Manuscripts, https://archives.nypl.org/mss/2955.

CHAPTER 11

1 An official history of Lehman Brothers gives the date of Mayer Lehman's arrival to New York as "late in 1867, on the eve of Mayer's coming." Lehman Brothers Bank, *A Centennial: Lehman Brothers 1850–1950*, 14.

2 The earliest recorded address for Mayer Lehman in New York, printed in *Longworth's New York City Directory* of 1868–69, was 363 West 20th Street.

3 Special correspondence of the *Cincinnati Gazette*, "Social and Political Condition of Western Alabama," September 30, 1865, reprinted in *National Anti-Slavery Standard*, October 21, 1865.

4   David Goodhart, "How My Lehman Brothers Ancestors Shaped America," *Times*, July 15, 2018, https://www.thetimes.co.uk/article/david-goodhart-how-my-lehman-brothers-ancestors-shaped-america-nvrklntdl.

5   C. Vann Woodward, *Origins of the New South, 1877–1913* (Baton Rouge: Louisiana State University Press, 1951), 29.

6   "Where Are the Great Slave Fortunes?" The Unz Review, June 13, 2020, https://www.unz.com/isteve/where-are-the-great-slave-fortunes.

7   Lehman Brothers, receipt for the purchase of ten enslaved people, Augusta, GA, 1863, Herbert H. Lehman collection, Box 81, Folder 17, Columbia University.

8   Roland Flade, *The Lehmans: From Rimpar to the New World, A Family History* (Würzburg: Verlag Königshausen & Neumann, 1999), 56.

9   *Report of the Select Joint Committee to Inquire into the condition of Affairs in the Late Insurrectionary States, Made to the Two Houses of Congress, February 18, 1872*, US Congress (Washington, DC: Government Printing Office, 1872), 317.

10   Morton Rothstein, "The Antebellum South as a Dual Economy: A Tentative Hypothesis," *Agricultural History* 41, no. 4 (1967): 380, http://www.jstor.org/stable/3740723.

11   Brazy, "An American Planter," 549.

12   Philipp Ager, Leah Platt Boustan, and Katherine Eriksson, "The Intergenerational Effects of a Large Wealth Shock: White Southerners after the Civil War," National Bureau of Economic Research, March 2019, https://www.nber.org/system/files/working_papers/w25700/w25700.pdf.

13   Deirdre Nansen McCloskey, "Slavery Did Not Make America Rich: Ingenuity, Not Capital Accumulation or Exploitation, Made Cotton a Little King," *Reason*, August–September 2018, https://reason.com/2018/07/19/slavery-did-not-make-america-r.

14   Statement of Sven Beckert, "An Enduring Legacy: The Role of Financial Institutions in the Horrors of Slavery and the Need for Atonement."

15   "The Devil and Tom Walker," Encyclopedia.com, https://www.encyclopedia.com/arts/encyclopedias-almanacs-transcripts-and-maps/devil-and-tom-walker.

16   For more details, see the NYC Landmarks Preservation Commission presentation "East Village/Lower East Side Historic District Designation Report," October 9, 2012, http://s-media.nyc.gov/agencies/lpc/lp/2491.pdf.

17   "Where Are the Great Slave Fortunes?" The Unz Review. See post 65.

18   John Syrett, *The Civil War Confiscation Acts: Failing to Reconstruct the South* (New York: Fordham University Press, 2005), 138.

19   Sarah Fling, "The Formerly Enslaved Households of President Andrew Johnson," White House Historical Association, https://www.whitehousehistory.org/the-formerly-enslaved-households-of-president-andrew-johnson.

20   DeNeen L. Brown, "40 Acres and a Mule: How the First Reparations for Slavery Ended in Betrayal," *Washington Post*, April 15, 2021, https://www.washingtonpost.com/history/2021/04/15/40-acres-mule-slavery-reparations.

21   "Two Warnings to the President," *National Anti-Slavery Standard*, October 21, 1865.

22   Du Bois, *Black Reconstruction*, 256.

23   *Boston Traveller*, printed in *Liberator*, September 1, 1865.

24   Richard Parker, "The Cotton Kings of Texas," *New York Times*, April 24, 2012, https://archive.nytimes.com/opinionator.blogs.nytimes.com/2012/04/24/the-cotton-kings-of-texas.

25   *Names of Persons Pardoned by the President: Message from the President of the United States, Further in Answer to a Resolution of the House of 10th December Last, Relative*

to Persons Pardoned by the President, April 15, 1865 to Dec. 10, 1866, 39th Cong., 2nd session, ex. doc. no. 116, 66–67.

26 "A Brief Review," *Elevator*, July 28, 1865.

27 "How the New Yorkers View It," *Corr. Independent Democrat*, printed in *Liberator*, October 27, 1865.

28 "The Pardon Mill," *Boston Traveller*, printed in *Liberator*, October 20, 1865.

29 William Lloyd Garrison, "Speech of William Lloyd Garrison, at the Annual Meeting of the Massachusetts Anti-Slavery Society," *National Anti-Slavery Standard*, February 8, 1862.

30 Elisha Weaver, "President Johnson Has Issued His Long Threatened Amnesty," *Christian Recorder*, September 14, 1867.

31 Samuel Childress, "Letter from Nashville: The Duty of the Government," *Anglo-African Magazine*, December 16, 1865.

32 Special Correspondent, "Social and Political Condition of Western Alabama," *Cincinnati Gazette*, September 30, 1865, reprinted, *National Anti-Slavery Standard*, October 21, 1865.

33 "In Memoriam: Mayer Lehman," 4, a document prepared on the occasion of his death, quotes from an obituary in the *New York Evening Post*, June 22nd, 1897. Accessible at: http://www.columbia.edu/cu/lweb/digital/collections/rbml/lehman /pdfs/0536/ldpd_leh_0536_0015.pdf.

34 J. Wilkes Booth, "Letter from the Murderer of President Lincoln," *Philadelphia Inquirer*, April 29, 1865.

35 Brazy, "An American Planter," 550.

36 "Restoration," *National Intelligencer*, March 21, 1866.

37 "Dr. Duncan, Late of Natchez, Miss.," *National Intelligencer*, February 1, 1867.

38 Gregory Rodriquez, "Amnesty Isn't a Dirty Word," *Los Angeles Times*, May 28, 2007.

39 "President Johnson, His Proclamation of Amnesty, and Its Effect," *Charleston Tri-Weekly Courier*, December 29, 1868.

40 *Daily News and Herald*, quoting "The President's New Policy," *Chicago Times*, September 10, 1867.

41 Sidney Denise Maxwell, *History of the Exposition of Textile Fabrics: held in Cincinnati, August 3[r]d, 4th, 5th, 6th and 7th, 1869* (Cincinnati: Gazette Co. Print, 1869), 69.

42 "Testimony of Frederick Wolffe," House and Senate Reports, 1661 H. rp. 262/2 Affairs in Alabama, investigation of murders and other acts of violence designed to limit vote in 1874 Alabama election, testimony, 271.

43 "Home News, the Weather, Prominent Arrivals, the City," *New York Tribune*, August 16, 1870.

44 *Real Estate Record and Builders' Guide* 5–6, no. 105 (March 18, 1870): 136.

45 Sarah Churchwell, "'The Lehman Trilogy' and Wall Street's Debt to Slavery," *New York Review of Books*, June 11, 2019, https://www.nybooks.com/online/2019/06/11 /the-lehman-trilogy-and-wall-streets-debt-to-slavery.

46 Peter Eisenstadt, ed., *The Encyclopedia of New York State* (Syracuse: Syracuse University Press, 2005), [p. 880-81], reprinted in "Biography: From The Encyclopedia of New York State: Lehman, Herbert H(enry)," on the website of New York State: https:// empirestateplaza.ny.gov/hall-governors/herbert-h-lehman.

47 "Moses Taylor," *Merchants' Magazine and Commercial Review* 50, no. 6 (June 1, 1864): 405.

48 Claudia Varella, "A Expensas de la Esclavitud: La Marca También de Moses Taylor & Co.," in José Antonio Piqueras, ed., *Plantación, Espacios Agrarios y Paisaje Social en la Cuba Colonial* (Castellón de la Plana: Universitat Jaume, 2017), 401.

49 Henry Louis Gates Jr., "The 'Lost Cause' That Built Jim Crow," November 8, 2019, *New York Times*, https://www.nytimes.com/2019/11/08/opinion/sunday/jim-crow-laws.html.

50 Mildred Lewis Rutherford, *A Measuring Rod to Test Text Books, and Reference Books in Schools, Colleges and Libraries* (Athens, GA: United Confederate Veterans, 1919), 5.

51 Chara H. Bohan, Lauren Y. Bradshaw, and Wade H. Morris, "The Mint Julep Consensus: An Analysis of Late 19th Century Southern and Northern Textbooks and Their Impact on the History Curriculum," *Journal of Social Studies Research* 44 (2020): 139–49; James W. Loewen, *Lies My Teacher Told Me: Everything Your American History Textbook Got Wrong* (New York: New Press, 1995). A summary of Loewen's findings is available in "Why Do People Believe Myths about the Confederacy? Because Our Textbooks and Monuments Are Wrong," *Washington Post*, July 1, 2015, https://www.washingtonpost.com/posteverything/wp/2015/07/01/why-do-people-believe-myths-about-the-confederacy-because-our-textbooks-and-monuments-are-wrong.

52 Conor Finnegan, "Pompeo Slams 'Rioters Pulling Down Statues' for 'Assault' on Tradition," ABC News, July 16, 2020, https://abcnews.go.com/Politics/pompeo-slams-rioters-pulling-statues-assault-tradition/story?id=71829243.

53 Sarah Schwartz, "Map: Where Critical Race Theory is Under Attack," *Education Week*, June 11, 2021, https://www.edweek.org/policy-politics/map-where-critical-race-theory-is-under-attack/2021/06.

CHAPTER 12

1 Bettye Kearse, "I Feared My Enslaved Ancestors Had Been Dishonored in Death—but the African Burial Ground in New York City Tells a Different Story," Time.com, March 24, 2020, https://time.com/5808542/african-burial-ground-history.

2 Leslie M. Harris, *In the Shadow of Slavery: African Americans in New York City, 1626–1863* (Chicago: University of Chicago Press, 2003), 1–2.

3 Telephone interview with Deadria Farmer-Paellmann, June 21, 2021.

4 "Our New York Letter," *Independent Statesman*, November 15, 1877.

5 *Trustees of Dartmouth College v. Woodward*, 17 U.S. 518 (1819), in John Marshall, *The Writings of John Marshall, Late Chief Justice of the United States, upon the Federal Constitution* (Boston: James Munroe and Company, 1839), 213.

6 W. Robert Thomas, "How and Why Corporations Became (and Remain) Persons under the Criminal Law," *Florida State University Law Review* 45 (Winter 2018): 520.

7 "1812: A New Bank Born in New York" and "1824: Quaker Mariners at the Helm," Citigroup, https://www.citigroup.com/global/about-us/heritage.

8 Arie de Geus, "The Living Company," *Harvard Business Review*, March–April 1997, https://hbr.org/1997/03/the-living-company.

9 Sarah Churchwell, "'The Lehman Trilogy' and Wall Street's Debt to Slavery."

10 Nick Moran, "CVS Health Year-End Revenue Tops $292B, Aetna Revenue Up 9%: 10 Things to Know," *Becker's Payer Issues*, February 9, 2022, https://www.beckerspayer.com/payer/cvs-health-year-end-revenue-tops-292b-aetna-revenue-up-9-10-things-to-know.html.

11 Tamar Lewin, "Calls for Slavery Restitution Getting Louder," *New York Times*, June 4, 2001, https://www.nytimes.com/2001/06/04/us/calls-for-slavery-restitution-getting -louder.html.

12 Peter Slevin, "Pre-Civil War Insurance Policies Paid Out for Lost Slaves: Aetna Inc. Reveals 'Legal' Practice," *Edmonton Journal*, March 9, 2000.

13 Robin Finn, "Public Lives; Pressing the Cause of the Forgotten Slaves," *New York Times*, August 8, 2000, https://www.nytimes.com/2000/08/08/nyregion/public-lives -pressing-the-cause-of-the-forgotten-slaves.html.

CHAPTER 13

1 Saidiya V. Hartman, *Scenes of Subjection: Terror, Slavery, and Self-Making in Nineteenth-Century America* (New York: Oxford University Press, 1997), 4.

2 *Farmer-Paellmann v. Fleetboston Financial Corp*, Civil Action # CV 02 1862, Class Action, March 26, 2002, https://casetext.com/case/farmer-paellmann-v-fleetboston -financial-corp.

3 "Plaintiff, Attorney Discuss Slavery Reparations Lawsuit," *American Morning with Paula Zahn*, CNN, March 26, 2002, http://www.cnn.com/TRANSCRIPTS/0203/26 /ltm.07.html.

4 "Chicago Makes History as 1st City to Pass Slavery-Era Disclosure Ordinance," *Jet*, October 21, 2002.

5 "Lehman Brothers Tells Chicago about Slave Purchase in 1800s," *Bond Buyer*, November 26, 2003, http://www.bondbuyer.com/news/lehman-brothers-tells-chicago -about-slave-purchase-in-1800s.

6 "Lehman Brothers Admits Past Slavery Ties," Associated Press, November 24, 2003.

7 "Lehman Brothers Tells Chicago," *Bond Buyer*.

8 Dan Mihalopoulos, "Firm Stands Firm on Slavery Ties," *Chicago Tribune*, May 4, 2004, https://www.chicagotribune.com/news/ct-xpm-2004-05-04-0405040314-story .html.

9 Rinker Buck, "Federal Judge in Chicago Dismisses Slavery Reparations Lawsuit," *Hartford Courant*, January 27, 2004.

10 CITY OF CHICAGO, ex rel. BOB BROWN (a. k. a. ROBERT ALFONZO BROWN), PLAINTIFFS; vs ARCHDIOCESE OF CHICAGO; WILLIS OF ILLI-NOIS; LLOYD'S OF LONDON, et al, Circuit Court of Cook County, Illinois, May 12, 2006. Copy with author.

11 Telephone interview with Bob Brown, September 22, 2022.

12 Salim Muwakkil, "Reparations Suit Leaves Opening," *In These Times*, February 2, 2004, https://inthesetimes.com/article/reparations-suit-leaves-opening.

13 Foner, "Slavery's Fellow Travelers," *New York Times*.

14 Michael Finnegan, "African Burial Ground Memorial Work Begins," *New York Daily News*, March 14, 2000.

15 Video call with James Lide, October 13, 2022.

16 "JPMorgan Says Predecessor Banks Had Links to Slavery, Apologizes," Associated Press, January 20, 2005.

17 David Teather, "Bank Admits It Owned Slaves," *Guardian*, January 22, 2005, https:// www.theguardian.com/world/2005/jan/22/usa.davidteather.

18 Al Swanson, "Commentary: Confronting Slavery's Legacy," UPI, January 21, 2005, https://www.upi.com/Defense-News/2005/01/21/Commentary-Confronting-slaverys -legacy/87851106343628.

19 Ken Magill, "From J.P. Morgan Chase, an Apology and $5 Million in Slavery Reparations," *New York Sun*, February 1, 2005, https://www.nysun.com/article /business-from-jp-morgan-chase-an-apology-and-5-million.

20 JPMorgan Chase & Co., *Annual Report 2005*, https://www.jpmorganchase.com /content/dam/jpmc/jpmorgan-chase-and-co/investor-relations/documents/ar05 -complete.pdf.

21 "Lehman Still Facing Challenges Over Chicago Slave Profits," *Bond Buyer*, September 14, 2005.

22 "Lehman Still Facing Challenges Over Chicago Slave Profits," *Bond Buyer*.

23 *Farmer-Paellmann v. Fleetboston Financial Corp*, Civil Action # CV 02 1862, Class Action, March 26, 2002.

CHAPTER 14

1 Clare Ruel, "Lloyd's Returns to Profit with £2.3bn in Full-Year 2021 Results," *Insurance Times*, March 22, 2022, https://www.insurancetimes.co.uk/news/lloyds-returns-to -profit-with-23bn-in-full-year-2021-results/1440696.article.

2 "Britain Grapples With Its Racist Past, From the Town Square to the Boardroom," *New York Times*, June 18, 2020. https://www.nytimes.com/2020/06/18/world/europe /uk-slavery-trade-lloyds-greene-king.html.

3 "The Transatlantic Slave Trade," Lloyd's of London, https://www.lloyds.com /about-lloyds/history/the-trans-atlantic-slave-trade.

4 Guy Faulconbridge and Kate Holton, "Lloyd's of London to Pay for 'Shameful' Atlantic Slave Trade Role," Reuters, June 17, 2020.

5 Lloyd's of London and Greene King to Make Slave Trade Reparations, *Guardian*, June 17, 2020. https://www.theguardian.com/world/2020/jun/18/lloyds-of-london -and-greene-king-to-make-slave-trade-reparations.

6 Bank of England database available at the Centre for the Study of the Legacies of British Slavery, https://www.ucl.ac.uk/lbs/firm/view/1116227371.

7 Tracy Jan, Jena McGregor, and Meghan Hoyer, "Corporate America's $50 Billion Promise," *Washington Post*, August 23, 2021.

8 "5 Questions About Reparations: Answered," Ben & Jerry's, June 11, 2020: https:// www.benjerry.com/whats-new/2020/06/reparations-questions.

9 Ta-Nehisi Coates, "The Case for Reparations," *Atlantic*, June 2014, https://www .theatlantic.com/magazine/archive/2014/06/the-case-for-reparations/361631.

10 1619 Project, *New York Times*, https://www.nytimes.com/interactive/2019/08/14 /magazine/1619-america-slavery.html.

11 Wendy Fry, "California Reparations Task Force Aims at More Than Dollars, Seeks Policies to Prevent Harm," *Cal Matters*, January 26, 2023, https://calmatters.org /california-divide/2023/01/california-reparations.

12 "Repair Can't Wait. Create Reparations Commission Now," Human Rights Watch, https://www.hrw.org/ReparationsNow.

13 "Georgetown Shares Slavery, Memory, and Reconciliation Report, Racial Justice Steps," *Georgetown University News*, September 1, 2016. https://www.georgetown.edu/news /georgetown-shares-slavery-memory-and-reconciliation-report-racial-justice-steps.

14 Maeve Glass, "Princeton and Slavery: Moses Taylor Pyne and the Sugar Plantations of the Americas," *Princeton Alumni Weekly*, November 8, 2017, https://paw .princeton.edu/article/princeton-and-slavery-moses-taylor-pyne-and-sugar-plantations -americas.

NOTES

15 The Princeton & Slavery Project, https://slavery.princeton.edu.
16 These and other quotes about Taylor and Citibank's founders were taken in 2020 and 2021 from the Timeline section on Citigroup's website, though those descriptions have since been removed, https://www.citigroup.com/citi/about/timeline.
17 "Citi Historic Records Review Summary," City Bank of New York (National City Bank of New York as of 1865), July 27, 2023, https://www.citigroup.com/rcs/citigpa/storage/public/Citi%20Historic%20Records%20Review%20Summary.pdf.
18 "Citi Historic Records Review Summary," City Bank of New York (National City Bank of New York as of 1865), July 27, 2023, https://www.citigroup.com/rcs/citigpa/storage/public/Citi%20Historic%20Records%20Review%20Summary.pdf.
19 Dana M. Peterson and Catherine L. Mann, "Closing the Racial Inequality Gaps: The Economic Cost of Black Inequality in the U.S.," Citigroup, September 1, 2020, https://icg.citi.com/icghome/what-we-think/citigps/insights/closing-the-racial-inequality-gaps-20200922.
20 The seven City Bank directors who enslaved Black people while serving at the bank were: Benjamin Bailey, Abraham Bloodgood, Samuel Tooker, Jasper Ward, Ichabod Prall, James Magee, and Edmund Smith. Sources include US Census Records, the Northeast Slavery Records Index, the New York Historical Society, and manumission records cited in Yoshpe.
21 Telephone interview with Amanda Yogendran, April 7, 2021.
22 "Citigroup Market Cap 2010-2023," Macrotrends: "Citigroup market cap as of July 18, 2023 is $90.06B." https://www.macrotrends.net/stocks/charts/C/citigroup/market-cap.
23 "About Princeton & Slavery," Princeton & Slavery Project, Princeton University, https://slavery.princeton.edu/about/overview.
24 "Recommendations," Brown University's Slavery and Justice Report, https://slaveryandjusticereport.brown.edu/sections/recommendations.
25 "Introduction," *Report of the Brown University Steering Committee on Slavery and Justice*, Brown University, 2006, https://digitalpublications.brown.edu/read/first-readings-2020/section/c1329de6-4340-4b99-8e43-7ee9751fb016.
26 Robert Miller and Jack Blackburn, "Bank of England Owned 599 Slaves for More Than a Decade, Historian Finds," *Times of London*, April 16, 2022, https://www.thetimes.co.uk/article/bank-of-england-owned-599-slaves-for-more-than-a-decade-historian-finds-gmcpmtffv.
27 "Slavery & the Bank," The Bank of England, April 29, 2022, at the Bank of England Museum, https://www.bankofengland.co.uk/museum/online-collections/blog/beginning-the-exhibition-slavery-and-the-bank.
28 Nicholas Draper, "Lloyd's, Marine Insurance and Slavery," Lloyd's of London, https://www.lloyds.com/about-lloyds/history/the-trans-atlantic-slave-trade/lloyds-marine-insurance-and-slavery.
29 Robert Miller and Jack Blackburn, "Bank of England owned 599 slaves for more than a decade, historian finds," *The Times*, April 16, 2022. https://www.thetimes.co.uk/article/bank-of-england-owned-599-slaves-for-more-than-a-decade-historian-finds-gmcpmtffv. See also The Bank of England, "Slavery & the Bank Print Guide," 42, https://www.bankofengland.co.uk/-/media/boe/files/museum/slavery-and-the-bank-large-print-guide.pdf.
30 Robert Miller and Jack Blackburn, "Bank of England owned 599 slaves for more than a decade, historian finds," *The Times*, April 16, 2022.

31 Nadine White, "Barbados Ambassador Calls On UK Government and Monarchy to Apologise for Slavery," *Independent*, January 16, 2023, https://www.independent .co.uk/world/barbados-monarchy-slavery-uk-government-b2262951.html.

32 Jasper Jolly, "ABN Amro Apologises for Historical Links to Slavery," *Guardian*, April 13, 2022, https://www.theguardian.com/business/2022/apr/13/abn-amro-apologises -for-historical-links-to-slavery.

33 Sarah Federman and Judith Schrempf-Stirling, "Why Corporate Success Requires Dealing With the Past," *MIT Sloan Management Review*, November 16, 2022, https://sloanreview.mit.edu/article/why-corporate-success-requires-dealing-with-the -past.

34 Jennifer Ludden, "Cities May Be Debating Reparations, but Here's Why Most Americans Oppose the Idea," *All Things Considered*, NPR, March 27, 2023, https://www .npr.org/2023/03/27/1164869576/cities-reparations-white-black-slavery-oppose.

35 Carrie Blazina and Kiana Cox, "Black and White Americans Are Far Apart in Their Views of Reparations for Slavery," Pew Research Center, November 28, 2022, https://www.pewresearch.org/fact-tank/2022/11/28/black-and-white-americans -are-far-apart-in-their-views-of-reparations-for-slavery.

36 Sarah Federman, "How Companies Can Address Their Historical Transgressions: Lessons from the Slave Trade and the Holocaust," *Harvard Business Review*, January–February 2022, https://hbr.org/2022/01/how-companies-can-address-their -historical-transgressions.

37 "Fourth Quarter and Full Year 2021 Results and Key Metrics," Citi, https:// www.citigroup.com/global/news/press-release/2022/fourth-quarter-and-full -year-2021-results-and-key-metrics.

38 Statement of Al Green, "An Enduring Legacy: The Role of Financial Institutions in the Horrors of Slavery and the Need for Atonement," hybrid hearing before the Subcommittee on Oversight and Investigations of the Committee on Financial Services, US House of Representatives, 117th Cong., 2nd session, April 5, 2022, https:// www.govinfo.gov/content/pkg/CHRG-117hhrg47476/html/CHRG-117hhrg47476 .htm.

39 Statement of William Darity, "An Enduring Legacy: The Role of Financial Institutions in the Horrors of Slavery and the Need for Atonement."

40 Federman and Schrempf-Stirling, "Why Corporate Success Requires Dealing With the Past."

41 "Deepwater Horizon oil spill," Britannica, July 7, 2023. https://www.britannica.com /event/Deepwater-Horizon-oil-spill.

42 "Deepwater Horizon oil spill settlements: Where the money went," National Oceanic and Atmospheric Administration, US Department of Commerce, https://www.noaa .gov/explainers/deepwater-horizon-oil-spill-settlements-where-money-went.

43 Quotes about the Hillman Family Foundations program came from the foundation's website: https://hillmanfamilyfoundations.org. Budget figures for the Hillman Family Foundations came from the foundation's 2019 IRS filing, posted through Cause IQ: https://www.causeiq.com/organizations/view_990/256065959/d172acee 55521388dceaac29f4d10d95.

44 Olúfẹ́mi O. Táíwò, *Reconsidering Reparations* (New York: Oxford University Press, 2022), 174.

45 Corky Siemaszko, "Sen. Mitch McConnell's great-great-grandfathers owned
    14 slaves, bringing reparations issue close to home," NBC News, July 8, 2019,
    https://www.nbcnews.com/politics/congress/mitch-mcconnell-ancestors-slave
    -owners-alabama-1800s-census-n1027511.
46 Ted Barrett, "McConnell Opposes Paying Reparations: 'None of Us Currently
    Living are Responsible' for Slavery," CNN.com, June 19, 2019, https://www.cnn
    .com/2019/06/18/politics/mitch-mcconnell-opposes-reparations-slavery/index.html.
47 Susan S. Kuo and Benjamin Means, "A Corporate Law Rationale For Reparations,"
    Boston College Law Review 62 (March 2021).

INDEX

Tulane University, 262
Turnbull, Nichol, 11–16, 18–19
  arrival in Georgia, 12
  cotton industry, 11, 13
  land holdings, 11
  listing and monetary value of enslaved
    persons, 15
  Marshall and, 23, 26
  runaway slave, 15–16, 18–19
Turner, Nat, 103
Twelve Years a Slave (Northup), 186

Underground Railroad, 185–87, 189, 199–200
Union Club, 204
Union Committee, 191, 194, 196–97, 203
Union Defense Committee, 205
Union Safety Committee, 197–202, 205
United Daughters of the Confederacy, 237
United States Gazette, 111
University College London Legacies of British
  Slave-Ownership project, 270
University of Pittsburgh, 225
University of the City of New York. *See* New
  York University
Unz, Ronald Keeva, 216
Unz Review, The, 216, 224
US Census Bureau, 152, 187
US Constitution
  Fifteenth Amendment, 209
  hypocrisy of, 5
  striking condemnation of slavery from,
    55–57
  Thirteenth Amendment, 211, 216
US Department of Agriculture, 134
US Department of Commerce, 152
US Department of Justice, 290
US Department of the Treasury, 27, 48–50,
  100, 151–52, 154, 162, 206
  See also Bank of the United States
US General Services Administration, 240
US Land Office, 131–32
US Navy, 174, 208, 210
US Supreme Court, 186
USDA (formerly, Bureau of Agriculture), 152

Van Leer, Anthony W., 139–40, 144–45
Van Rensselaer, Stephen, 91, 110
Varella, Claudia, 236, 276
Vesey, Denmark, 58, 83, 125
Vianna, José Lima, 173
Vicksburg Whig, 114
Victory (ship), 76
Virginia Theological Seminary, 273
Volvo, xix
Vroom, G. B., 30

Walker, David, 83–86, 103, 125, 184
Wall Street. *See names of specific capitalists,
  businesses, and industries*; white capitalist
  elite

War of 1812, 25–27
Ward, Samuel Ringgold, 78, 109, 189–90, 193
Washington, George, 5
Washington Post, 271
Waters, Hayden, 77, 109
Watt, James, 15
Webb, James Watson, 69, 106
Webster, Daniel, 190, 199
Weeks, Ezra, 7
Weld, Theodore Dwight, 122
Weston family, 33
Whelan, Charles, 121, 123, 125
white capitalist elite, xvi–xx
  abolitionist exposure of, 102–3, 120–27
  about-face in commitment at outbreak of
    war, 204–9
  American Colonization Society, 74–78
  backlash against abolitionists, 127, 182,
    187–202
  colonization scheme, 64–69, 71, 74–78,
    82, 85, 89
  commute to counting houses, 92, 170
  corporation boom, 40–41
  cotton price surge and subsequent
    collapse, 96–100
  deforestation, 133–34
  dying off of early generation, 109
  dynastic wealth through marriage, 40
  European immigration, 85–86
  industrialists moving south, 135
  lack of expenditure for direct benefit of
    Black people, 87–88
  Lincoln's council of financiers, 206–7
  losses from self-emancipation and
    abolitionism, 187–88
  mansions and marble, 90–92, 126, 200
  membership in manumission societies, 8,
    38, 62–63
  merchant princes, 90–93, 126, 200
  Merchants' Exchange Building, 40, 168
  moral contradiction and duplicity, 5–6, 8,
    38, 63, 125, 208–9
  names left out of story of slavery, xix
  northern slavery aristocracy, 40–41, 50–51
  overview of Wall Street businessmen in
    1820s, 2
  percentage who were enslavers, 43
  postwar disenfranchisement efforts, 209
  postwar freedom to prosper, 213–14
  privilege not to question their privilege's
    origins, 52, 57–58
  profiting from war, 208
  protecting segregation and white privilege,
    181–82, 188–202
  reduced concentration of families in
    control of slavery, 130
  reinvention and second act, 125, 212,
    226–27
  sponsoring breakup of the union, 204
  survival through market collapse, 97